Rethinking America's Past

Rethinking America's Past

Howard Zinn's

A People's History of the United States

in the Classroom and Beyond

ROBERT COHEN AND SONIA E. MURROW

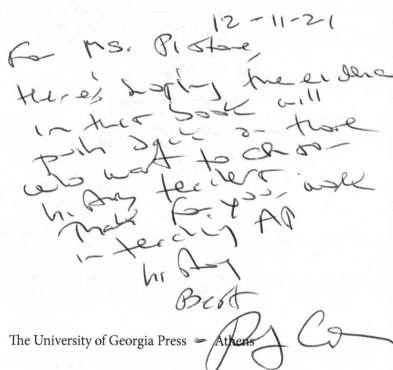

The University of Georgia Press ∾ Athens

This publication received generous support from the Stephen M. Silberstein Foundation.

Howard Zinn letters and other material from his papers archived at
New York University's Tamiment Library / Robert F. Wagner Labor Archives,
Copyright © The Howard Zinn Revocable Trust

Library of Congress Cataloging-in-Publication Data
Names: Cohen, Robert, 1955 May 21– author. | Murrow, Sonia E., 1964– author.
Title: Rethinking America's past : Howard Zinn's A people's history of the
United States in the classroom and beyond / Robert Cohen and Sonia E. Murrow.
Description: Athens : The University of Georgia Press, [2021] |
Includes bibliographical references and index.
Identifiers: LCCN 2021021083 | ISBN 9780820360331 (hardback) |
ISBN 9780820360348 (paperback) | ISBN 9780820360355 (ebook)
Subjects: LCSH: Zinn, Howard, 1922–2010. People's history of the United States. |
Zinn, Howard, 1922–2010—Study and teaching (Secondary) | United States—
History—Study and teaching (Secondary) | United States—History—
Textbooks. | United States—Historiography.
Classification: LCC E175.8 .C56 2021 | DDC 973—dc23
LC record available at https://lccn.loc.gov/2021021083

For my children, Lev and Talia,
and my mother, Hope

And in memory of Tom Hayden

It is a . . . profoundly important thing we are trying to accomplish, to look at the world from other points of view. We need to do that as we come into the twenty-first century, if we want this new century to be different, if we want it to be not an American century, or a Western century, or a white century, or a male century, or any nation's . . . century but a century for the human race.

❧

If the colonial period of our history constitutes our birth and infancy we were not "born free." We were born amidst slavery, semi-slavery, land monopoly, class privilege, and class conflict.

❧

It was easy to detect the control of the German scholars or the Russian scholars, but much harder to recognize that the high school texts of our own country have fostered jingoism, war heroes, the Sambo approach to the black man, the vision of the Indian as savage, and the notion that white Western Civilization is the cultural, humanistic summit of man's time on earth.

❧

The schools teach about the Declaration of Independence, . . . that we live in a democracy and that there is equality and justice for all. At the same time, the schools do not give . . . young people . . . the information that shows how these ideals are being violated every day.

❧

Consider how much attention is given in historical writing to military affairs . . . and . . . how little attention is given to antiwar movements . . . to those who struggled against the idiocy of war.

❧

As a result of omitting, or downplaying, the importance of social movements of the people in our history—the actions of abolitionists, labor leaders, radicals, feminists, and pacifists—a fundamental principle of democracy is undermined: . . . that . . . the citizenry, rather than the government . . . is the ultimate source of power . . . that pulls the . . . government in the direction of equality and justice.

CONTENTS

Introduction 1

CHAPTER 1. Origins and Appeal
11

CHAPTER 2. Before *A People's History*
46

CHAPTER 3. In High School Classrooms
63

CHAPTER 4. "Dear Mr. Zinn": Student Voices
94

CHAPTER 5. Not Just for Kids
129

CHAPTER 6. Teachers: A People's Pedagogy
158

CHAPTER 7. Retrospectives and Reviews
179

CHAPTER 8. On Stage and Screen
238

Acknowledgments 267

Notes 269

Index 309

Rethinking America's Past

INTRODUCTION

Most historians hope that their research and writing (as well as their teaching) will resonate with their students and colleagues but realize that in a culture as relentlessly ahistorical as America's, the chances are slim that their books will get much attention from the general public. So Howard Zinn's success in attracting millions of readers to *A People's History of the United States* (1980), his revisionist introduction to the American past, is extraordinary.[1] Some of those readers, inspired by Zinn, would go on to become leading historians, among them Robin D. G. Kelley, who holds the Gary Nash Endowed Chair in American History at UCLA. Kelley, whose many publications include a labor history book, *Three Strikes*,[2] coauthored with Zinn, recalled the influence that *A People's History* had on him as a young scholar-activist and Zinn's enduring appeal:

> In 1981, near the end of my second semester as a freshman at California State University, Long Beach, I decided to declare History as my major. I had gone through at least four majors during that first year, among them Philosophy and Political Science, because like so many Black kids of that generation, I saw myself as an activist—a revolutionary. I toyed with law school, political theory, a lifetime of re-reading Marx and Engels, but nothing compared to understanding the past. As far as U.S. historians go, Howard Zinn changed the game—for me and for most of my colleagues and comrades. He exposed the barbarism of the colonizer when the colonized were presumed to be the barbarian in need of civilization. He revealed the racist foundations of American "liberty" and yet always demonstrated that working people and other subjugated and oppressed people kept the ruling class on the run—either on the plantations or factories, the Northern plains or the Mexico border, or Cuba and the Philippines. Yes, he was the outstanding popular historian of social justice movements, the working class, oppressed peoples, but perhaps most crucially, Howard Zinn was a critic and chronicler of the inhumanity of war. He committed his life to ending war and writing books in which antiwar activists were the heroes, not tank commanders, the cavalry, or fighter pilots. Imagine a history book that sells over a million copies that doesn't sell war? He was quite courageous in his complete condemnation of war. He once wrote: "After

my own experience [as a bombardier] in that war [World War II], I had moved away from my own rather orthodox view that there are just wars and unjust wars, to a universal rejection of war as a solution to any human problem."[3]

Kelley's words capture why Zinn's *People's History* emerged as America's best-selling and most iconoclastic introductory history book in the 1980s and why it has had steadfast appeal. Decades before the emergence of Black Lives Matter and the tearing down of Confederate statues, Zinn was tearing down myths promoted by nationalist politicians and school textbooks. In place of traditional textbook tales of heroic explorers opening up the "New World," *A People's History* begins with a chapter on Columbus as the emblem of genocidal conquest, war, and slavery. Rather than treat racial slavery as an exception to America's forward progress, Zinn offered a far different version of American exceptionalism, arguing that "there is not a country in world history in which racism has been more important, for so long a time, as the United States. And the problem of 'the color line,' as W. E. B. Du Bois put it, is still with us."[4]

Similarly, the tragic consequences of U.S. militarism—such as the bloody conquest of Mexico and the Philippines, the nuclear incineration of Hiroshima and Nagasaki, the carpet bombing and chemical warfare inflicted on Vietnam—comprised so central a theme in Zinn's pacifist-inflected history that when the book came out in the Reagan era, most school system leaders would not consider adopting it. *A People's History* was also too controversial for school officials because of its indictment of the inequities of American capitalism and Zinn's celebration of working-class rebellions against it. But the radicalism that alienated education leaders made Zinn's book an underground classic among those who, like Kelley, were influenced by the social movements of the Long 1960s, becoming critical of social inequality and America's unending wars. Zinn's book spoke to those who had marched against racism, war, sexism, and class exploitation, as well as to the coming generations influenced by or awakening to the critical sensibility that was a legacy of that turbulent time.

It was, however, not only the content but the form of *A People's History* that made Zinn's book so popular. The book was written with a clarity and verve that made it accessible both to such well-read historians-in-the-making as Robin D. G. Kelley and to high school students, who prior to reading Zinn had likely never read a history book from cover to cover. Although when *A People's History* was published, President Ronald Reagan was the one known as the Great Communicator, far to his left Zinn demonstrated communicative skills that were equally impressive, and unlike Reagan, whose lines were fed to him by a teleprompter, Zinn wrote the words that made him so popular. At a time when the Left had retreated to academia—as Todd Gitlin put it, "marching on the English department while the Right took the White House"[5]—Zinn was passionately committed to speaking to the broader public. Zinn knew that the groundbreaking scholarship generated by historians of the African American experience, women, U.S. imperialism, and labor in the Long 1960s had been cloistered in academe. He wanted it to reach high school teachers and their students, workers, people of color, prisoners, and millions of other Americans he hoped would learn from it that any progress toward social justice had resulted from people's grassroots struggles.

Howard Zinn's papers in NYU's Tamiment Library offer extensive evidence—carton after carton of reader letters to Zinn—of how effective he was in leaving readers moved by A People's History. Zinn exposed readers to the ugly, exploitative underside of America—some for the first time, generating shock and outrage. Zinn proved effective too in valorizing resistance movements: his engaging and lyrical introduction to those often forgotten movements of the eighteenth-, nineteenth-, and twentieth-century United States inspired readers to believe that protest by people like them could make a difference in the struggle for social change. The letters to Zinn were written by a diverse and multiracial array of people—leftist and liberal political organizers, artists, writers, filmmakers, actors, academics, prisoners, soldiers and sailors, disability activists—young, middle aged, and elderly. We were particularly struck by the large number of letters from teachers and students because they relate directly to our own work as historians based in schools of education who prepare undergraduates and graduate students to become high school and middle school history and social studies teachers.

What the Zinn archives make evident is that to understand the impact of A People's History on history education one must analyze the book not only as an introductory work but also as a tool for teaching in history classrooms, a milestone and yardstick in the history of history education, a barometer of educational reform, and a presence in American popular culture. So our study offers a diversity of approaches to capture this multilayered history of the impact of A People's History: (1) historiography (i.e., historical writing), as we look, in chapter 1, at the origins of A People's History and, in chapter 7, at the way critics in 1980 and historians retrospectively view A People's History as a historical work; (2) the history of education, as we show in chapter 2 how history education's persistent failure paved the way for the success of A People's History as an alternative to that tradition of failure; (3) a historical teaching and learning case study, as we explore in chapters 3 and 4 the way a teacher used A People's History in high school history classes for more than a decade, documenting a thorough classroom record of student responses to Zinn and debate-oriented historical pedagogy; (4) the history of educational reform, as we probe in chapter 6 how an activist teacher reform movement helped to popularize *A People's History*; and (5) cultural and political history, as we explore, in chapter 8, the way *A People's History* influenced American popular culture and, in chapter 5, what adult letters to Zinn tell us about American culture's relationship to historical knowledge, particularly with regard to the history of dissent.

Since the Zinn papers offer empirical evidence of the impact that *A People's History* has had on teaching and learning history, we can do what late twentieth-century reviewers of the book (in the absence of such evidence) could not: explore the impact of *A People's History* on readers of all ages and its usage and effect in history classrooms. We also assess how well Zinn's book stands up as a work of history and as a teaching tool beyond the classroom: on stage and on film. We can learn from Zinn—no matter how one feels about his brand of history—what it means to be successful in engaging students with U.S. history and how it was possible for Zinn and the teachers who taught *A People's History* (in tandem with and in conversation with conventional textbooks) to make historical classes sites of animated discussion, debate, and intellectual engagement.

In spotlighting the impact of *A People's History* on teaching and learning in history classrooms we are referring to the teachers and students who have made use of the book, primarily in high schools. But it is important not to exaggerate how widely used *A People's History* was by teachers in the three decades between its publication in 1980 and Zinn's death in 2010, the period on which we focus in this book. Those teachers who assigned *A People's History* were often inventive, dynamic, and, according to student letters to Zinn, highly effective, and one can admire them as grassroots curriculum reformers, but they nonetheless constituted a minority of the history teaching profession. In most school districts in the United States, Zinn's book was—as he was well aware—considered far too radical to be adopted as an official school textbook (or anti-textbook). That is why education historian Larry Cuban, in his landmark study of history instruction in two urban school districts, never mentioned Zinn or *A People's History*.[6] This reflects a persistent challenge that dedicated reformers face in transforming school systems that are institutionally, pedagogically, and politically conservative, and therefore highly resistant to change.[7] Thus, while there are in the Zinn archives many letters from teachers and students praising *A People's History* for transforming their teaching and learning of American history, we found no such letters from public school principals, school board members, or anyone else in education leadership expressing admiration for *A People's History* or committing to order it for the schools they oversaw. Initially, then, Zinn's book came into schools piecemeal from individual teacher initiative—that is, from the bottom up. And we'd expect no less, that for such a paradigm-shifting work there had to be a people's movement to champion a people's history. Indeed, eventually teacher-led organizations would generate curriculum materials that incorporated Zinn's *People's History* into the classroom practice of reform-oriented teachers (which we detail in chapter 6).

While wary of exaggerating Zinn's influence on history education in schools, we also want to be careful not to understate either the scope or endurance of that influence. Although ours is a study of the impact Zinn's *A People's History of the United States* had on history teaching and learning from its publication in 1980 to Zinn's death in 2010 (grounded in the archival collection documenting that impact—Zinn's papers—that spans those years), we want readers to bear in mind that Zinn's classic work continues to have a significant impact on American education almost a decade after his passing. So examining how Zinn helped to change history education has contemporary as well as historical importance. One could argue, in fact, that—though not dominant nationally in history classrooms—Zinn's bottom-up approach to American history has grown more popular among teachers over the past decade.

This recent surge in popularity has many sources, including the impressive success of two relatively new means of making people's history more accessible to teachers (and students): the publication of *A Young People's History of the United States* (2007)—which for the first time adapted Zinn's book for middle school and upper elementary students—and the online history education resources provided by the Zinn Education Project.[8] Dan Simon of Seven Stories Press estimates that sales of the *Young People's History* connected to schools is twenty thousand to thirty thousand books annually. Deborah Menkart of the Zinn Education Project finds that close to one hundred thousand teachers use the project's website.[9] Other factors sustaining and expanding Zinn's presence in the schools include the way the multicultural education and ethnic studies movements and the backlash against them (a key part of America's culture wars),[10] along with the Trump administration's regression toward nativism, misogyny, and white supremacy, have fueled teacher interest in Zinn's inclusive, egalitarian, and critical approaches to the American past.

To some university-based historians it may seem odd that almost half our book focuses on history education and Zinn's impact on it at the high school rather than college level, especially since Zinn was himself employed as a professor rather than as a high school history teacher. But part of what made Zinn so distinctive among history professors was that he cared deeply about secondary education, its failure to engage students with history, and the tendency of school officials to shut out dissident views of the American past and present. That is why the major educational initiatives he helped to create, the Zinn Education Project and the Voices of a People's History theater program, targeted high school teachers and students. It is also why Zinn, acting as a people's historian rather than an academic, spoke so frequently at high schools (and corresponded with high school teachers and students), seeking to open them up to his critique of the American warfare state. For example, during the early days of the war in Afghanistan, Zinn spoke to a Massachusetts high school class about that war and provoked a parental backlash by equating this U.S. military intervention with terrorism. This made headlines, leading to invitations to speak at seven other high schools in the state—and Zinn accepted *every one* of those invitations.[11] With the high school student population far larger, more working class, and more racially diverse than its college counterpart, Zinn saw its students and teachers as a natural constituency for the inclusive people's history that he championed.

Since Zinn understood that his *People's History* would not become an official text in high schools, he wrote appreciatively to and about teachers who dared to bring his book into their classrooms[12]—in an almost underground fashion—by photocopying select chapters and having students use those chapters to challenge their conventional U.S. history textbooks. Some of these teachers had their students write Zinn letters making such comparisons. Many of their letters have been preserved in the Zinn papers, offering a unique window onto Zinn's impact at the high school level. The letters provide a rare glimpse into the way young students viewed not only Zinn's book but also the history education they received in school prior to encountering A *People's History*. These classroom sets of high school student letters to Zinn are also the most balanced letters he received because they came from classes that included (mostly conservative) critics, distinguishing them from college students' and other adults' letters that came almost exclusively from those whose admiration of Zinn had led them to take the individual initiative to write him. Thus our high school focus evolved out of these uniquely illuminating sources and Zinn's own concern that the historical profession had done little to address the inadequacy of high school history textbooks and history teaching and learning.

As in the past, A *People's History* remains controversial, evidenced not only by the persistence of conservative attacks on it in the media but also in the realm of book orders, where a form of antiradical political correctness raised barriers to school access to Zinn's book. Dan Simon has experienced this firsthand as the publisher of Zinn's *Young People's History*, observing that as of November 2019,

> I do not think that either Howard's voice, or his view of history are less radical now than in the past, or perceived as less "dangerous" or subversive. It seems to me that on a regular basis we hear from someone at a school wanting to see it adopt AYPHotUS [A *Young People's History of the United States*], only

to have it blocked at a higher level. And even more ominously, we hear from entire school districts interested in adopting AYPHotUS . . . [but then,] mysteriously, somewhere along the way the school district adoption ends up being blocked. This happened for example in Portland, where in fact some five or six years ago a larger order came through for thousands of copies. But it was not repeated.[13]

With the issue of whether *A People's History* should be assigned in public school classrooms remaining contested, the historical evidence of its beneficial educational impact presented in our book should be of particular interest to the public, teachers, and those involved in leading schools and school systems.

Education at its best is not confined to classrooms, schoolhouses, or college campuses; it also encompasses popular culture. Theater, film, and television can, as Howard Zinn realized, serve as powerful vehicles for mass history education. Zinn used these venues as well as protest music to teach millions of Americans in the early twenty-first century about the history of dissent and mass protest. He worked with accomplished actors such as Danny Glover, Matt Damon, Marisa Tomei, Josh Brolin, Viggo Mortensen, and Kerry Washington; popular musicians like Bob Dylan, Bruce Springsteen, and John Legend; and poets such as Martin Espada and many others to bring *A People's History* and its critical and dissident sources to life on stage and screen.[14] Anthony Arnove, Zinn's collaborator in this work, generously shared with us his extensive files on these cultural and popular initiatives, enabling us to end our book with an in-depth account of Zinn's projects in popular history education and entertainment—work that Zinn, then in his eighties, pursued with the energy of a teenager. Our hope is that the story of these initiatives will encourage other historians to collaborate with artists to bring critical history into popular culture venues—to push back against the national tendency toward historical amnesia, especially with regard to the successes and possibilities for democracy in action as embodied in nonviolent protest movements.

Zinn, who has often been misrepresented by the right as un-American, portrayed social movements glowingly in his *People's History* because they were part of an American tradition of dissent and resistance he admired, even loved—with its deep commitment to interracial democracy, economic equity, peace, and social justice. The capaciousness of this egalitarian vision, Zinn's eloquence in evoking it (drawing on the even greater eloquence of dissenters from Frederick Douglass to Emma Goldman to Langston Hughes) resonates with democratic idealism even today—despite Donald Trump. So Zinn's book continues to sell, continues to be attacked by conservatives, continues to help fill theaters with audiences moved by the readings of the dissenting historical voices that Zinn selected. As Pulitzer Prize–winning historian Eric Foner observed recently, "the main point is that we are still discussing Zinn's *People's History* forty years after it was published, which is quite a tribute to the book."[15] Zinn's book lives on as part of America's dissident culture and the continuing struggle to keep the democratic ideal alive in a nation beset by extreme inequality and a money-driven, unrepresentative political system, presided over until recently by a billionaire president flirting with white nationalism and authoritarianism.[16]

Though Zinn did not live to see the Trump presidency, the emphasis of *A People's History* on inclusive democratic politics, people's movements, and progressive change from below is the polar opposite of Trumpian authoritarianism—as embodied in the Great Leader, "I am your voice" mantra of Trump's chilling acceptance speech at the 2016 Republican Party convention.[17] In this sense Zinn can be seen as the anti-Trump, whose historical work calls America back to its highest ideals of interracial and participatory democracy. Had more Americans absorbed the narrative *A People's History* offered of the U.S. failure to live up to those democratic ideals—in the eras of "Indian removal," slavery, anti-labor violence, Jim Crow, McCarthyism, and the collapse of the New Deal order—might they have been inoculated against the delusional nostalgia of Trump's "Make America Great Again" campaign slogan?[18] Has the choice of American educational leaders to avoid dissenting history texts and political controversy in their schools contributed to the larger failure to attain historical literacy in America's public schools? We leave it to readers to answer these questions, but as you do so it is worth considering the connection between this record of school failure in history education and Trump's professed "love" of "the poorly educated."[19]

Zinn saw historical study as foundational to democratic struggle and hoped that the stories of protest and resistance in *A People's History* would help inspire readers to become active working for a more democratic America. In one of his last interviews, Zinn acknowledged that the activist ethos he imparted in *A People's History* distinguished him from conventional historians, that "it might be considered an unprofessional thing for a historian to write a history that somebody else interprets as a call to action. But to me, the historian is a citizen before he [or she] is a historian. The historian is a human being before he is a historian. . . . I see the historian as somebody who intervenes, whose work should lead other people to think they are not simply passive instruments [of political and economic elites.] . . . Democracy requires an active citizenry. Therefore, you might say the writing of history should itself be a democratic act. It should promote democracy by giving people the idea that they too can participate in history."[20] Thus it is almost impossible to divorce the value of *A People's History* as an instrument for challenging conventional textbooks in U.S. history, for stimulating debate and engaging pedagogy in classrooms, from Zinn's politics and activist ethos and his search for a usable past.

A People's History shows us too that despite one's remoteness from political power, an activist-intellectual like Zinn could, through the power of his ideas and the eloquence of his prose, have far-reaching impact on American culture and education. It is the story of that impact that we hope to illuminate in these pages.

As important as Zinn is to our story, his impact on history teaching and learning was never a solo act. If our archival research has revealed anything it is that inventive teachers were as important as Zinn himself in bringing history to life in the classroom. Such teachers proved themselves daring and successful in using A People's History in debate-oriented pedagogy in history classrooms, provoking students to engage in historical thinking. The evidence for this in the Zinn papers—in the form of extensive student and teacher letters to Zinn—is simply overwhelming. Such archival evidence explains what we had long observed but never quite understood before: the enthusiasm of high school teachers about A People's History. And to this day, Zinn's critics have failed to confront this evidence, failed to study the views of teachers and students on Zinn.

Of course, even the most thought-provoking historical works have flaws, and that includes Zinn's. We hope that the more compelling and evenhanded criticisms of A People's History in these pages will encourage Zinn's admirers to consider the weaknesses and limitations of his work. Our view is that A People's History works best not as a tool for some new orthodoxy but rather as a companion piece to more conventional textbook and introductory overviews of American history, where the assumptions, narratives, and conclusions of both are compared and debated. This is, in fact, the way Zinn has been most commonly used by innovative teachers aiming to teach their students to analyze conflicting historical interpretations, on the basis of evidence and reason, while asking critical questions about the United States and its past.

We see this approach to the teaching of American history—where students analyze competing historical interpretations, especially those of radical versus non-radical historians, along with conflicting primary sources—as a sure path to exploring the richness, complexity, joys, and tragedies of that history. Promoting a recognition that historical study worthy of its topic is neither a trivia game for teens nor a prep regime for standardized tests nor a nostalgia trip for sentimental adults. It is instead an exercise in critical thinking, which in the American case yields engagement with the startling reality that, as James Baldwin memorably put it, "American history is longer, larger, more various, more beautiful, and more terrible than anything anyone has ever said about it."[21]

Unlike Baldwin, who urged us to grapple with the complexities and contradictions of the nation's past, President Donald Trump at his 2020 White House Conference on American History argued for a superpatriotic, cheerleading version of U.S. history. His speech at that conference promoted intolerance of dissenting views of American history by slandering teachers and historians who foregrounded the role of racial and class conflict in American history. Without offering evidence, he accused teachers of promoting a "twisted web of lies in our schools," indoctrinating students in a version of history that has led them to hate America. This was, he claimed "a form of child abuse in the truest sense of those words."[22] Referring to the mostly nonviolent nationwide Black Lives Matter protests against police violence as "left-wing mobs" fomenting "violence and anarchy," Trump again without evidence charged that "left-wing rioting and mayhem are the direct result of decades of left-wing indoctrination in our schools." A key source of this alleged indoctrination named by Trump was Zinn, whom he depicted not as a historian but as a propagandist: "Our children are instructed from propaganda tracts, like those of Howard Zinn, that try to make students ashamed of their own history."

It is no accident that Zinn was the only historian Trump denounced by name and that, along with the 1619 Project (whose controversial curriculum places slavery at the center of the American experience), Zinn's work was made to sound like a serious threat to American patriotism. If one equates patriotism and Americanism as Trump does, with unreflective boasting about American greatness, Zinn would indeed seem threatening, for his *People's History* demands of us (as does the 1619 Project) a critical reckoning, a rethinking of the American past. Zinn beckons us to confront rather than evade the gap between our nation's inspiring democratic ideals and its failures to live up to them. Yet, contrary to Trump's accusation, Zinn was not a propagandistic purveyor of shame. For Zinn also narrated the struggles of egalitarian idealists to push America's government leaders toward policies consistent with the nation's democratic ideals. So it was just as possible to come away from reading Zinn feeling pride in the courage of antiwar activists as it was to feel shame about the massacre at My Lai. Zinn's goal, however, was not evoking pride or shame but rather promoting critical thinking about the past (and present) that could yield engaged democratic citizenship. History classrooms in a democratic society ought to be free and open enough to discuss the strengths and weaknesses of Zinn's and the 1619 Project's version of the American past as well as those of less critical versions of that past, so our historical dialogue is large and deep enough to encompass both the tragedy and the beauty of which James Baldwin wrote. This book is intended to convey Zinn's contribution to that historical dialogue.

CHAPTER 1

Origins and Appeal

Howard Zinn ranks as one of America's leading popularizers of its history. His *People's History of the United States* has been the best-selling popular survey of American history in the late twentieth and early twenty-first century, having sold more than 3,300,000 copies as of October 2019.[1] Remarkably, Zinn's antiwar, antiracist, anticapitalist *People's History*, published initially in 1980, became a best seller at a time when American politics was leaning rightward, during the Reagan era—a time of soaring military spending, retreat from civil rights enforcement, and enactment of the regressive economic agenda of big business. From 1980 through and beyond Zinn's death in 2010, *A People's History* sold an increasing number of copies with each passing year, the opposite of the normal trajectory of book sales.[2] Indeed, in 2003, on the occasion of the celebration of the one millionth copy sold, Hugh Van Dusen, Zinn's editor at Harper and Row (now Harper Collins) attested that in all his years in publishing he had never seen a book continue to expand its readership in this way annually, which in the book business was akin to defying the laws of physics.[3] The popularity of *A People's History* impacted the publishing world, as other presses sought to emulate its success by adopting the "People's History" tag for other books and the radical history approach that Zinn had used. One of these publishers was the New Press, whose "People's History" volumes, on everything from the American Revolution to U.S. sports history, Zinn endorsed.[4] The dissident speeches Zinn featured in *A People's History* would be performed by famed actors, actresses, musicians, and writers at theatrical events across the United States, culminating in a film version, *The People Speak*, which reached an estimated nine million viewers when it aired on the History Channel in December 2009.[5]

A People's History has also had a major impact on history teaching and learning, especially in high schools. Even though *A People's History* was considered too radical to be adopted by public school districts, innovative teachers beginning in the 1980s discussed and circulated in class photocopied chapters from Zinn's book and used them as a contrast to the corresponding and often boring chapters in their mandated textbooks.[6] Even today, Zinn's history, with its emphasis on the role of classism, racism, gender inequality, and imperialism in the American past, continues to attract tens of thousands of teachers who connect with it online through the Zinn Education Project's curriculum resources—a project endowed by a former Zinn student and staffed by talented, grassroots teacher-organizers who worked closely with Zinn in launching the project.[7]

This book explores the impact *A People's History* has had on history teaching and learning in schools, among the general public, and in popular culture. But before we delve into that impact we must start with Zinn himself, the key source of this educational and public rethinking of American history. So this chapter probes how Zinn understood the popularity and wide appeal of *A People's History* in the late twentieth- and early twenty-first-century United States, and it examines the book's origins and intentions and what the "people's history" approach to the American past meant for him. We also look at the first glimmerings of that appeal, via the internal reviews (the publisher's readers' reports) of Zinn's initial efforts to write a people's history of the United States, since those reviews—even when offering criticism—predicted that the book would fill a significant gap in the realm of accessible American history writing.

That the growing popularity of *A People's History* took its publisher by surprise is evidenced by the fact that Harper and Row gave Zinn only a small advance for the book and committed to a modest initial press run of five thousand copies.[8] Van Dusen even had to lobby to convince the press to bring the book out quickly in paperback, since there had been no expectation of robust sales. This is quite understandable since introductory histories almost never become best sellers.

The book's surprising popularity led Zinn and Van Dusen to ponder the reasons for it. Both came to link the success of *A People's History* to the impact that the 1960s had in fostering dissident politics and cultural change and the persistence of the critical antiwar and social justice ethos disseminated in that tumultuous era. As Zinn recalled in 2008,

> I remember sitting down [with Van Dusen], and asking "How come? Why is this happening?" And the answer, it was an encouraging one. The answer to it was: well people are hungry for a different and bolder, and yes even more radical view of our society, a more critical view. One that citizens should have of their society. In other words, the movements of the '60s had created a new kind of spirit, and that spirit translated itself into a desire for things in the culture, whether it's books or plays or movies . . . that would reflect their new experience. So we concluded that this still is the answer to . . . the question of why people are still buying *A People's History* in large numbers is that the

state of society is one that's not pleasing to people. They are not pleased with the wars that are going on. They are not pleased by the economic inequality in a country which is the wealthiest . . . in the world. They are not pleased with the discrimination on race, on sex, or against immigrants, and so on. And in a situation like that they are looking for something that's written that will corroborate their own instinctual desire to protest against what's going on. So our surprise at the success of the book began to dissipate as we began to think about why this was happening.[9]

Van Dusen also cited the impact of the 1960s on teachers in explaining why sales of *A People's History* increased each year. In 1991 he wrote Zinn a letter attributing the book's impact in high schools to "a generation of teachers who grew up in the 60s." Those teachers "naturally wanted to assign the book—one of the very few which matches their view of history and which students love" since it is "wonderfully readable and gripping."[10] Harper and Row incorporated into its marketing of the book this idea that teachers (as well as general readers) had become receptive to a more inclusive, critical reading of American history. Thus a fall 1991 Harper ad presented *A People's History* as connecting with this democratic revolution in historical understanding (and scholarship), contrasting Zinn's book with traditional textbooks' out-of-date elitism:

Recently, as a passing glance at even the editorial pages would reveal, there has been a seismic shift in the way history is viewed and taught. To the surprise of many, and to the chagrin of some, certain historians have been putting forward the idea that history does not consist solely in the conduct and decisions of kings, generals, diplomats, religious leaders, and captains of industry of European descent. In fact (shock! horror!), women, people of non-European backgrounds, the poor and working classes have actually always existed. While this was probably an opinion held by some for many years at a purely instinctive level, it was not one easily verified by the history books most of us were forced to slog through in grammar school, high school, and beyond. All this is by way of preface to saying that we at Harper proudly publish Howard Zinn, whose pioneering classics A PEOPLE'S HISTORY OF THE UNITED STATES . . . and THE TWENTIETH CENTURY . . . stand as essential antidotes to establishment and exclusionary views, and deserve to be mentioned in the context of both Black History Month and Women in History Month—and for that matter the [500th] Anniversary of Columbus's arrival in the New World.[11]

The '60s generational explanation of his book's popularity was attractive to Zinn in part because it accorded with his admiring view of social protest movements and of the most recent heyday of such movements, the 1960s.[12] Here Zinn was embodying the communalism of the 1960s social movements of which he had been a part (as a civil rights and antiwar movement veteran), crediting the book's popularity not to his own skills as a writer but to the critical spirit and mindset that was a legacy of those movements.[13]

This view of the book's popularity matched up well with Zinn's memory of why he had written *A People's History of the United States* in the first place, which was also deeply connected to the 1960s and its protest movements. As Zinn recalled in 2008,

> I decided to write *A People's History* . . . [after] teaching history for years, and we were going through and past the movements of the '60s, the southern [civil rights] movement, the antiwar movement, the women's movement . . . all sorts of movements of the '60s, the prisoners' movement, gay and lesbian movements. And people coming out of those movements were looking around for a history of the United States that would connect with the kind of spirit they felt, having been involved in those movements. They couldn't find that spirit in traditional history books because they'd been in movements of ordinary people striving against the power of the Establishment. And they saw, as I did when I was studying history, . . . the regular, traditional, orthodox books as representing really the voice of the Establishment . . . the voice of the presidents and generals . . . "the important people." [Post-sixties Americans were] looking for something that represented what they were feeling, having come out of those movements. And so they kept asking me as a teacher of history . . . if I knew of a book [introducing U.S. history] that was . . . a progressive, radical . . . critical view of American history. And there really wasn't. And so I thought "Well, I'll write it. And then I started to write it."[14]

In Zinn's telling, then, the genesis of *A People's History* came from people—movement veterans and others influenced by the protests of the 1960s—who "kept asking" him to "recommend a . . . one-volume history of the U.S. written from the point of view that would reflect the sensibilities of the '60s . . . their movements . . . and I couldn't find a book that would do it. I think that's what happens very often. If you can't find a book that does what you want, you write it."[15]

Zinn was so eager to credit people and movements of the 1960s with generating the demand for *A People's History* that in explaining his book's origins he spotlighted them rather than the '60s generation of New Left historians, who had produced the new social history (raising the banner of writing history "from the bottom up"), and histories critiquing U.S. imperialism and militarism that he would draw on in writing *A People's History*. According to Zinn, because of "the movements of the '60s, people began to rethink all sorts of issues: women's history, labor movement [history], [and the history of] war and antiwar movements. And the traditional textbooks and traditional books on American history didn't satisfy them. So . . . they were looking for this [more critical] point of view."[16]

Along these same lines, Zinn cited not the example of other radical historians or his own historical training but his involvement with the southern Black freedom struggle of the Long 1960s with shaping his bottom-up approach to writing history, focusing on people at the grass roots as opposed to government officials.

> What I saw in the South . . . amazing scenes [of courageous organizing against racism]. I was going from Atlanta, Georgia, to Selma, Alabama, to towns in Mississippi, and I was seeing remarkable scenes going on, and talking to extraordinary people. And I thought, this is not being captured [by the media or by academic books]. And I kept that in mind [in writing *A People's History*]. . . . I wanted to tell the story of this country from the standpoint of people who had been omitted, and to bring in events and vignettes that took place in our country that would not ordinarily make their way into the history books.[17]

Zinn's crediting of the southern Black freedom movement of the 1960s with inspiring his egalitarian, "people's history" approach to historical study has merit when one considers how that movement changed the focus of his writing. Zinn's first book, *La Guardia in Congress* (1959), read like a traditional Columbia University doctoral dissertation of the 1950s, which is how it originated, in that it was a top-down political history of an elected political leader.[18] It was quite a contrast to his innovative and bottom-up account of the Student Nonviolent Coordinating Committee, *SNCC: The New Abolitionists* (1964), which he wrote after he had been teaching at Spelman College, a historically Black college for women in Atlanta, and had served as a mentor to his students and other SNCC activists in the freedom movement.[19] His involvement and historical interest in the movement led him to do pioneering oral history work documenting this student movement.[20] Zinn's oral history interviews on the Deep South movement sit-ins against racial segregation and its voting rights and Freedom Rides agitation became the heart of his SNCC book, the first book on this central organization of the southern Black freedom struggle.[21] So the movement had helped turn Zinn's attention from the political elite to community-based dissident politics and protest, rendering him among the first American historians of the 1960s to approach history from the bottom up.

On the other hand, Zinn was already predisposed toward a democratic ap-

proach to history by his own social and political background, and so biograph-
ically the roots of Zinn's inclination toward people's history predate the 1960s.
Born in 1922 to a Jewish immigrant working-class family, Zinn was radicalized
in his youth during the Great Depression. Keenly aware of the tremendous gulf
that separated the wealthy from those like his family who worked hard but lived
in poverty, Zinn grew up "class conscious," as he put it.[22] So much so that he
was drawn to those radicals who most scathingly criticized and challenged that
inequity (and agitated against the fascist menace long before others in America did so), young communists in his Brooklyn neighborhood. Though Zinn
never became a party member, he attended a Communist-led demonstration
in Times Square as a teen and was knocked unconscious by one of the police
officers who broke up the event, which Zinn later cited as contributing to his
radicalization. He realized, "The state and its police were not neutral referees in
a society of contending interests. They were on the side of the rich and powerful.
Free speech? Try it and the police will be there with their horses, their clubs,
their guns, to stop you."[23]

Zinn's labor as a youth in a variety of working-class jobs, from waiter to ship-
yard worker, deepened his identification with workers and the labor movement.
Thus it is not surprising that after learning from a song by the radical folksinger
Woody Guthrie of the 1914 Ludlow Massacre, a major event in American labor
history left out of his school textbooks, Zinn chose at Columbia University even
in the conservative 1950s to write his history master's thesis on that massacre.[24]
He retained a lifelong interest in labor history, a sympathy for the working class,
and hostility to the inequities of capitalism, all of which would figure prominently in his *People's History of the United States*. For Zinn, issues of class and
social inequality were not mere abstractions but were personal and deeply felt,
since they harkened back to his youth and his family's hardships. One can see
this in Zinn's memoir, where, in commenting about his father's working-class
experience, Zinn angrily mocked the folklore of capitalism and the assumptions
foundational to the American dream of individual success, which he viewed as
insulting to the memory of such hardworking laborers:

> All his life . . . [my father] worked hard for very little. I've always resented
> the smug statements of politicians, media commentators, corporate executives
> who talked of how, in America, if you worked hard you would become rich.
> The meaning of that was if you were poor it was because you hadn't worked
> hard enough. I knew this was a lie, about my father and millions of others,
> men and women who worked harder than anyone, harder than financiers and
> politicians, harder than *anybody* if you accept that if you work at an unpleasant
> job that makes it very hard work indeed.[25]

In the end, Zinn's own experience and the sensibility he brought to writing *A People's History* reflected the insurgent radical politics of not only the 1960s but also the 1930s. In this way, he is one of the few popular writers shaped by both the Old and New Left. From the Depression era, his working-class roots, and proximity to the anticapitalist Left, Zinn had a strong awareness of class as a central and historical dividing line and source of social tension and protest. And from the 1960s, with Zinn's involvement and writing about the Black freedom movement, he gained a strong awareness of race as an essential and historical source of conflict, with racism and the struggles against it central to understanding American history. The 1960s also awakened Zinn to the role of gender in history, as he fostered and admired the activism of his students at Spelman against not only racism but also the paternalistic regimentation of campus life and restrictions imposed on their freedoms because they were female.[26]

On questions of war, imperialism, and foreign policy, Zinn brought an even more unusual multigenerational lens. In these areas, Zinn is best known as a figure aligned with the New Left, a leading critic in 1960s America of the Vietnam War, and author of a popular and early book urging the immediate withdrawal of U.S. military forces from Vietnam.[27] Zinn traveled as part of an antiwar delegation to the Paris peace talks to speak with the North Vietnamese delegation, and he was part of a similar delegation to North Vietnam, obtaining the release of three American pilots.[28] Zinn was also involved with the Pentagon Papers case and hid in his house some of the government documents for Daniel Ellsberg before they were published. Zinn became one of the nation's most prominent antiwar speakers.[29]

But Zinn's disillusionment with war and the U.S. military began long before the Vietnam debacle. Zinn was one of few authors who as a combat veteran from World War II—in which he served as a bombardier—came out of "the Good War" with a deep skepticism of the military and an almost pacifist outlook on war. This outlook grew from Zinn's troubled conscience, when he learned that well after the outcome of World War II was certain (three weeks before the war ended) he had been part of a bombing run that dropped the chemical weapon napalm on the French village of Royan, killing German soldiers, awaiting the surrender of their army, and French villagers as well.[30] This painful memory (and horror over the nuclear incineration of Hiroshima and Nagasaki), as much as the Vietnam tragedy, was foundational to the antiwar theme that dominates Zinn's accounts of U.S. military ventures in his *People's History*.[31]

The origins of *A People's History* are, then, intrinsically linked with Zinn's radical politics, which emerged from his own experiences from the 1930s through the Long 1960s. And Zinn's brand of radical activism and writing was such that it yielded a degree of candor that was almost unheard of within the American historical profession. Zinn did not believe historians could or should be neutral in their writing. He thought their pose of neutrality was dishonest, as in those textbooks he had read in high school and college that feigned neutrality but were in reality "white man's history" that neglected Black and Native American history and were so conservative that they never mentioned such prominent dissidents as Emma Goldman or the antilabor brutality of the Ludlow Massacre.[32] Zinn would be explicit that his sympathies in *A People's History* were with those who had been oppressed by American racism, capitalism, and imperialism and those who resisted such oppression. So Zinn's radical politics as well as his willingness to reject the conventions of history and textbook writing distinguished him from the authors of most introductory works on U.S. history at the time of the writing and publication of *A People's History*.

Zinn brought to this enterprise a political agenda that was the opposite of antiquarianism or history for its own sake. Zinn wanted his book both to resonate with those who in the 1960s had learned to think more critically about American society and to teach others why they too ought to think more critically about the United States, past and present. As Zinn explained in 2004, "I wanted in writing *A People's History* to awaken a great consciousness of class conflict, racial injustice, sexual inequality, and national arrogance."[33]

Zinn thought that by focusing—as most other introductory American history books and textbooks had not—on organizing and resistance to oppression, his *People's History* could deepen readers' understanding of U.S. history and inspire them to support people's movements for democratic change in their own time. "I wanted," Zinn stressed, "to bring into the light the hidden resistance of the people against the power of the establishment: the refusal of Native American people to simply die and disappear; the rebellion of black people in the antislavery movement and in the more recent rebellion against racial segregation; the strikes carried out by working people to improve their lives."[34]

Activism and politics not only motivated Zinn in writing *A People's History* but also influenced the timing of his writing of the book. Zinn's activism against the Vietnam War in the 1960s and early 1970s made it impossible for him then to take on a project so ambitious as *A People's History*. As Zinn recalled, during the Vietnam era even his writing was "wrapped up" in that antiwar struggle. "I wrote a book [titled] *Vietnam: The Logic of Withdrawal*. I wrote a book about civil disobedience." The latter originated as rebuttal to U.S. Supreme Court justice Abe Fortas's book *Concerning Dissent and Civil Disobedience* that had condemned draft resistance. "My writings were all geared to . . . immediate necessities [of antiwar organizing], and I didn't have the leisure to sit down and do what I . . . had in mind, to write the kind of radical history that would become *A*

People's History of the United States." So the writing of that history would have to wait until the late 1970s, after the war and the movement against it had ended.[35]

Zinn's public discussions of the genesis of his work popularizing radical history were incomplete, however, since he did not mention that his initial idea for *A People's History* was for a book series he proposed editing, rather than for a single-volume *People's History* that he would author. Zinn articulated this vision in a proposal he sent to Daniel Okrent, then a young editor at Alfred Knopf, in May 1972. The idea was for a twelve-to-fifteen-volume series of books to be published "in celebration of the 200th anniversary of the Declaration of Independence."[36] Even though the proposal was never acted on, it is a revealing document that gets at Zinn's inception of the term "people's history" and how he envisioned popularizing a democratic and anti-elitist approach to the writing of American history.

Zinn told Okrent that he chose "People's History" for the title of the book series because "it comes closest to the theme of the series," without sounding "outrageously radical considering how often we see textbooks labeled 'A History of the American People,' and yet speaks clearly to new approaches, new consciousness among so many young teachers in schools and colleges." The new approach, of course, necessitated breaking with the "customary telling of history from the top down, through study of national policy, leaders, moguls." Zinn wrote, "It really has to be different (justifiably so, not for the sake of sensationalism) to attract great attention. And that crucial difference, as I see it, is to tell the history of the United States from the standpoint of the various parts of the population who are either given their token chapter in the standard text, or ignored altogether as a group. There is a large public now ready for this."[37]

Among the most striking aspects of the proposal was Zinn's stress on making this People's History series accessible.[38] Though there were some professional historians on the list he included of possible contributing authors, Zinn was critical of the academic writing style that too often left historians disconnected from the public and unable to reach a mass readership. So Zinn proposed that an author in this series need "not be necessarily a professional historian, but someone who can be depended on to be factually accurate, a lively raconteur, neither academic jargon nor sensationalism—I think of Barbara Tuchman as a model."[39] Thus, in discussing the volume he wanted to focus on "working people," Zinn noted that "most academic labor historians are real dull." So he was inclined toward popular writers for that volume, naming radio host and oral history writer Studs Terkel and novelist Harvey Swados as possible authors, along with his friend and radical historian Staughton Lynd. Similarly, for the volume Zinn envisioned as being titled *The Accused*—"a history of civil liberties and constitutional law and political hysteria, from the Alien and Sedition Act, to the Harrisburg trial and Pentagon Papers case"—he suggested as a possible author "this fellow [E. L.] Doctorow who wrote *The Book of Daniel*," the historical novel whose protagonist was the son of Julius and Ethel Rosenberg. And for the volume on farmers, "from Bacon's Rebellion through the grape and lettuce strikers of today," he wrote, "maybe we can find some young John Steinbeck." Zinn was also open to using journalists and thought famed Vietnam War correspondent Jonathan Schell would be an excellent choice to do a volume on the "history of militarism and wars from the standpoint of the American GI, sailor, marine."

Zinn was keen to have books in the series that conveyed critical perspectives on race relations, written by authors of color. Indeed, the first category in his book series proposal was "Indians look at American history," in which he hoped a Native American historian would offer "a savage account (read into it what you like!) . . . of the interaction between Indians and the dominant white society, from the Columbian explorations to now." He wanted either his friend Vincent Harding, a prominent African American historian and civil rights activist, or Black novelist John Oliver Killens to write a volume on the Black experience. "This is the model," explained Zinn, "to range through American history, focusing on some group, through the eyes of that group, and[,] as often as possible, having a member of that group do the telling, or[,] if not, have enough documentary material so that the viewpoint[s] of those people come through powerfully."[40]

Transcending nationalism, much as he would in his single volume *People's History of the United States*, Zinn envisioned foreign policy volumes that would focus not on the view from Washington but from those on the receiving end of U.S. military and economic intervention. "Imagine telling the history of American involvement in Latin America, from the Monroe Doctrine though the Dominican intervention, through the eyes of Latin-Americans." Zinn thought Brazilian scholar-journalist Márcio Moreira Alves would be an ideal choice to write this kind of historical volume on U.S. intervention in Latin America.[41]

This inclination to break with a parochial and nationalistic approach to analyzing U.S. globalism is consistent with Zinn's politics, educational work, and his approach to history. Most obviously it is connected to his willingness as an antiwar activist to see the Vietnam War from the anticolonial Vietnamese perspective. But even earlier, at Spelman College he had headed the non-Western studies program, rejecting Eurocentrism and advocating what later would be called multicultural education. At Spelman, Zinn had been close to African students, sharing their enthusiasm for ending colonial rule. As a young professor, Zinn had spent a year at Harvard on a fellowship studying Asian culture and history. So Zinn was well-equipped and inclined to see the United States from a global perspective, influenced by critiques of U.S. globalism and neocolonialism.[42]

What is evident from his people's history book series proposal is that by 1972 Zinn—though not yet realizing that a one-volume people's history would be much more accessible than a people's history book series—had already worked out the approach he would employ in the late 1970s to write his *People's History of the United States*. That approach, in a nutshell: U.S. history from below, minus American nationalism, deeply critical of racism, war, capitalism, and political and economic elites, written with the flare and clarity of leading novelists and journalists, avoiding the leaden prose of academia.[43] Virtually every chapter and major topic covered in *A People's History of the United States* was anticipated in Zinn's earlier book series proposal.

Of course, the series proposal was more ambitious than what could be covered in a single volume. However, the breadth of *A People's History of the United States* mirrors the scope and originality of Zinn's thinking about ways to introduce Americans to their dissident past and the varied forms of oppression and resistance that textbooks omitted. For example, one volume Zinn envisioned for his series would have been devoted to young people, others to the elderly, women, cities and city people, and radicals. A topic rarely covered in history textbooks, prisoners, would have been explored in a separate volume. Zinn, who was a critic of the penal system and a prison abolitionist, thought that a people's history should offer a book-length study of "people in jail, probing such questions as What were jails and punishment like in colonial days? What about the abolition of imprisonment for debt movement? What of the development of the modern jail in the 19th century?, that which we still have with us today? What documentary materials can be dug up on the local jails, state penitentiaries, federal prisons: day-to-day life, diaries, memoirs, prison rebellions, all the way up through Attica?"[44] Zinn suggested that this volume might also cover other areas of confinement, including mental institutions. "I think of Foucault's *Madness and Civilization*," he wrote, "about the development of those institutions in France. Should the sick in hospitals be included too—the institutionalized in general? I'm not sure at this point. There's a value to focusing on prisoners. There's another value to saying: here are all the people we lock up and put away for one reason or another."[45]

On literature and culture, Zinn had a volume in mind that would narrate the history of "neglected writers and thinkers. . . . I am thinking of people's literature: the oral tradition, folk music." The goal of this book would have been "getting at the underside of the literary and cultural history of the country. Humor, popular art & entertainment. Unpublished poetry or self-published poetry."[46] As a possible author of this volume, Zinn suggested poet Denise Levertov.

While Zinn could not fit everything in his one-volume *People's History*, the sensibility that shaped it can be traced to his 1972 book series proposal. For example, while Zinn did not have the space in *A People's History* to offer the multicentury history of prisoners that he recommended in his series proposal, he did include in it a passionate and empathetic history of the prison rights movement that placed the Attica prison rebellion of 1971 into historical perspective.[47] Similarly, though he lacked the space to devote a chapter to people's literature, folk music, and folklore, the words of dissident poets and novelists loom large and are embedded throughout *A People's History*. Thus, Zinn titled his chapter on the Black freedom movement of the 1950s and 1960s "Or Does It Explode?" from a line in "Lenox Avenue Mural," the famous poem by Langston Hughes. The chapter's opening four pages introduce readers to the Black experience through African American poetry by Hughes, Claude McKay, Countee Cullen, Gwendolyn Bennett, Paul Laurence Dunbar, and Margaret Walker, the prose of Richard Wright, and the satirizing by Black performers Bert Williams and George Walker of white minstrel shows. "It was," as Zinn pointed out, "all there in the poetry, the prose, the music, sometimes masked, sometimes unmistakably clear—the signs of a people unbeaten, waiting, hot, coiled."[48]

While Zinn's book series proposal articulated key components of his approach to popularizing America's neglected history of militarism, racial, class, and gender oppression, and dissent, it also signaled the limitations of his approach. In the proposal's discussion of an international affairs volume, Zinn, as we have seen, was keen to have U.S. foreign policy studied from the perspective of those victimized by the United States, including Latin Americans, Asians, and Africans. But instead of striving for a new synthesis of that history from the perspectives of both those impacted by U.S. policy and the Washington elite who made policy, Zinn was rejecting the latter. "The point here," Zinn wrote, "is to do a history of American foreign policy, but not as it is customarily is done, from the top, for the Pentagon Papers approach or the presidential diary . . . [or] memoir approach."[49] This is not to say that Zinn had no interest in the Washington elite. He certainly would cover enough of its thoughts and actions to document its abuses of power. But as the series proposal indicated, he saw his main contribution as additive—in this case adding the views of those outside the United States and elsewhere in illuminating the views of dissidents, the oppressed, and mass protest movements that challenged those in power—rather than synthesizing top-down and bottom-up history.[50]

Zinn was not interested in having the people below share the spotlight with those with political and economic power but wanted the spotlight shifted from the elite to the people. This can be seen clearly in his 1972 book series proposal and its volume on the history of soldiers. Zinn was enthused about this volume since he saw that it would bring out unconventional, surprising topics.

> Let's have a history of militarism and wars from the standpoint of the American GI, sailor, marine. Hard to do, but there must be a lot of documentary stuff here. Also a necessary supplement to the volumes on foreign affairs written through foreign eyes. Not Theodore Roosevelt on the Rough Riders, but some soldiers writing about Cuba, or about the crushing of the rebels in the Philippines. The closer we get to the present day, the more material; we could fill a volume with stuff from the ordinary GI's on Vietnam: look at the Winter Soldier hearings.[51]

Note that here Zinn was not saying "let's compare the bottom-up view and critique of American militarism from the common soldier with Teddy Roosevelt's top-down view glorifying war." He was saying instead, "*Not* Theodore Roosevelt on the Rough Riders" (emphasis added), meaning that the top-down view in this case was not even worth including. And in this case Zinn meant it literally, as he chose not to mention Roosevelt's Rough Riders in *A People's History*.

Zinn's understanding of the way that social change worked in America had a lot to do with his own relative lack of interest in elite politics. For Zinn, it was not the major political parties but democratic movements that pushed for real change, and so the important actions for historians to study were those of such movements. One can see Zinn's disdain for the two-party system and the national political elite it empowers in the way he responded in 2008 to a question about the U.S. presidential race:

> When somebody says to me, "I've read your book [*A People's History*]. Who do you want to be President?" Well, first of all, my heart sinks. This person has read my book! This person hasn't understood that for me, sure it's better to have A than A prime, B or B minus; I say, "Some presidents are somewhat better than others, but the whole point of the book . . . the really important thing, is not who sits in the White House, but who's picketing the White House" . . . not what laws are passed by Congressmen, but what people are out on the streets demanding Congress do this, do that, stop the war, raise the minimum wage, and so on. The important things in history, the important struggles for justice and equality, are not initiated by the White House. And one of the things that history . . . teaches us, if we look at it carefully, is that these initiatives for change have always come from below . . . from social

movements. And presidents, congressmen, and supreme courts have had to react to that. And therefore the job of citizens is to create the kind of climate, ... atmosphere, spirit ... agitation in the country, that will cause whoever is in the White House, to be forced to react to it.

I don't tell people not to vote, ... who to vote for, even though there are gradations of good and bad.... But I tell people to support their candidate for one minute ... that they're in the voting booth, think about the election, but in all the time before you get into that voting booth, and all the time after, be out there in the streets.[52]

These attitudes reflected Zinn's experience as an activist as well as his study of history. In the Black freedom movement of the early 1960s, Zinn saw firsthand a supposedly progressive Democratic president, John F. Kennedy, initially reluctant to take meaningful action to support the movement, protect its activists, or stand up to segregationists. And so Kennedy began his presidency lethargic on civil rights, much as his Republican predecessor had been. Indeed, a central theme of the report Zinn wrote on the Albany, Georgia, civil rights struggle for the Southern Regional Council (1962) was the failure of the Kennedy administration and its FBI to assist the Black community and Martin Luther King Jr. in securing their constitutional rights from the segregationists who were trampling them.[53] Zinn was equally critical of the Johnson administration's failure to protect Freedom Summer voting rights volunteers from being brutalized and killed by Mississippi racists, and he observed that it was only after years of pressure and sacrifice that the freedom movement finally got these presidents to support civil rights legislation. Similarly, in his decade of activism against the Vietnam War, Zinn found both the Democratic president Lyndon Johnson and his Republican successor Richard Nixon devoted to the anticommunist crusade in Vietnam and determined to continue waging an increasingly unpopular war. Zinn noted that here too it took years for a persistent and militant mass movement to win, finally helping to end the war.[54]

Along with Zinn's own activist experiences in the 1960s, he was also left unimpressed with major party and presidential leadership by his reading of the classic indictment of that leadership, *The American Political Tradition* (1948), by Richard Hofstadter—who Zinn praised as one of the "great American historians" of the twentieth century. Zinn thought Hofstadter correct in stressing that, despite their differences rhetorically, conservatives and liberals were both adherents of "nationalism" and shared "a willingness to go to war" and a reverence for "capitalism ... the market, and private enterprise." This meant to Zinn that whether liberal or conservative, Democratic or Republican, U.S. presidents were not inclined to "make any serious changes in the social structure," "do away with poverty," or challenge what President Dwight Eisenhower termed the "military industrial complex."[55] Such change, if it was to come, would have to be initiated from below, by activists and movements out in the streets demanding change, peace, and social justice, and they, rather than status quo–oriented politicians, ought to be center stage in *A People's History*.

⌒

When Zinn realized in the mid-1970s that a single-volume people's history would be far more accessible to the public than a large series of books, he began to work on a prospectus for such a work, which he initially titled *Struggle for Democracy: A People's History of the United States*. The prospectus for his book confirms what Zinn said later in interviews, that its impetus for came from his having been "approached by teachers, neighbors, friends . . . on countless occasions" to recommend "a good, plainly written one-volume history of the United States, which is up to date in what it covers and in its viewpoint." Zinn explained that what those people meant by "up-to-date-viewpoint" was "an approach to history which incorporates the sharp criticism of government policy that has become widespread in the past fifteen years, not just among radicals, but among millions of Americans. (See polls of the past few years, which show, after Vietnam and Watergate, a huge number of Americans disillusioned with government leaders and official myths)." Zinn thought that "history these days should reflect the new consciousness of the history of the underclasses in America—native Americans, blacks, working people, women (one might add GI's, old people, children), those overlooked in the telling of history, which has traditionally centered on the doings of the powerful and successful."[56]

Zinn was aware that social historians in academia had already been exploring this new perspective on the past, but he knew they had made little headway in reaching a mass audience. "Among professional historians, we have [heard] more and more talk about (and disputes about) 'history from the bottom up,'" he wrote. "There have been scattered attempts to emphasize that kind of history, but no comprehensive history of the country in one volume written from that point of view." Zinn's one-volume American history would be "held together by a unified interpretation of the American past and a strong, provocative point of view," he said. "It has been in my head for years, and finally I would like to put [it] down, in language intelligible to the reading public."[57]

Since Zinn was pitching his book idea to a leading publisher, Knopf, he naturally emphasized the uniqueness of the work he was planning. And it is true that the sweeping, accessible survey of the American past from a bottom-up, antiwar, and antiracist perspective he was proposing was unique at that time.[58]

But it is not true that there had been only "scattered attempts," as he put it, at writing history from that perspective. Indeed, long before Zinn began writing *A People's History* there had been major works that had done so, such as Jesse Lemisch's, Staughton Lynd's, and Alfred F. Young's studies in the 1960s of the American Revolution.[59] In 1968 *Towards a New Past: Dissenting Essays in American History*, edited by Barton Bernstein, was published, bringing together the best of New Left bottom-up and anti-imperialist scholarship in history.[60] Francis Jennings had recast colonial history from the Native American perspective in *The Invasion of America: Indians, Colonialism and the Cant of Conquest* (1975). New feminist scholarship had yielded important works, such as Gerda Lerner's *The Grimke Sisters of South Carolina: Pioneers of Women's Rights and Abolition* (1971), and a generation of scholars of new labor history, inspired by the great British radical historian E. P. Thompson's pathbreaking work, *The Making of the English Working Class* (1966), had been probing working-class culture and protest.[61] Herbert Gutman's *The Black Family in Slavery and Freedom* (1977), John W. Blassingame's *The Slave Community: Plantation Life in the Antebellum South* (1972), Lawrence W. Levine's *Black Culture, Black Consciousness: Afro-American Folk Thought from Slavery to Freedom* (1977), and numerous other works explored the African American experience under slavery, building on the work of W. E. B. Du Bois and other pioneers of Black history.

And a generation of New Left diplomatic historians, alienated by the Vietnam War, created a wave of new scholarship questioning Cold War ideology and the nationalistic assumptions that had led most U.S. historians to write as if the United States was faultless in fomenting the Cold War. In response, the infuriated cold warrior Robert James Maddox published in 1973 *The New Left and the Origins of the Cold War*, with seven chapters, each devoted to attacking a major Cold War revisionist, seeking to discredit this new radical scholarship. Zinn knew of such radical scholarship and would cite and draw on it in his *People's History*, but as the first popularizer of this history, there were times, as in this book proposal, when he would give the impression that he had invented it, which he had not.[62]

Even at this early point in the planning of *A People's History*, Zinn displayed an awareness of a central tension in the writing of such a radical history. Being "sharply critical of the American past" could sound "cynical" and leave readers either despairing or cynical themselves about the American past and future. Zinn proposed to avoid that trap by rescuing "from the archives the overlooked heroes and heroines and popular struggles which suggest possibilities for the American future."[63]

This approach was grounded in Zinn's long-standing belief that for people's history to inspire new generations of activists, "history should not leave us with a dark and hopeless vision. There is too much of that already. There are too many pessimists, too many cynics." In people's history, he said, "we need to see how courageous men and women in their time" stood up for peace and social justice and thus gain "the good feeling of standing alongside people who fought back: the irrepressible Mark Twain pointing his finger at the American imperialists, . . . Jack London arguing for socialism, W.E.B. DuBois pioneering the fight for black people, Charlotte Gilman telling of the economic and sexual exploitation of women, Emma Goldman speaking magnificently for anarchism, against war, for our freedom to love and to live our lives as we choose."[64]

Zinn was convinced that even though the mass protest movements "did not take power away from the business and military interests in the country," they did succeed in keeping "alive the spirit of resistance and unity against arbitrary power." Thus it was up to those who wrote people's history to "keep this story" of resistance "fresh in our memories" and to "pass that spirit to whatever generation will make a new America." This meant that a people's history should be realistic about the problems of the past while also offering stories to inspire and empower readers, suggesting to them that resistance has a noble past and can have a promising future. The lesson is that in American history "there were years of suffering and brutality, and only days of magic. . . . But we can have more of those days. . . . It is up to us."[65]

Zinn's book prospectus showed his desire to avoid getting bogged down with chronology. He wanted to probe the history of oppression and resistance beyond the usual chronological chapter cut-off points so that key themes in U.S. history would not get truncated or overlooked altogether. Zinn thought a textbook-style race through time trivialized important events and conversely gave undue attention to already well-known events, thus evading hard historical truths. This is what Zinn was referring to when he warned in his book prospectus that

> the strictly chronological approach is not ideologically neutral; by fragmenting the crucial issues it becomes easier to avoid those troubling conclusions which come from continuous attention to a problem. For instance, official policy on the race question becomes more clear and more vulnerable to criticism, as one sticks with it, across the centuries. And the complicated ways of resistance of blacks, subtle or overt, become impressive when viewed over a period of time, through slavery and "freedom." Similarly with other issues.[66]

Zinn would later find it impractical to dispense with a chronological sequencing in *A People's History* (since it would be easier to read his work alongside conventional textbooks if the structure of both was the same). But one can see remnants of Zinn's desire to organize the book thematically by the way he combined major events and eras into a single chapter. Thus the Civil War and Reconstruction are explored in the same chapter, as are World War II and the Cold War—something one never sees in conventional textbooks.[67] And Zinn would offer important generalizations and questions about American history that far transcended the chronological boundaries of the single chapter in which they appeared. Thus in the opening page of A People's History's chapter "Drawing the Color Line," on the enslavement of Africans in America, Zinn wrote, "There is not a country in world history in which racism has been more important, for so long a time, as in the United States. And the problem of 'the color line,' as W. E. B. Du Bois put it, is still with us. So it is more than a purely historical question to ask: How does it start?—and an even more urgent question: How might it end? . . . Is it possible for whites and black to live together without hatred?"[68]

The "tentative outline" that Zinn provided for an introductory chapter he intended to include in A People's History illuminated his approach to the book and American history and so is worth reviewing, even though in the end he did not write a formal introductory chapter (but instead opened the book with his iconoclastic Columbus chapter). Initially Zinn had planned in an introductory chapter to make three key points. The first was that "history writing is necessarily selective, and therefore cannot avoid a point of view."[69] This meant including "a lucid, terse discussion of the critical questions of objectivity, neutrality, values"—which Zinn would end up providing in his Columbus chapter via his critique of Samuel Eliot Morrison's classic and mostly flattering biography of the explorer.[70] The second point: "The viewpoint of this book will be forthrightly that of the people left out of the standard histories, or given token attention, or dealt with patronizingly, or seen as passive victims. Ours will not be the usual situation in which the historian invited himself to sit with the mighty and so sees the past from the lofty perch of Presidents."[71] Here again (as we saw in his people's history book series proposal) Zinn used the additive rather than synthesizing approach, adding the view from below and eschewing the view of lofty presidents. This highlighted his egalitarianism—that he would not privilege the elites' views over the views of "the people," including those the elite oppressed—but it can also be read as impatience with elites that limited his empathy and understanding of them. Zinn conveys his approach clearly in the first chapter of A People's History when he breaks away from the Columbus story to announce that he prefers to "tell the story of the discovery of America from the perspective of the Arawaks, of the Constitution from the standpoint of the slaves, of Andrew Jackson as seen by the Cherokees, of the Civil War as seen by the New York Irish," and so on.[72]

The third and final point in Zinn's tentative outline is in some ways the most interesting—and is not articulated in the opening chapter of *A People's History*. It summarizes his view of the contrast between elite and nonelite history, explains why the latter interested him more, and shows us the way he saw the role of conflict in American history. Zinn wrote that when you take a bottom-up approach to American history, "the standard argument among historians" over whether "consensus or conflict" has been more characteristic in society "looks false and confusing." Zinn credited Richard Hofstadter's "wonderful book" *The American Political Tradition* for disproving "the myth of real conflict" at the top of society and the U.S. political system. But Zinn argued that Hofstadter erred in leaving "vacant the history of opposition from below—perhaps because writing in the late Forties, he was not impelled to be aware of those currents." Thus Zinn concluded, "The real conflict [in American history] has not been among liberals and conservatives, Jacksonians and Whigs, Republicans and Democrats—but between all of them and those people who were so excluded they did not even merit attention as contending forces."[73]

Zinn thought that, if viewed from their point of view, those excluded from power—"by far the great majority [of the American people]"—were "in constant opposition to the dominant groups."[74] Nonetheless, this opposition was, in Zinn's words, "scattered and ineffective" because the establishment was powerful, clever, and brutal, dealing with such dissent "by force and deceit," using "a variety of political techniques and cultural conditioning to hold on to power and undermine resistance, pushing potential rebels into quiescence or collaboration" yet "never totally subduing the opposition."

In his proposal Zinn argued that the virtual erasure of the history of dissent from American memory via the antiradical "mass education system and mass media" undermined the prospects of serious change. He viewed this as a form of "cultural pacification." By playing down "the amount of rebellion, dissent, conflict in American history" the U.S. educational system promoted "the myth of one big, happy consensual American family," papering over class differences and other forms of inequality and division with such misleading unitary terms as "national interest and national security."[75]

Zinn envisioned *A People's History* not as romanticizing dissent or exaggerating "the amount of overt opposition" but shattering the myth that those outside the elite could be subsumed under an American capitalist consensus. "The point" of a people's history, wrote Zinn, "is to make clear that the country is not one family united by a common interest, but consists of (a) privileged groups, and (b) the rest of the country, whose opposition has never been strong enough to make this country a true democracy, but whose expressions. . . . illuminate the history of this country as a struggle for democracy not yet achieved."[76]

Zinn's plan to challenge the myth of capitalist consensus did not stem solely from academic interest. The myth needed to be shattered to inspire activists struggling in late twentieth-century America to build protest movements. For Zinn, top-down history was objectionable because it enabled the elite who owned most of the property to act as if they owned the nation's very history—a mind-set he found troubling and inappropriate for a democratic society. As Zinn later put it, "[The top-down] approach to history . . . in every society serves the interests of the privileged and powerful, because by ignoring ordinary people, it reinforces their feelings of powerlessness. We are not surprised when the narratives given to the public in totalitarian states deify the leaders and reduce the citizenry to ciphers. But we are startled when it is suggested to us in liberal democratic societies such as ours, boasting freedom of expression and a pluralism of ideas, there is a similar exaltation of leaders, with everyone else barely visible."[77] Ever the optimist, Zinn thought the history he was writing, of resistance by "the victims of our expansion, blacks, working people . . . women . . . suggest[s] a coming conflict[on behalf of social justice, peace, and participatory democracy] more fierce than any that has yet taken place in our 200-year history."[78] That is why in outlining his book's final chapter in the late 1970s, not foreseeing Reagan's presidency and the nation's shift rightward, Zinn described a continuation and possibly decisive acceleration of the movements for social change that had been so central to the United States in the 1960s. Thus Zinn promised in that last chapter to discuss what might be

> a climatic joining in our time of the various strand[s] of the people's struggle for democracy, and against those who have thus far controlled the economy, the politics, the culture. Blacks, native Americans, working people of lower and middle classes, women, have rebelled [separately] but with portents of alliance-through-necessity. Also scattered upsurges of prisoners, consumers, tenants, welfare recipients, speaking by implication for the old, the institutionalized, the illness-ridden—a Brechtian ensemble of the dispossessed. All these, disunited, surging and ebbing uncertainly, mollified often by gestures and symbols, fearful of punishment gestating inside a rich, armed empire. The empire, however, seems to have reached its limits in the outer world and is falling back. Also, it may be reaching the limits of ingenuity in maintaining its control inside the country, judging by indices of crime and economic disorder. We might cautiously sketch the outlines of a possible democratic society in the America of the 21st century.[79]

Agree with it or not, Zinn's conflict-centered view of history from below was exciting (even theatrical—as with the Brechtian reference above) and original for an introductory American history targeting not academics but the general public. And it was not just that Zinn wrote with verve but also that his timing was perfect, in writing a radical history that millions of Americans would prove eager to read in the aftermath of the Long 1960s.

It is not surprising, then, that all six outside readers for Cambridge University Press, the first publisher to whom Zinn sent his single-volume book proposal, responded enthusiastically. Though the reviewers were anonymous, all appear to have been historians and aware of the chasm between the work of new radical scholars, those stirring up the profession by stressing the underside of American history, and the dull introductory textbooks whose authors seemed oblivious to this rethinking of the American experience. As one reader prophetically asserted, "The general reader who was weaned on [Samuel Eliot] Morison and [Henry Steele] Commager [or other conventional U.S. history textbooks] or Thomas Bailey's diplomatic history [which painted a benign picture of U.S. foreign policy] in high school or college and who wants to know what really happened . . . is ready and eagerly waiting. So also is the college survey clientele. And I would add, so is the high school teenager but for the stranglehold which is maintained over what he is allowed to read in U.S. history. But maybe, out of school hours, he may pick up a paperback Zinn."[80]

An anonymous reader on the Princeton faculty proved equally prophetic in recognizing that "the point of view Zinn holds will . . . be controversial and unpopular in many circles," especially among mainstream historians and conservatives certain to be offended by his radical criticism of America's failings. But this reader thought such controversy would be "all to the good as a teaching device" since it would offer students the opportunity to compare Zinn's revisionist account of the American past with more conventional counterparts. "Certainly [Zinn's] is a point of view that has real legitimacy, and that represents the perspective of an increasing number of younger historians. But whether one agrees or not, the book would promise to be just the kind of provocative teaching tool that would interest me."[81] This is precisely the way, as we will see in chapter 3, high school teachers would view *A People's History* as they used it to challenge conventional textbook history.

The most balanced and perceptive reader's report at Cambridge University Press came from a historian was who was "very impressed with both the proposal and the prospects for a successful book . . . [that would attract] a large market . . . not simply among students in college courses, but [also] in a more general readership interested in American history."[82] That positive assessment, the reader explained, stemmed in part from "admiration for Mr. Zinn," whose books and articles attested to his "ability to present original and provocative ideas in the clear, intelligible fashion necessary in reaching a wide audience." The reader shared with Zinn the belief that a critical look at American history in an accessible introductory work was long overdue.

But this reader detected a problem with Zinn's assumptions about both elite political history and the history of conflict between the elite and the masses. This reader thought Zinn was too dismissive of electoral politics and the conflicts among those who wielded political power, too wedded to the notion that those outside the elite were in a constant state of turmoil and protest. This reader found it simplistic of Zinn to posit a consensus at the top of American society and constant conflict between the top and those at "the bottom" or "the excluded."

> Is it really true that (p. 6) "the great major[i]ty" of Americans have been in "constant opposition to the dominant groups?" Rather, it seems to me to be the challenge to delineate when consensus did reach far down into the lower classes, and when class or racial conflict did predominate. The idea of "constant opposition" is, in fact, a fundamentally ahistorical idea, since it excuses the historian from investigating when conflict did and did not exist, and why it was stronger at some times and in some regions than others. . . . Zinn does mention . . . that "a variety of political techniques helped to contain social conflict." But his outline shows a singular desire to avoid all consideration of [electoral] politics. Now I am well aware that "traditional" [historical] writing has emphasized politics to the exclusion of the topics Zinn will be dealing with. But this does not make it correct simply to reverse the equation and argue that politics does not need to be considered at all. The political system has played a fundamental role in American history, particularly in this context, the role of linking people from all parts of the social scale in a common ritual and a common set of rights, while excluding those seen to be outside the body politic—blacks and women, for example, in the 19th century. Zinn does have a chapter entitled "The Politics of Class Conflict," but it seems there will be much more of the latter than the former in it.[83]

One must bear in mind that this reader was responding to a brief book proposal, not the finished manuscript, and so had no way of knowing that Zinn's book would not ignore electoral politics. Nonetheless, as we saw in Zinn's earlier book series proposal, Zinn was decentering electoral politics in the American historical narrative because he believed the major challenges to the status quo came from below, from movements outside the electoral system. So this reader was correctly sensing that in positing a consensus among the governing class, Zinn was writing them off as sources of major social change (and representing at best very narrow policy choices, Tweedledee and Tweedledum) and consequently would display little interest or empathy in A People's History even for the reformers among them.

The reader's critique was also perceptive in challenging Zinn's notion of "constant opposition" from below to ruling class oppression since American history is filled at least as much with acquiescence as resistance to the status quo. However, for an introductory text, this stress on persistent opposition made for an exciting, action-packed, and at times inspiring narrative—especially since most textbooks so downplayed class conflict that many readers had simply never heard of many of the tumultuous events Zinn would portray in A People's History. So while there are indeed problems with the notion of "constant opposition" in history, Zinn's People's History would not offer a theory but instead a detailed narrative, packed with dramatic stories and eloquent quotations illustrating oppression and resistance to it, which seemed revelatory for novice readers of history, especially compared to standard textbooks.

The last steps en route to publication of A People's History came after Zinn shifted his pitch from Cambridge University Press to Harper and Row. Zinn's editor at Harper recalled the book proposal as "brilliant," and when Zinn submitted the manuscript, the readers' reports on it were equally effusive.[84] "Stunning," was the way Robert C. Twombly—architectural historian and biographer of Frank Lloyd Wright—characterized the Zinn manuscript in his report for Harper. Twombly thought Zinn's People's History had "superbly achieved its objective of uncovering 'the underside'" of the American past, telling "the story of the American people in all its unvarnished complexity and variety." Zinn, he wrote,

> in his strikingly original text, . . . avoids the commonly accepted categories around which American history has traditionally been organized. Discussing colonial America, for example, he does not begin with the familiar story of expanding Europe and swashbuckling adventurers, their American outposts, settlement of . . . colonies, the slow growth of liberty, and its inevitable struggle against a tyrannical England. . . . Rather . . . [it] is about reds, blacks, and working class whites . . . a social history of working people, minorities, women, children, and the ways their lives were affected by forces over which they had little control but against which they repeatedly struggled. . . . Zinn fleshes [out] a much more accurate, realistic, and complete picture of life as actually lived in colonial America than if he had concentrated on the . . . leaders . . . of the period.

Twombly provided analysis of A People's History in comparison to the college textbooks assigned to introduce undergraduates to the American past. He deemed those textbooks literary and educational flops (the same as could have been said about high school history textbooks). The "standard [textbook] histories by prominent historians—the first ten that any editor or historian could mention—simply turn students off." By contrast, he said, "Zinn's book . . . has a better chance than any of the competition . . . of making history real and alive, especially to introductory students." The difference was not only due to the new and exciting vista on the American past that came from Zinn's approach to history but also to Zinn's "lively . . . writing style," which Twombly connected to Zinn's political passion and compassion—and his refusal to embrace typical textbooks' colorless tone of political neutrality. Zinn, as Twombly pointed out, took "many opportunities to editorialize" on historical events, inserting himself into the narrative as no textbook author would. Though unconventional, such insertions worked well, Twombly noted, since they were "clearly indicated, un-confusing, and help make the book more alive to the reader by making the author a real person."[85]

Zinn was, in effect, inventing a new approach to the historical survey book, rejecting the stance of objective reporter of historical information in favor of what Twombly aptly labeled "advocacy history," in which the author explicitly identifies with the oppressed of the stories he narrates and makes clear that he is "an actor in an ongoing struggle who, enriched by the people about whom he writes, lends his talents to the modern version of the causes for which they fought." Twombly thought it took considerable skill to accomplish all this without becoming "sentimental or propagandistic," and he wrote that Zinn had managed this feat through "rich . . . documentation" and analysis in which "his argument is solidly grounded. . . . I know of no other history of the United States that gives such a full and careful picture of the way life was lived by people who are not usually the central figures in the story, that is the American majority." Zinn's *People's History*, Twombly concluded, was "brilliant, original, and humane . . . a unique kind of American history and ought to be gotten into as many hands as possible."[86]

The other Harper reader, George Kirschner, was as fond of Zinn's manuscript as Twombly had been, praising *A People's History* as "beautifully written, fluid, and supple. The opening chapter, particularly is really elegant both in idea and in phrasing. . . . The publication of this book will be an immense contribution to the study of American history." Kirschner's review stressed the book's potential in high schools, noting that "the entire book reads easily, and somewhat quickly. I feel that high school students will have no difficulty with the text at all. They will . . . be able to follow the threads of the complex argument."[87]

Kirschner, in his review, failed to recognize that Zinn's book would be deemed too radical to be adopted by most school systems and so in assessing the manuscript mistakenly assumed it would replace standard textbooks. Kirschner was thus most concerned about coverage and that Zinn had "occasionally assumed more historical knowledge than his readers actually have." So, to ensure student knowledge of events or people Zinn did not cover, Kirschner recommended "a comparative time line that would show the 'traditional' historical events (Presidents, major legislation) alongside the events of Mr. Zinn's narrative . . . ground[ing] students who are often ignorant of traditional history and historical personages." He also recommended that, like textbooks, Zinn provide "visuals" and a bibliography.[88] None of these suggestions, save a bibliography, was acted on by Zinn or his editors because they saw the book not as a comprehensive or illustrated textbook but as an alternative to one.[89]

Kirschner was most perceptive about how effective Zinn's book could be in high school history classes. He understood that the book was a superb vehicle for challenging old assumptions about the American past. And he realized how important the teacher's role would be in this process. Kirschner predicted that one of the greatest challenges of the book would be

> not to the students, but to the teachers. The book insists that teachers must face not only the realities of the American historical experience, but [also] the serious work of combatting myths and sterile interpretations in their classrooms. It will be difficult to use this textbook without really getting to work, . . . encouraging students to test and question, to use their intelligence to the fullest. When that kind of work is going on in the classroom, it is not only the most difficult for a teacher, it is also the most rewarding.[90]

As we will see in our high school case study (chapters 3–4) on the initial use of *A People's History*, Kirschner's prediction proved accurate, since using Zinn's book was challenging for teachers as it pushed them to find ways to get students to engage with historiographical debate, radical criticism of U.S. war-making and capitalism, and other topics often omitted from school history education.

Kirschner was also astute in recognizing that there was something special about the opening chapter of *A People's History*. Much of what was most novel and thought provoking about *A People's History*, (most praised by its admirers and castigated by its detractors) was exemplified in its first chapter, "Columbus, the Indians, and Human Progress." Zinn later noted that his treatment of Columbus was "the most explosive thing in the book." And when Zinn began receiving letters from readers from across the United States, "a disproportionate number of them were about Christopher Columbus." Zinn quickly realized that although there are a lot of things in the book that people never heard of and lots of new angles . . . that people never saw [before] . . . what I said about Columbus was the most startling because every American has learned about Christopher Columbus . . . from elementary school on, . . . Columbus the great adventurer, navigator, . . . brave man, religious, a hero. Well, there are all these cities named after Columbus, all the statues of Columbus. . . . So when I said that . . . sure Columbus was a great navigator, . . . a brave man, but he was also . . . the first ruthless imperialist. . . . I mean, he kidnapped Indians. He was greedy for gold to satisfy his financiers back in Spain. And in search of gold, he drove the Indians, mutilated them when they didn't bring him gold, kidnapped them and brought them back to Spain because he had to have something to show his . . . supporters back in Spain. And that essentially began a campaign which resulted in the genocide of the indigenous people of the island of Hispaniola, where he and the Spaniards did a lot of . . . their marauding, the island which is now Haiti and the Dominican Republic.[91]

It was through the letters he received from a teacher on the Columbus chapter that Zinn first realized how controversial *A People's History* was and how challenging it could be for high school teachers (especially in the Reagan era) to teach. Soon after *A People's History* was published, Zinn received a letter from a California high school teacher. In a later interview on C-Span, Zin recalled,

She was using my book . . . as a supplement to the regular text, because there was a time . . . when using my book was just not accepted . . . especially in high schools, where there's more rigid control of textbooks. But she was using my book . . . in a way it was used very often. The teachers would photocopy chapters, and it sounded like samizdat-like . . . like the underground: photocopy chapters and hand it out to the class. Well, . . . [a] student brought the chapter on Columbus back home. Her mother looked at it and went into a fit and asked for an investigation of the teacher because . . . this was just outrageous to her that anybody should say these things about Columbus.[92]

While Zinn was correct that his presentation of Columbus was "explosive" and set his book apart from conventional textbooks, knocking Columbus off his pedestal was only one part of what made the first chapter of *A People's History* distinctive and memorable. As Twombly smartly noted, Zinn's book was innovative in form as well as content, in the way Zinn flashed back and forth between past and present, history and historiography, fifteenth-century narrative and contemporary moral reflection on America's troubled history of imperialism and racism. Zinn's "Columbus, the Indians, and Human Progress" embodied the moral urgency of the civil rights and antiwar movements—in which he had been deeply engaged—and cast the Columbus myth as symptomatic of America's failure to consider the human toll that brutal Western conquerors inflicted on people of color in the name of "human progress." So, after dramatically telling the story of Columbus's brutal mistreatment of the Arawaks and the disastrous decimation of the Native population of the "New World," Zinn then pulled back to discuss how schools, textbooks, and modern America itself distorted the Columbus story by romanticizing it, obscuring the ugly historical reality and grim legacy of Columbus and his successors in conquest. "The European invasion of the Indian settlements in the Americas" began with "conquest, slavery, [and] death. [But] when we read the history books given to children in the United States, it all starts with heroic adventure—there is no bloodshed—and Columbus Day is a celebration."[93]

In this opening chapter, Zinn also took aim at the classic biography of Columbus by Harvard historian Samuel Eliot Morison for romanticizing Columbus, highlighting the explorer's "indomitable will, his superb faith in God," and his "outstanding . . . seamanship," while minimizing the importance of the genocide of Indigenous people that Columbus unleashed. Zinn accused Morison of burying the story of Columbus's crimes "in a mass of other information," which "is to say to the reader with a certain infectious calm: yes, mass murder took place, but it's not that important; it should affect very little what we do in the world." Defying the historical profession's taboo on presentism, Zinn insisted on the contemporary relevance of the distorted heroic Columbus narrative and how it continued to be told. He deemed such hagiography "deadly" since it encourages an "easy acceptance of atrocities as a deplorable but necessary price to pay for progress (Hiroshima and Vietnam)," which is "one reason these atrocities are still with us."[94]

Zinn used the Columbus story to introduce his overall approach to history, insisting that there is an "inevitable taking of sides which comes from selection and emphasis in history." Morison and traditional texts sided with Columbus; in dissenting, Zinn cited the existentialist Albert Camus: in a world of "victims and executioners, it is the job of thinking people not to be on the side of the executioners." And this folds into Zinn's discussion of the counternarrative that frames *A People's History*—justifying his decision to tell "the story of the discovery of America's from the viewpoint of the Arawaks" and all of American history from the perspective of those oppressed by the powerful as well as of others who were critical of that oppression.[95]

Zinn's placement of this discussion of his "bottom-up" approach to history was remarkably unconventional, in that he had "decided on no introduction, preface, foreword" to *A People's History*. Instead he would get "immediately into the narrative and then, halfway through the first chapter, [would] stop and consider what's going on here," revealing the focus of the book, his political perspective, the distinction between people's history and traditional top-down accounts of the American past, and why he favored and practiced the former. Zinn realized that this was "an unorthodox approach."[96] But it added to the chapter's impact, combining its revisionist take on Columbus with an unconventional pause in the narrative, in order to reveal the assumptions of its author. It was as if a filmmaker stopped a movie midscene to confide to viewers the ideas and cinematic techniques undergirding the film being screened. This was all the more powerful since Zinn—by dispensing with an introduction or preface to the book and jumping right into the Columbus narrative—was explaining his historical approach once readers had already gotten a sampling of its results in the opening pages of A People's History.

The contrast between Zinn's historical approach in his opening chapter and normal textbook fare, between Zinn and the conventions of the historical profession, could not have been more dramatic. Textbook authors and historians in their texts stay in the past. If they are writing about Columbus, they stick to his era, whereas Zinn insisted on placing Columbus in the context of war-making and the cant of conquest that continued into what was then the present, the twentieth century. He also switched back to the twentieth century to condemn the way American schools (and a national holiday) continued to venerate Columbus, something textbooks had never done. While textbook authors and historians tend to avoid linking their telling of the past to moral arguments, Zinn, as we have seen, insisted on doing so, even justifying it as an ethical imperative, as articulated by Camus, whom Zinn paraphrased.[97] (Invoking Camus on political morality was another dramatic departure from textbook "neutrality.") While textbooks and historians strive to sound balanced and objective, Zinn argued that balance and neutrality were impossible, so he openly discussed his biases. Whereas textbook authors avoid historiographical debate, Zinn quickly engaged in one about Columbus with Morison. Whereas textbooks were often jointly authored and lacked a personal voice, Zinn—as Twombly noted—let readers know who he was, what his intentions were, and what moral choices he made in writing history. Thus, readers felt they knew Zinn and were inclined to find him and his views interesting, whether they agreed with them or not.

Zinn's unconventional introduction to American history reflected not only the distance between himself and textbook authors but also his alienation from the mainstream of the historical profession. Early in his career, Zinn encountered the stuffy elitism of leading historians when, during the late 1950s, the Southern Historical Association rejected his petitions to stop holding its meetings in hotels that discriminated against its African American members.[98] And when, in the early 1960s, Zinn attempted to get Columbia University's oral history center—the nation's leading oral history project—to fund interviews with SNCC organizers, he found its leader uninterested in documenting this historic Black-led student protest organization.[99] Zinn participated in the effort by fellow radical historians in 1969 to get the American Historical Association to oppose the Vietnam War, a move that failed because many members claimed this would violate their professional obligation to be politically neutral.[100] All of this contributed to Zinn's break in *A People's History* from the tendency of professional historians to write history so to mask their biases, avoid explicit moral judgments and presentism, and publish academic prose that played well within the profession but put off general readers.

In *A People's History*, Zinn was intentionally writing for the public, not for other historians. This concern with reaching beyond academia was not new for Zinn. As we have seen, back in 1972 while Zinn was still thinking of *A People's History* as a book series, he stressed the need to choose authors who could connect with general readers. This stress on accessibility reflected Zinn's democratic politics and his years of work as an organizer in mass movements. His classic antiwar work *Vietnam: The Logic of Withdrawal* (1967) had been designed to be a quick read, with the feel of a political pamphlet, intended to convince readers of the need for an immediate end to the war; it sold some forty thousand copies.[101] His *Disobedience and Democracy* (1968)—which sold about seventy thousand copies—was also geared to the public, whom Zinn sought to convince that the antiwar movement's use of civil disobedience was justified, rebutting Justice Fortas's book that sought to discredit draft resistance.[102] Zinn's history of SNCC had been written to document its antiracist organizing and awaken the public to its courageous work against the violent Jim Crow regime. *SNCC: The New Abolitionists* sold between twenty-five thousand and thirty thousand copies and had five printings by the early 1970s. So Zinn's publication record was more that of a politically engaged writer-activist than academic. Even back in the early 1960s, when historian Staughton Lynd joined Zinn on the Spelman College faculty, Lynd quickly realized that "the most remarkable thing about Howard as an academician was that he was always concerned to speak, not to other academicians, but to the general public. Soon after arriving in Atlanta, I asked him what papers he was preparing for which academic gatherings. This is what I supposed historians did. Howard looked at me as if I was speaking a foreign language. He was one of two adult supervisors to the Student Nonviolent Coordinating Committee and was preoccupied with the question of how racism . . . [might] be overcome."[103]

Though Zinn's *People's History* did have a panoramic quality and explored key themes and events in American history from Columbus through the late twentieth century, he avoided the burden of being comprehensive, which tended to make textbooks tediously long. Zinn's earliest interest in textbooks and curricular matters emerged not from what they covered but what they left out. Back in graduate school, as we have seen, Zinn was outraged when he learned of the Ludlow Massacre, the 1914 murder of striking miners and their families, and learned it not from a textbook but from a Woody Guthrie song. So Zinn's introductory history would highlight such working-class tragedies and struggles that textbooks neglected and devote entire chapters to Native American struggles, women's rights, labor, and the socialist movement.[104] Focusing on telling stories of oppression and resistance from below left Zinn with room to include extensive quotations from dissidents in U.S. history. This helped give his *People's History* a literary quality and documentary feel that was unusual in an introductory work—featuring an absorbing narrative, with stirring stories as opposed to the encyclopedia-like feel of most history textbooks. Zinn could focus on this kind of people's history without concern that doing so would alienate a textbook publisher, state textbook adoption boards, or school administrators because he did not seek to publish his book with a textbook publisher.

A People's History has its critics. How could it not? After all, Zinn's was an anticapitalist history of a nation that regarded its past as a capitalist success story, an antiwar book about the world's leading military superpower, a history unflattering to the two-party system in a nation committed to that system, and a narrative that stressed class divisions in a nation with extreme income inequality, with Zinn also highlighting American racial and gender inequity. Finally, it was a history written in ways that criticized how U.S. history had been written by professional historians.

No matter how one views *A People's History*, there is now evidence that enables us to go beyond our own view and to grapple with the impact of this influential introductory work of history. Thanks to the opening of Zinn's papers at New York University's Tamiment Library, archival evidence has become available that explains why Zinn wrote the book—as we have seen, along with extensive correspondence and other documentation on the public's reaction to it. This evidence allows us to understand the book's surprising emergence as a best seller and its impact on history teaching and learning. Reading through the Zinn papers, we have been struck by the many letters from readers describing the book as intellectually transformative, even life changing. Many readers found *A People's History* immensely significant and engaging because of Zinn's approach to writing critical history, the extensive quotations he provided from dissenters, and the questions he raised about America's social order and war-making, which were so different from anything they had experienced in their history classes and textbooks.

Typical of reader messages to Zinn was one from a Massachusetts under-graduate who read *A People's History* as a high school student. "You have been a hero of mine," this reader wrote in 2001, "[who] opened up a whole new way of viewing not only my country and its government, but also the effect my country has on the rest of the planet."[105] A Hampshire College student thanked Zinn for having "destroyed . . . [the student's] fairytale version of American history."[106] A former high school dropout wrote to Zinn that reading *A People's History* had changed his life, motivating him to pursue a career as a history teacher. A history teacher from a South Dakota Indian reservation e-mailed Zinn in 2006 that she had received "an early morning wake up call" from one of her Native American students. The student, she reported, "said it was my fault that he hadn't slept the night before. Actually, as I pointed out to him, it was your fault! He started read-ing the book and could not put it down!"[107]

This last student's reaction calls to mind historian Timothy Patrick McCar-thy's observation that one of the key appeals of Zinn's book was that it enabled "so many Americans—workers and women, farmers and feminists, socialists and students, immigrants and indigenous people, communists and civil rights activists—to see themselves as agents of history for the first time" and to share Zinn's critique of (and anger toward) the sources of their oppression.[108] This can also be seen in the letters to Zinn from Latinx students in a Chicago second-chance high school, one of whom wrote to Zinn, "[*A People's History of the United States*] made me change my perspectives. I watched the common people who have been exploited, victimized, and oppressed . . . watched the struggles, fights and ways that common people stood up to the oppressor. It really em-powers you to make sense of the world and want to change it. I will have to take action on any issue that matters to me to try to make something good out of it. For example, I support immigrants by marching with them."[109]

Similarly, singer-songwriter Bruce Springsteen, the son of a New Jersey blue-collar worker, in crediting Zinn's book with helping inspire him to write *Nebraska*, his most overtly socially conscious album, said, "[*A People's History*] had an enormous impact on me. . . . It gave me a sense of myself in the context of this huge American experience and empowered me to feel that in my small way I had something to say. It made me feel a part of history and gave me life as a participant."[110]

Such testimonials on behalf of *A People's History* speak to the power of Zinn's prose and how inspiring his radical history could be, which made him for many "the people's historian." But perhaps Zinn's perspective on the book's popular-ity is the most persuasive, that the book's success was less about him than it was about the democratic mass movements of the Long 1960s that stirred him. It was these movements that sparked the historiographical revolution that inspired Zinn and a generation of radical historians to turn their attention from elite history to the history of the majority: women, African Americans, Native Americans, and workers, and to write critically of America's abuse of power on the international stage. In this sense, the popularity of Zinn's book can be seen as a validation of the social movements of the 1960s and of the inclusive historical scholarship they generated, attesting that many people preferred a more democratic, critical approach to history.

The many letters to Zinn from teens as well as adults and elders suggest that what Zinn had written was new, exciting, and eye opening. *A People's History* was viewed this way in part because, as we have seen, the new social history and New Left historiographical revolution (of which Zinn was a participant), which had generated such excitement and controversy in the historical profession, had not found its way to the general public until Zinn wrote his book. But there was another reason Zinn's book stood out so. That has to do with the failure of history education in U.S. high schools in the early, mid-, and late twentieth century to truly engage students, to teach them to think historically, to debate and interpret history. As we will see in chapter 2, the failure and unpopularity of high school U.S. history textbooks and pedagogy paved the way for the success and popularity of *A People's History of the United States.*

Timing, organization, and popular culture played important roles in the success of *A People's History.* Timing was important in part because those touched by the movements of the 1960s and 1970s were, as Zinn discussed, ready for a radical rethinking of America history. Also, as Zinn's editor pointed out, 1960s youth by the 1980s were part of the nation's teaching force, in a position to bring *A People's History* to new generations, their students. And timing mattered with regard to teachers in another respect too. Alienated by Reaganism, Reagan's new cold war in Central America, and by the top-down educational "reforms" of the 1980s, including crude reliance on standardized testing, teachers began organizing for democratic educational change. This paved the way for an authentic teacher-led reform movement that stressed Freirean pedagogy in schools as a vehicle for progressive change, teaching beyond the textbook, and the development of inclusive, multicultural curricula. For social studies and history teachers who were part of this movement, *A People's History* aligned perfectly. And, as chapter 6 shows, veterans of this movement would promote the use of Zinn's book by their colleagues and in the early twenty-first century founded the Zinn Education Project, one of the most successful online progressive history education projects in the history of American education.

But even before this movement coalesced, innovative high school history teachers on an individual basis brought *A People's History* to their students.

These teachers saw that conventional textbooks were dull and recognized that comparatively teaching Zinn versus the standard textbook could foster intellectual engagement in their classes. Our case study of the classes of one such teacher in chapters 3 and 4 shows that whether students were liberal, conservative, or neither, they found *A People's History* stimulating, and their debates about it provide exciting examples of student thinking about history.

An indication of the broad appeal of *A People's History* is the way it has resonated with major figures in popular culture, from movie directors and actors to musicians, novelists, and poets. A clear sign of this came in 1998, in a memorable scene in the Academy Award–winning movie *Good Will Hunting*, when the protagonist, played by the actor Matt Damon, raves to his court-ordered therapist that *A People's History* is a book that will "knock you on your ass." *A People's History* would soon appear in television shows and in other feature films, reaching more people than had bought Zinn's best-selling book and having an unprecedented impact on popular culture for a U.S. history book. Accounts of this impact and related theater and movie projects—culminating in 2009 with the History Channel broadcast of *The People Speak*, a documentary film of the readings of dissident speeches from *A People's History*—are provided in chapter 8.

With the book's success came a measure of celebrity for Zinn that drew new readers. After *A People's History*, he would publish a memoir, *You Can't Be Neutral on a Moving Train* (1994,). The memoir was made into a documentary film with the same title by Deb Ellis and Denis Mueller, narrated by Matt Damon, which was short-listed for an Academy Award in 2004. Zinn toured the country discussing the memoir, *A People's History*, and the latter's successor, coedited with Anthony Arnove, *Voices of a People's History* (2004), which compiled progressive and radical speeches from the American past in and beyond those quoted in *A People's History*. Zinn published and spoke widely about *Declarations of Independence* (1990), his penetrating critique of American ideological orthodoxies. He went on in the final decades of his life to publish more than a dozen books of essays and interviews that often focused on contemporary political conflicts and wars. Even into his seventies and eighties, Zinn was a prominent speaker who crossed the country agitating against the U.S. wars in Iraq and Afghanistan and the "war on terror." He used his celebrity to promote his vision of an America free of militarism.[iii] Most often he would appear on such media as National Public Radio and alternative radio shows like *Democracy Now*, as he was considered too radical for most major networks. But as the war crises heated up it was even possible to catch Zinn (in 2005) on Jon Stewart's *Daily Show* denouncing George W. Bush's Iraq War.

Zinn eventually become an eminent figure of the American Left, with a national following much like that of his friend Noam Chomsky. Zinn's eloquence as a speaker denouncing the U.S. wars of the early twenty-first century, along with his charismatic optimism, compounded the popularity he had already achieved with *A People's History* and his other writings.[112] In this era, for example, fans attending a Pearl Jam rock concert heard lead singer Eddie Vedder tell the crowd that Zinn should run for president. At a Santa Cruz, California, demonstration in January 2005 protesting the reelection of Iraq War initiator George W. Bush as president, the crowd collectively took "an oath of office as President Pro-Tem of the United States," and "since no Bibles were on hand, a copy of Howard Zinn's *A People's History of the United States* was used."[113] While Zinn's visibility came out of political conviction and was not part of a marketing strategy to promote *A People's History*, there is no doubt that his prominence helped to attract yet more readers.

The final source of the appeal of *A People's History* is its most inadvertent—the steady stream of attacks on the book from the Right. With their ability to garner headlines and media coverage, such right-wing figures as Rush Limbaugh and David Horowitz, conservative publications such as the *Wall Street Journal* and *National Review*, and antiradical organizations such as Accuracy in Academia helped draw attention and interest in the book. So did right-wing politicians, most notably Mitch Daniels who in the aftermath of Zinn's death in 2010 sought covertly as governor of Indiana to find ways to ensure that *A People's History* would be banned from the classrooms of his state. When in 2013 the private correspondence documenting this censorship attempt was exposed by Associated Press reporters, a major scandal ensued that embarrassed Daniels and led copies of *A People's History* to fly off the shelves of Indiana bookstores and to increased borrowing of the book from the state's libraries.[114]

The enduring popularity of *A People's History*, then, is connected to many aspects of recent U.S. history: the history of the historical profession itself and how it and America were changed by the social movements of the 1960s, the history of educational reform in the late twentieth and early twenty-first century (including teachers' search for more engaging curricula and pedagogy), the history of American popular culture, and the history of the American Right and Left. It would take more than one book to probe in depth all these sources of Zinn's appeal. We make no claim to offer such a comprehensive history, and this chapter is intended only to introduce readers to the origins and appeal of *A People's History of the United States*. Our book's broader goal is to help move the conversation about Zinn and *A People's History* beyond the polemics of his detractors and admirers, assessing the book's impact on history teaching and learning in and beyond the classroom, with views grounded in archival sources and other historical evidence. *A People's History of the United States* has now managed to engage millions of readers in studying and debating American history for four decades, and there is much to be learned from probing why this is so in a nation where history is consistently rated the most unpopular school subject.

CHAPTER 2

Before *A People's History*

One of the keys to the popularity of Howard Zinn's *A People's History*—and especially its appeal to inventive teachers—is the landscape of educational failure that predominated in high school history classrooms on the eve of its publication in 1980, as evidenced by reported lack of interest in history, its low status alongside other areas of study, and adult Americans' general ignorance regarding U.S. history and government.[1] U.S. high school history textbooks assigned in the 1960s and 1970s were often poorly written, dull, overweight tomes (some close to a thousand pages), which few students would read voluntarily.[2] These tedious books, combined with equally disengaging pedagogy, which emphasized memorization of names and dates (not historical interpretation, debate, and the cultivation of high-order thinking skills) helped to make history the least popular subject among high school students.[3]

This failure in high school history is in many ways perplexing when one considers that the sixties and seventies were the era when a revolution in historical scholarship—the new social history, inspired by the Black freedom movement and the other major protest movements of this period—was generating much excitement at the college level.[4] At universities across the country, labor studies, women's studies, African American studies, LGBTQ studies, and New Left revisionist history of American expansionism and war were being taught for the first time, offering students a new and critical reading of the American past. But this new scholarship could not make its way to the high schools except in a diluted form. The social and radical history bubbling up on campus became flat by the time high school textbook authors got done abridging it. Textbooks might add some minor references to Blacks or women or gays and lesbians (often in sidebars, not integrated into the narrative), but the result was often tokenism that did little to change the focus or lessen the dullness of textbooks.[5]

Similarly, despite attempts at pedagogical reform, with buzzwords like "the new social studies," the history classroom generally lacked innovation, so that focus on covering large amounts of material and memorization, breeding poor understanding and retention of historical knowledge, remained the norm.[6] This chapter is devoted to introducing readers to the evidence of that failure, enabling us to see why Zinn had little, if any, competition. His *People's History* offered high school students and teachers an engaging introduction to American history and provided critical perspectives on U.S. capitalism, imperialism, war, and racism at the same time that other historians and textbooks avoided such inquiry.

A People's History connected high schools for the first time to approaches pioneered by the new social historians, to the New Left critique of American imperialism, and to other views increasingly prevalent on college campuses. But in the twenty-five years prior to the book's publication, most U.S. history textbooks were uncritical surveys that maintained uncritical and flat classroom instruction. This was the result of a number of factors including textbook market demands, the politics of curriculum formation, and the limits of school reform.[7] Back in 1995, education historians David Tyack and Larry Cuban, in their classic history documenting the glacial pace of educational change, describe the nature of school reform as "tinkering" at best, with change often like "fireflies, flickering brightly but soon fading." Regardless of countless efforts to change schools across the twentieth century, there existed continuity in "structures, rules and practices" that shaped instruction and preserved old and ineffective methods and practices.[8] More recently, in another important study of schooling, Cuban in 2016 reported finding little change in this depressing theme of limited and failing educational reform: "Pervasive and potent processes within the institution of schooling preserve its independence to act even in the face of powerful outside political forces intent upon altering what happens in schools and classrooms. Reformers seeking to 'transform' schooling see such adaptations as failure; less self-interested observers see this as how organizations adapt politically to their environment."[9] What reforms were implemented in classrooms served as minor additions to a deeply embedded "grammar of schooling."[10]

Changes made to history textbooks in the years prior to publication of *A People's History* conform to the pattern of slow and superficial school change described by Tyack and Cuban, "tinkering," largely cosmetic and inadequate. While publishers eventually included more nonwhite people in their U.S. history textbooks, the basic structure of those books did not change.

Why didn't high school history textbooks change in the 1960s and 1970s to match the changes on college campuses noted above? Conservative critics viewed academic history as a "plaything" of the Left but had little to complain about concerning high school history instruction. For one thing, most historians were isolated from that world.[11] Their absence in shaping high school history curricula was detrimental. Academic historian Gary Nash was unusual because he actively engaged in efforts to improve pre-college history instruction. Nash attributed the shortcomings to ignorance: "Most teachers were unfamiliar with the rich new work of social historians." Thus, most students were "deprived of new perspectives in race, class and gender issues that might have helped them more intelligently confront the social upheavals of the 1960s."[12]

The failure to bring to high schools the new social history explored by university-based historians was a result of schools' and school boards' own history of conservatism, especially the schoolhouse tradition of reducing historical study to bland forms of civic education aimed at achieving social consensus. Frances FitzGerald in *America Revised: History Schoolbooks in the Twentieth Century* (1979) documented this tradition, in which textbooks have been used to promote perspectives on race, ethnicity, gender, economics, and social class with all the sharp edges removed ostensibly to serve the goal of "unifying" the nation.[13]

In 1979 sociologist Jean Anyon's study of U.S. high school history textbooks used during the two decades prior to the publication of *A People's History* identified the prevalence of hegemonic ideologies in them. The textbooks, she asserted, presented conservative, antiradical views of American social reality as objective history. When comparing textbook narratives, Anyon concentrated on how specific topics were addressed in covering the period from Reconstruction to World War I. Anyon identified how "school knowledge" (textbooks included) was associated with maintaining the power of dominant social and economic groups. She concluded that "textbooks not only express the dominant groups' ideologies, but also help to form attitudes in support of their social position." This is accomplished, she argued, by the presentation of class-blind perspectives as "truth" and the absence of deep examination of content and opposing viewpoints.[14]

Anyon linked the stability of American capitalism to the "lack of working-class consciousness" that followed from such conservative textbook narratives ignoring discussion of social class. Such warped history fostered political passivity, thus helping to preserve the power and influence of big business. Anyon found in U.S. history textbooks of the 1960s and 1970s repeated instances where capitalism and its beneficiaries were presented as benign, even generous (Andrew Carnegie donated money to build libraries), while at the same time the working class, immigrants, and minorities were minimized (Carnegie's exploitation of workers is not mentioned, nor was there focus on working-class empowerment). One might expect that, while describing the period of rapid industrialization at the end of the nineteenth century, textbook writers would make the labor movement and the working class central to the narrative. But the day-to-day experiences of industrial workers were nearly absent from textbooks published during this period, including how they responded to low wages and poor working conditions.[15]

U.S. history textbooks published in the sixties and seventies denied the legitimacy of radical methods of social, political, and economic change, including socialist organizing. While socialism constituted an important response to capitalist industrialization and offered a critique of its ensuing inequality in many countries, and although the Socialist Party of America was influential, with nearly 150 members elected to state legislatures between 1910 and 1920, the majority of textbooks Anyon surveyed said very little about the party, its platform, and popular support for it.[16]

When they did say anything about the labor movement, these textbooks neglected the history of industrial and anticapitalist unions like the syndicalist Industrial Workers of the World in favor of more mainstream craft unions. So during the sixties and seventies the most-referenced labor organization in U.S. textbooks was the American Federation of Labor (AFL), and the violent labor upheaval and class warfare in the coalfields of the early twentieth century was ignored. The AFL embraced the corporate order and advocated bargaining over wages rather than pushing for fundamental change to the unequal social structure. Similarly, the majority of textbooks published in the two decades before *A People's History* praised cooperation between unions and business owners while failing to highlight cooperative relationships among activist workers.[17]

This muting of the history of labor struggle during the age of industrialism in the United States not only distorted reality but also removed the inherent drama of these events. Textbooks airbrushed or left out most of the life-and-death class conflicts of the era. The period of industrialization between the Civil War and World War I was one of intense conflict between business owners and the industrial workforce. But textbooks presented brief narratives unsympathetic to workers' efforts to organize and fight for their rights. Nearly all of the books Anyon reviewed present the same three strikes—the railroad strike of 1877, the Homestead Strike (1892), and the Pullman Strike (1894)—all of which were considered by labor to be setbacks that led to the demise of some unions and diminished middle-class support of unions in general. Anyon argued that the effect was to cast doubt on strikes as a viable tool for working-class agency and social justice. However, most of the books present the 1902 anthracite coal strike, resolved after President Theodore Roosevelt intervened, as successful, giving the impression that government intervention was benign, appropriate, and perhaps the best remedy in labor disputes, although in most of its interventions government sided with business against striking workers.[18]

Most of the textbooks Anyon reviewed promoted the idea that industrial workers were responsible for their poverty, the result of their own failures and not a consequence of fundamental economic arrangements.[19] This kind of ahistorical individualism in textbooks left students without data to analyze inherent inequity in both the context of labor and in capitalism in general. Ultimately, Anyon believed, this version of history undermined the sense of agency among working-class students and corroded hope for social change. "The symbolic legitimation of powerful groups in the textbook version of economic and labor history may have the least favorable consequences for the inner-city poor," she wrote.[20]

Economics and labor history were not the only topics poorly presented in U.S. history textbooks published prior to 1980. Textbooks of the 1960s and 1970s failed to critically assess the history of U.S. foreign policy. In many seventies textbooks America's role in the world, including in foreign wars, was treated with minimal reference to antiwar movements. These textbooks gave the impression that the Vietnam War came to a close because President Richard Nixon and Henry Kissinger deliberately planned its end. Most, with their patriotic frames and uncritical descriptions of the U.S. international role, did not prepare students to understand why historians would spotlight failures and contradictions in U.S. foreign policy. While there were a handful of books highlighting critical questions—one was *As It Happened*, by Charles Sellers (McGraw-Hill, 1975), which prompted students to consider whether U.S. foreign policy was "responsible" or "arrogant" (as its approach was based on assumptions of dominance and superiority)—the vast majority of textbooks published in the 1970s reflect a laudatory view of U.S. actions on the world stage while omitting connections between the military and industry and ignoring foreign powers' perspectives on U.S. foreign policy.[21]

The treatment of women and gender in history was another area sorely neglected in the textbooks of the 1960s and 1970s. Textbook reviews covering the twenty-five years prior to the publication of *A People's History* with a focus on women's history concluded that women were largely omitted from most narratives.[22] For the dozens of index listings for men, there were few for women, with almost no women quoted at all in the majority of books. Illustrations included only men in some cases, or in other cases far more men—and men of higher status—than women, who were most often depicted in gendered roles such as housewife, and from the middle and working class. Stories of women were almost never highlighted in case studies provided in textbooks. Textbooks of the early 1970s dealt poorly with the Nineteenth Amendment and the struggle for women's suffrage, and according to one textbook review there was no mention of the leaders of the movement. Women were also excluded from explanations of law and the courts. Depictions of women working outside of the home were omitted, which might lead students to think that most women did not do such a thing.[23] Textbooks published in the early 1970s failed to acknowledge the existence of second-wave feminism, a social and political movement of major importance. In their study of civics and government textbooks assigned in U.S. high schools, Jennifer Macleod and Sandra Silverman expressed unease over the "narrow, stereotyped image of women as housewives, passive and dependent, defined by their husbands' occupations." When in the early 1970s Myra and David Sadker asked hundreds of high school seniors to name twenty famous women in American history, the average student could name only four or five, underscoring textbooks' unequal treatment of women and inadequate coverage of gender issues.[24]

U.S. history and civics textbooks were slow to change, but some that were published years before *A People's History* appeared in 1980 did begin to reflect shifts inspired by the sixties, especially in the area of diversity. The civil rights movement upended the image of a homogeneous American society, bringing forth hard questions about America's shifting identity. School boards across the country accepted the view that the United States is a multiracial, multiethnic, multicultural society and that diversity must be reflected in textbooks. However, presenting a heterogeneous America to schoolchildren raised new and challenging questions. Was the United States like Yugoslavia, with a complex and fragile dynamic among ethnic and cultural groups? Was there a dominant culture in the United States, and, if so, was it beneficial to the entire U.S. citizenry? A review of popular textbooks assigned in the 1960s reveals textbook narratives grappling with these questions, though the outcome was the result of "tinkering," with little significant or meaningful improvement.[25]

Education scholars, noting the superficiality of textbook reform, developed an analytic framework for assessing the limits and possibilities for meaningful change in textbooks. Overall, in the twenty years prior to *A People's History's* publication as well as in the period following, history textbooks accounts can be seen as existing along a continuum ranging from American hegemony and Eurocentrism (highlighting "common heritage") to American multiculturalism (highlighting diversity). James Banks, Catherine Cornbleth, Dexter Waugh, and other scholars identified frameworks that describe multicultural historical narratives since the 1960s, such as "additive," "revisionist," and "transformative" approaches.[26] These three approaches each foreground American diversity but assert different theoretical and philosophical positions on the nature of historical narrative. The additive approach merely adds to an existing Eurocentric immigrant American narrative in the form of heroes, holidays, and contributions.

This increases social and cultural diversity in curricula, but ultimately the additions are superficial embellishments. Even as recently as the 1990s, California's state history curriculum promoted a pluralistic version of American society but omitted analysis of existing and dominant racial and cultural hierarchies. According to Cornbleth and Waugh, "In this master narrative, hierarchy was flattened, race faded away, and everyone became immigrants."[27]

A more meaningful multicultural revisionism goes beyond the additive approach by presenting a diversity of voices and experiences as part of a more integrated core narrative. A history from the bottom up, as opposed to traditional political, military, and economic history, incorporates the experiences and voices of workers, women, Blacks, Native Americans, Chicanos, and other marginalized groups. But, as Cornbleth and Waugh suggest, there is more than one form of multicultural revisionism:

> Revised stories, with a different focus or theme than conventional histories, vary in the extent to which and how they are multiculturally revisionist. While more inclusive than the older syntheses, they usually operate from a single interpretive framework or story line. The single story line provides coherence at the expense of the diversity of the peoples and cultures whose stories are being told. In contrast, a second variety of revisionist multiculturalism, characterized by multiple perspectives, would accommodate and highlight diversity at the expense of a single story line. It would make the interests of various individuals and groups explicit rather than giving the appearance of being interest free.[28]

The most radical approach, transformative multiculturalism, sometimes called "reciprocal history," rarely made it into textbooks. This approach draws on the work of Sylvia Wynter and Toni Morrison and is rooted in a Black studies cultural model aimed at probing predominant systems of knowledge. Breaking down what she calls America's "race- and class-biased hierarchy" and reconceiving it as a "community of communities based on reciprocal recognition," Wynter proposes in her 1992 book *Do Not Call Us Negroes*, making change in society through "reinterpretation." "Reinterpretation" includes reframing history writing to ensure that its lessons enlighten all Americans—illuminating power and class dynamics, and the racism and oppression that shape the American story—so that members of every group can view themselves as actors, whether beneficiaries or oppressors.[29] Transformative multiculturalism requires that dominant groups recognize their privilege and also how they themselves have been shaped, limited, and otherwise imprinted by racism and sexism. This approach was seen by school boards as far too radical.

Overall, the textbooks fashioned to respond to the changes in society during the 1960s and 70s did not go beyond the additive approach and in no way were transformative. These textbooks continued to offer a nationalistic narrative similar to earlier versions, with a few more nonwhite and female faces added in.[30] Unlike what Zinn would do in *A People's History*, they failed to engage readers and encourage them to think critically and deeply about their nation.

Though there were efforts, then, to reform history textbooks starting in the 1960s, the vast majority adopted in individual states failed to fully and accurately reflect American diversity. This was true for a variety of reasons and was made certain because of the textbook adoption process. American regionalism and education federalism shaped how books were written and marketed to school districts. An element of American education since just after the Civil War, textbook adoption policy was first put in place by former Confederate states mandating that their account of the war be presented in schools.[31] Thus, from the start, history textbook adoption was influenced by regional forces and was intensely political.[32]

While more inclusive texts did appear after the early 1960s, such as Houghton Mifflin's *Land of the Free: A History of the United States*, by John Walton Caughey, John Hope Franklin, and Ernest R. May, the adoption of such texts was contested at the state level.[33] Those like California state superintendent of public instruction Max Rafferty, who was involved in the California adoption dispute over *Land of the Free*, argued that history teaching needed to "cultivate patriotism" and that the textbook, with its critical treatment of American slavery and racism, was antipatriotic. Rafferty and his supporters favored so-called "factual" history and condemned purported "interpretive" history, which they claimed biased historians were pushing in the schools. As the controversy heated up, Rafferty threatened to ask Governor Ronald Reagan to bar *Land of the Free* from California schools unless the authors made substantial changes to it. Rafferty got intimately involved by suggesting edits. In the case of the Reconstruction chapter, subtitled "The Union Is Restored, and with It White Supremacy," he asked that the subtitle's reference to white supremacy be removed.[34]

In May 1964, a United Civil Rights Council (UCRS) member praised *Land of the Free* before the California State Board of Education. "Negro Americans for, lo, these hundred years have sought in vain to hear some faint echo of their achievement mentioned in the textbooks of the public schools," read the UCRS statement. As the conflict brewed, the Houghton Mifflin California representative reassured Rafferty and his colleagues that the new version still advocated the principle that textbooks "play a unique role in helping to unify the nation."[35]

While the textbook was criticized for being too radical, critics on the left argued that it reflected a markedly patriotic view of the United States. Reading through *Land of the Free* today, its laudatory tone comes through, even in its introduction, which asserts that Americans "take for granted that government will not be a party to any discriminatory action based on race, color, religion, or politics. . . . If there is a unifying feature, it may well be our acceptance of the national commitment to liberty and . . . freedom. We agree that we want a government of laws that apply equally to everyone. We do not want a government that gives favors to a select few. We agree that there should be no such thing as a second-class citizen. All should have equal rights and fair treatment."[36]

Such textbook controversies demonstrate how difficult it was for even moderately critical textbooks to win state adoption. Similar conflicts took place in other states, from Michigan to Mississippi, where even non-radical attempts at a more racially integrated history proved controversial, and publishers retreated in fear of losing sales. But Black organizers and communities of color kept alive the reform impulse, battling to eliminate racial bias in textbooks in the 1960s. A widely publicized 1962 campaign in Detroit, led by the Black advocacy organization Group on Advanced Leadership (GOAL), called for the immediate withdrawal of a textbook they argued presented slavery favorably.[37] GOAL was later joined by the local chapter of the NAACP, and other city school districts and organizations representing racial and ethnic groups nationwide began to look closely at textbooks for racial, ethnic, or religious bias.[38]

During this period Adam Clayton Powell Jr., the congressional representative from Harlem and chair of the House of Representatives Committee on Education worked to extend desegregation of schools to curricula, advocating more multiracial textbooks. To this end, he introduced a bill linked to the Elementary and Secondary Education Act (ESEA), bringing Congress into this highly fractious area. Because of Powell's efforts, some ESEA funding was put toward textbook revision. Nonetheless, education scholars would find that though there were changes made to textbooks in the 1960s and 1970s, in most cases "major ideological frameworks" were not significantly altered. According to Michael Apple and Linda Christian-Smith, dominance was maintained through compromise and the process of "mentioning," with new topics named but not developed in any depth.[39]

Disputes over how U.S. history was depicted in textbooks were highly charged because such presentations revealed how Americans understood their past. "It quite literally defines who we are," observed education historian Jonathan Zimmerman.[40] This was evident in battles over a Mississippi textbook published in 1974, a decade after the *Land of the Free* adoption controversy in California and six years before the publication of *A People's History*. The dispute was provoked by James Loewen's critical state history, *Mississippi: Conflict and Change*. Loewen's frank treatment of racial conflict, as well as descriptions of the contributions Black Mississippians made to the state, raised the ire of conservative critics. Thus, the state's schools refused to adopt the textbook. While a lawsuit was brought before the State Education Department led by the NAACP Legal Defense and Education Fund, Loewen, and concerned educators and parents, the publisher stayed out of the lawsuit and subsequent debates. In fact, textbook publishers almost always chose profits over principle, shying away from more progressive authors in adoption controversies. Publishers also have a history of deleting passages that school and state officials have deemed offensive.[41]

While textbooks in the 1970s did begin to refer to the struggles of nonwhites in American society, FitzGerald argues that they did not explain why these groups struggled. For example, they did not mention how the Bureau of Indian Affairs exploited Native Americans and tribal lands. There was little or no discussion of institutionalized racism, and only a few texts portrayed actions for equal rights led by women or racial, ethnic, and religious groups. While textbooks published in the 1960s and 1970s included more photographs and graphics than ever, making them more visually attractive, they rarely showed more than a token nonwhite person or two, such as Martin Luther King Jr., and largely ignored the oppression and comparative poverty of people of color in the United States.[42] Controversial textbooks such as *Land of the Free* and *Mississippi: Conflict and Change* attest that there were some attempts before Zinn's to have textbook narratives more fully reflect the diversity of American life. However, the vast majority of American history textbooks published in the sixties and seventies did not adequately address racial, ethnic, class, and religious conflict, and, when they dealt with diversity, their approach was usually additive, with no attempt to recast the master narrative.

Social studies education as led by education professors, progressive school leaders, and professional organizations in the sixties and seventies shifted the field toward emphasizing values, problem solving, and, according to critics, the promotion of "liberal" pedagogies. Unsurprisingly, these efforts—referred to as "the new social studies"—drew strong reactions from conservatives, who claimed they were overly critical of the U.S. government while promoting left-leaning perspectives and policies. The field's largest and most influential professional organization, the National Council for the Social Studies, failed to secure public confidence for such reform, with critics claiming that the NCSS reduced complex phenomena to solvable problems and reinforced ahistoricism. Some asserted that with the decrease of history being taught explicitly in the schools, replaced by newfangled versions of the social sciences, historical understanding by the nation's children had become "disjointed and shallow."[43] In response to the new social studies failure, by the mid-1970s, conservatives, including "back to basics" proponents, worked to influence the content of U.S. history textbooks. Many feared that if they did not take control of the social studies curriculum, American teenagers, soon to be voters, would remain ignorant of American history and thus one day put the nation at risk.

Nevertheless, the 1980s were marked by two prevailing and simultaneous trends in curriculum making—one "conservative" and the other "progressive," the first supporting American hegemony and espousing objectivity in history, the second promoting inclusivity, the need for multiple perspectives, and critical analysis. The degree to which these currents made a mark on textbooks—and curricula reconfiguring—varied across states and regions. Both trends involved scholars, textbook authors, publishers, and school boards. The most influential conservative trend led to textbooks during this period increasingly promoting privatized solutions to social and economic problems. Free-market and privatizing approaches were closely aligned with archetypal American motifs stressing common heritage, individualism, and the Protestant work ethic. But as these themes became more pronounced in textbooks, their narratives became more jingoistic, dogmatic, and tedious.

During this period, right-leaning politicians and the think tanks that informed them reiterated the themes espoused by curriculum conservatives, including the idea that multiculturalism challenged American unity and would weaken the nation. In 1984 William Bennett, head of the National Endowment for the Humanities and later of the Department of Education under President Reagan, referred to principles that were derived from "great epochs of Western civilization" as "the glue that binds together our pluralistic nation."[44] And with publications such as Diane Ravitch and Chester E. Finn Jr.'s *What Do Our 17-Year-Olds Know? A Report on the First National Assessment of History and Literature* (1987), concern increased about what was widely considered to be shallow history education in schools and its consequences for the nation.[45]

The idea that common stories about the United States would serve as "glue" for Americans was repeated again and again in debates about what history should be taught in the schools. Those involved in writing and publishing history textbooks in the 1970s and 1980s often promoted a common culture while neglecting social, economic, and institutional elements that uphold structural inequalities in American society.[46] According to Loewen and other textbook critics, this resulted in depriving students of critical perspectives on American history and society. Almost ten years after the publication of *A People's History*, education historian Lawrence Cremin described this trend as reminiscent of a previous era: "Every indicator in the early 1980s pointed toward the beginning of a new nationwide Americanization movement not unlike the one that flourished during the second and third decades of the century, and toward a return to definitions of what it meant to be an American that closely resembled those of the earlier era."[47]

Foes of multiculturalism during the 1980s, including Arthur Schlesinger Jr., Lynne Cheney, E. D. Hirsch, and Diane Ravitch, emphasized common heritage and uniformity and largely succeeded in shaping U.S. history curricula.[48] This was happening at the same time that inventive teachers were desperately trying to enliven school history, since study after study showed that American schoolchildren not only rated history at the bottom of all their subjects but also performed poorly on national history tests.[49]

The backstory presented here helps explain how inadequate (and mind-numbing) textbooks contributed to the poor state of history education in the early 1980s, irrespective of attempts by individuals of different political stripes to improve it. The gap between policy adoption and actual implementation in classrooms varied widely—"from an inch to a mile," Larry Cuban wrote. After years of teaching history in Cleveland and Washington, D.C., public high schools, Cuban reached the conclusion that "reform ideas, talk, and organizational changes directed at improving how and what teachers teach may affect what happens in schools but may not reach inside classrooms."[50] This has certainly been the case with history education in the context of national and state policies aimed at improving it since the 1950s.

Education reforms from above, most originating in the federal government, were affected by the Cold War and U.S.-Soviet relations after World War II. The National Defense Education Act (1958), the Elementary and Secondary Education Act (1965), and "A Nation at Risk" (1983)[51] all involved intense and extensive reassessment of K–12 American education, resulting in priorities for reforming schools, including improving the teaching of subject areas. However, despite attempts at pedagogical reform from above, improving history education proved to be complicated and elusive.

Demographic and political currents unleashed by the 1960s seemed conducive to educational change. Fifteen years before the publication of *A People's History*, in the mid-1960s, influenced by the Black freedom movement, government initiatives such as President Lyndon Johnson's War on Poverty and the Elementary and Secondary Education Act of 1965 promoted equity and achievement by low-income students. This reform impulse, enhanced by the passage of the Civil Rights Act of 1964, drew idealistic college graduates into work as secondary school teachers. These young teachers aspired to expand educational opportunity to low-income students of color, end racial segregation, and battle against sexism and racism in their textbooks and curricula. They also were eager to work with immigrant students, including those who spoke a first language other than English. As Cuban described, inspired by their teaching experience in urban schools, with high rates of poverty and with students of color the majority, these teachers demanded change—and in many cases carried this out on their own. "The history of race and enduring poverty that children experienced within families and in a city mattered greatly to what happened in schools and classrooms."[52]

In her study of National Teacher Corps members who taught in urban schools serving poor communities during the 1960s, historian Bethany Rogers, through interviews with Teacher Corps members, captures the ethos shared by many who were teaching at the time. "[T]eaching in the inner city . . . was my way of being able to react to the society that was willing to take us and keep us in Vietnam . . . that was willing to assassinate leaders who were different, that was willing to accept the capitalist drive."[53] For these educators, teaching was an opportunity to respond personally to social and political concerns of the day. Many of them sought to do this by engaging students in study of U.S. history that supported critical examinations of government (including foreign policy), class, race, gender, and the economy. But, as we have seen, textbooks critical of U.S. history were generally unavailable to high school teachers at the time. Thus, it was African American literature, not U.S. history textbooks, that volunteer teachers used as they pioneered an antiracist curriculum for Black students in the Freedom Schools that accompanied the historic Mississippi Freedom Summer voter registration crusade led by the Student Nonviolent Coordinating Committee (SNCC) in 1964.[54]

Teachers, of course, mattered as much as the textbooks, curricula, and education policy problems discussed above. Inventive history teachers were of great importance in creating the need and opportunity for Zinn's *A People's History* and its challenge to the status quo in history education. Unfortunately, many educational histories focus so much on textbooks and curriculum reform that they offer very little information about what history teachers actually taught young people in their history and social studies courses and why.[55]

Larry Cuban is one of the few education scholars to avoid this error. His *Teaching History Then and Now* (2016), focusing on two high schools where he once taught, goes the deepest in exposing what and how history teachers have taught over the last fifty years in American schools. Regarding both goals and methods, Cuban distinguishes between conventional and unconventional history teachers. Cuban described conventional history teachers as being committed to the "heritage" approach, using "the past to re-create the present" and rooted in civic and national goals. "Beyond the U.S. flag in every classroom and Pledge of Allegiance, examples of the heritage purpose at work in schools are lessons that focus on the Founding Fathers of the Revolutionary period and heroes such as Davy Crockett, Abraham Lincoln, Frederick Douglass, and Susan B. Anthony to recoup from the past a legacy that all American students should know."[56] Educators and others who support this approach believe that high school history classes must emphasize American progress, American exceptionalism, and common experiences among U.S. citizens. During the twenty-five years prior to the publication of *A People's History*, the majority of U.S. history textbooks reinforced the "heritage approach" while state education departments and school districts instructed school administrators and teachers to purchase them.

But other history teachers more closely aligned with the work and methods of professional historians employed teaching methods Cuban termed "historical," centering on interpretation and analysis.[57] In this approach, history was presented through multiple viewpoints and students encouraged to develop high-order thinking skills, such as analyzing different perspectives on historical events, assessing primary documents and other sources, understanding historical context, and making claim-evidence connections.[58] With the "historical" approach, which Cuban described as more "student-centered" than the heritage approach, students learn that history is "an interpretation of the past, not a telegram that yesteryear has wired to the present."[59] In some cases, teachers who implemented the historical approach were innovators in their school communities or members of informal or semiformal organizations that sought to promote "critical thinking" or "social justice" through their teaching.[60] At the center of their work was a commitment to exposing students to a range of sources, multiple perspectives, and varied interpretations, all while emphasizing history's contested nature.

Teachers who supported the "historical" approach were not a monolithic group. For example, some viewed themselves as progressives or even radicals, aiming to decenter the conventional narrative through the use of competing sources. Commitment to social change and activism informed the teaching goals for many, and the pedagogical and curricular choices they made reflect these goals. Other teachers who carried out the historical approach were primarily concerned with the work of professional historians and the developing historiography.[61] Teachers who employed this approach wanted students to examine historians' biases and made this a critical topic of analysis.[62]

The textbook analyses of Anyon and FitzGerald, the educational reform critiques of Tyack and Cuban, the history of history teaching by Cuban, and the other educational scholarship we have reviewed offer clues as to why by 1980 there was a pressing need and even hunger for a book like Zinn's *A People's History*, a book that provided a new kind of introduction to American history and a radical departure from conventional textbooks. This scholarship documents that history textbooks and reform efforts were failing badly, leaving students as bored with and disengaged from school history as their parents had been in their own school days. And innovative teachers, such as those Cuban found favoring the "historical" over the "heritage" approach, were dissatisfied with this legacy of failure. They aimed to move beyond memorization of names and dates and overreliance on poorly written and dull textbooks, and they wanted their history classrooms to reflect the analytical rigor, debates, controversy, and high-order thinking skills of professional historians. For such teachers, *A People's History* offered a vehicle for this critical approach. In this sense, the success of *A People's History* in attracting innovative teachers was a product of the failure of conventional textbooks and the low-quality classroom teaching they supported.

This failure of textbook history would prove enduring, and so some teachers would continue to seek other sources, such as *A People's History*, as alternatives to standard textbooks long after the 1980s. As James Loewen indicated in his 1995 book *Lies My Teacher Told Me: Everything Your American History Textbook Got Wrong*, well into the 1990s U.S. history textbooks in high schools remained woefully inadequate. Loewen's detailed examination of twelve widely used textbooks revealed that they promoted Eurocentric, laudatory, and false views of American history and were horribly dull to read. When Loewen updated his textbook review for the second edition of *Lies My Teacher Told Me* in 2007, he found that textbooks remained inadequate. In preparing this second edition, Loewen could not stomach reviewing twelve more textbooks. As he put it, "I read only six new books, partly owing to publisher consolidation, but also because reading them is so tedious. . . . Nothing could get me to read another dozen high school history textbooks. . . . They are just too boring."[63]

The review of history textbooks and pedagogy presented in this chapter has focused on how the deficient state of history education set the stage for the popularity of *A People's History* soon after its initial publication in 1980. But Loewen and others remind us that there remained a lack of competition for *A People's History* well into the 1990s and the early twenty-first century.[64] Thus, history teachers would use *A People's History* as an important adjunct to their official textbooks. Dissatisfaction with standard textbooks was so widespread that Loewen, like Zinn, would reach the best-seller list. By 2018, *Lies My Teacher Told Me*, which had won an American Book Award in 1995, had sold nearly two million copies—most likely aided by a blurb from Zinn on its cover urging "every teacher, every student of history, every citizen" to read Loewen's book.[65]

This is not to say that most history teachers today remain stuck in the rut of the 1970s. Pedagogies that encourage students to use the skills employed by professional historians have become increasingly popular with teachers since the early 2000s, with programs such as the Stanford History Education Group (SHEG), founded in 2002 by Sam Wineburg, a pioneer in the field of historical cognition, along with his colleagues Daisy Martin, Chauncey Monte-Sano, and others. In order to "enrich students' intellectual experience in the history classroom," SHEG carried out research, worked with schools and districts, and provided free materials for teachers and students, including its popular guide *Reading Like a Historian: Teaching Literacy in Middle School and High School History Classes* (2013).[66] The wide reach of the program is impressive, with six million downloads of their *Reading Like a Historian Curriculum*.[67]

Today SHEG is one of many projects supporting efforts to get students to think (and read and write) like historians. Teaching students to think historically is also supported by the National History Education Clearinghouse and the Historical Thinking Project, the latter founded by Peter Seixas, a scholar of curriculum and pedagogy at the University of British Columbia. This thrust in social studies education has made its way into state curricula and curriculum guides, codifying it as an integral part of social studies instruction in many states.

SHEG's publications represent a notable advance over the textbook-centered history pedagogy of the twentieth century. The cover of SHEG's popular *Reading Like a Historian* workbook alerts readers that it is "aligned with Common Core State Standards," underscoring its foregrounding the development of skills— analysis of sources, contextualization, corroboration, generalization, consideration of multiple viewpoints, and questioning of accounts. Yet there is a political timidity in this approach. While students taught under the SHEG model are encouraged to "think like a historian," this pedagogical reform does not encompass deep analysis of historical content, systemic criticism of U.S. governmental policy, or emphasis on history from the bottom up. SHEG materials do not support debates about ideology, class conflict, and militarism that Zinn highlights. SHEG's evasion of such debates and criticism can be seen in its workbook's presentation on teaching the Cuban Missile Crisis, which asks students to consider "how our understanding of history changes [the] more distant we are from an event."[68] In this way the proposed essential question—"Why Teach about the Cuban Missile Crisis?"—is approached with a narrow and relatively trivial discussion of temporal matters (e.g., whether we understand this event today bet-

ter than Americans did in 1962) instead of exploring the pivotal historical debate over whether President Kennedy's cold warrior approach to foreign policy
helped bring the world to the brink of nuclear holocaust.[69] Thus, while the work
of the Stanford History Education Group conforms to Larry Cuban's "historical"
approach to history education (centering on teaching with primary documents
and how historians carry out their work), SHEG steers clear of questions that are
central to a people's pedagogy and history (discussed more fully in chapter 6).

The letters that students and teachers wrote to Zinn in the closing decades of
the twentieth century provide evidence that teachers attempted to support critical thinking about U.S. history in their classrooms well before the creation of
SHEG in 2002 and other twenty-first-century curricular reforms. For example,
a teacher at the center of the case study in our next chapter, Bill Patterson, assigned select chapters from A People's History in his classroom in the 1980s and
1990s (as did other innovative teachers) to foster debate about the standard textbooks' version of the past in order to highlight multiple perspectives in history,
an essential aspect of the "historical" approach. Patterson and other teachers
were initially doing such teaching solo, without the sophisticated sourcing and
scaffolding aids that SHEG would later produce with its team at Stanford. These
teachers were not only using professional historians' skills and approaches, they
were also promoting critical, even radical alternatives to the status quo in teaching history.

This brings us to pose two questions that are pertinent to history education today, when A People's History of the United States remains popular among
teachers and their students. What impact did A People's History—with its explicit and radical politics and rejection of the posed neutrality of textbooks—
have on the process of history teaching (and learning) in the classrooms of a
teacher who made extensive use of it from the 1980s through the turn of the
century? And what can historians, teachers, and others concerned about history
education learn from the responses of students to encounters with A People's
History in the classroom?

CHAPTER 3

In High School Classrooms

Since its publication in 1980, Howard Zinn's *A People's History of the United States* has generated an enormous amount of criticism, especially (but not exclusively) from the Right. Conservatives have repeatedly expressed fears that Zinn's book—which they denounce as anti-American because of its unyielding criticism of U.S. capitalism, militarism, racism, and classism—is being used by teachers for indoctrination. Such attacks on the book have outlived Zinn. As referenced in chapter 2, news of Zinn's death in 2010 motivated Indiana's governor Mitch Daniels to explore the possibility of banning Zinn's "false" and "anti-American" history from the classrooms of his state.[1]

Missing from such denunciations is evidence of the ways *A People's History of the United States*—whatever its flaws—has been used in the classroom by history teachers. Such evidence is now available thanks to the opening of the Howard Zinn archive at NYU's Tamiment Library, which contains extensive teacher correspondence and hundreds of student letters and e-mails to Zinn concerning the role that his *People's History* played in their history classrooms. This chapter offers an illustrative case study of how *A People's History* has been used in high school history classes. It focuses on the teaching and learning of history in the classes of Bill Patterson, a teacher who worked in public high schools in two largely conservative, white, middle-class Oregon suburbs. In an unusual collaboration between students, teacher, and prominent historian, each year from the mid-1980s until the early twenty-first century, Patterson had his students, high school juniors, write Zinn to discuss their reactions to chapters of *A People's History* and compare them to the conventional school-mandated history textbook that they also read.

This case study will be followed by a chapter that offers an extensive sampling of the student letters. Our goal here is not to resolve the debate about the merits and flaws of Zinn's interpretation of American history (those are probed in chapter 7). Rather, we offer an evidence-based history of the impact of *A Peo-*

ple's History in high school classrooms with a mind toward teaching students to think historically.

Innovative and effective history teachers encourage students to ask analytical questions about the past, use evidence to answer those questions, go beyond names and dates in considering the record, take into account the context in which sources were created, and compare points of view of the actors involved. Such teachers are inclined against traditional textbooks whose approach stunts such critical thinking and engagement.[2] (As we showed in chapter 2, this is not a new problem). Most U.S. textbooks at the time when Zinn was writing *A People's History* gave students the impression that history consisted of one uncontested narrative that they had to memorize, leaving them unaware of the importance of critical analysis of competing historical interpretations. Those flat textbooks contributed to a preponderance of disengaged students and complaints that history was boring, complaints documented by the letters that Patterson's students wrote to Zinn.

Though *A People's History* has been praised and criticized for its role in history education in America's high schools, the most vocal supporters tend to be innovative teachers, and the harshest critics tend not to have spoken with them. Critics have drawn negative conclusions about *A People's History* without talking with teachers or gathering other primary source data about how teachers use *A People's History* or how students who have read it (or parts of it) view their learning experience.[3] Critics tend to analyze *A People's History* as a solo textbook, but this is misguided since the book is usually used comparatively. Zinn has most frequently appeared in high school classrooms via photocopies of his book's most provocative chapters—such as the one about Columbus—which teachers have provided to augment textbooks and spark debate.

While *A People's History* provides teachers an opportunity to enliven history for students, it has, as noted, been considered too radical to be adopted by school districts. Contrary to right-wing alarmists who imagine that Zinn now dominates history instruction in schools, his book has never attained the status of state-mandated textbook. As Bill Bigelow, a veteran teacher and codirector of the Zinn Education Project, explains, "There is no way that one can consider *A People's History of the United States* to be a mainstream text in school districts in the country, if by 'text' we mean a book assigned to all students as the main course material. In fact, we are unaware of any school district that has adopted Zinn in place of a standard Pearson or Houghton Mifflin Harcourt textbook. Critics of Zinn who imagine . . . that somehow *A People's History* . . . is now the new orthodoxy . . . [are] simply wrong."[4]

Teachers' letters to Zinn in the first thirty years after its publication demonstrate that *A People's History* had been a tool for innovation, dissent, and debate rather than a dominant text in high school history. Teachers who in the 1980s started to bring *A People's History* into their classrooms were part of a reform effort countering the failure of traditional textbooks, rote pedagogy, and standardized tests. Alternative approaches were desperately needed to bring history to life, and later in the 1980s a more organized reform movement emerged, with activist teacher organizations like Rethinking Schools (1986) and Teaching for Change (1989) and their publications. Reform-oriented history teachers would embrace *A People's History* and in the twenty-first century be part of the online organizing of the Zinn Education Project (discussed in chapter 6).

In the early eighties there were hundreds of teachers besides Bill Patterson who brought *A People's History* into their classrooms, some of whom also corresponded with Zinn about their use of his book. Secondary school teachers at the time taught during a period of intense upheaval and change, when terrorism rocked Europe, assassinations and war shook South Asia and the Middle East, and a global recession hit. Ronald Reagan and Margaret Thatcher pushed for supply-side economics including decreased regulation and lower taxes, which provoked debates on methods for economic recovery and growth. Americans felt the pinch directly or otherwise worried about how a struggling U.S. economy would affect them. During this period, many Americans agreed that it was time to transform U.S. politics and economics, and a rightward shift came with the Reagan landslide in the presidential election of 1980, which gave forty-four states to the former governor of California. This worried many moderate, liberal, and left-leaning teachers. Perhaps more than teachers of other subjects, history teachers in the 1980s were on the front lines of these political developments and taught about them.

In response to the tumultuous domestic and global context in which they worked, teachers sought ways to help students become engaged citizens. Some of these teachers had come of age and were shaped by Long 1960s social movements that raised probing questions about U.S. racism, sexism, imperialism, and capitalism. For them, investigating multiple perspectives while applying critical analyses to a range of topics seemed essential to rigorous, meaningful study of the U.S. past and present. These teachers realized that fostering critical readings of the American past necessitated the decentering of standard textbook narratives and they found *A People's History* a useful tool in this process.

Between 1980 and Zinn's death in 2010, hundreds of secondary school teachers wrote to Zinn, conveying dismay about the grim state of history education in U.S. schools, including the tedious textbooks their schools mandated. One teacher described her school's standard textbook as "one-sided," with a "boring and trite" historical narrative.[5] Another charged that the textbook provided by his school distorted history by leaving out facts essential to a critical understanding of the past.[6] Teacher Laura Vantine, in a 1980 letter, told Zinn that the standard textbook she was required to use in her Hamilton, New York, school made her cringe.[7] As a corrective, she had suggested the school use *A People's History* alongside the textbook. A North Carolina high school teacher wrote Zinn, "The textbook I must use for the political systems classes I teach is almost pure propaganda." Teacher Ben Honoroff of Brooklyn, New York, called his textbook a collection of "flat blurbs."[8] California teacher Michael Presser bemoaned required textbooks that "exclude[d] facts and information essential to reaching any reasonably informed conclusion," such as on the Vietnam War.[9] Presser expressed concern that his school's textbook ignored the Johnson administration's deceptions in connection with the 1964 Gulf of Tonkin incident, which was depicted uncritically as an unprovoked attack that led to escalated U.S. military involvement in Vietnam. Presser's attempt to address this problem involved assigning a chapter from a world geography textbook along with Zinn's chapter "The Impossible Victory: Vietnam," from *A People's History*. This enabled him to complicate for his students this milestone event in the history of the Vietnam War.

Reform-oriented teachers from the 1980s onward turned to Zinn to go beyond their textbooks to enliven, extend, and deepen their history courses. Zinn was for these teachers via *A People's History* a provocateur who inspired students to ask deep questions about their government, its foreign policy, and the experience of women, people of color, and working-class and poor people in American history. Teachers' letters to Zinn attest that his radical approach enabled them to engage their students in thought-provoking debates—in which Zinn's indictment of U.S. imperialism, militarism, classism, racism, and sexism was compared with the triumphalist version of American history found in most high school textbooks.

Of equal or even greater value are the letters students wrote to Zinn, since very few sources exist that enable us to hear directly from high school students, reflecting on their experiences learning history and reading history textbooks.[10] Fortunately, the Zinn papers include hundreds of letters by students who wrote to Zinn after reading sections of *A People's History* (along with corresponding chapters in conventional U.S. history textbook). Many letters offer thoughtful, detailed, and revealing accounts contrasting textbooks and Zinn's book, and compare tedious history classes centered on a textbook with lively, engaging classes in which Zinn's book was used to challenge the textbook, encouraging students to decide between competing historical interpretations.

The largest set of such letters sent to Zinn came from Bill Patterson's high school juniors. Patterson asked his students, as a culminating class activity, to send Zinn their thoughts, criticisms, and questions about *A People's History*, and over the years many did so. Zinn saved more than a hundred of those letters, and they now offer a store of evidence in which students discuss their initial encounters with Zinn's book, historical debate, and their questioning of textbook history.

In the course of overseeing his students' writing letters to Zinn, Patterson himself corresponded with Zinn from the mid-1980s through the late 1990s.[11] Patterson's purpose in writing was to insure that Zinn would not mind receiving scores of letters from students (Zinn welcomed them) and to thank him for reading them and for writing responses to some. Patterson commented in these letters about his motivations and goals in assigning chapters from *A People's History*. They offer, along with his students' letters, contemporaneous evidence of why and how he made use of Zinn's book in his classes.

Patterson's letters also illuminate the educational and political environment in which he was teaching and reveal someone dedicated to effective history education, concerned that the public school system, with its various mandates, undermined meaningful teaching and learning. Referring to some of the obstacles he encountered in his work, Patterson wrote Zinn, "As you are probably aware, it is sometimes difficult to present any kind of history in a public school setting, considering material handed to you, class size and how public schools tend to condition a young person's mind." Patterson was determined to overcome these obstacles, explaining to Zinn his "attempt to facilitate a thoughtful atmosphere" in his history classes and expressing thanks to Zinn for writing a book that "helped immensely" in this effort and for Zinn's welcoming of student letters.[12] Patterson was critical of the school systems' devotion to standardized testing, which he saw as "dumbing down the quality of learning (and teaching) in the social studies area"—especially with their emphasis on memorizing names, dates, and other details.[13] In contrast, Patterson emphasized discussion, debate, conceptually oriented historical reading, and a final writing assignment that required students to compare and analyze historical arguments.

Patterson's letters to Zinn explained that he had assigned several chapters of *A People's History* together with the required textbook "for the sake of exposure to a variety of interpretations and attempting to nurture independent thought." *A People's History* became a central part of Patterson's history curriculum because he observed that it promoted critical thinking skills and fostered lively debate. Instead of sleepy class sessions in which students were disengaged, Zinn and his book, in Patterson's words, "provoked spirited (sometimes rowdy) discussions in class," enhancing student interest in history. Students who disagreed with Zinn's radical take on American history, no less than those who agreed with him, tended to find these sessions intellectually stimulating since Zinn's writing was accessible and his ideas so new to them. As Patterson told Zinn, "over the course of the school year, no matter if a student 'loved' you or 'hated' you, they all looked forward to what you had to say on a topic."[14]

Although Patterson did not adhere to a formal educational philosophy, his Zinn-versus-textbook assignments were designed to promote "the 'art' of inquiry," as Patterson put it in one letter to Zinn, an attempt to teach students to research and assess conflicting views, so as "to get at the truth . . . a skill desperately needed as these young people approach adulthood."[15] His inquiry approach to teaching involved students' referencing multiple sources while carrying out historical investigations driven by their own questions.[16] This approach echoed the work of education philosopher John Dewey, who identified inquiry in learning as a process of reflection that was encouraged by some "perplexity, confusion or doubt."[17] As the two U.S. history texts presented students with contrasting views of history, Patterson's students were propelled to "demand . . . the solution of a perplexity," which supported learning and a critical perspective on the past.[18] This is what Patterson meant when he explained to Zinn, in his second year of using Zinn's writing to challenge textbook history, "Your book, A People's History, helped in providing the students the chance to investigate various topics, form conclusions, and articulate how they came to those conclusions."[19]

In Patterson's classes, Zinn's book was used selectively in a handful of debate-oriented units in which Patterson would distribute photocopied chapters of A People's History—on Columbus, Andrew Jackson and the Indian Wars, the Mexican War, the Gilded Age and Progressive Era, World War II and Vietnam—that offered the most dramatic contrast with the class textbook. Students would then compare the history presented in that textbook—Addison-Wesley United States History—with Zinn's critical interpretations and debate the relative merits of the contrasting versions of the past. Exposure to vastly differing texts would enable his students to view what is at the heart of the discipline: interpreting and weighing evidence and making logical conclusions.

Their correspondence revealed that both Zinn and Patterson realized that Patterson's use of A People's History in his conservative school district was not only innovative but also daring. Zinn at one point asked whether Patterson had experienced any pushback or censorship attempts from local educational administrators or parents. Patterson replied that he hadn't received any pressure to stop, speculating that this might have been because he and his students seemed to be "(unintentionally) 'low key' about Howard Zinn outside of the classroom. As a result, I really wonder how many folks in the community (including the board of ed.) are aware that I use your book. Certainly some administrators are aware, for in the process of teacher evaluation they inevitably see my supplemental materials. There have been no problems so far." Patterson assured Zinn that he would not put up with any censorship but would insist on his right to assign chapters from A People's History even "if questioned or threatened by the powers that be." This stance, Patterson explained to Zinn, "is a result not necessarily of any extreme ideological bent on my part, but for the sake of [student] exposure to a variety of interpretations and attempting to nurture independent thought. As you know, at times this task collides into formidable barriers in our society."[20]

This correspondence suggests that if Patterson had a pedagogical motive for assigning Zinn, it was not leftist indoctrination but nurturing independent-mindedness in his students. This was a natural inclination for Patterson since, as his letters to Zinn show, he was himself independent minded. This at times led Patterson to challenge the assumptions of the conservative communities in which he taught. Patterson wrote to Zinn that acquainting students from his conservative community with what for them were new and more critical ways of looking at American history generated such lively debate in his classrooms that it amounted to "stirring the pot." "Using your readings makes the job [of teaching] that much more rewarding," he added.[21]

Patterson in his correspondence comes across as a self-confident teacher who grew even more so over the course of his career. After a decade of assigning Zinn's book in his classes, Patterson started to involve his students' parents in class discussions of the book, despite potential controversy. By 1999 Patterson was having his students ask their parents to share in writing their reactions to the Zinn readings, and these were used to further enliven class discussions. Patterson shared these parent responses with Zinn and reported that he had received "good parental feedback (both critical & complimentary)."[22]

Patterson believed his students would gain through exposure to A People's History and a conventional textbook both content knowledge and skills including historical analysis and interpretation.[23] His decision to assign chapters of Zinn underscores his knowledge of how to teach, what content to teach, and to what ends, developed over time inside and outside of the classroom.[24] Patterson's pedagogical choices were guided by his concerns that anonymous and authoritative textbooks with "words and ideas that have first been run through a blender," as one teacher-scholar described, contribute to an impoverished conception of history.[25] Such concerns are supported by studies and noted in the literature of history education reform.[26]

The student letters to Zinn, as shown in the next chapter, provide extensive evidence that Patterson's assigning of contrasting texts resulted in students engaging in "meaning over memory" as they pondered simultaneously different historical narratives about the same events.[27] While Patterson provided his students with historical facts, he was most interested in fostering critical thinking about history. In place of disengaged students with little to say about bland textbook narratives, Patterson found that when he assigned Zinn alongside the textbook it provoked "spirited discussion."[28] Patterson later looked back on his teaching as having been centered on student participation and the clash of ideas: "I . . . have always appreciated argument and discussion. . . . I don't think many people have this skill of discussing and getting down to the roots of issues."[29]

In our interviews with Patterson in his retirement, he shared extensive details about his background, rationale for assigning *A People's History*, and the context in which he taught, with Zinn as part of his curriculum from the 1980s onward.[30] Patterson's entry into history teaching in the early 1970s was not a straight line. He studied psychology as an undergraduate at Pacific University in Forest Grove, a small school in Oregon. He started in education as a wrestling coach. "Strangely enough I basically got the job as a result of coaching. I coached wrestling. I used to wrestle, high school wrestling, college wrestling. I was pretty accomplished in that and there was a reputation and all that." Some of his colleagues were initially skeptical that someone with his coaching background could excel at history teaching. There was, as Patterson recalls,

> a great film back in the 1980s, it was called "Teachers." One of the characters was this guy "Ditto" and all he did was pass around worksheets, and kids fell asleep or kids did their work with worksheets. . . . One day in this movie . . . Ditto the teacher, who normally sat at his desk and read the paper, choked to death, died, and the kids didn't even know it. . . . So when I got there in our social studies department in '75 a couple, three, of the teachers thought "that's just the way coaches are. They just pass out worksheets."

Patterson knew of the coach-teacher stereotype, and he understood their concern. "I empathized with them. And they . . . got to know me and they found out I was a little bit different."

Although Paterson had studied psychology in college, he had also been interested in history and historical debate. "[Historiography] was always my interest. . . . It was easy for me at a very early point to take a person out of it and not become really judgmental about this person or that person. It became very obvious to me . . . that human beings are just human beings. They're very interpretive." This way of thinking was in line with how he viewed people's natural tendency to hold on to perspectives that made sense to them while confirming personal beliefs. Patterson was fascinated by exposure to multiple perspectives on events in general, which led him to consume news from varying sources. "I listen to Fox News. I listen to Al Jazeera America, I listen to all of them, and it's so interesting, and they all have their different perspectives."

Patterson explained how he came to incorporate A People's History into his classes in the early 1980s, after seven years of teaching, as a contrast to the standard textbook.

> When I ran into A People's History in '83, '84, and started to use it, this may sound weird, I thought the worse the basic textbook, the better. . . . In my time, from 1975–2005, the textbooks were pretty lame, to say the least. . . . And my attitude was, as time went on, the lamer the better. They made Zinn and others a little more credible. . . . [In] thirty years of teaching I was always unimpressed with textbooks. As time went on, they were good to use in that you could bounce off them and make supplemental readings like the Zinn chapters from A People's History a little more meaningful. Ironically [as a point of contrast] the textbooks became more and more valuable."

After three or four years of using Zinn as a supplemental reading, Patterson engaged his students more directly in examining point of view in historical narrative. He described his teaching strategy:

> I really got into the idea when I introduced the textbook as clarifying "Exactly what are you reading here?" You've been brought up with the idea that this [textbook] is the Bible, but let's . . . ask ourselves: "Who writes these books?" And we tossed that around to the point where, "Yes, people write these textbooks, a group of people write these textbooks, and they could fall victim like everybody else to their own prejudices." I can't remember how I worded it. But after a couple of years with Zinn I started to introduce the basic textbook in that way.

Patterson explained that his decision to use Zinn was consistent with his prior approach to teaching. "I was always searching for supplemental stuff . . . alternative points of view, that was my nature. When I ran into Zinn . . . it was like the perfect storm. . . . The whole idea of skepticism about anything that I read in a textbook. . . . The textbook adoption meetings were so bizarre to me. Like "what's the best textbook?" Give me the worst text. I don't care. . . . When

I ran into Zinn . . . I was ready for him. Ready to use *A People's History* in the classroom."

Bringing students to understand the interpretive nature of history was a central goal for Patterson. "If it [history] is taught right, then the kid leaves the classroom at the end of the year or the end of the semester knowing it's interpretive." For Patterson, assigning Zinn in tandem with the standard textbook was in line with his natural inclination to notice and highlight varying perspectives. "[*A People's History*] was a real complement to what I was thinking already. And it then became obvious that in my opinion historians or people in general, they have their everyday experiences, they report what they want to report, they share their own story. And it's all interpretive." And for Patterson, historians were fallible humans with their own interests and perspectives. "It goes back to Zinn. You select and invariably omit what you want to. . . . It was just so valuable."

Patterson believed that understanding the contested nature of historical interpretation was crucial, not only because of its value in grappling with the complexities of history but also for teaching the habits of mind that would enable students to become critical readers and thinkers in other areas of life. He thought that once students learned to be skeptical of what their history textbooks told them, they would apply those critical thinking skills "when they watch[ed] the news," since they would realize that the media is rendering interpretations that had to be critically assessed rather than blindly accepted. And "when they [heard] their own friends report on something," they would also be ready to ask critical questions since even personal reportage is interpretive.

Patterson started using Zinn in the classroom at a point in his career when he felt more confident. "It's interesting that when Zinn came into my life, into my classroom, it was about eight years into my teaching. And I've often thought it takes five, six, seven years to be a good teacher. So it just came at the right time." Patterson's pedagogical approach evolved over time. He knew he was ultimately interested in engaging students in debate, but his use of Zinn at first involved improvisation. "There were no parameters at the beginning . . . as I think about it . . . I winged it. And as I saw the back and forth initially on . . . whatever chapter we were doing, I would . . . monitor, and if some person was coming from some weird angle, as a teacher you just get good at doing that stuff naturally. I knew discussion was my thing. . . . But I did not at the outset specifically state. 'OK this is what we're going to do, these are the rules.' I was never into that. That's not me."

Patterson saw his role not as siding with Zinn or the textbook but instead doing as much as he could to get students to question both, to facilitate engaging discussion and debate. His pedagogical stance was that of disrupting easy or im-perceptive class consensus: "I was always the devil's advocate. Whenever I saw the kids going towards one sentiment, I'd be against it. . . . That's how I went at it. And I loved [it], it was always fun. Any discussion, if somebody would come in with a Zinn point of view on whatever topic that we were dealing with, I could play devil's advocate with them and against them. I loved to have the kids a little confused with me. 'OK, the teacher is giving me Zinn, but every once in a while he's not with Zinn. He's kind of arguing against Zinn's point of view.'" Patterson wanted students to see that neither side had a monopoly on the truth. "I didn't want the kids to leave the classroom thinking I was a Zinnite."[31]

The results were quite successful, in Patterson's view. "For the most part, the kids got a kick out of the health . . . of the discussion, whatever can provoke dis-cussion. . . . So in that sense *A People's History of the U.S.* was a tool, a tool that I could use to promote that idea even more. . . . It's just this guy who came along and with his great stuff, and it was to create discussion and debate. And so what if he is right or wrong?" For Patterson, its value was not necessarily "to change their thinking" but to "kind of provoke [and end] the dead [historical] thought."

It is evident when reading Patterson's students' letters to Zinn that he was able to convey through his pedagogical stance the difference between his pri-vate view and his classroom position on Zinn, as the students freely dissented and argued with their teacher and with Zinn on a range of topics and ques-tions. In Patterson's interviews, as in his letters to Zinn in the 1980s and 1990s, he acknowledged that teaching with *A People's History* was potentially provoc-ative because of how conservatives in the local and school community might respond. Exposing adolescents to Zinn's radical take on American history in-volved some risk. But Patterson was not overly concerned about this. In fact, he was somewhat amused by the idea of being called out for assigning a radical historian to his students, and he did not let political considerations push him to revisit his decision: "Really, in my gut I had no concern about the administra-tion, parents, public. I knew, you know yourself in your gut, when you're doing right. You don't have to fret on anyone coming down on you. At that time if I was to have been hauled in I would have just kind of smiled and almost laughed at them, what a joke this is that I am even being called on the carpet. That was my attitude."[32]

Although both communities where he taught were conservative, Patterson felt that in the 1980s there was at least some dialogue between opposing camps, as opposed to the stark and acrimonious divide that exists today on cultural, po-litical, and economic issues. "Back then . . . a guy like Ronald Reagan would be a puppy dog compared to a guy like Ted Cruz. So back then conservatives were a little more receptive. You could talk with them. . . . I could talk with them about Howard Zinn, and they would go 'Hmm,' where today it would be 'GRRRR!' I think that people, especially liberal, left-leaning [ones], forget how conservatives back in the day were nothing compared to how they are today."

Certainly some parents were critical of Patterson's use of Zinn in the classroom, but Patterson did not shy away from them. When one parent went to the administration claiming Patterson was "anti-American and non-Christian" for teaching with Zinn, Patterson engaged the problem openly and head-on. When his principal suggested he invite the parent to his classroom, Patterson was open to it. "I thought, 'that's a cool idea.' So I did. And I didn't mince words, when he came in, the father. I just did what I usually did. And the guy came in. He didn't come into his son's classroom. He came into the same class but not his son's. And then afterwards he came up to me. He had two words for me. He said, 'You're good.' He walked right out, and I've never heard from him since." Patterson did not change his approach to teaching with *A People's History* when this parent sat in. "I didn't fake it. I just did what I normally did. The reason I give that example is [that] that was my attitude. I went balls-out. I loved what I did. I wasn't ever, ever concerned about parents and what they thought. Call me naïve."

Patterson gives credit to a teacher colleague for giving him the idea to have students write to Zinn after reading chapters from *A People's History* alongside the standard textbook. After some thought, he decided to give the assignment for extra credit. "But it turned into more than that. It was more than extra credit. The attitude [among students] was 'Yes, this is what I want to do.'" He described how he incorporated Zinn into the overall course: "It was so simple. As I read *A People's History* it was just . . . so easy to incorporate. Columbus [in the textbook] and then [Zinn's] Columbus. The Founding Fathers and the Founding Fathers. Jackson and then Jackson. It was just very easy to me." He assigned chapters he thought would be most engaging, instructive, and decentering for his students alongside the standard textbook: "It was just my gut, what was the most interesting chapter. What I emphasized chronologically."

While Patterson gave his students freedom to decide what topics they wanted to write to Zinn about in their letters, he did require that they include specific references to content in *A People's History* or in the standard textbook. "The only second draft I would require was if they were too general or they did not specifically refer to whatever chapter or chapters [we were studying], to make it meatier. . . . I tried to impress upon them to make it substantive."

Patterson took the same approach in class discussions. He didn't want students to emote but to explore and debate historical issues in a serious way, drawing on the conflicting accounts they had read. "You've got to watch [out] that discussion at the high school level doesn't become this bullshit session where nothing gets done," Patterson noted. "You've really got to control that." It was crucial to "make sure that your kids have some sense of facts and foundation," and then you can debate competing historical interpretations in an informed way. And because Zinn in *A People's History* was so up front about his biases and disagreements with standard textbook fare, Patterson felt, "Oh, my God, this is just the guy I need."

Just getting high school juniors to read their history textbooks can be a challenge. And here Patterson was expecting students to read a second account on top of the required textbook. Patterson found, however, that class debates on Zinn versus the textbook were so thought provoking that they motivated even reluctant students to do the extra reading. Was Columbus the brave discoverer of "the New World" or murderous and greedy slaver? Did an expansionist United States instigate the Mexican War, or was Mexico the aggressor? Students wanted to know enough about the issues to participate in the debates, to develop their own views on Zinn, the textbook, and historical truth. Patterson did recognize workload realities by assigning only select Zinn chapters—the half-dozen or so that seemed best suited for debate—so that students were reading Zinn periodically rather than every day. This made the debates special events to which students looked forward. They provoked not only intense discussions but also, as Patterson put it, "appreciation for complexity," igniting student curiosity because the students were "[no longer] quite sure what [was] the truth."

The teaching methods Patterson employed when assigning Zinn alongside the textbook were creative and effective, as is evident in the student letters to Zinn. His students became deeply engaged with history. They had been provoked to read both the textbook and Zinn carefully and critically and to participate actively, even passionately, in their class's lively discussions and debates. Plus they became confident enough about their learning to correspond with the historian whose work they had studied.

However, as Patterson himself was the first to admit, his approach to history teaching was not without flaws. Patterson could have done more to give his students intellectual tools, including terminology, to deconstruct historical interpretations. He might have made the "work of history [more] visible and open to students" by showing them, among other things, that interpretation was distinct from facts and evidence but made use of both.[33] While some student letters indicate clear comprehension of the interpretive nature of history, others did not appear in full command of this key concept. For example, some of the letters refer to Zinn's narrative as his "opinion" instead of historical interpretations grounded in sources, evidence, and analysis. Few students used the terms "evidence" or "primary source." Many of the letters reveal students assessing the reliability of their sources by comparing them to other accounts but without the proper terminology (e.g., "primary source" and "evidence"). Since Patterson did not emphasize the role of sourcing in historical writing, this was something the students attempted to address but not with much sophistication or depth, save for a few students who were clearly more advanced.

Patterson, reflecting years later, thought he might have done a better job teaching how history is constructed: "I don't think I did a real good job with that. We may have taken a look, or I may have shown them a couple of times . . . the notes and references [of a history book]. . . . It didn't, reflecting back on it, seem that important with that age group, but . . . if they were to pursue it in college, that would be very, very important for them to understand. But at the time these were juniors in high school, that was my call. Maybe I was negligent in that area." Patterson's students would have been better served if they had access to more terms and concepts to use to bolster their capacity for historiographical analysis. Such analysis would also have been made easier had Zinn had footnoted *A People's History* so that students could probe his sources directly. But still, Patterson was swimming against the tide in an era before the Common Core Standards and other mandates designed to promote skills development in the content areas.[34]

Educational research suggests that teachers' content knowledge influences their capacity to support historical thinking among their students.[35] Such research illuminates Patterson's teaching practices and their limitations, including that his pedagogical choices were informed by his own knowledge of history and at times constrained by his lack of familiarity with the historical context of Zinn's work. While Patterson conveyed to his students that Zinn was an unorthodox historian, he was unable to communicate to them that Zinn was part of a new social history revolution of the 1960s, with its stress on history from the bottom up, and the New Left's critique of American imperialism. Consequently, Patterson's students were not sufficiently encouraged to do what historian E. H. Carr suggested was essential to any deliberate study of history. "Study the historian before you begin to study the facts. . . . By and large, the historian will get the kind of facts he [or she] wants."[36]

Patterson understood that there were distrusting critics who assumed teachers assigned Zinn to indoctrinate their students. He thought that such critics both in the 1980s and more recently, as with Governor Daniels in Indiana, were ignorant of how and why teachers used Zinn's book in their history classes. Patterson recognized that the most vehement critics of *A People's History*, whether adults or his own students, were influenced by a sense of nationalism they held and felt Zinn lacked. "And it goes back to patriotism. . . . Pride in my opinion just gets in the way on a personal level or a national level, just gets in the way all the time. . . . The idea of patriotism undercuts critical thought." Patterson found it "shocking" that Daniels would call for banning Zinn from the classroom, seeing it as "a reflection of his ultra-patriotism, bizarre, absolutely bizarre," and calling to mind, as Patterson put it, "that old Samuel Johnson phrase, 'patriotism in the last refuge of a scoundrel.'" Patterson believed that if one did not agree with a work of history, one should discuss and debate it. Having seen the peda-gogical and historical value of such discussion and debate in his own classroom, for Patterson the idea of banning *A People's History* seemed absurd.

Consistent with his pedagogy, Patterson did not find it unreasonable for Daniels, or anyone, to question why he and others used *A People's History* in their history classes. So, when asked how he might respond to the charge that whoever is teaching Zinn is trying to indoctrinate students, Patterson replied that such criticisms merited evidence-based dialogue, not defensiveness: "Ac-tually I would love to have a one-on-one conversation with someone like him [Mitch Daniels]. . . . And I would ask him why do you think I included Howard Zinn in my curriculum? . . . Why do you think I brought Zinn in to complement the textbook version of history? . . . To give him a chance to respond." Since Zinn had worked so well as a part of his history teaching, Patterson was con-fident that he could demonstrate to anyone (as he did to that initially skeptical parent who came to observe) that in his classroom *A People's History* served to deepen student interest and knowledge of history.

Patterson was nonetheless serious about ensuring that Zinn would be the ob-ject of critical inquiry, not veneration, in his classroom. He was aware that some admiring students saw Zinn's narrative as reflecting THE TRUTH in history. He was as concerned about students taking this uncritical view as he was about ad hominem attacks bred by nationalism. Patterson, speaking of Zinn and how he approached teaching Zinn's work, imparted the view that, "OK, this guy's new. He's bringing in new ideas [that are] against the textbook, but don't necessarily believe it's the gospels. I really wanted to get that across too."

Because the student letters reflect a range of views across the political spec-trum, it is evident that Patterson's students felt free to debate, to disagree with Zinn, and to consider multiple perspectives on events and narratives. Patterson was impressed that many of his students were open to learning alternative views on history, even though they had been raised in communities that were largely conservative. Actually, in some cases this conservative backdrop rendered po-litical and historical dissent and debate all the more stimulating since Zinn, as the first leftist historian they had ever read, seemed so novel and fun to discuss.

It was, in Patterson's view "a real credit to the kids that despite the overall demographic of both of the towns [where Patterson taught], these kids, they were up for it. They came, all of them from pretty good families. Yes, maybe [at home] they were indoctrinated in a way, [but] at the same time they were up for a new thought. They were receptive. I did have good kids."

Patterson was aware during the 1980s and 1990s that trends and policies in education, including an increase in state testing, did not necessarily lead to improvements in teaching and learning. When asked if he saw himself as a "bottom-up educational reformer," Patterson replied that he was sympathetic but not a leader in reform efforts: "In my thirty years [as a teacher], as time went on I don't think I saw myself as a reformer but as someone who played around the system. I was all for reforming the system but I wasn't a major player in it. . . . You know, Bill Bigelow [of *Rethinking Schools*] was incredibly involved in reforming the system, and I was part of that underground movement, I went to meetings and things like that. But I don't know if I had what he had."

Though he viewed standardized testing as detrimental to history education, during his years in the classroom Patterson did not actively fight against testing. "I figured . . . I could get away with what I was doing and then they will still take these tests—and I didn't regard them as too important. 'OK, they can take the test.' But then I can do what I really wanted to do. It didn't really have to do with being successful in tests." He was aware, though, that there were teachers and activists around him who were directly involved in education reform. "There were some really, really very bright, progressive [ones]. Nowadays they would be considered radical. They were great, incredible teachers that were doing [exciting] things in the classroom. In terms of assessment, way beyond what I did or what I could do, what I really wanted to do. I really give them a lot of credit. What I did is stuff I was pleased with. I gave traditional tests, but I didn't really care too much about them. But some of these guys, Bigelow and the others, they were real pioneers, gutsy people who did really good work . . . Better work than what I did."

While Patterson did not view himself as an activist or a radical teacher, he was shaped by the events of his lifetime, including the fight for African American civil rights and other social justice movements, and these resonated with him. As discussed in chapter 1, Zinn's editor at Harper and Row thought one reason *A People's History* became a best seller was that it resonated with teachers who had lived through the 1960s civil rights and antiwar movements. These teachers, he suggested, had finally found with Zinn a history of the United States that reflected their own values and experiences. Patterson responded to this idea, that his decision to use Zinn in the classroom reflected a generational experience on his part:

I was a kid in the fifties, . . . grew up in a pretty conservative environment as far as my dad was concerned. . . . I was born in Southern California, [then] lived [at ages] six to twelve in Oregon, then in Hawaii from thirteen to eighteen. But my brother and I became of the same ilk, totally opposed to what my dad was all about. . . . Yeah, it might have been a generational thing. But I think it was much more than that. My brother and I . . . there are some real similarities in the way we think. . . . We can appreciate complexity and have a real resistance towards absolutisms. And it's not in a real militaristic way. . . . This gut feeling that what you see is not necessarily what is. You know that line, "There's something happening here, but you don't know what it is."[37] It resonates with my brother and [me] in the way we look at and do things. I think this rolled right into when I was teaching and looking at this stuff and going "hmm," and then Howard [Zinn] comes along, and "Oh, my god, this is cool," and everything unfolded.

Patterson saw his pedagogical stance in the classroom as guided primarily by his inclination toward robust argument, not by a political stance he may have held.

I don't regard myself as some radical or anything like that. I . . . have always appreciated argument and discussion. And I don't think [that] many people have this skill of discussing and getting down to the roots of issues. And so that's what I've always been interested in. Just the spirited discussion, and not taking it personally. . . . To organize your thoughts the best that you can. And Howard Zinn came along, and he . . . was a tool. I do have to admit that much of what he had to say, coming from that underdog point of view or not the victor's point of view was appealing, . . . but he was a tool more than anything else, and that's all that I'm interested in, have been interested in. I don't like "left," "right," "liberal"—those terms are too abstract for me.

Patterson also appreciated Zinn's candor, the way he was up front about his biases in A People's History, which made the book useful in awakening students to the idea that historians' writing is influenced by their point of view. Patterson thought it good teaching, not revolutionary politics, to use Zinn's book. But Patterson's appreciation for inquiry-based learning, his interest in exposing students to thought-provoking interpretations that they'd never encountered before, certainly set him apart from most of his colleagues. And as the letters show,

Patterson's students were intrigued by his stance in the classroom, with some trying to pinpoint his political orientation.

How students responded to Zinn's biases and his radical version of American history was up to them. All Patterson asked was that they ground their analysis in a careful comparative reading of Zinn and the textbook and argue on a substantive historical basis. Many of Patterson's students who wrote to Zinn were able to do that. Their letters reveal how they viewed Zinn's interpretation of American history, how they saw their textbook's version of that history, and what it was like for high school juniors to encounter historiographical debate for the first time.

There is something profound and intimate about the letters written by these young people, in the way they illuminate the process of historical teaching and learning.[38] These letters were an organic part of actual classroom activity, written voluntarily. They offer us the unmediated words and thoughts of high school learners. As researchers, we would have preferred to view every letter that Patterson's students sent to Zinn, instead of just the 121 letters that we found (there is no way to know why more of the letters did not get saved and archived). But if this archival collection—like most—is imperfect and incomplete as a record of how Patterson used Zinn in his classroom, it is nonetheless a far better paper trail than exists on most teaching strategies employed by an individual teacher in a public high school. Despite their limitations, the letters, together with our interviews with Patterson, offer illuminating evidence about the impact that exposure to contrasting narratives and interpretations can have on student engagement and learning in high school history classrooms.

The letters attest that Patterson's students understood that Zinn was not being held up as the final arbiter of history, rather that select chapters from *A People's History* had been assigned "for the purpose of comparison to the textbook and for debate."[39] In fact, Zinn exposed students right away, in the first chapter of *A People's History*, to the idea that history involved sorting out conflicting interpretations and to the notion that a historian's view of the past was often influenced by one's ideology, political assumptions, and those that prevailed in the time in which the historian was writing. He illustrated this, as we have seen, by criticizing Samuel Eliot Morison's biography of Christopher Columbus, which valorized Columbus as a courageous explorer while slighting the significance of his brutal mistreatment of the Indigenous people in the Caribbean. Zinn pointed out that history had most often been written from the victors' point of view, as with Morison on Columbus, but that he in *A People's History* would look at history from the other side. In one of the most well-known passages from his book, cited earlier, Zinn explained his radical break with standard textbooks. His phrasing was so explicit that students with little or no historiographical background could recognize that his was a different approach to American history than any they had experienced: "I prefer to tell the story of the discovery of America from the viewpoint of the Arawaks, of the Constitution from the standpoint of the slaves, of Andrew Jackson as seen by the Cherokees . . . of the rise of industrialism as seen by the young women in the Lowell textile mills, of the Spanish-American War as seen by the Cubans. . . . And so on, to the limited extent that any one person, however he or she strains, can 'see' history from the standpoint of others."[40]

For virtually all of the hundreds of high school students who wrote to Zinn, including Patterson's, this approach to U.S. history represented a dramatic break with the version of history they had received in their classes and textbooks since grade school. Seeing how different Zinn's history was from their textbooks led them—haltingly, at first, and in diverse ways and with varied levels of sophistication—to begin thinking about historical methodology and to question the relationship between evidence, bias, and historical conclusions. For most, this was the first time they understood that historical truth was contested, historical narratives selectively constructed, and history a critical discipline.

⸎

In his history classes, Patterson paired Zinn's A People's History of the United States with a conventional textbook in order to contrast historical narratives.[41] Assessing the learning outcomes of this approach to history teaching raises two important questions: 1) How does assigning contrasting texts in the same course impact students' capacity to develop the skills necessary for historical thinking? 2) How does exposure to an introductory work, with a critical and revisionist interpretation, impact students' ability to develop skills that support historical thinking? To answer these questions, we probe students' historical understanding as expressed in their letters. To preserve the privacy of these students, we do not mention their last names, the dates of their letters, or, when quoting, the name of the school in which they were enrolled.

The letters were written by high school students who were, to use education scholar Bruce VanSledright's term, "intelligent novices."[42] Together they illuminate the process by which Patterson's students learned history in the context of their prior knowledge and beliefs, their perspectives on government and society as they were shaped by race, class, gender, religion, and political orientation, and their reading chapters from A People's History alongside a standard textbook.[43] The letters provide evidence of ways that contrasting texts engage students in developing historical thinking as they bring to light explorations of historical relativism and objectivity (skills required for critical analysis in history) and draw on their prior historical assumptions, reading, and lessons. They also illuminate the learning that may result when a historian serves as both intellectual and political provocateur, as well as offering a window through which to observe challenges inherent in the process of young people learning history.

The voices in the letters range from confident to hesitant, and student reactions range from unsympathetic and intensely critical to appreciative and laudatory. Some students express personal epiphanies, while others express concern about Zinn's revisionist historical narrative. Regardless, the letters together show how Patterson's students had come to better understand the interpretive and contested nature of history, how their interest and engagement in history had been sparked, and why history now mattered to them.

Patterson was, as we have seen, confident that giving students multiple perspectives on people and events would provide a starting point for critical thinking about history. And the student letters attest that he was correct on this. For Patterson's students it was intellectually stimulating, even thrilling, to become aware that history involved critical thinking and debate about conflicting interpretations. One student, who told Zinn that she found his writings "very educational," added, "Until I read one of your writings I never even stopped to think about the fact that our History books were only giving us one viewpoint on all the issues. I didn't realize that there were so many controversial happenings to be written about."

Requiring that they read conflicting accounts of historical events and actors was initially disorienting to some of Patterson's students. This plus Patterson's debate-oriented approach to teaching history was so novel to students that it took some time to become accustomed to it. Many students expressed that in history classes prior to Patterson's they had not been taught that historical interpretations could be criticized. They were ignorant of the existence of debate among historians and had believed historical understanding consisted of memorizing facts.[44] The thought process they often went through as they first encountered Zinn's accounts of textbook heroes such as Columbus and Andrew Jackson tended to proceed in two stages. First there were varying degrees of cognitive dissonance and reluctance to entertain the possibility that an account contrary to their traditional history textbooks could be valid. This was followed by a stage of inquiry and critical reflection, sometimes combined with criticism of their previous textbooks and teachers.

Reading *A People's History* alongside the textbook led these students to realize how uncritical their prior history classes, teachers, and textbooks had been. This realization yielded dismay at what they began to see as their own limited education. One student had initially been "shocked" by Zinn's revisionist portrait of Columbus because it was at odds with what she had been taught about him. But as she began to consider the evidence presented in *A People's History*, she realized the source of her shock: "I had never heard that part of the story before." This, in turn, led her to realize that the portrayals of Columbus she had previously been given in school had left her "incredibly close-minded, perhaps even brainwashed." Similarly, a boy named Alden found Zinn's portrait of Andrew Jackson at odds with the textbooks and wrote, "The facts you presented make me understand how brainwashing our textbooks can be."

Another boy, Chris, was equally taken aback by Zinn's depiction of the Mexican War as a "war of aggression" involving war crimes by U.S. forces. This view contradicted the textbook's portrayal of U.S. expansionism as benignly spreading "the republican form of government across the continent." Chris wrote to Zinn, "[Your writings] are necessary to balance out the brainwashing effect of the textbook. The text can only include the positive events in history. Your readings give the bare facts. . . . We need people like you to continue to write the truth." A student named Alison wrote that prior to reading Zinn, "[Such narratives] were not available to me in my previous twelve years of schooling. All this time I have been deceived . . . given only favorable information about the [U.S.] government and history." The result was that she had "grown attached to glamorous victories and blinding patriotism." The critical insights offered by Zinn led another student to reflect, "Since the first grade I have been taught to see the clean side of [American] history." Only with Zinn and Patterson's approach had he come to see "the other side of history." One girl characterized her pre-Zinn history education as being "sugar-coated" by unreflective teachers—"since the third grade."

Though a mostly white suburban student body, there were a few students of color in Patterson's classes, and they and others who had personally experienced racism were impressed by how Zinn highlighted racial discrimination and the struggle against it. They expressed concern about the conventional textbooks' lack of emphasis on the subject. For example, a Japanese American student whose parents were interned by the United States during World War II, and so was aware of "how unfair Japanese Americans were treated," praised Zinn as the only historian she had read in school "who tells the side of the minority."

Assigning texts that contradicted each other also engaged students in explorations of relativism versus objectivity, a critical discussion in the field of history. The letters demonstrate that many of Patterson's students were initially confused about how to engage ideas of relativism and historical truth and the knowledge that historical interpretations were subject to criticism. Those who read Zinn and accepted his interpretations were now comfortable relying on Zinn's insights to question the conventional textbook's history. But the process did not end with critiquing the textbook for some of the more sophisticated students. It led them to raise questions about Zinn's historical interpretations too. One girl, after thanking Zinn for enabling her to recognize that the textbook supported an uncritical view of American history, added, "Sometimes I feel your writing is just as bad at omitting all the details as the original textbook." She credited Zinn with modeling independent historical questioning and interpretation, helping her to weigh historical events and interpretations of them "by [her] own standards." And she directed this new critical capacity toward the textbook and Zinn's book alike.

Patterson's more perceptive students began to consider sources and to make determinations about those sources. This process placed them in a position to ponder that they, like professional historians, made determinations informed by personal experience, bias, and perspective, underscoring the contested nature of history, and puncturing notions of a singular historical truth. Patterson described his approach and ultimate goal: "The main point is anything to provoke . . . a little confusion, anything to provoke against the idea of an absolute truth. That was important to me."[45]

Textbooks are designed to be comprehensive, authoritative, and politically moderate so as to be adopted by school boards and state education officials. Zinn, in contrast, opted not to be comprehensive but instead selected events to narrate in order to spotlight particular themes that he found most important—especially imperialism and class, race, and gender inequality. On these topics he offered extensive quotations and stories that engaged readers in the colorful drama of history, as opposed to the decontextualized, dull summaries presented in textbooks.

Zinn's version of U.S. history for most students was new and surprising. Though the students were unlikely to have known this, Zinn was seeking to connect the public with an approach to historical writing that university-based new social history scholars had pioneered in the 1960s. Many admired the way Zinn, as one put it, "always take[s] the side of the underdog." Another compared Zinn's work to the exposés of the Progressive Era, telling him, "I see you as a muckraker." Whether students agreed or disagreed with Zinn's historical narrative, they acknowledged that his book was more accessible and engaging than their textbook. This was true because Zinn chose to infuse his writing with controversy, lesser-known information about U.S. history, history "from the bottom up," and, finally, his own point of view.

Zinn's talent as a writer of popular history contributed to the book's capacity as a powerful tool for inquiry-based instruction, drawing students into *A People's History* (even if they disliked Zinn's politics) and in this way rendering it a sharp contrast to their textbook. For example, one girl who disagreed with Zinn, commented: "For the most part I am offended by how you criticize some of the greatest leaders in history. However, our history books are so boring that it is nice to read something else." One student wrote to Zinn, "The accounts you give are in much more detail and much better interpreted than the regular textbook we are using. Your writing brings us directly to the event just as if we were alive and involved in it." Throughout the letters to Zinn, students commented about the quality of his writing, as they noticed Zinn had done something different and with success.

Many students were provoked by Zinn to discuss the question of his biases. This is not surprising since early in *A People's History* Zinn was explicit about his perspective, politics, and philosophy. His was a dramatic contrast to impersonal multiauthor textbooks that rarely provide interpretive claims.[46] Zinn announced in chapter 1:

> My viewpoint, in telling the history of the United States, is different: that we must not accept the memory of states as our own. . . . The history of any country, presented as the history of a family, conceals fierce conflicts of interest (sometimes exploding, most often repressed) between conquerors and conquered, masters and slaves, capitalists and workers, dominators and dominated in race and sex. And in such a world of conflict, a world of victims and executioners, it is the job of thinking people, as Albert Camus suggested, not to be on the side of the executioners. . . . If history is to be creative, to anticipate a possible future without denying the past, it should, I believe, emphasize new possibilities by disclosing those hidden episodes of the past, when, even if in brief flashes, people showed their ability to resist, to join together, occasionally to win.[47]

Zinn's approach to writing history, then, was radically different, in form as well as content, from the textbook because he included a "meta-discourse" in his writing and so exposed readers to his "ideas, beliefs, hesitations and judgments."[48] For nearly all of the students who wrote to Zinn, this approach was entirely novel in a history text. Some students' reaction to Zinn was rooted in the degree to which they were willing to accept his meta-discourse as a valid approach to writing history.

Some of Patterson's students were upset with Zinn for what they deemed his overly critical tone. One, who credited Zinn with helping him to see American history in a new light, nonetheless asked Zinn why he chose to "always write . . . every bad thing that America did," saying that it "would be nice to hear the brighter side of things that America did in history." "You seem to have a very negative, one-sided outlook on our country," complained another, even though she said she found much of Zinn's history illuminating. "Have you ever written something positive about the United States?" she asked. Her rebuke reflected her developing skill in thinking critically about historical interpretations. But Zinn in *A People's History* coupled his often scathing portrayals of the political and economic elite with positive depictions of protest movements and organizers who championed peace, minority rights, and the interests of workers. This student was so offended by Zinn's criticism of the U.S. government that she overlooked that a key theme of *A People's History* was that democratic idealism and virtue rested with ordinary people.

Regardless of whether a student seemed inclined in favor of Zinn or against him, the letters show that Zinn's text provoked them to engage with his historical evidence and conclusions. Even among the students who found fault with Zinn's tone, there was a willingness to share with him disagreements and questions regarding specific historical arguments. For example, some students wrote Zinn that they were impressed by his treatment of Columbus or Andrew Jackson but then would take issue with his discussion of other topics—especially those linked to their sense of patriotism—such as wars involving the U.S. armed forces. One typical in this regard praised Zinn for his vivid account of the brutality of Indian removal but then objected to his discussion of the desertions and war crimes by U.S. troops in the Mexican War. She rebuked Zinn for "[making] it sound as if we were (the army) gross, dirty cowards!!! In any war there are rapes, and soldiers that break and run away. That is part of . . . war. In any country this would have happened." These responses revealed students struggling with Zinn's critical narrative as it challenged their understanding of patriotism. This student personalized Zinn's criticism of U.S. troops, referring to soldiers as "we" even though they died more than a century before she was born. She demonstrated a similar identification with the Jacksonian generation of American soldiers who had driven Indians from their lands. However, she found Zinn's description of the mistreatment of the Native Americans so "disgusting" that she wrote, "[I am] very embarrassed to admit that America could do that!"

Some of the most perceptive criticisms of Zinn came in response to his indictments of big business leaders and capitalism. One objected to Zinn's characterization of Gilded Age industrialists as greedy robber barons, responding that such business leaders as Carnegie had a strong work ethic. "[They] started with little and worked their way up to become very wealthy men. They provided jobs for many and encouraged others to improve themselves . . . [and so] were good role models for others." Such students saw that Zinn's socialist inclinations kept him from portraying a positive side of big business, corporate titans and the profit motive they embodied that fueled American economic growth. These high school juniors proved both willing and able to counter Zinn's socialist assumptions with their own arguments, demonstrating that adult critics of *A People's History* who assume that youth would be manipulated by Zinn's radicalism were mistaken.

A review of the student letters to Zinn affirms that in *A People's History* Zinn was a provocateur able to stimulate intense interest and debate, which is why Patterson noted that his students—whether they "loved" or "hated" Zinn—were engaged in his classroom. Because Zinn provoked readers, the letters are filled with questions and criticisms. Some students took him to task for using the term "genocide" to characterize Columbus's impact on the Arawaks, for drawing an analogy between the U.S. internment of the Japanese Americans in World War II and the Nazi concentration camps, for casting doubts on the democratic character of the victorious Allies in that war, for claiming that the atomic bombings of Hiroshima and Nagasaki were unnecessary, and for portraying the Vietnam War as driven by U.S. imperialism.

Among Patterson's students, those most vehement in their criticisms of Zinn were a small number who tended to ground their views of historical events in conservative ideology. They saw patriotism as synonymous with loyalty to U.S. policy and thought of history as a school subject that should reinforce pride in their country's political and economic systems, leaders, wars, military, and foreign policy. Strong criticism of the United States was for most of this group unacceptable, and so they tended to dismiss Zinn as unpatriotic or communist. One, who signed his letter, "Young Patriot and Lover of the United States of America," wrote that he was "angered" and "disgusted" by Zinn's argument that the atomic bombing of Hiroshima and Nagasaki was not necessary to end World War II and by his critique of the Spanish American and Vietnam Wars as imperialistic. Matt called Zinn's "opinions" "an insult to this great country of ours" and added, "The United States . . . is the finest country to ever exist and you should be thanking God that you live here. Remember, thousands of men died so you would be able to express your opinion. It is sad that you don't seem proud of it. . . . This is America. LOVE IT OR LEAVE IT!"[49]

The anger evident in this letter (and others like it) was a sign that no matter how much students disliked Zinn's view of history, they found it engaging and provocative. Indeed, Patterson told us that he vividly remembered the author of the angry letter to Zinn quoted above and recalled that though this student was hostile to Zinn's views, he enjoyed and looked forward to debating Zinn. Patterson remembered, "[He] was an interesting guy, very bright guy. Really had some problems with Howard Zinn. And he was very up on the terminology, 'left' and 'right,' 'liberal' and 'conservative.' . . . Really gung ho, he was always chomping at the bit: 'OK, when are we going to read Zinn's account on that?' Whatever unit or chapter we did. He was always ready, always ready for Zinn."

So even some of the most ardent student critics of Zinn were learning from their encounters with his views. Some of them seemed to have worked the hardest to develop their skills so they could debate Zinn effectively. James, who was among the angriest of Zinn's critics in Patterson's classes, wrote an extensive and probing critique of Zinn. James wrote Zinn, "[I find your] assaults on [Andrew] Jackson's character insulting." He accused Zinn of being anachronistic in judging Jackson by the standards of the late twentieth century rather than those of Jackson's time. James questioned Zinn's use of evidence and even analyzed Zinn's biography in an attempt to locate the source of his hostility to the U.S. government and military, speculating that Zinn, as a disillusioned World War II veteran, used history to lash out "against the same government that made you experience the horrible things that you did while in the Eighth Air Force bombing that German encampment and the French village with napalm." James's letter reflected clever argumentation grounded in his reading beyond what had been assigned. Most impressively, James enlisted Zinn's own words from the introduction to another of his books, *Postwar America, 1945– 1971*.[50] "I could not," James wrote, "have said it better [than you have] in the first sentence of that introduction, 'Any book of history is, consciously or not, an interpretation in which selected data from the past is tossed into the present according to the interest of the historian.' Mr. Zinn, I ask you sincerely, what is your interest?"

Patterson's students usually managed to express their anger toward Zinn's history in ways that were substantive, serious, and not merely denunciatory. Amanda, whose letter will be included in the next chapter and who had been infuriated by Zinn's criticism of Columbus, engaged his arguments on Vietnam and U.S. internment of Japanese Americans, conceding that internment was "inexcusable" and that Zinn was convincing in arguing against U.S. involvement in Vietnam, though she did take issue with other aspects of Zinn's interpretation of both these events. Here we can observe her grappling with the idea of multiple perspectives on historical events, something Patterson fostered in class. He also encouraged students to be open to dissent, to the point where Amanda wrote Zinn, "Even though I may have many questions and we may disagree. . . . You aren't a 'sheep' (as Mr. Patterson would say) that follows the average crowd, and I admire you for that. I appreciate the fact that your writings challenge our normal [beliefs]." Patterson, as evidenced in the student responses, was successful at supporting some students to go beyond an emotional response to Zinn, and in the process many were able to transcend biases that had previously limited their capacity to be open to dissenting perspectives.[51]

The student letters to Zinn illuminate how complicated it can be to teach students new to historiographical debate how to develop an analytical framework for assessing such debates. With students ignorant of historiography and the contested nature of history, one of their tendencies in their letters was for those who admired Zinn's critical take on American history to view him as a heroic "lone ranger" who single-handedly changed, even revolutionized, our understanding of America's past. Since Zinn was the first revisionist historian whose work they had read, it was not surprising that students viewed *A People's History* this way. "Our country as well as all countries need someone like you to speak from the victim's point of view," wrote one student to Zinn, and many other letters to Zinn made it sound as if Zinn had invented revisionist, radical history. The problem with this is that Zinn had not. Nor was Zinn alone in raising concerns about triumphalist textbook history. It is evident in the students' letters that they did not comprehend Zinn's place in the larger historiographical context.

It would have been a challenge, because of time limitations and complexity, for anyone teaching a U.S. history course for high school juniors to have covered the historiographical revolution of the 1960s. Nevertheless, it is important to understand that Zinn was part of a generation of historians conditioned by their own experiences (with Vietnam, the civil rights movement, and other protest movements, for example). This contextualizes Zinn's work and renders it more amenable to analysis than it would be if seen as the writing of a heroic individual struggling to reveal the "truth" in history. Such a critical frame would have been useful to ensure that students' admiration for Zinn's effectiveness in refuting textbook depictions not lead to idolization. The way some of Zinn's student admirers enthused about him suggests the need for a teaching strategy that includes critical analysis of Zinn's (and others') revisionist work.[52]

Patterson's students' letters can best be understood by placing them in four analytical categories indicated in the chart below. These reflect the letters' varied tone and content, ranging from ones praising Zinn's writings to those who criticized them most vehemently, even questioning Zinn's motives. What is striking about the letters is the degree to which they show that the vast majority of students took seriously the endeavor of writing them. In their letters, students made arguments for or against interpretations offered in Zinn or their textbook (or both). As indicated by the list below, students were almost evenly divided between those who accepted Zinn's view of history and those who questioned his conclusions. This bespeaks a healthy intellectual dynamic in which both the textbook and Zinn's anti-textbook were being critically interrogated.

1. Enthusiastic supporters: students who   59
    embraced Zinn's view of American history

2. Supporters with concerns: students who approved   22
    of Zinn's critical take on the American past yet
    had reservations about some of his conclusions

3. Moderate critics: students who, though they valued   13
    having the opportunity to read Zinn's book since it stood
    in such stark contrast to their conventional U.S. history
    textbook, expressed concerns about Zinn's tone,
    motivations, and many of his conclusions

4. Severe critics and skeptics: students who were sharply   26
    critical or strongly doubtful of Zinn's entire historical
    narrative, many of whom saw his work as offensively
    unpatriotic and questioned his motives

Different as the pro- and anti-Zinn responses may seem, and however divergent they may have been politically, many of the best pro and con letters shared a concern with evidence and an ability to use evidence to test the conclusions historians drew. Zinn's student critics used evidence from their textbook and other sources to question Zinn's conclusions, while Zinn's admirers employed evidence from *A People's History* to challenge their textbook's historical conclusions. Some students questioned both Zinn and the textbook. This was quite an achievement, when one considers that these students were juniors in high school.

One can see their youth and inexperience as writers in the spelling and grammatical errors in their letters to Zinn. Yet shining through amid these imperfections is the development of genuine critical thinking, interrogation of texts, and an attempt to glean historical truth out of competing interpretations. How well Patterson as a teacher and Zinn as a historian succeeded in provoking such engagement is evident. "[As I] read these articles," one wrote, referring to photocopies of Zinn chapters on Columbus and on Andrew Jackson and Indian removal,

> these became more than just a supplement to my textbook. They gave me the ability to weight certain aspects of historical events to my own standards. Which is more important; Columbus' discovery of America, or the extinction of a race of people? As a student I appreciate the opportunity to see more than

just the narrow textbook view of history. Textbooks seem a very dispassionate source of information, yet you have written that many historians have colored history with their own ideology. My question to you is, are you not also subject to . . . tainted ideology? Is your own view any less narrow than those you criticize? Perhaps it is my role as a student to extract the pieces of information from each extreme to create an objective vs. subjective view of history. Without benefit of your information this would most certainly not be possible.

Zinn's student critics sometimes displayed modes of expression that reflected their youth and immaturity. Some asked whether Zinn was making up his facts. Others went in for ad hominem attacks, asking Zinn whether he was a communist or an atheist or why he hated America. But the best of these critical students took their anger at Zinn and channeled it into pointed and meaningful questions. Zinn would later recall the tone of those unhappy that he had cast the U.S. government and its war-making in so negative a light: "[They asked] how I got such information, and how I arrived at such outrageous conclusions."[53] Some tried to use their letters to Zinn to rebut what they had read in *A People's History*. A number of them, for example, raised on stories of American heroism in World War II, insisted that the United States dropped the atomic bombs on Hiroshima and Nagasaki not to impress the Soviets as the first act of the Cold War (as Zinn suggested) but to force the Japanese to surrender and end World War II.

The vast majority of Patterson's students included comments in their letters indicating that they understood that secondary sources are constructed by authors for particular purposes. Thus, the students who accused Zinn of having an "agenda" were actively involved in source attribution as they accused Zinn.[54] Conversely, many students realized that their conventional textbook also was written for a particular purpose, as when some students wrote that they believed their textbooks attempted to inculcate unthinking patriotism and even to "brainwash" them. These students showed evidence of critical thinking while they assessed the perspective of textbook authors, deliberately evaluating their social and political position when writing history.

In Zinn's book there are two key historical themes: oppression by the powerful and resistance by the oppressed. The oppression theme is certainly negative and iconoclastic toward traditional American political heroes and leaders. Zinn is extremely critical regarding oppression initiated by the government, the rich, and the military. The resistance theme, on the other hand, is positive, even hopeful, and people whose movements to challenge oppression and champion equality are the heroes of *A People's History*. Zinn accentuates their heroism through his literary flare and extensive quotations from an array of eloquent and powerful speeches and writing by American dissenters. As with most read-ers of *A People's History*, both themes registered with Patterson's students. Some students would note with pleasure and agreement Zinn's championing of "the underdog." So, for them, the positive theme resonated. But by far the biggest waves generated among students by Zinn came from his criticism of American militarism and capitalism and the way he foregrounded racism and imperial-ism, which represented a dramatic departure from their prior historical edu-cation, a challenge to their sense of patriotism and to values promoted in their communities.

Sadly, too many high school students today do not appreciate or enjoy learn-ing history in school.[55] When asked, students describe their history education as learning names and dates, taking multiple-choice tests, and often receiving from teachers one-dimensional explanations.[56] Therefore, it is not surprising that on the National Assessment of Educational Progress (NAEP) results released in 2014, the most recent available data prior to publication of this book, students performed more poorly in U.S. history than in any other subject. Nationwide, only 12 percent of high school students were "proficient" in U.S. history.[57] It is reasonable to conclude that students are not effectively learning the subject and most likely are alienated by how it is taught.

Supporting secondary students in developing skills required for critical anal-ysis of texts and society, through rigorous and meaningful study of the past, can result in their engagement in the discipline, help them get ready for college, and prepare them for democratic citizenship.[58] It is also worth noting that critical analysis aligns with goals of the highly promoted Common Core learning stan-dards. The Patterson case study presented in this chapter suggests that assigning a revisionist social history text such as Zinn's *People's History* alongside a stan-dard textbook in a high school history course can accomplish at least some of these goals.

Whether by using Zinn's or another alternative text, the teacher who ex-poses students to multiple interpretations of the American past encourages students to interpret history themselves. This is why Patterson, a talented, debate-loving history teacher, made Zinn's *People's History* a part of his cur-riculum for nearly two decades. And it is a key reason why to this day Zinn remains popular with high school history teachers—with more than 100,000 educators signed up with the Zinn Education Project website and over 280,000 following the Zinn Education Project Facebook page and receiving its regular feeds.[59] Without meaning to do so, Patterson, by having his students write to Zinn, seeded the creation of an archival collection on his classroom teaching that documents the power of historical debate to enhance student learning in social studies classes.

Whatever its flaws and limitations, *A People's History of the United States* has been a uniquely valuable book for getting students to move past the widely accepted assumption promoted at least implicitly by many high school textbooks that there is one uncontested view of American history. As the student letters to Zinn demonstrate, *A People's History* engages students, angers and inspires them, and prods them to think critically about how historical evidence is used and conclusions reached. Moreover, *A People's History* encourages students to question assumptions about American virtue. It requires them to confront the arguments of a historian who sees the United States as a society that, from its founding, has been torn by class divisions, racial unrest, and gender inequities, and marred by imperialism and war. Judging by the online comments of teachers accessing materials from the Zinn Education Project (with twenty-five thousand teachers registered), *A People's History* retains its appeal for many teachers and their students. Indeed, in the present, when high school history teachers are put under great pressure to promote critical literacy skills through the reading of divergent sources and viewpoints, Zinn and the debates he promotes seem more timely than ever.

The success of *A People's History* in engaging Patterson's students was a collaborative outcome: inventive, debate-oriented pedagogy on Patterson's part combined with Zinn's thought-provoking writings, which brought history to life in the classroom. Patterson's teaching was, as we have seen, not flawless, but his basic approach was effective in getting the most out of his students, their textbook, and *A People's History*. Zinn without Patterson would not have made for such a powerful classroom experience. Nor would Patterson have been able to achieve the same without Zinn.

Overall, historians and textbook authors have shown little interest in understanding why *A People's History* became a best seller and so popular with teachers and students. Patterson's students' letters to Zinn make it clear that they were stimulated by his candor about his political bias and his philosophy of history. They appreciated his relating the present to the past, his selective (rather than exhaustive) coverage of topics, his challenging of conventional thought (calling out historians whose work he deemed problematic, like historian Samuel Eliot Morison), his criticizing of traditional heroes, and his shifting the spotlight from government to dissidents and the common people.

As this chapter and the next one demonstrate, if we respect students by assigning them historical writings that engage and challenge them, prioritizing critical thought over encyclopedic coverage, they will respond with interest and insight. If we respect students, we will encourage them to think critically about a range of historical sources and interpretations. History classrooms should be as enlivened by controversy as history itself has been.

CHAPTER 4

"Dear Mr. Zinn"

Student Voices

When we first encountered in the Zinn papers the letters Bill Patterson's students wrote to Howard Zinn about their reactions to *A People's History*, we were startled and gratified. Usually education researchers have to work long and hard to probe the classroom teaching and learning process, designing research instruments and seeking ways to observe that process without their presence as observers altering it. And such in-class research is confined to the present since a researcher or research team has to be there to document it. These student letters to Zinn, however, enabled us to examine one teacher's history teaching methods and assess the impact on history learning over the course of a decade and a half. The sources are the learners themselves via the letters in which they reflect on their teacher and their readings, often comparing these with their prior experiences in history classes.

These letters are valuable because they take us inside the classrooms where Zinn's introduction to American history had been used for years. In the decades of debates by historians, politicians, and pundits about Zinn's *People's History* and its impact on education, no one had considered evidence documenting that impact from the perspective of students who had read and discussed Zinn's book in their history classes.

In chapter 3 we used these student letters, Patterson's own correspondence with Zinn, and our interviews with Patterson to analyze the way history teaching and learning worked in this teacher's classrooms. Our goal in this chapter is to bring readers even closer to the experience students had with Zinn's book by spotlighting their own writings about that experience. In chapter 3 we quoted about twenty of Patterson's student letters to Zinn to illustrate reactions to Zinn's book and Patterson's use of it in his debate-oriented pedagogy. We offer in this chapter a sampling of complete letters to Zinn by Patterson's students so readers can have a fuller encounter with these narratives and form their own judgments about the strengths and limitations of their educational experience.[1] This means

turning to documentary history, drawing from the Zinn archive as large a selection of these letters as we have room for—it would require an entire book to
include all 121 student letters from this collection. Our choice of letters for this
chapter was determined by their clarity in expressing student views on Zinn's
book and their detailing of what transpired in the class discussions and debates. We wanted to illuminate both teaching methods and learning outcomes
that made *A People's History* a significant part of the history courses taught by
Patterson.

A key advantage of complete letters is that they enable us to witness intellectual strengths and weaknesses that excerpts cannot convey so effectively. Regarding strengths, one can observe in these letters students enacting genuine
critical thought, using Zinn to question and pose alternatives to the textbook,
and using the textbook or outside sources to offer alterative interpretations to
Zinn's—or doing both.

As you examine these student letters there are a number of contextual matters to consider. It makes sense to keep in mind how new these high school
juniors were to serious historical study. Unaccustomed to new and critical interpretations of the American past that contradicted prior learning and old assumptions, some students responded emotionally in their letters, whether eu-
phorically or angrily, as they grappled with the cognitive dissonance. They were
in the early stages of sorting out the connections between arguments, evidence,
and conclusions, so some would refer to Zinn's historical arguments as "opinions" rather than as interpretations of the past that were grounded in historical
evidence. Engaged as they were with history, they were nonetheless novices in
assessing historiographical disputes and exploring what it meant to view history
as a scholarly discipline and a way of thinking critically about the American
past. So as you read the letters you can consider how to measure the depth and
limits of the students' learning.

One might judge among such limitations a moralistic element that some of
the pro-Zinn letters exhibit, asking whether it enhances or impedes historical
understanding. Such moralism might give pause to professional historians, as
when, for example, students, after reading Zinn, went from revering Andrew
Jackson as a democratic hero to denouncing him as a racist Indian killer and
slave owner. This too is connected to the students' inexperience in dealing with
historical complexity, their lack of awareness that historical figures can be contradictory, exhibiting both admirable and offensive qualities, and that historians
generally aim to understand and contextualize rather than celebrate or condemn their subjects.

But this problem is also connected to the fact that conventional textbook his-

tory at the high school level often imparted a simplistic triumphalism via laudatory images of America and its traditional heroes, a kind of textbook moralism.
So it was both natural and logical for students exposed to Zinn to refute that
textbook view in moral terms. And it is true that moral judgments do affect the
interpretations that historians offer. For example, ever since 1975 when Michael
Rogin made Indian-killing central to his classic work on Andrew Jackson, Old
Hickory's racist violence has overshadowed and badly damaged his reputation
among many historians as the embodiment of frontier egalitarianism.[2] So it may
not be so much the students' moralism as their youthful lack of subtlety in expressing it that makes some of their conclusions seem overly emotional. Nonetheless, for novices, such emotion, whatever its effect on historical judgment,
can be read as a sign of engagement with history, a central mission of introductory history classes. On the other hand, some readers may see in this tendency
confirmation of the charge made by Zinn's critics that in reversing the roles of
"good guys" and "bad guys" he trades in the same kind of simplistic history that
he aims to refute in traditional textbooks.

If Zinn's admirers among these student letter writers tended to be moralistic, their conservative counterparts expressing anger tended in their critical
letters to have been experiencing a kind of tug-of-war between their nationalist
assumptions and historical curiosity. On the one hand, Zinn's critical history
offended their sense of patriotism (for some, superpatriotism), their pride in
America, and tempted them to dismiss Zinn. But on the other hand, his interpretations in A People's History were so provocative that most could not resist
engaging with Zinn and attempting to refute his arguments. These contrary im-
pulses are reflected in the tone and content of the letters to Zinn by the angriest
of his young critics, who would combine ad hominem insults and intolerant
statements—charging Zinn with being a communist or urging him to "move to
Russia"—with earnest and sometimes effective attempts to rebut his critiques of
American leaders, institutions, and wars. So the reader is placed in the position
of judging the pedagogical utility and problems with generating emotion—in
this case anger—to motivate historical learning.

Readers might also ponder whether generating some anger was an inevitable
part of discussing a radical historian's view of American history in a conservative community. Zinn was, after all, bringing a critical historical lens to students
for whom this was not merely new but contrary to the civic myths upon which
they had been raised. As historian Renee C. Romano explains,

> All nations have their own civic myths, but these foundational stories have
> been particularly important to the United States, whose diverse population
> includes people from many different ethnic, national, religious, and racial

backgrounds. Traditional American civic myths promote patriotism and conceal the violence of continental and global expansion by portraying the United States as an exceptional nation built on ideals of liberty and equality. They teach that all Americans have equal opportunity for life, liberty, and the pursuit of happiness, and that success depends only on hard work and individual merit. These traditional narratives by necessity downplay elements of American history that do not fit neatly within a story of freedom, liberty, and individual opportunity. They minimize and even ignore the significance of slavery, racial violence, the dispossession of native land, gendered exclusions, and class conflicts in America's past.[3]

And with regard to Zinn, the angriest letters in this chapter attest that, as Romano reminds us, when American history moves "beyond the limited sphere of academia" it becomes "a political minefield whenever representations of the past . . . undermine this celebratory account."[4]

Zinn's nationalistic student critics tended to become the most defensive or irritated with him on questions of foreign policy and war. Most often, this was connected to the patriotic theme of sacrifice Americans made for the nation when they served, risked, or lost their lives in the armed forces. And it was also the function of the sense of national mission that these students had grown up with— a belief that the United States had an exceptional history, beginning with "a heroic conquest of the land and its original inhabitants," in the words of historian Paul Buhle. In this view, "the steady spread of democracy from border to border and sea to sea" inevitably came next. "It culminated in the current nation being uniquely suited by history, perhaps by divine destiny, to make the rules of the planet and carry them out when necessary. Every sacrifice made, by Americans and others, was justified by that end. Even when . . . atomic and finally thermonuclear war threatened to wipe out civilization, the sense of rectitude remained firmly in place."[5]

Although the letters of Zinn's conservative student critics may seem to have little in common with those of their classmates who tended to agree with him, readers might consider at least one similarity. Both sides of the debate about Zinn (and A People's History versus their textbook) displayed concern about fairness. Students who wrote to Zinn complaining about his historical narrative felt that his critical view of the American past was so one-sided that it was unfair. Their classmates who appreciated A People's History, on the other hand, saw their textbook and prior history classes as so uncritical that the historical accounts in them were unfair to Native Americans, Mexicans, workers, and others—so for them it was Zinn who was the agent of fairness.

But Patterson's classroom was clearly intellectually stimulating, and it is evident that Patterson encouraged debate and dialogue. Some of this debate stemmed from students' skeptical view of some or all of Zinn's historical interpretations. One can tell from their letters that student critics of *A People's History* were learning how to air their opposing views without inhibition. The repetition of similar phrases about the one-sidedness of Zinn's book suggests that some student critics were echoing what like-minded classmates had said about *A People's History*. So, while some students might have been be swayed by the arguments of classmates who found *A People's History* convincing, others come away from such discussions with a critical take on Zinn reinforced in class. It is striking that high school juniors not only debated Zinn's historical interpretations with their classmates and teacher but also displayed the self-confidence to challenge and debate Zinn himself, a professional historian.

Sometimes, however, such confidence was misplaced. Conservative student counterarguments to Zinn based on vague, nationalistic assumptions generally fell flat. This was the case, for example, with students who sought to dismiss the problem of war crimes in Vietnam (My Lai) and the Mexican War by asserting that "war is hell," as if every soldier who engaged in combat commits such crimes and as if there were no code of military conduct. Or by arguing that since everyone who served on the front lines of war is a hero, their integrity and motivations must not be questioned—that such questioning is slanderous and unpatriotic. In such moments one sees the pitfalls of the debate format, as these students felt compelled to "win" an argument with Zinn at the expense of historical complexity and accuracy. However, these exchanges do underscore that in letters to Zinn some students were beginning to at least consider the contradictions that exist between blind patriotism and human rights.

The most common complaint about *A People's History* among his student critics was that it was too "negative" about America's history. Readers can judge for themselves whether Zinn's telling of American history was, as these students charged, overly cynical and negative. Or whether these students were too attached to what they had learned prior to reading *A People's History* to be able to consider a different and more critical narrative. Zinn weighed in on this question in an exchange of letters with one of Patterson's students, Amanda, who held fast to the heroic mythology about Columbus and who sought to justify, on national security grounds, Japanese American internment during World War II. In his letter to Amanda, Zinn reviewed Columbus's misdeeds and the injustice of Japanese internment, inviting her to confront the evidence so as to face some unpleasant truths about the American past. Though Zinn responded to numerous other students in Patterson's classes, this is the only such response that has survived in his archive. This correspondence between Amanda and Zinn (see first letter below) reveals the experience of one student for whom thinking crit-ically about American history proved difficult.

Intellectually some of the strongest critical student letters to Zinn focus on particular eras, conflicts, or historical figures and challenge Zinn by offer-ing alternative interpretations that they found more convincing. Although the students rarely cited sources, it is evident that they drew them from various places—their textbooks, communities, families, et cetera. And in a number of cases their counterarguments to Zinn were plausible, as, for example, when they claimed that his interpretation of World War II underestimated the role antifas-cist idealism played in motivating Americans to join that struggle or chided him for not taking seriously enough the oppressiveness of the communist regime the United States battled against in Vietnam.

Just as Zinn's critics sometimes proved adept at constructing historical argu-ments, so did student critics of the textbook. And one should not assume that Patterson's high school juniors were wrong or exaggerating in their unflatter-ing comments about their textbook. The first textbook Patterson assigned them to study and compare with Zinn, *Addison-Wesley United States History*, was skimpy on some key topics and lacked the critical edge that Zinn provided.[6] On Columbus, for example, the textbook offered three pages and only a vague (and unexplained) reference to his "mistreatment of the Indians."[7] Zinn, on the other hand, made Columbus and the fate of the Indigenous people he conquered and enslaved the key focus of an entire chapter, detailed with primary and second-ary source quotations.[8] The contrast was equally striking between Zinn's cov-erage and the textbook's superficial and essentially uncritical treatment of the Mexican War.[9] Zinn's detailed chapter on that war depicted it as a U.S. war of aggression.[10]

Pleased as we are about being able to share these letters, we are aware that they, like all historical sources, must be read critically, and with an understand-ing of the ways in which this correspondence originated.[11] It is possible, for ex-ample, that students may have been inclined to view *A People's History* favorably because their teacher assigned chapters from it, or that students wrote letters to Zinn that expressed more admiration than they really felt. There is also in-equality inherent in the process of a high school student writing to a prominent author of a book they have read in school, in that the author seems a kind of celebrity they might be wary of offending, especially since many of them hoped Zinn would reply to their letters.

Such potential problems with bias are real and ought to be kept in mind as you read the letters. In our view, these issues with potential bias are offset by the way Patterson conducted his class—welcoming, almost insisting on debate, playing devil's advocate, and making it clear to students that their letters should express to Zinn their views, no matter what they were. Again, though no sources are free of bias, we think these letters constitute authentic student expressions of their views of Zinn's *A People's History*, their textbook, and their experience in history classes—a conclusion we welcome you to test.

As noted, these letters to Zinn were written by Patterson's students in the two suburban Oregon high schools where he taught. To preserve the privacy of the writers, we have deleted the names of their schools from the letters as well as the students' last names. For the same reason we have deleted the dates of the letters, but all were written in the decade and a half in Patterson's teaching career from 1986 to the early twenty-first century, the period when he assigned Zinn in his history classes.

The letters from Patterson's students reveal a process of historical discovery that was far from flawless and certainly not easy. As the letters document, the process had a major impact on many of students, who learned to see the American past and present critically for the first time and to explore major disagreements about history and politics. In the course of publishing our initial findings concerning this correspondence, we received e-mails from several of Patterson's former students.[12] They viewed him as an inspiring teacher whose class sessions using *A People's History* opened their eyes to new ways of thinking about history and the world. They ranked those sessions with Patterson and Zinn as among their most memorable educational experiences.

Some of Patterson's former students even viewed this experience as life changing. This was the case, for example, with Rebecca Mayer, who had been a student of Patterson's in 2000 and read our article about Patterson's use of Zinn in his classes.[13] Mayer wrote,

> [That class] had a huge impact on my life. . . . I remember feeling a mixture of shock and excitement reading the chapters of A People's History that Mr. Patterson provided. Shock, because it did feel like the previous 12 years of history education were full of lies. Excitement, because as an avid reader, I was thrilled by the idea of new, undiscovered stories. One of the things I've always appreciated about Mr. Zinn's work is that it's not that he was trying to simply disprove previously held ideas about American history, . . . that he was trying to supplement it by giving voice to the voiceless. Yes, you got familiar stories from a different POV [point of view], but there were also stories that were omitted from traditional history texts or, at best, footnotes to the bigger events.
>
> The Sacco-Vanzetti affair was one of these that sticks out in my memory. Not only was the story new to me, but the concept that someone could be

convicted of a crime that they may not have committed. I realize that for an 18-year-old to just be discovering this is naïve, but remember, I grew up in suburban, middle class . . . Oregon. I was shielded from these concepts for a long time, especially by parents that believed that honesty and hard work were the number one measure of a person's worth. They judged the world in a black and white manner, and the logic worked for my young mind. I was a good kid who followed the rules and rarely questioned authority, because in my experience, authority had been trustworthy. The Sacco-Vanzetti affair was especially important to me, because I remember at the time, I was never able to decide in my head if they were truly guilty of murder or if they were framed. This grayness really irritated me . . . for a long time. It didn't work with my black and white logic. And over time, I was able to expand my reasoning to accept several conflicting ideas and let them battle out in my mind. The greatest change happened when I was able to accept that there was not always a clear winner in the battle for truth. That each idea might hold a kernel of the truth and that it's important to keep searching for different points of view.

Traditional history education in public schools doesn't allow for discussion and student opinion. It was very much a teach-to-the-test style. Because of Mr. Patterson, I chose to major in history in college . . . , and I was surprised even then that we were expected to express our interpretations of the material. Apart from my class with Mr. Patterson, my education . . . had not prepared me for this. We have young students memorize facts but don't dive in as to why those facts are worth knowing.

I do remember the debates Mr. Patterson had us participate in. . . . We talked about the debate in class and he was so supportive of the points I was attempting to make. I think Mr. Patterson wanted us to see that history is not something . . . devoid of emotion, and the lessons we learn from it don't have to fit within a multiple choice selection.

I've often wondered if that was the point of introducing us to Zinn's A People's History. To show us that history is not just dates to memorize and presidents to immortalize, but a record of all human life. It's messy and ugly and painful right alongside the beauty and success and glory. I ended up focusing on Native American and Latin American history in college. . . . I loved it all. Like in Mr. Patterson's class, we were encouraged to ask questions and to fight for our interpretations.

The best teachers make you want to learn more, Mr. Patterson did that. . . . I never want to be a person that is 100% certain about something and refuses to consider an alternative. . . .

This has . . . helped me in what became my career. I am a public librarian.

. . . By the very nature of the job, we have to make sure that the selections we make cover a variety of stances. . . . I am able to analyze a collection and find the holes, regardless of my personal opinion on the topic. I want everyone in my town to be able to find the information they need with no judgment, whether explicit by staff disapproval or implicit by lack of resources.[14]

At this point, there is no way of knowing (without a national search for the alums) how many of Patterson's students shared Mayer's sense that Patterson and Zinn helped transform and improve their high school educational experience and even shaped their subsequent intellectual development, college major, and professional career. We make no claims about her typicality but offer her memoir to indicate how powerful the combination of Patterson's pedagogy and Zinn's history was to this student—and was likely to others.[15] Note that Mayer's message focused at least as much on Patterson as on Zinn. The role of *A People's History* in the teaching and learning process is as much about the teacher (and the students) as it is about Zinn.

The letters from Patterson's students can offer us only a snapshot from an earlier time, so unlike Mayers's memoir they speak to short-term rather than long-term impact. As our analysis in chapter 3 and our preface to the letters here suggest, we are impressed with that impact. But the best way for you to see whether you agree with that analysis is to judge for yourself, in reading the twenty-two letters included below. We have arranged the letters into three sections, where students offer their most revealing comments on 1) Zinn's calling into question their prior history education and textbooks; 2) historical methodology; and 3) the quality of Zinn's prose. Together this selection imparts the range of student views of Zinn and the impact that debate-oriented class sessions, using his *People's History*, had on their understanding of history.

To maintain the authentic, unfiltered student voices in these letters, we have presented them as close to verbatim as possible. We want you to experience the letters in the form that they were read by Zinn. Toward that end we have minimized use of "[*sic*]" and other bracketed insertions, and we have not pointed out inaccuracies in their historical arguments. Readers should therefore not assume that all their facts are straight or that quotes and even paraphrases that the letters attribute to Zinn are accurate (see note 8). These are, after all, the writings of high school juniors inexperienced in historical writing and analysis.

Reading these letters today, in the wake of the Trump era, it is especially important to consider Patterson's determination to promote historical and political dialogue. The hyperpolarization promoted by Trump has reduced American politics to a kind of Right-Left political tribalism, in which demonization has replaced dialogue. In such an era it seems crucial for educators to teach their students to engage with those with whom they disagree and to try to judge opposing arguments on the basis of evidence and reason. As ad hominem attacks and intolerance in some of these letters attest, such dialogue was not easy, and not all of the students proved capable of staying at the level of evidence-based dialogue.

I. COPING WITH COGNITIVE DISSONANCE

Letters highlighting the radical break Zinn represented regarding students' prior history education and textbooks (presented by alternating critical and admiring letters)

Letter 1

Dear Mr. Zinn,

My name is Amanda . . . and I am a junior at T. High School. I am in Mr. Bill Patterson's first and second period U.S. History class. Throughout the first part of the year we have been reading and studying your writings. At the beginning of the year I was very confused when we were learning about you. One of the first packets we read was the one you wrote on Christopher Columbus and the Indians. This piece made me mad. To me Christopher Columbus is a hero. Children of all ages look up to him. In grade school we used to recite a poem stating, "In 1492 Columbus sailed the ocean blue," just to remind us of what a strong, courageous and confident man he was. We learned about how he became very close with the Indians, by trading goods and helping one another. In your writings you state that basically Columbus was an indecent person, and that he captured the Indians and tried to keep them under control so they wouldn't get in the way of Columbus's "fame." I strongly disagree with every word in that section of your book, and I want you to know that I have and will always look at Christopher Columbus as a hero and an adventurer that wasn't afraid to stand up for what he thought was true.

The next reading that really caught my eye was "A People's War." I must say that even after how disgusted I was after reading about Christopher Columbus and the Indians, you and I have somewhat of an agreement on "A People's War." I like your point on Executive Order 9066. I think it is inexcusable to have the authority to take the Japanese out of their homes even though they are currently U.S. citizens. However, have you ever thought of what if one of the Japanese wasn't a citizen? What would we do then? We would have absolutely no idea. They could be sneaking the Japanese government information and clues to where the U.S. would strike next, and that would cause more deaths then we already had. If the Japanese weren't being hurt then I think the Executive Order 9066 was a benefit to the U.S.

[In] "The Empire and the People," I find the question, "how did President McKinley reach his decision to acquire the Philippines," an interesting one. You say in your writings that he preached [prayed] to God and asked what he should do. Are you implying that he was confused and was honestly torn between what to do on this decision? Or are you stating that he should follow his conscious [conscience]?

The final writing I would like to make comments on is "The Impossible Victory: Vietnam." You state in the very first paragraph that it was the U.S. technology against the Vietnam[ese] and human power, and the human power won. I agree with you one that the U.S. shouldn't have been there, but was it possible that at the beginning our intentions were good?

Well, Mr. Zinn, even though I may have many questions, and we may disagree on a few things I believe that you are a very honorable man with good thoughts that you like to share. You aren't a "sheep" (as Mr. Patterson would say) that follows the average crowd, and I admire you for that. I appreciate the fact that your writings challenge our normal believes [beliefs]. Thank you for your time. I would love it if you could take some time to write me back a quick little message. I have enjoyed studying your writings.

Sincerely,

Amanda

Response to Amanda from Howard Zinn

Dear Amanda,

Sorry to have taken so long to reply to your letter, but I have been traveling a lot while my correspondence has piled up, and I am just beginning to make my way through the pile.

I appreciate your honest disagreements with the things I say in my "People's History of the U.S." Let me take them up one by one.

On Columbus. You say "I strongly disagree with every word in that section of your book and I want you to know that I have and will always look at Christopher Columbus as a hero and an adventurer that wasn't afraid to stand up for what he though[t] was true." When you use the word "disagree" do you mean that you don't believe that Columbus mutilated, tortured, enslaved, killed Indians in pursuit of gold? I didn't make that up. It's not a matter of debate. That is what he did. His own journal shows his attitude towards them. His most admiring biographer, Samuel Eliot Morison, says he was guilty of "genocide." So my next question is: assuming those facts are true, do you still think he should be seen as a hero? An adventurer, yes. But a hero? Do you hold up someone as a hero who you think is guilty of treating other people with brutality[?] Can you imagine someone coming from another planet to this one, someone with enormous destructive weapons, killing everyone on this planet, and be hailed back on his home planet as a hero because he discovered our planet, and emptied it of its people, and made it open for conquest and habitation by his home planet[?] What would you think of such creatures who would consider someone like that a hero?

As for your point on Executive Order 9066 putting Japanese men, women, children, some born here, some not born here, in concentration camps: you say "what if one of the Japanese wasn't a citizen? . . . They could be sneaking the Japanese government information and clues to where the U.S. would strike next. . . ." Do you mean to say that whether you are a citizen or not determines whether you would be a spy? And how in the world is a Japanese person in California going to sneak information across the Pacific to Japan? And do you lock up two hundred thousand people because one of them might possibly be a spy? Now one in every two hundred Americans has a criminal record, that means in every two hundred thousand Americans a thousand have a criminal record. Should we lock up those 200,000 to make sure that someone among them does not commit a crime? Amanda, there is such a thing as hysterical fear, which leads to depriving people of their liberty, even their life, even if they haven't done a thing wrong, but because you imagine they might (because of their ancestry or skin color or whatever) possibly do something wrong. Do you realize that you would be living in a totalitarian state? Frankly, I am shocked by your attitude. It is not kind, humane, or democratic. You should read the autobiographies of Japanese people who as youngsters experienced the cruelty of their families being wrenched out of their homes and thrown into camps, not because they did anything wrong, not because there was any chance of them doing anything wrong, but because they were Japanese. Not much different from killing six million Jews simply because they were Jews. Suppose you are Irish, and live in England, and the English decide to round up all Irish and put them in concentration camps, on the ground they might possibly be secretly helping the Irish Republican Army? And an English person responded to your anger by saying: oh, you never can tell, one of these Irish might give away secrets.

Was McKinley "confused . . . honestly torn . . . asking if he should follow his conscience in deciding to take the Philippines"? He probably was not sure what to do, but there was great pressure from corporations and other political leaders, and all those who wanted the United States to have an empire, to have more colonies, to control more international trade, to have military bases. And so he made the decision which resulted in an ugly war against the Filipino people, who wanted independence, not American control.

Were our intentions good at the beginning in the Vietnam war? I suppose you mean the intentions of the government, because the American people did not know what was going on. The intentions of the government are quite clear, and they were not good—the intention was to have a base in Vietnam which the United States would control, and our government was willing to make war to have that base. It certainly did not have the intention of letting the Vietnamese people decide for themselves who should run their country, because we would not let them have elections in 1956, as was promised by the Geneva Accord of 1954. We knew Ho Chi Minh and the Communists would win that election, and our government will not allow free elections if it thinks those elections will bring to power someone we don't like. Not very democratic, is that?

This is the "quick little message" you hoped I would write. Thanks for reading my stuff! Best of luck in your studies.

Howard Zinn

Letter 2

Dear Mr. Howard Zinn:

You don't run across many writers like you in an average day, that's for sure!

The first day I stepped into Mr. Patterson's history class we were told we would be reading and studying your writings, and that we would either hate you or love you.

Contrary to my very first opinions, I ended up loving your work. I find it quite a pleasure to be able to write to you, since all of the other great writers of America seem to be, unfortunately, dead.

Since the third grade the teachers have been teaching us the history of our country in a rather "sugar-coated" way. I am so pleased to be finding out what *really* happened! For instance, the real story about "America's founder," Christopher Columbus and how he treated the Indians that were on the island his boat bumped into. After I found out the real story I must admit I was quite embarrassed that we have a whole day dedicated to this man who did not even know he discovered America. And, of course, the true story about George Washington, which was quite contrary to what we were taught all through grade school and junior high. Also, the Valley Forge "episode." We were taught that George Washington braved it through and was right there with his men coaxing them along, and being a "savior" to them, when actually he was inside a comfortable, warm hut while his freezing men were planning a mutany against him.

I still love this country just as much and realize it was a different time back then, and maybe those instances were acceptable. I just wish our history books would tell us both sides and not only what they want us to know! That is not right! It's not the American way.

I would just like to thank you for telling us all the truth— keep doing it, please!

You are a great American, as well as a great writer!

Thank you,
Stephanie

Letter 3

Mr. Zinn:

"ARE YOU NOW OR HAVE YOU EVER BEEN A MEMBER OF THE COMMUNIST PARTY?"

These words were spoken several times by a judge named McCarthy who would denounce any and all public figures having any contacts with either the party or its members. This period was a disgrace to our society and serves as an example to us of what can happen when we charge guilt by association! But like so many other examples in history, people tend to forget them as long as they do not conflict with their own personal lives. My U.S. History teacher has used excerpts from your book, "A People's History of the United States" and through those I have noted that you forget some of these lessons.

There is a great lesson to be learned that I would like to share with you in Kahlil Gibran's book, "The Prophet." He (the prophet) is asked by a teacher, how to teach people things. The prophet's reply is, "If he [the teacher] is indeed wise he does [not] bid you enter the house of his wisdom, but rather leads you to the threshold of your own mind." These words could be applied when, for instance, trying to report a part of history. Instead of trying to press your own bitter version of our countries history on us, why don't you try to let us come to this conclusion on our own? In chapter seven of your book 'People's History' you are very persistant in your own views yet perhaps you forget the element of time. It is much easier to solve a problem two-hundred years later. Right off the bat you charge president Jackson guilty by being the son of a land speculator when you write, "John Donelson . . . ended with

20,000 acres of land. . . . His SON-IN-LAW (emphasis mine) made twenty-two trips out of Nashville in 1975 [1795] for land deals. This was Andrew Jackson." You go on to make several other unsubstantiated assumptions with, "Jackson was a land speculator, merchant, slave trader(?), and the most aggressive enemy of the Indians in early American history." Let us come to that last decision by ourselves. Don't push your opinions on us since you have no more credit with us than any other text-book publisher that as you imply tend to protect the American government by cushioning the facts. I personally find your assaults on Jackson's character insulting. Who are you to say that if you were in the same position with a whole section of your country preparing to leave and with political and financial pressures as well as your own morals and values being questioned that you would have had the foresight to see that moving the indians would be as hazzardous as letting them stay. Actually in the entire chapter, you fail to prove that the president was responsible for the deaths on the Trail of Tears.

A second thing is that you tend to criticize Jackson for wanting the [Indians] to adopt the characteristics of the white people. Is it not reasonable for a man to innocently believe that everyone should be as 'superior' as his own race? Think of what parents do when they raise their children. They try to shape their children into their personal morals and values. (i.e. . . . How many four years olds really are spiritually lifted when they pray?) Parents also spend a great deal of time, as does society in general, in telling children that they should leave their immature playful ways behind them and eventually grow up? Sound familiar? Perhaps it was by instinct that the whites (assuming themselves superior) try to shape the Indians out of their 'savage' ways. If ignorance is a sin we shall all burn in Hell! (Or whatever equivalant).

Another thing that I think you do purposefully that offends me is the way you add a quote from another person but then paraphrase at the end of the quote what the person goes on to say. . . . It is odd how these quotes seem to depict exactly what your point is in paraphrase but the actual words that you quote give no such conclusion. An example is when you give a large quote by a Dale Van Every where he says, "in the long record . . . known as the Great American Desert." In this paragraph he describes how horrible the removal was for the indians and how the land was so much part of their life. Then you go on to say that, "According to Van Every . . . Indians and the whites had settled down, often very close to one another. . . ." Show me that he says it because in the quote you present that is not what he says.

And so we journey to yet another chapter—8 "We Take Nothing By Conquest, Thank God." Please, must you always be sarcastic? In this chapter you point out that the Mexican War was a horrible thing. What war isn't. You also mention [one U.S. Army officer writing] that "They (the unruly volunteer soldiers) had driven away the inhabitants, taken possession of their houses and were emulating each other in making beasts of themselves. Cases of rape began to multiply." That is why wars of anykind are so horrible. You above most should know considering that you were in one. But that is just that, no matter how immoral, disgusting, and unfair it may be, a war with rules of conduct would not truly be a war but rather a sadistic game played by governments that were not in war with each other since obviously they would be in cooperation to enforce these 'rules.'

I must admit, you are a hard person to figure out. At some points I figured you were an antagonist who was trying to stimulate ideas in others minds just for the awareness but at other times I could feel real emotion coming out as if you had a personal stake in it. In all truth[ful]ness proclaiming that Polk had it in for the Mexicans from the very start and was an active part in provoking the war only to justify destroying the Mexican control over the desired land would be as fair as I proclaiming that the reason you write this material is a way for you to leash [lash] out on the same government that made you experience the horrible things that you did while in the Eighth Air Force bombing that German encampment and the French village with napalm. In closing I would like to share with you a sentence that summarizes my entire letter. I could not have said it better and surprisingly enough the quote is by you in the first sentence of your book, "Postwar America: 1945–1971." The sentence is this: "Any book of history is, consciously or not, an interpretation in which selected data from the past is tossed into the present according to the interest of the historian." Mr. Zinn, I ask you sincerely, What is your interest?

Cordially,
James

Letter 4

Dear Mr. Howard Zinn

My name is Jim. . . . I am a junior at T . . . High School. This year I entered our junior history class very optimistic and ready to learn. We have gone through learning about America from the very beginning. My teacher, Mr. Patterson hands out packets of readings from different people through the years. One packet that we received was written by yourself, As Long as Grass Grows or Water Runs. Your writings are different from others we have looked at. You give the other side to the movements of America. My teacher asked us to re-

spond to your reading. We are supposed to give a positive or a negative response to the writing. I chose the positive side. In the next paragraph you will
read why I agree with which the manner you wrote with.

I chose your writings to be a positive source of American history. In our
history books we are given only an overview of how Andrew Jackson pushed
the Indians out of their own land and we took it. In your writing You seemed
to be giving us a look at Jackson's personality. I felt like I really knew what his
next move was going to be. Whereas in our history books we can not really
get a feeling of the whole ordeal. After reading my history [text]book on this
chapter I had to go over it again to memorize it. That is what it felt like, memorizing. Your writing was real interesting to read after I had already read the
[text]book. I found a lot more information for debate topics. Which happened
to be a major assignment in class. Mr. Patterson handed out your pamphlets
[photocopies of select chapters from *A People's History*] which gave us a different point of view.

I am really glad that my teacher gave us your writings to give us a different
side to our country and the way our personalities have been in history. Your
outlook gave me interest about our country. It makes [me] wonder if our country is not only put on a pedestal for us to be proud of, but is it taught to us in
our history classes as a religion? Is what we read in our books really the whole
truth? Apparently not.

Yours truly,

Jim

Letter 5

Dear Mr. Zinn,

I am a seventeen year old junior attending T . . . High School in . . . Oregon. I
have a wide range of interests that vary from all sports to doing well in school.
One of my primary interests is in the field of politics, foreign policy and the
like. I am currently enrolled in a U.S. History class with whom I consider to be
an exceptional and yet very vocal instructor. This teacher has included many
different things in our studies, with many of your writtings playing a major
role. While discussing your work and opinions, Mr. Patterson very often sides
with the radicals by expressing agreement with your ideas. I feel that there are
times when he says what he says simply to provoke thought or to obtain a reaction from the students. Nontheless, I'm convinced that he is usually sincere
in his statements of agreement. The majority of our class also shares the same
train of thought. However, Mr. Zinn I am writting to you because I am a defi-

nite exception to this case. I have yet to agree with any of your philosophies that I have read so far this year. There are even times when I am simply disgusted with your liberal opinions and consider them an insult to this great country in which we live.

From the very start, there have been many things that you've said that angered me. Perhaps one of the most aggravating were your statements about the bombing of Hiroshima and Nagasaki that put an end to World War II. It is obvious that you are appalled by this occurance and state many suggestions why. For instance, when relaying projected American casualties if an invasion of Japan were to take place, you said that the estimated 1 million dead or wounded "were pulled out of the air to justify the bombings." I'd like to know how you got such an absurd idea, and how you would back it up. On the other hand, if you look at the size of Japan, the Japanese attitude toward surrender, and the previous island battles of Okinawa, Iwo Jima, and Sai Pan, [you can] surmise that, if anything, these were conservative predictions.

Secondly, it should be made known to all people, once and for all, that we dropped the bombs, not to impress the Russians, but to end the war quickly. By doing just so, more lives were saved in the long run. The United States gambled with a weapon it knew very little about, and we should all be very thankful that we did. Consider the fact that more lives were lost in a single fire bombing raid on Tokyo than lost in Hiroshima.

There is one last statement you made on this topic that very much disturbed me. In asking why we dropped the second atomic bomb on Nagasaki, you expressed the idea that perhaps, since this was a different type of bomb, the people of Nagasaki were victims of a scientific experiment. How dare you, Mr. Zinn! I simply cannot comprehend the kind of attitude it takes to say such a horrid thing about the government of your country which you should be so happy to live in. The reason for the second bomb was simple. After Hiroshima, the Japanese chose not to surrender, or even acknowledge what had happened. So after five days, we were forced to drop our final bomb on the city of Nagasaki in hopes of totally eliminating the chance of loosing more American lives. Remember, this was total war.

I hope it is clear that this issue is only one of many that we dissagree upon. The Spanish American War and Vietnam are others. In conclusion Mr. Zinn, I find your liberal and seemingly anti-American attitude very disapointing. The United States, though imperfect, is the finest country to ever exist and you should be thanking God that you live here. Remember, thousands of men died so you would be able to express your opinion. It is sad that you don't seem to be proud of it. If you and your kind don't like it here, please leave. A great nation with a glorious history such as this will do very well without you. I grow sad to think that there are people like yourself living in this country. For this is a haven that I would gladly give my life for, but if I did there would be people like you that would not appreciate my sacrifice at all. Remember, this is America, LOVE IT OR LEAVE IT! Thank you for your valuable time,

Sincerely,
Matt
Young Patriot and Lover of the United States of America

Letter 6

Dear Mr. Zinn,

I am writing in regards to the booklets that [are] being distributed to our U.S. History class to read.

As I read through the material and related them to the textbook and lectures used in class, I saw an obvious contrast. We often refer to our textbooks as a source of information and your writings have made me look twice.

It has made me come to realize that our "glorious and perfect nation" might have some fault. The great leaders in the past are described as righteous people who can . . . do no wrong. In reality it is hard to believe. Because it is smuggled in a bright red, white, and blue [school-mandated U.S. history] book with a big, beautiful eagle on the front, the content of this 832-page book is rarely analyzed by a high school student. Your writings help to identify the opposing fact which is needed to make a decision of whether this person did more harm or good to our country.

Out of the several writings of yours I have read, I found that *As Long as Grass Grows or Water Runs* has effected me the most. In reading about the Indian removal, it brought to my mind our Sophomore class studying the Holocaust last year. I don't think the Holocaust should be compared to anything but reading about the thousands of Indians killed in a "removal" effort brings similarities to my mind.

I agree with your writings, and I don't think a veil should be hung over the hard facts. We deserve to know the facts and we have a right to know. I want to commend you on your work, I think more of it is needed in the schools today.

Thank you for sharing your work with us.

Sincerely,
Rebecca,

Letter 7

Dear Mr. Zinn,

You say that the great heroes of America, like Christopher Columbus and Thomas Jefferson are not the great heroes that have been portrayed to us in grade school and middle school. Why exactly is that? When I was in grade school and middle school, I learned that these people, Thomas Jefferson and Christopher Columbus were people who did great things.

I am in high school and the teacher in my U.S. History class gave me the readings that you have written from your research saying horrible and disgusting things like the killings, raping and the enslaving that Christopher Columbus and his men did to the Arawaks. You also wrote about the enslavement of blacks and how Thomas Jefferson perpetuated this by having his own slaves. You say that what he did was wrong and I agree but during this particular time it was the way of life to have slaves no matter how you or I disagree, it was the way of life at that time and in that place. I don't agree with you on the fact that he was a man who did total wrong.

You speak about these people as if they did so much that was wrong. You blame the texts [conventional U.S. history textbooks] for being bias[ed] and one sided, but you too are bias[ed] and one sided. Yes, I have found that throughout history there have been many times where people have committed barbaric crimes, but there is nothing we can do about the past except recognize it for what it is and make sure those same things don't happen again. These people may have done wrong and they may have done things that are unforgivable but they are human beings too that make mistakes. These people have made an impact in history and have created a positive effect. They didn't do all bad, where is the good that they did, why haven't you also written about the good things with the bad things? I agree with you that some incidents in history are unforgivable and wrong and I get sick just thinking what America has done to people in the past and even now. America is not perfect but I can't do anything about the past, I have to worry about the present and future and make sure that things that happened in the past don't happen again.

People today in general dwell too much on things that are sick and insane when they should be dwelling on the good things in life. I believe that if you want to be happy in life you need to put your attention on the good things. When I say that I don't mean to forget about the problems of the world today because it is good to know about them so you can find away to handle them but not to get so wrapped up in them that you become miserable. What you're doing is great. It is nice to know another side of the story so you can try to find the truth but getting information that is only one sided is not the whole story. If you can't get both the good and the bad in one it is hard to find the truth. Thanks for listening to me.

Sincerely,
Jessica

Letter 8

Dear Howard Zinn,

My name is M'Lissa . . . and I am a junior at T . . . High School. I am in Bill Patterson's U.S. History class and we have based most of our class on looking at what you have to say about history. I have to say that I am very pleased to have finally read history from a different perspective. Through social studies and history that I have previously taken, compared to your view, nothing has ever been told from the victim's point-of-view.

Take for instance, when you wrote about A People's War? The United State's image is to step forward and defend helpless countries, as our history [text] book will tell us. You suggest though, that for the record of world affairs, that we have been misled. You bring across the impression that we (U.S.) have been hypocritical. "It had instigated war with Mexico and taken half of that country. It had pretended to help Cuba win freedom from Spain, and then planted itself in Cuba with a military base, investments, and rights of intervention. It had seized Hawaii, Puerto Rico, Guam, and fought a brutal war to subjugate the Filipinos" (399). You suggest that we have had a history of invasion and a long record of intervening for our own purposes. This seems to make so much sense to me. You also suggest that the U.S. was a democracy with certain liberties however, "Blacks looking at anti-Semitism in Germany, might not see their own situation in the U.S. as much different" (400). America is supposed to [be the] home of the free, land of the brave, and yet we still deny certain people their democratic rights and remain like this.

I know that you are only presenting a different view of history to us, but it seems to make perfect sense to me. In A People's War, you also say that if China got their independence and self-determination "Our general diplomatic and strategic position would be considerably weakened—by our loss of Chinese, Indian and South Sea markets as well as restrictions upon our access to the rubber, tin, jute, and other vital materials of the Asian and Oceanic regions" (402). You suggest that we could not let China get its independence because we needed access to that area for our own economic purposes. What other logical reason could the U.S. have had for not letting China receive its independence? Makes sense to me.

When you wrote of the Cold War, you say "The Marshall plan of 1948 had an economic aim: to build up markets for American exports" (424). We wanted control all over the globe and what better reason to give economic aid to countries that needed it so they could build themselves up for our advantage.

We had to help other countries with social reform, and yet you still say that it was only for military aid to keep [in] power right-wing dictatorships, enabling them to stave off revolutions. The U.S. had to keep their influence some way, and I agree with you that our only goal is to profit for ourselves.

I hope that after of [sic] Mr. Patterson's class, I do not come out too narrow-minded. I do not want to think in just one way. I think that it is good to see more than one point-of-view to our history. I have really enjoyed reading your work and value it very much when it comes to discussing our history. I personally feel that our history books need to be rewritten, told, and questioned from more than one perspective.

Sincerely,
M'Lissa

Letter 9

Dear Mr. Zinn,

My name is Mark. . . . I'm a junior at T . . . High School, in . . . Oregon. I have recently been taking a class with Mr. Patterson in U.S. History [where our focus] is your published work. I must say that most people in the class don't like what you have to say. To be honest, half the time I strongly agree with and support your ideas. The other fraction of the time I am left frustrated and angry because what you have to say makes no sense to me whatsoever.

An example of work that I have agreed with that you have written is the piece "As Long as the Grass Grows and the Water Runs." I like your point that shows Jefferson to be an insensitive person (I have a better term for him, but it's not printable.), the government to be cold-hearted and Andrew Jackson to be "insensitive" also with regard to the banning and mobilization of Native Americans. The point I like the most of all is when you discuss Daniel Boone and Davy Crockett integrating with the Native Americans, proving that if the government would have left the Native Americans alone, the white man would not have had a problem with their being around.

The pretty . . . [part] of this letter ends now. It is time to challenge you. When I read "The Socialist Challenge," it left me dumbfounded and angry. When you mentioned these terrible business[es] trying to make a profit, I just laughed. Businesses are supposed to make a profit. That's why they're there. With all due respect, Mr. Zinn, I think you're a socialist. In "The Socialist Challenge," you mentioned certain tycoons getting ahead in life, owning 90% of the wealth. In discussing the businesses, [it] appears to me that you spoke from an extreme socialist point of view. I must tell you. If it's socialism you believe in, I think you're wrong. Only in a perfect society would socialism work. With laborers running things, everything and everyone must be equal. This goes against human nature. Socialism is very similar to communism and I must say that both turned into the same thing. Russia and China are examples of communism gone bad turning into dictatorship.

Leaving on a positive note. I respect you in many ways. I respect your firm beliefs and your extreme writing style. History did not stop where you did in your writing. There is more to be written, and I must say I would love to see you write another book. My sister once wrote you and she received a letter in reply. I would be grateful if you could do the same for me.

Sincerely,
Mark

Letter 10

Dear Howard Zinn,

Some Americans are really proud to be an American. There is nothing wrong with that, I think it is really important to be proud, but with this they feel everything that the United States does is good, they never see the dark side. Since I am from South America, I have different points of view in the class; I see most of the things in different ways. It is like you are talking about the Nazis in the class where you have a German person, it is almost always a different point of view.

There are several people in my history class that really do not like you, they feel you hate Americans because all your texts show the dark side of the story. Some of them think you should move out of the country.

In one of your texts, "Columbus, the Indians, and Human Progress" [it] is really good the way that you tell us the story because when they teach in middle school about Columbus they tell he was, a brave and good man who discovered the New World. He discovered a new world, which was a progress, but he also destroyed a race, he just wanted goods from their lands and the Indians were so nice to the white man. In one of Columbus' messages he wrote: "As soon as I arrived in the Indies, on the first island which I found, I took some of the natives by force in order that they might learn and might give me information of whatever there is in these parts," and the Indians really gave information about gold.

Another text that I really liked is the one about the Filipino Resistance. I really agree when they talk about the reason they wanted the Philipines, everything was about land, economic reasons. There they have so much products because of the fertility of the soil, which some of them would be impossible to have here.

I am not against Americans, I am just against the books that never show the dark side and the people that don't accept what their people did, because I really accept what my people who came from Portugal did, they killed a race.

I think your texts are the best, your book A People's History of the United States is the best book I have ever read, I really appreciate your work and I'm sure when I show my friends in Brazil your work they will become a big fan of your books. Your book is the kind of book that you can't stop to reading.

Yours sincerely,
Ariana

II. STUDENTS ON HISTORICAL METHODOLOGY

Letter 11

Dear Professor Zinn —
This letter concerns two of your articles [chapters] I have recently read; Columbus, the Indians, and Human Progress and As Long as the Grass Grows or Water Runs. These articles were given to me as part of an assignment in my U.S. History class. As I read these articles, they became more than just a supplement to my textbook. They gave me the ability to weight certain aspects of historical events by my own standards. Which is more important; Columbus' discovery of America, or the extinction of a race of people? As a student I appreciate the oppurtunity to see more than just the narrow textbook view of history. Textbooks seem a very dispassionate source of information, yet you have written that many historians have colored history with their own ideology. My question to you is, are you not also subject to that same tainted ideology? Is your own view any less narrow than those you criticize?

Perhaps it is my role as a student to extract the pieces of information from each extreme to create an objective vs. subjective picture of history. Without benefit of your information this would most certainly not be possible. I would really appreciate any response you might have regarding the issues raised.

Sincerely,
Kassie

Letter 12

Dear Mr. Zinn,

Hi! My name is Stacey. . . . I am a Junior history student at T . . . High School in . . . Oregon. I have enjoyed reading several chapters of your book. It has been a source of many discussions in my American History class—sorry to say, not everyone sides with you. These discussions have been the main reason why history is one of my more enjoyable classes. Everyone seems to have an opinion!

Although I have enjoyed reading your work, I must say you seem to be pretty harsh sometimes on the choices of the government. You don't seem to believe in the political choices that were made. In Chapter 8 [on the Mexican War] you ask, "Where was popular opinion?" You say that there were no surveys taken, and the majority of the people did not vote. Are you implying that the government was not always acting for what the people wanted, and did things without the people's input?

Doesn't the government know a little bit more than the average American white man did? You mention more than once that today's history books don't tell what really went on or at least they don't tell the whole story. Why do you think they don't tell the whole story?

I have one question I would like to ask you, not concerning politics, but your feelings on the positions of women, blacks, and Indians. In the beginning of Chapter 7 [on Native Americans in the Jacksonian era], you say that the women were needed, so they were dealt with, but the Indians were not needed, and they were an obstacle. How do you feel about the places or positions of women, blacks and Indians then and now?

Thank you for letting me know what I haven't been learning in my history books.

Sincerely,
Stacey

Letter 13

Dear Mr. Zinn:

I am responding to writings in your book *A People's History of the United States*. My U.S. History class is presently reading and commenting on selected chapters. In reading chapters 1, 7, 8, and 11 I was filled with mixed feelings. I believe you are a very good writer and you make your point very well. I feel a good example of your superb writing is in Chapter 8. titled "We Take Nothing by

Conquest, Thank God". You make Col. Hitchcock look like a good guy, but only to show how much of a hypocrite he is.

Through reading and growing up, I have learned and been taught many things. One of these things is by exaggerating and piecing together any evidence or facts, you can make it say whatever you want. By distorting and twisting the truth you can make America seem proud and happy or shameful and lonely. I believe in trying to write and make a point you do this in some of your examples and illustrations. In chapter 7, titled "As Long as Grass Grows or Water Runs", you make America seem as if they were out to get the Indians and harass and pester them. I don't feel this way about the U.S. I feel that America was on a forward progress and the Indians just happened to be in the way. Think about if we had not progressed into the west, what would have become progress now? Would we be living in tee-pees?

Through reading selections of your book, I have learned many things. Many new ideas and facts were presented that were unknown to me before. In chapter 7, you portrayed Jackson as a slave holder, executioner, and a land speculator. The facts you presented make me understand how brainwashing our textbooks can be. Another example of this is in chapter 8. The newspapers make the war with Mexico seem good and a justified cause. They did not show the broken families, killed Mexicans and the bloody earth. This also shows me how distorted the press can be. After all, who wants to have a rebellious and cheating country? Wouldn't it be wonderful if education presented both sides?

Sincerely,

Alden

Letter 14

Dear Mr. Zinn,

My name is Hayley . . . , and I am a Junior at T . . . Highschool. This year in my history class I have been given the opportunity to write to you from my U.S. History teacher, and I've decided to take this chance to tell you what my feelings are on your work.

First, let me start out by saying your articles [chapters from *A People's History*] have definitely taught me to widen my tunnel vision on American history. Before I was presented with your work I was used to being given the history [text]book and memorizing the fact that United States is right in everything we do. I truly resent how the textbooks present the history stories, but I also must add sometimes, I feel your writing is just as bad at omitting all the details as the original textbook. I realize that in order to present a good paper on most subjects, you must be biest [biased] to either side but, I feel that sometimes you go overboard with your down playing the American government and soldiers. For instance, in your article, "The Impossible Victory: Vietnam," I did not respond well to the way you put down the soldiers for many of their actions. I feel that you should understand the stress they and their leaders were under and respect that fact. I know that you were also a soldier, in World War II and for that reason I am even more surprised at your reaction to Vietnam. The Vietnam vets need all the support they can get even after the war. They are still suffering from the traumatic situations they were put in as young adults. Usually, you write the opposite of which every other journalist or historians write so it would have been a nice change for you to try to find the good aspects of the Vietnam [War] or at least backup there efforts. I feel you should of used you[r] wonderful writing abilities and your hypnotic way of presenting topics to persuade people to feel positive about there war vets.

On the other hand I truly appreciated your comments on Christopher Columbus in "Columbus, the Indians, and Human Progress." Let me first start off by saying I enjoyed your title choice of this report. It really forces you to search for the meaning and truly understand the piece. This article is truly refreshing. I have never heard of an account of Christopher Columbus from a negative aspect. This aspect of him leaves me confused. I do not understand why he is so looked upon as a heroic and great founder of this land if in fact he was none of the above. Maybe this is a question you can answer for me or at least give me some insight on how you found your information to prove this point. I am very interested in a background on how you find all your information to write all of your articles. Most of your works that I have read are always new and shocking details. I was just wondering where you come upon all of these facts and stories?

I hope none of my comments have offended you or led you to believe that I do not appreciate the hard work you put in into finding and presenting all of the facts that the textbooks omit. Through your writing you have taught me to always look for the other side of the story, before I conclude . . . [my] perception of the event. This is something I can always use throughout my life. Once again I thank you for your work you put into promoting awareness of the victims. I appreciate you taking the time to read my comments, and I am looking forward to a response from you on my thoughts.

Sincerely,
Hayley

Letter 15

Dear Mr. Zinn,

I'd like to commend you on your writings. They are overall excellent but with some exaggeration. Your work has been definately against America and Americans. Your writings say the opposite of the text[book] and give us another side of the story.

In one of your writings, (COLOMBUS, THE INDIANS, AND HUMAN PROGRESS) you mentioned that in two years, one-half of the 250,000 Indians on the island Haiti had been killed through murder, mutilliation, or suicide. Being one of the smaller islands in the world, I personally don't think that Haiti is big enough to support a population of 250,000 Indians. But I do agree that the Spaniards put an impossible task on the Indians and used God as their reason for their wrong doing. The Spaniards also probably doctored up the history books to cover their tails.

In your piece, "WE TAKE NOTHING BY CONQUEST THANK GOD," I agree that the Mexican war was our fault. We marched our troops into their (disputed) territory that, in the past was inhabited by their people, which said to them that we were going to attack them. The text[book] says that they attacked us but it was really the other way around, we invaded them. When we found Colonel Cross with a crushed skull, dead, we shouldn't of blamed it on the Mexicans as fast as we did. It could of been anybody, a crazy kid, a peace seeking American, a drunk Mexican or American, or his horse could of bucked him and stepped on him while he was lying on the ground.

I'd like to ask you a few questions.

1. Where do you get your facts for your material?
2. Are the facts real or just a load of bull?
3. Do you have a fan club? If so how many members does it have?

Well, I'd appreciate it if you'd please answer my questions, and any comments about the rest of the letter and mail it back to me.

Thanx,

Brad

III. ZINN'S WRITING STYLE

Letter 16

Dear Mr. Zinn,

I am writing to you as a high school student in . . . Oregon. In this years history curriculum your writings are included as a second point of view. Your sarcasm is enjoyed immensly by our class. Some enjoy supporting your theories, and others of course, tear it down. As for myself, I support your theories.

During the first part of our course, we learned about the exploration of North and South America. Your writing Columbus, the Indians, and Human Process [Progress] really opened my eyes to the inhumane character of Christopher Columbus and his troops. We now set aside a day each year to celebrate a rapist. Your writing should be required reading in every history class in the nation. We should not be blinded by misleading information and facts.

The second reading we used was "As Long as the Grass Grows and Water Runs", again, [this] was an eye opener. This reading made me realize that taking the Indians land was wrong and unconstitutional. The government was a lying party back then, and I have always believed that we were totally justified in taking their land.

One fact about you bothers me. You seem to use God's name in vain. Are you an Atheist or something to that effect? You rip Christianity and other religious groups. If you don't like relig[i]on I think you should keep it to yourself because it offends other people.

We are presently working on the Civil War and I look forward to reading more of your theories.

Sincerely,
Glenn

Letter 17

Dear Mr. Zinn,

I am a junior at T . . . High School in . . . Oregon. For the last semester I have been attending Mr. Patterson's U.S. History class. In that time I have had two great teachers, Mr. Patterson and yourself. I have not only read your packets [of select Zinn chapters] I received in class, but taken it upon myself to read your book.

I admire any author who has the dedication to write such a long writing, however, your piece contains not only length but is intelligent, obviously well researched, and logically put together in such a way that it is not only history but a story with war, violence, greed, deception, and fantasy. The very elements that together create the kind of literature I enjoy to read on my own time. While reading I found myself overcome with the realization that all of the events you wrote about were real, not a character in a book, but real experiences that happened to real people, just like me.

I have become exposed to so many theories and ideas that were not available to me in my previous twelve years of schooling. In place of encouraging me to make my own opinions by present[ing] all the facts, I had been shown only a glimmer of honesty, the slender bit of knowledge that I never doubted as anything less . . . [than] absolute facts. I had grown attached to the glamorous victories and blinding patriotism. All this time I have been deceived either out of the ignorance of others who were given only favorable information about the government and history, Or intentionally or to quiet possible thoughts of rebellion, disbelieving authority, or even to protect me from the horrors of mankind. Teachers are often too eager to point to Germany during the times of Hitler and the holocaust, even though in our history we reflect the actions of Nazi Germany.

Our government has either promoted or looked the other way when events such as the genocide [of the] American Indians (Columbus, the Indians and human progress), Japanese internments camps (A People's War?), the inferiority of women (Surprises), treatment of Blacks in the south (Or does it explode?), the presence of our troops in the Philippines (The Empire and the People), and the massacre at Mylai (The Impossible Victory: Vietnam). That is only a few instances in which we mirror behavior that is presented as evil.

I have learned that there is never a real truth. There are only [infinite] perceptions of everything anyone has ever experienced or [been] exposed to, not only in our time, but also the views and opinions of all people that have ever existed. In addition, that perception is based on the environment, education, and self image of each individual. So all I can really do is become as well educated as I can and discover my own truth through my own personal experience and learning. So, I thank you, Mr. Zinn, for helping me to have the basic knowledge of my past that will help me apply level judgement. To what government and authority tells me. To not to settle for an easy answer, but to look deeper and find my own personal truth.

Sincerely,

Alison

Letter 18

Dear Mr. Howard Zinn,

I am writing you to let you know how I feel about your writings that I have read. First, I must tell you that you are a very talented and persuasive writer. I really enjoy your work. Sometimes I agree with you and sometimes I don't. The latest work of yours that I have read is from the book "A People's History of the United States." I read Chapter 7, "As Long As Grass Grows Or Water Runs". This is one of your writings that I was in agreement with. We did many cruel and inhumane things to the indians. Until I read your writing I had never thought about how cruel we really were. I myself believe that all races should be treated the same, and I have experienced some of the prejudice still in todays society. You see, I have a very good friend who is black. He Graduated last year so I don't see him very often but I do still care about him. Last year after he sung the solo in a choir concert at school I went up to him and gave him a great big hug! Well, my gaurdian's boss just so happened to be at the same concert and he recognized me. The very next day he went into my gaurdian's office and in a discreet way he told, M . . . that if he can't control his kids that he would never be promoted. Of course I was informed of this. It really placed a lot of burden on my shoulders. I really related to this writing. I feel that we are lucky to be able to read work such as yours because there are two sides to every story and we have a right to know the good as well as the bad. As I mentioned before I do disagree with some of your writings. I do feel that we did some things right in making this country. People now seem to have no feelings towards the U.S. as a country, even those who live in it. I myself love this country for all its good and all of its bad. I do pay attention to the news and I see all the hurt that is spread but I try my damdest to make the U.S. a better place. I would like to thank you for taking the time to read my letter. Please keep up the good work.

Sincerely,
Donna

Letter 19

Dear Mr. Zinn,

I am a student at T . . . High in . . . Oregon, and have a few comments regarding your view of American history.

Obviously I cannot desagree with your facts for if they were not legit you would not get away with all the books and articles you put out. I can however disagree with the tone and minipulation, let me rephrase that, attempted minipulation you try to inflict on your readers. In almost all your accounts of U.S. History you find you find it necessary to throw in some kind of sarcastic or milicious tone which only can be defined as shock value. That is fine for a Stephen King novel, but not for an educational piece on our history. Even if everything I learned as a child and a young adult are not true at least they are trying to make this country stomachable and not a place where just [anyone] with a pen can contort the thoughts and opinious of young people. With the only goal being to revolt against a system under which millions of people are content almost every day of their lives.

Unfortunately it is difficult to meet you to better understand your motives for having the views and opinions that you have. All that I can judge you on is what I read and hear.

It will be equally difficult for you to understand why I feel the way I do about your writings. So to help you understand, I will use some examples from my point of view.

In your piece "Robber Barons, and Rebels" you portray characters such as J. P. Morgan and John D. Rockefeller as scum of the earth and that it was some kind of grand plan to provide an unhealthy and dangerous working environment when it simply turned out that way as the events of time and sircumstances, and although I cannot agree with the way fat cats like Morgan and Rockefeller dealt with their company policies it was not their desire to make anybody suffer. The simple fact is if Morgan and Rockefeller did not do what they did someone else would have.

In your piece "Columbus, the Indians, and Human Progress" you portray Columbus as a cold blooded murderer, rapist, and slave owner. When you very well know that those practices were perfectly acceptable, and once again bringing me to the question of why you would try to make this event more dramatic than it actually was, at that time.

I am not totally against all that you have written, I do fully respect your account of President Andrew Jackson's plan to move the Indians where ever necessary. In your account, "As long as the grass grows, or the water runs" as I am a great adversary of racial prejudice in that era.

I sincerely appreciate this opportunity to express my opinions to you. I would greatly appreciate a responce if your schedule allows you to.

Sincerely yours,

Ryan

Letter 20

Dear Mr. Zinn,

I am writing as a concerned high school student who has read many of your writings. I am presently a junior at T . . . High School who has come to thouroughly enjoy the history of our great country, the United States of America. But one question had come up in my mind that interests me. Mr. Zinn are you proud to be an American? Don't get me wrong about the knowledge between us, but it appears to me that you think our country has had a history of crude treatment. In your writing "A People's Way [War]", you compared executive order 9066 to the way Hitler treated the Jews. You took a negative side of things. I know everyone is entitled to their own opinion, but being a professor I would think you would be a bit more positive with regards to our country.

Another question I have for you is the way you are with your students. Do you preach them or teach them? In your writings you appear to preach rather than give out information. You do have a lot of facts throughout your writings, but it appears to me you like to preach. You express our country's economic necessity very much in your writings. In "War is the Health of the State," you said our entrance for war was for our country's economic necessity. But the way you described it was in a preaching matter [manner].

I am not criticizing your writings Mr. Zinn, but I am very curious with your style of writing. I really do enjoy reading your information while taking great interest in them. I would appreciate your response and look forward to reading more of your work.

Sincerely,

Ron

Letter 21

Dear Mr. Zinn,

My name is Dan . . . and I am a student at T . . . High School in . . . Oregon. In our Alternatives to violence U.S. History class, we have read some of your work that pertains to our curriculum. Even though I like your style and think you are a gifted writer, I regret to say that I disagree with the content of your work. It is my opinion that you have as much a right to say your opinion as I do mine, and I applaud you for speaking it. Your writings also offer a point of view that is not the general one which we are taught, and I like being given a choice of what source to believe instead of one just being shoved down my throat.

I have not read all of your writings so there might be instances that answer my question, which I have simply not read yet. The question I would like to ask you is, has the U.S. Government ever done anything good at all, and if so, was it just a byproduct of American greed? I must say that I support your opinion on Vietnam whole heartedly, but why is there such a large problem with the U.S.'s involvement in World War II? In "A People's War" [you] point to the fact that the diplomats and business men wanted to move in on European markets which, when you look at those markets in those times, who wouldn't? Anyway diplomats and business men are not in charge of the country. Diplomats did what they did for political advancement and business men did what they did to advance their careers. Basically, they were taking advantage of what the government was doing. From my point of view, when you assault the actions done, it is individual's actions you assault, not the government's.

I notice that I have disagreed with what you think and I hope that you do not take offense to it. If you do take offense then I apologize. One more thing that I would like to say is thank you for your writing. It taught me to compare and contrast the validity of the sources we draw from. I really don't have that much more to say, save keep up the good work.

Sincerely,

Dan

Letter 22

Dear Mr. Howard Zinn,

Hello, my name is Marcy . . . , and I attend T. High School. . . . My Junior U.S. History class reads and studies a few of your writings. For the most part I am offended with how you criticize some of the greatest leaders in History. However, our history books are so boring that it is nice to read something else. You do give a side of history which is interesting to learn.

One of your readings, "Columbus, the Indians, and Human Progress" informed me that Columbus and his crew raped women and took and killed Indian prisoners all out of greed for gold. However, if you were Columbus, would you want this written about you?

Another writing, "We Take Nothing By Conquest, Thank God" was an even better eye opener. How can you put down one of our Presidents, who was leading Americans who wanted to populate and institutionalize 'the land'? The U.S. had every right to expand because it was our manifest destiny; although it may have not been correct in the way we did it. If it wasn't for Polk, we might not be here.

The third reading, "As Long as the grass grows", points out that Thomas Jefferson was a liar, and a cruel man because he took the Indians land away. It was not the Indians land. Did it have their name on it? It was the peoples land, and would belong to those who populate and organized it because GOD made it their manifest destiny to expand, and improve on it. If GOD would have left it up to the Indians, it would likely still be prairies, without growth, and with nothing to show for what GOD has given us.

In conclusion, I enjoyed your readings and wished to learn more about the real Viet Nam [war] (next semesters reading). This kind of interest in your writings undoubtedly explains why you are in the business of authoring the horrible truth about some of our greatest heroes. In closing, I would like to know the source of your information and your opinion on why these 'facts' have not been published in school textbooks. I look forward to your response at your earliest convenience.

Sincerely
Marcy

This cartoon, like the many letters from his former students at
Spelman College and Boston University in Howard Zinn's papers,
attests to Zinn's popularity as a teacher and his role in inspiring civic
engagement among his students—many of whom became active in the
civil rights and antiwar movements. Howard Zinn papers, Tamiment
Library and Robert F. Wagner Labor Archives, NYU. (Courtesy of the
estate of Howard Zinn)

Howard Zinn's devotion to improving history education in high schools was evidenced by his many school speaking engagements, like the one recorded here in 2002 in a class at Chicago's Dr. Pedro Abizu Campos Puerto Rican High School. This school visit was included in the biographical documentary film on Zinn, *You Can't Be Neutral on a Moving Train* (2004), by Deb Ellis and Denis Mueller (narrated by Matt Damon). Photo by Judy Hoffman (production still from *You Can't Be Neutral on a Moving Train*). (Courtesy of Deb Ellis)

Howard Zinn with Bill Bigelow at the National Council for the Social Studies convention, Houston, 2008. Bigelow was one of the teacher organizers with whom Zinn worked most closely in popularizing people's history. (Photo courtesy of Deborah Menkart)

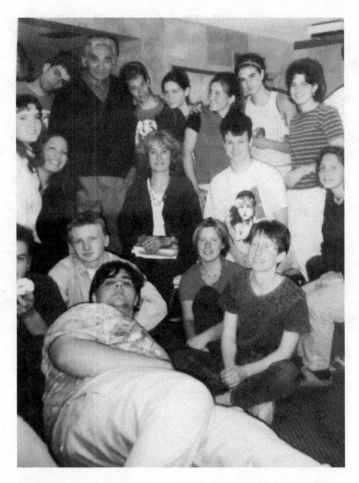

Howard Zinn with Sheila Wilensky and her honors U.S. history class
from Mount Desert Island High School, Bar Harbor, Maine, late 1990s.
(Photo courtesy of Sheila Wilensky)

**From Executive Producers Howard Zinn, Anthony Arnove
Josh Brolin, Matt Damon, and Chris Moore
Comes the documentary THE PEOPLE SPEAK**

**Please join Howard Zinn, Jim O'Hagen, Kerry Washington,
Anthony Arnove, and Chris Moore
<u>Tuesday February 10th</u>
for dinner and a sneak peak at the film.**
http://www.thepeoplespeak.com/

Cocktails at 7:00 pm with a buffet dinner at 7:30pm. At 8:00pm we will be
showing about 20 minutes of the film. We should be done by 9:00pm.
Post Factory NY: 161 6th Ave. at Spring Street, 11th floor, NY, NY 10013 212.627.1662

This documentary is based on Howard Zinn's seminal works <u>A People's History of the United
States</u> and <u>Voices of a People's History</u>, written with Anthony Arnove. We have two goals for
the evening. First, we hope to raise awareness with activists in the NY area who might be
interested in using the doc for organizing and their own fundraising. Second is to raise some
money ourselves to finish the doc. So, yes, we will be asking for money but it is not required in
order to attend, so please come. We acknowledge this is one of the worst times to be raising
money. We also acknowledge that one may feel that there is less need for a documentary
about the voice of The People when we have just elected Barack Obama to the White House.
However history has taught us that it is only through pressure from The People on those in
power that real progress can be accomplished. This documentary is being made to celebrate
those voices from the past who made this country what it is today, and to inspire new voices to
keep driving for the United States to live up to -- and extend -- its promise.

Poster for *The People Speak* film fund-raiser, with Howard Zinn,
Anthony Arnove, Chris Moore, Kerry Washington, and Jim O'Hagen,
New York City, 2009. The film "featured the words (in letters,
songs, poems speeches, and manifestoes) of rebels, dissenters, and
visionaries" from American history, drawn from Zinn's *A People's
History of the United States* and Zinn and Anthony Arnove's *Voices of
a People's History of the United States*. Howard Zinn papers, Tamiment
Library and Robert F. Wagner Labor Archives, NYU. (Courtesy of the
estate of Howard Zinn)

Howard Zinn with Josh Brolin and Danny Glover during the filming of *The People Speak*, at Emerson College Cutler Majestic Theater, Boston, 2008. Photo by Greg Federman (production still from *The People Speak*). (Courtesy of Voices of a People's History of the United States)

Kerry Washington during the filming of *The People Speak*, at Emerson College Cutler Majestic Theater, Boston, 2008. Photo by Greg Federman (production still from *The People Speak*). (Courtesy of Voices of a People's History of the United States)

Howard Zinn with Anthony Arnove during the filming of *The People Speak*, at Emerson College Cutler Majestic Theater, Boston, 2008. Zinn and Arnove codirected *The People Speak* with Chris Moore. Photo by Greg Federman (production still from *The People Speak*). (Courtesy of Voices of a People's History of the United States)

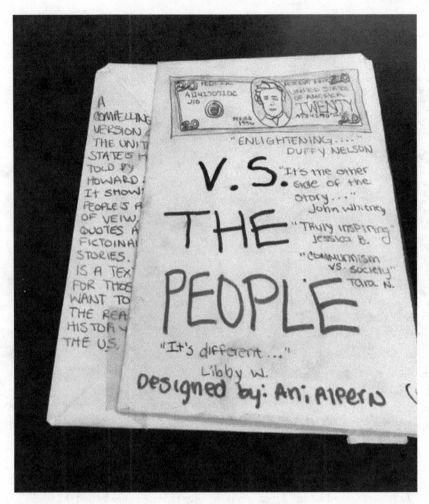

A student-created book cover for *A People's History of the United States*. This was one out of more than a dozen book covers that students designed for Zinn's book as part of a class assignment. Such illustrations, along with the many letters young students sent Zinn, document his book's popularity with students and its success in engaging them in historical study and debate. Howard Zinn papers, Tamiment Library and Robert F. Wagner Labor Archives, NYU. (Courtesy of the estate of Howard Zinn)

Dear Professor Zinn,   Sept. 12, 1989

Six years ago, when I was a junior at Northfield Mount Hermon, I read _A People's History of the United States_ in my US History Survey course. Your book had an enormous impact on me and I wrote to you to thank you for opening my eyes. I still have the letter you sent to me in response.

Last spring, I substituted at the local highschool in my hometown of Hamilton, NY and I came across a history text in a junior year US History Survey course that made me cringe. I'd hoped times had changed. I visited that teacher a few weeks later with _A People's History_ under my arm. I suggested he read it.

Last week I began graduate school at Tufts in their M.A.T. program. I went to buy the texts for Education 172: Class, Race & Gender in the History of US Education. Imagine my delight when your book was included on the shelf, under my professor's name! I am reading it anew with a more mature yet equally zealous avidity.

Among other exciting coincidences, I have discovered a video of your debate with Buckley on Reform vs. Revolution. This is my next endeavor.

I want you to know that your work has had a profound effect on me and I am indebted to you for the new avenues you've shown me.

Sincerely,
Laura Vantine

Laura Vantine's letter indicates the way _A People's History_ could prove transformative for students, in her case helping to foster interest in history first as a high school student, then as a teacher education graduate student, and finally influencing her approach to history as a teacher. Zinn wrote back to her, and they corresponded several times. Howard Zinn papers, Tamiment Library and Robert F. Wagner Labor Archives, NYU. (Courtesy of the estate of Howard Zinn, and Laura Vantine)

December 1, 1994

To:
Mike Nguyen
Kevin Huynh
Ruth Miza
Thuy Vu
Yi Zhanq
Laura Duran
Hanako Ueda
Michael Ng
Kelly Paige Hoffman
Jill Trangmoe
Roshunda Stewart
Richard Ramirez
Brando Horn
Gania (?) Vazquez
Theresa Juarez
Linh Tran
Maria Nevarez
Aura Jiminez
Peggy Meherin
Rosaura Cabrera
Norma Hernandez
Jennifer Stearman
Bourzou Khanverdi

Please forgive me for not replying to each one of you personally, but I am overloaded with work, so I must address you as a group. I have read every one of your letters, and I am tremendously impressed with how thoughtful they are. You seem to have been stimulated by what I wrote in my essay "The Use and Abuse of History", and I am happy about that, because that's the reason I wrote it, to get young people to think, to be independent, to understand that anything you read in a history book (including mine!) is just part of the story, and it is your responsibility to look for those parts that are left out.

I thank your teacher, Thomas Doyle, for taking the trouble to accumulate your letters and send them to me. I'm sure he is an excellent teacher! I wish you all the best of luck. Maybe some day I will be in your part of California and I can meet with all of you together.

Sincerely,

Howard Zinn
29 Fern St.
Auburndale, Mass. 02166

Howard Zinn letter to students in Thomas Doyle's high school history class in California. Given Zinn's hectic schedule, it is striking how often he took the time to respond, as he did here, to student and teacher letters about *A People's History* and his other writings that were used in schools. Howard Zinn papers, Tamiment Library and Robert F. Wagner Labor Archives, NYU. (Courtesy of the estate of Howard Zinn)

Howard Zinn teaching antiwar lessons in *A People's History of American Empire* (Metropolitan Books, 2008). Ever eager to foster critical thinking about U.S. war-making and imperialism, Zinn collaborated with historian Paul Buhle and cartoonist Mike Konopacki on this graphic history that has sold more than eighty thousand copies. Illustration by Mike Konopacki. (Courtesy of Paul Buhle and the estate of Howard Zinn)

Rock star Eddie Vedder at a Pearl Jam concert, during the Iraq War, with a "Zinn 4 Prez" poster. Vedder, a friend of Zinn's, admired both his historical writing and antiwar activism. Howard Zinn papers, Tamiment Library and Robert F. Wagner Labor Archives, NYU. (Courtesy of the estate of Howard Zinn)

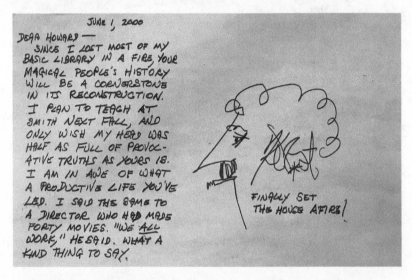

Note and sketch from novelist Kurt Vonnegut to Howard Zinn. These World War II veterans became friends because, as Zinn put it, "we had things in common: the second world war, bombing, books, the future of the world . . . [and] a profound hatred of war." Howard Zinn typescript of memorial remarks on Kurt Vonnegut, Howard Zinn papers, Tamiment Library and Robert F. Wagner Labor Archives, NYU. (Courtesy of the estate of Howard Zinn)

CHAPTER 5

Not Just for Kids

Since *A People's History* offers an introductory overview of American history and people associate introductory works with students in history courses, there has been a tendency to connect Zinn's book with youth. Indeed, the popularity of *A People's History* with students has led some critics to portray Zinn as a kind of pied piper of the young, which has been expressed most heatedly by Zinn's ardent detractors who fear his book undermines young people's faith in American capitalism, exceptionalism, and foreign policy. This is why some have sought to bar the book from history classrooms. But even moderate critics, such as Harvard historian Jill Lepore, have mocked Zinn on the grounds that his *A People's History* popularized a simplistic version of the American past whose melodramatic and iconoclastic distortions appeal to immature teenagers. Lepore's assessment of *A People's History*, offered in the pages of the *New Yorker* on the occasion of Zinn's death in 2010, compared Zinn to Holden Caulfield, the rebellious fictional adolescent created by J. D. Salinger, contending that reading *A People's History* at fourteen was "like reading *The Catcher in the Rye*, at the same age ('history's so goddam phony'). . . . It's swell and terrible and it feels like something has ended, because it has."[1] This is a common put-down of *A People's History* among critics, that the book appeals to adolescents enamored with dissent and opposition because teens are by nature dissenting and oppositional—and tend to see things in black and white.

But this portrayal of Zinn as a pied piper of youth does not hold up alongside the extensive letter collection in the Zinn archives by adult readers of *A People's History*, which show that its appeal is too complex to be understood as the result of a youth movement. These adult letters refute the notion that Zinn's book was transformative only for young people occupying one of Erickson's stages of human development and that Zinn's perspectives are something one grows out of. The letters sent to Zinn from 1980, the year *A People's History* was published, through the early twenty-first century show that it was equally impactful for adults. Lepore also overlooked the reality that young people exposed to *A*

People's History were most often introduced to Zinn because an adult, a teacher, assigned selections from Zinn's book to them.

A "smells like teen spirit" reading of Zinn's popularity is also contradicted by *A People's History's* sales history. The book was deemed too radical to be adopted by school districts or most individual schools and got into schools primarily via photocopied chapters assigned by teachers, and most of its sales were to adults in bookstores. Hugh Van Dusen, Zinn's editor at Harper, estimated in 1994 that only 20 percent of the sales of *A People's History* were to high schools.[2]

The Zinn archives contain letters to Zinn from a wide array of adult readers of *A People's History*, including high school teachers, college professors, undergraduate and graduate students, parents, grandparents, and others with an interest in history and politics. Readers who wrote to Zinn also include prominent progressives, such as Ron Kovic, Victor Navasky, Oliver Stone, Howard Fast, Tim Robbins, Ralph Nader, Bill Moyers, Susan Sarandon, Viggo Mortensen, Jane Fonda, Pete Seeger, Jonathan Kozol, Naomi Klein, Colin Firth, Don Delillo, and Mumia Abu-Jamal. Former students of Zinn's wrote to him, including those from Boston University, reflecting on their experience in his classes and how they were influenced by reading *A People's History*. There are letters to Zinn written by military veterans and by at least fifteen prisoners, many of whom Zinn corresponded with over time, showing interest in their cases. Zinn saved all of these letters. The adult letters are distinguished from the student letters referenced in chapters 3 and 4 in that they were not part of a teacher-generated project but initiated by a personal desire to communicate with the author of *A People's History of the United States*.

The large collection of adult letters conveys the ways these readers personally connected with *A People's History* and Zinn's other published works and, for many, Zinn's activism. Evident and striking is the enthusiasm with which the vast majority of the adults wrote to Zinn, as they shared personal stories, epiphanies, fears, hopes, and commitments, along with the respect and admiration they had for Zinn as a historian-activist. Also striking is the fact that adults wrote to Zinn referencing *A People's History* consistently across a thirty-year period, from the year it was first published to the year of his death, attesting to the book's longevity and impact on adult readers beyond its initial launch.

Overall, adult readers connected to *A People's History* via either education or politics. Some wrote to Zinn after reading *A People's History*, sharing responses that were of a purely intellectual nature; they were attracted to history from the bottom up. Other adults wrote responses that were more overtly political; they were drawn to *A People's History* because it either attracted them to radical politics, to activism, or affirmed their already dissenting politics. More than half the

adult letters conveyed to Zinn that reading his history was personally transformative. For some, the transformation was connected to their new understanding of U.S. history, while for others it pertained to an activist ethos, connecting
with Zinn's own political work or their interest in pursuing activism. Sometimes
it was both, as was the case with one who wrote Zinn, "Thank you, thank you,
thank you for writing this book. I am a 60 year old man who has unfortunately
never read a true history of the United States until now. It was almost like you
unscrewed the top of my head and blew out all the fog. I have always been apa-
thetic regarding politics but your book has changed me. You have dislodged my
apathy and made me downright angry. . . . I am currently helping to organize a
peace group in Grants Pass, Oregon."[3] This is not the kind of response an ordinary U.S. history survey book generally elicits, nor is it the response of a Holden
Caulfield.

For this Oregonian and others inspired to activism by Zinn, *A People's History* represented something new in their lives; it served as an introduction to a
critical, leftist view of history and society. But for more adults, including those
who had already been politically active, *A People's History* affirmed their dissident politics. The majority of letters attest that reading *A People's History* was
inspirational, regardless of the letter writer's political views before encountering
the book or their desire to engage in activism after reading it.

While the student letters in previous chapters refer exclusively to Zinn's *People's History*, many adults were moved to connect with Zinn after reading his
other books and articles too or hearing his lectures or radio and television interviews. They were more familiar with his political activism and his broader
reach and impact. By the 1990s, many adults who wrote to Zinn had read his
book critiquing American ideology, *Declarations of Independence* (1990); his
memoir, *You Can't Be Neutral on a Moving Train* (1994); his antiwar writings
in *Z Magazine*, the *Nation*, and the *Progressive*; or attended talks he gave on
college campuses and bookstores. Approximately half the adults who wrote to
Zinn indicated that they had engaged with his other work beyond *A People's
History*. Not surprisingly, these adults had a more sophisticated understanding
of Zinn's contributions to historical and dissident writing than did the high
school students.

Among the constant stream of letters adults sent to Zinn from 1980 to 2010,
the theme of failed school history curricula appears most frequently. Those
who stressed this theme were inspired to write to Zinn because the engaging
American history presented in *A People's History* was such a contrast to the dull
and largely uncritical history instruction they had experienced in their school
years—whether that had been in the 1940s, 1950s, 1960s, or 1970s. In many ways,

this collection of letters is like a museum of educational failure, as again and again adults recount for Zinn the inadequate history education they received.

Many expressed disappointment that their schooling had deprived them of a critical perspective on American history. This left them all the more appreciative of Zinn's book for providing views from new and illuminating vantage points. As a woman from East Texas wrote to Zinn in 2001, "My husband and I just recently purchased PEOPLE's [History]. . . . Thanks for giving us all a different and very fresh look at the history we were taught in the 60s both in high school and college."[4] A People's History ignited in adult readers a new interest and even passion for history to the degree that they had been motivated to write Zinn. The cognitive dissonance experienced by many adult readers of the book (reminiscent of that expressed in many of the student letters to Zinn) led them to congratulate Zinn. As one typical adult wrote, "[A People's History] reversed that which I had learned before."[5]

Regardless of the age of the adult letter writers, many considered themselves to have been shortchanged by their history education. They expressed anger and consternation at the realization provoked by Zinn's book that the American history they had been taught in school consisted of "lies" or "sugar-coated" narratives. They praised Zinn for deepening their history education: "I want to thank you for the alternative education I have received by reading your exceptional book: A People's History of the United States. I was blown away with the posture you took juxtaposed to what I was taught in Burbank school system in California about American history. You really opened my eyes with the information you provided regarding the 50s, Vietnam, Watergate, the defiance of the War Powers Act, and the loony Reagan presidency."[6]

Adults conveyed to Zinn that his book had offered them a first look at some of the hard "truths" about American history ignored by the schools and textbooks of their youth.[7] A Colorado woman wrote, "I'll be real honest. When I first read your book, A People's History of the United States, I was really angry. . . . The fact that I went through 17 years in our public educational system without ever being told the truth about Columbus, the real class struggles, or the Ludlow Massacre (just to name a few) is very alarming to me. My husband is a native of Colorado and had never heard of the Ludlow Massacre before."[8] A midwesterner wrote, "[History] as it should be told was greatly stifled in my schooling. . . . A PEOPLE's HISTORY is the greatest piece of American Non-Fiction that has ever been written. It should be required reading for every single American. . . . Thank you so much for this book. You should mail a copy to the White House every four years . . . maybe they'll get the picture someday."[9]

Some adults wrote to Zinn about their difficult school experiences, including dropping out, and how reading *A People's History* motivated in them a new passion for education. One wrote Zinn, "I read [*A People's History*] shortly after dropping out of high school and getting my GED and it changed my life. Since then, I have wanted nothing else but to teach history. I remember principally dropping out because I knew something was wrong with the school system, and that I was not gaining any real . . . knowledge from attending. I see principally why that was is because of the way things were taught. Your book inspired me to venture back into the gaping intellectual black hole that is the public secondary school system, and teach history."[10] Another reader considered how things would have been different for him if had he been assigned *A People's History*: "It would have made for some amazing debates and enriched the quality of my high school education tremendously. . . . I normally do not write letters to authors I do not know, but your book challenged me almost like no other. . . . I just wanted to tell you as I finish the last pages of the last chapter, that I wished your text was introduced to me while I was taking AP U.S. History in high school.[11]

Many adult letters to Zinn expressed surprise: *A People's History* had showed that history wasn't boring but could be exciting, even transformative. A Texas man, e-mailed Zinn:

> I remember very vividly the first time I opened *A People's History* of the United States. By the time I turned page 150, I had to leave the book alone for almost a month while I absorbed what I had already covered. Your words reached me when I was very nearly a tabula rasa. I had taken the mandatory courses in history in high school and college but nothing more, and I didn't particularly enjoy those. It turned out that what I had considered boring about what I had been taught was less an expression of the subject or the teaching for that matter but more a result of the vacuousness of the ad campaign itself. . . . Finishing *A People's History* took nearly a year and a half as I had to take frequent breaks to allow my paradigm to shift. (Helen Keller a socialist? Columbus a tyrant?).[12]

Similarly, the graduate of a suburban high school outside Boston explained to Zinn that his history courses there had been "devoid of feeling and . . . not engaging." "When I reflect upon my World History class freshman year . . . , I am left with the sour taste of dissatisfaction. . . . Facts and objective text-book opinions dominated the class. Stories and anecdotes were never told."[13]

Others wrote to Zinn that in their classes American history had been whitewashed, focusing narrowly and uncritically on Anglo-Americans and political elites. A Minnesota woman in 2005 told Zinn, "[In my high school] we had studied to death the great acts of Indo-European patriotism and exploration. Skipping over any detail on Frederick Douglas[s] or Harriet Tubman my teachers felt that the mention of these individuals was merely enough. . . . By only giving mention the teacher essentially said that that was all these people were worth. . . . Events like colonizing the [Americas] and Manifest Destiny were acted upon by rich white men but the deeper history, [the] dirty little secrets, reveal[s] a thicker, richer past worth studying."[14]

Elders, including retirees, wrote Zinn, expressing a belief that the antiwar and egalitarian ideals in A People's History and in Zinn's own activism offered hope and inspiration that crossed generational lines. As one wrote, Zinn's book led him to "aspire to a more just, peaceful and equitable social future." An eighty-one-year old former attorney from Colorado, who was "a long time admirer of [Zinn's] work and activism for peace and justice," described himself as a "contemporary who has shared a lot of history with you." He thought Zinn's historical insights could be of great benefit to children his grandson's age. "[I am] helping to home-school an eleven-year-old grandson in history," he wrote, "[and] I am discouraged by the standard school texts that glorify Kings, generals and other oppressive leaders of the ruling classes." "Thus this letter," he continued. "It would be so good if you could . . . do a history of the U.S. for children from the same view point as your great book for adults so that youngsters could understand the class nature of oppression and injustice and aspire to a more just, peaceful and equitable social future."[15] Others also wrote to Zinn about their interest in exposing their grandchildren to the kind of historical narrative Zinn provided in A People's History that had been lacking in their own education.

A World War II veteran wrote to Zinn, "I'm not certain what defect in my habits is responsible for my having missed [A People's History] all these years, but I am grateful something changed enough for your book to burst into my consciousness." He mentioned to Zinn his "thirty years of teaching economics," and he noted, "[There were] a few years as a soldier (when you were also), a few years of marching in anti-war parades in the sixties, and a gradual transformation from devoted shill of capitalism to an intemperate socialist." He concluded: "[I am going to] immediately purchase twenty copies of A People's History of the United States and distribute them to my five children, ten grandchildren, and five special friends. If any one of them asks what seems to be wrong with the United States, I'll know he or she hasn't done his or her reading and I'll recommend studying chapters one through twenty. If any one of them asks, what can be done, I'll read chapter twenty-one aloud, even at the dinner table, where I will also toast to your good health and long life."[16]

Some of the most cosmopolitan letters came from Zinn readers born outside the United States. For them, reading A People's History served as a corrective to the simplistic portrayals of the United States they had been exposed to overseas. One who had moved from Israel to the United States in 1971 described how eye-opening *A People's History* had been as he completed "the American puzzle." "I consider myself lucky to have come across your *People's History*," he wrote. "Reading it was like finally attending the U.S. orientation class I seem to have missed when I landed at O'Hare in 1971. You have no idea how attractive America is made to look from afar. My descent to reality was long, steep, and involved several crashes which, however[,] managed to dislodge my head out of my a—."[17]

These education-centered letters from adults offer a contrast to Lepore's dismissing *A People's History* as being best suited for immature teens. If there is angst in such letters, it is not of the teenage variety but of adults feeling deprived of a truthful and meaningful history education. This is counterbalanced by hope, expressed most poignantly by grandparents, that future generations, in the wake of Zinn's book, will have a better experience with history education than their own.

Teachers who encountered *A People's History* were inspired to assign it to their students for some of the same reasons that stimulated such praise by other adults. They admired its accessibility and its revisionist, bottom-up narrative, and they appreciated Zinn's foregrounding of his political perspective and his critique of U.S. policies at home and abroad. Especially they noted the alternative it provided to the standard narrative of American exceptionalism, democratic progress, capitalist virtue, and benign role on the world stage.

Some college-level instructors shared with their high school counterparts dissatisfaction with the quality of writing in most U.S. history textbooks and saw *A People's History* as an attractive alternative. In 2000, for example, a community college professor in Southern California wrote Zinn that a textbook she had used the previous year, *The Enduring Vision*, was good compared to most but boring: "Most of my students didn't read much of it." Though she was "a little nervous" about assigning *A People's History* (owing to its "boldness in discussing class conflict"), she had done so since she thought students would find it more readable than the textbook. "Well that certainly happened!" she told Zinn. "I get only positive comments from the students about the book, even from students who don't completely agree with your views."[18] A Virginia Tech history professor reported that Zinn's book was the first she had ever used that was so popular with her students that most did not sell it back to the campus bookstore at the semester's end.[19]

With high school teachers, the textbook issue loomed especially large because, unlike for college professors, their history textbooks were mandated by their schools and districts rather than chosen by themselves. Thus, by far the most common theme across the high school teacher letters is dissatisfaction with the mandated textbooks. These teachers found their students bored by textbooks that watered down important controversies in American history involving classism, racism, and sexism. A Vancouver teacher wrote, "'Regular' history presents the accomplishments of those who generally represent about five percent of the population. . . . You present a much greater percentage."[20] A Minnesota teacher noted that women were nearly nonexistent in her textbook, unlike *A People's History*: "Your text included over eighty references to the sexism women face in our nation."[21]

Most teachers wrote to Zinn that they used his book comparatively with a textbook—much as we documented in Bill Patterson's Oregon classrooms discussed in chapters 3 and 4. A teacher in a suburb near Racine, Wisconsin, thanked Zinn for providing a contrast to Daniel Boorstin's conventional textbook, *A History of the United States*.[22] "[Your book was] so useful to my attempts to balance my U.S. History classes," she told him.[23] An AP U.S. history teacher in Tacoma had a class set of *A People's History* that she regularly paired with the standard textbook, by Michael Allen and Larry Schweikart's, *A Patriot's History of the United States*.[24] "My hope, for next year, is to develop a unit on the Industrial Revolution from our class set of *People's History* and then examine Allen's [chapter] "Sinews of Democracy" to look at how culture shapes government. This should be even more interesting than using the text[book] as the conservative point of view. . . . It is great to let the students question the text and work through responses that require analysis of data, not just vague generalizations."[25]

It is impressive that teaching Zinn's radical history versus a textbook worked so well in different high school settings and with students of varying skill levels. At a Seattle school, a teacher described her students as "working-class, African American, and former 'drop-outs.'" She recounted how engaged her students were by reading Zinn along with the textbook. "Sometimes we read no more than two pages when lively discussion erupts. I think we would be the envy of most high school teachers. . . . This is critical thinking in action. Isn't it amusing that the educational bureaucracy moans about how we teachers are slacking off and neglecting critical thinking skills and then spends millions of dollars on approved texts?"[26] Similarly, a teacher who wrote Zinn in the 1990s described her successful use of *A People's History* at her middle and high school for "students who were unable to function in a 'normal' school setting. . . . Most of the students were labeled as Emotionally Disturbed, Behavior Disordered teens. . . . Most were abused and abusive, involved in drugs and alcohol, had some connection with the court system . . . had no trust in anything, including themselves." She had used what she termed a "compare and contrast" approach in which her students read selections from *A People's History* alongside the standard textbook and thereby became energized to read and debate history:

> The class saw the American Revolution through different eyes; the eyes of the oppressed. We looked at the rich being able to buy substitutes to fight for them and compared it to today, to gangs. . . . Your book allowed me to bring history into today, to help students to look at human behavior and relationships. To encourage them to look at their history, the impact it had on them and how it could influence their future. The powerless were able to identify with those in history, to rage against the authority who should have made better choices.[27]

Though no teachers quite matched the longevity of Bill Patterson in having their students write Zinn letters about *A People's History* decade after decade, some who used the Zinn-versus-textbook teaching strategy did over shorter time periods have their students correspond with Zinn. Thomas Doyle, a teacher in a California magnet high school, had his students write Zinn as a culminating assignment in his classes from at least 1994 to 1998. His student letter writers were from diverse settings, ranging from advanced placement honors classes to ESL classes (with recent immigrants learning history while mastering English as a second language).[28] Doyle noted, "[My students had] grown tired of a text that required strict memorization of facts, and they find your interpretations of the past insightful."[29] He enjoyed comparing *A People's History* chapters to the textbook. "Of all the historians I assign," Doyle explained, "your works are always the most popular among my students, for your direct engagement of the human and moral issues never fails to ignite debate. I routinely use your chapter on WWI in regular classes, to give them an alternative to the traditional accounts."[30]

Some teachers' letters indicated that though they were enthusiastic using Zinn's historical insights in their teaching, they did not always concur with his views or want to push a political agenda in their classes. A Wisconsin teacher wrote to Zinn in 2000, "I just wanted you to know that you have heavily influenced me as an educator. I have read most of your books and although I do not always agree, I find the perspectives challenging and important. I will use your facts and perspectives in my classroom to challenge my students to understand differences and most importantly I will challenge them to think."[31] The teacher from Milwaukee who appreciated using Zinn in contrast to Boorstin's textbook explained, "Your third chapter was just what I had been needing." It had helped push students to think about the dynamics of war more deeply: "[Many of my students think] that any suggestion that war is avoidable is big-hearted and empty-headed." Then he shared with Zinn questions and reservations about politicizing his classrooms: "Is it appropriate for a teacher to openly challenge these orthodoxies, and if so, how is it best done? I do not want to indoctrinate them with my theories of non-violence, but I am equally averse to leaving these perverse beliefs alone." Similarly, a Missouri teacher wrote Zinn about indoctrination and teaching history, concluding he had most likely not been guilty of pushing his own agenda in his classroom. That teacher wrote, "Although my students hold a healthy disregard for Andrew Jackson and his policies and know that Christopher Columbus was no hero, I don't think I have radicalized any of them with my prejudices and views."[32]

In their correspondence with Zinn, college history teachers were more disposed than their high school counterparts to mix criticism with praise of Zinn's *People's History*. Almost all these professors had a high regard for Zinn's book as an innovative work that made accessible a critical, inclusive version of the American past, but many of them had their own knowledge base of radical history and used it to offer Zinn corrections and additions for the book's next edition. Among the most memorable of these was one sent by Roxanne Dunbar-Ortiz of Cal State Hayward's Native American Studies Department in 1981. Decades later, Dunbar-Ortiz would publish *An Indigenous People's History of the United States* (2014), which she credited Zinn with helping inspire.[33] In her 1981 letter to Zinn she called Zinn's book "brilliant," especially its discussion of Indians, Blacks, "the invasion of Mexico, and . . . imperialism." She wrote Zinn that she had "just finished reading with great satisfaction" the final essay exams of her class, which consisted of mostly working-class and "multi-national/ethnic" students who loved *A People's History* and learned effectively from it. But Dunbar-Ortiz urged Zinn to rethink some of the terminology he had used, suggesting that he drop "Negro" for "Black" (Zinn mostly used "black" but sometimes used "Negro" in his coverage of Reconstruction) and that he "not refer to Indians as among the 'excluded' groups in the colonial and early national period, when they were separate peoples and not national minorities."[34] Similar letters came from professors combining praise for *A People's History* with suggestions that he include gay and lesbian history, the struggle for disability rights, more coverage of the West Virginia coal wars, the Latinx struggle against discrimination, and the massacres of Native Americans.[35]

Unlike many college history courses, high school history classes are often housed in the field of social studies, which promotes forms of civic engagement and service learning. Teachers who viewed their historical teaching in this vein wrote that they were inspired by *A People's History's* activist spirit. They were delighted to have access to a book that made it possible for them to link history with civic engagement and activism. For Zinn and many of the teachers who wrote to him, it mattered that students—no matter their class or skin color—knew that real change in America often comes from below, when people organize to resist oppression. Both Zinn and these teachers thought that many textbooks failed to portray this as fundamental to American history. The teachers wanted their students to read about, in Zinn's words, the "human cost" of what may at first glance seem the "exciting story" of capitalist "financial ingenuity" and "the use of government for class purposes, to serve the needs of the wealthy and powerful, [which] has continued throughout American history, down to the present day."[36] Typical was a teacher who wrote Zinn about the empowering message he hoped his students learned from history. "While I have only recently begun reading your work, I find the ideas within it to be the ones I try to pass on to my students, in particular, the idea that we are not just recipients of history, but interpreters and agents of it."[37]

High school teachers who wrote to Zinn often agreed with him that elite-centered history ran contrary to democratic education and posed a barrier to politically engaged citizenry. They agreed with him that "the result of having our history dominated by presidents and generals and other 'important' people is to create a passive citizenry, not knowing its own powers, always waiting for some savior on high—God or the next president—to bring peace and justice."[38] A ninth-grade Boston humanities teacher thanked Zinn for showing her students at "an inner-city school with a high poverty population" that "once in a while, the wretched of the earth do find a voice in history."[39]

Many high school teachers who wrote to Zinn were committed to reforming history education. This meant incorporating history from the bottom up into their teaching and challenging nationalistic myths perpetuated by their textbooks. This could be politically sensitive when done in conservative regions—which is one reason Zinn expressed admiration for teachers who dared to use his book in the face of pushback. For example, a teacher from California wrote to Zinn that she had been "accused by fellow teachers of teaching 'revisionist' history." "I respond by gladly admitting [this]," she said. "As any good historian knows, historical research is constantly undergoing scrutiny and revision. History to me is a dynamic and evolving discipline that should bear microscopic evaluation. . . . I particularly enrage a fellow history teacher, and native Texan, when in my classes I dispel some of the myths of the Alamo."[40] Tom, a Wisconsin high school teacher, wrote to Zinn in 2000 that the textbook provided by his school was Boorstin's *History of the United States*, and his use of select chapters from *A People's History* to challenge Boorstin was considered controversial in his school setting. "I have," this teacher confided to Zinn, "been chastised publicly by parents for teaching your book, [and] my name among some of the students is 'Tomrade.'" However, he persisted. "[Your book is] so very useful to my attempts to balance my U.S. history classes," he wrote. "This conservative bunch thinks that any suggestion that war is avoidable is big-hearted and empty-headed," he said. Nevertheless, he was determined to encourage questioning by his students.[41]

Although college professors enjoyed greater academic freedom than their high school counterparts, they too knew political heat from assigning Zinn. Conservative media, politicians, and organizations such as Accuracy in Academia in the 1980s, and with their successors in this century, made headlines going after professors associated with the Left, and Zinn and his book were prime targets. While there is no evidence that professors risked their jobs by assigning *A People's History* to their students, high school teachers in conservative regions were aware that it was daring to assign Zinn. As with the undaunted high school teacher above, untenured college professors showed daring in their determination to use *A People's History* to provoke their students to question traditional assumptions. This can be seen, for example, in the case of an adjunct professor of economics in Utah who in 2004 wrote Zinn, "I've been using your book as a major text for the past ten years despite confronting what must surely be some of the most conservative students in the nation. I'll continue using it [even though] . . . Utah . . . has given the Republican candidate for the presidency a higher percentage of the vote in the presidential elections than any other state. We liberals could hold our state convention in a phone booth. You get the picture."[42]

Equally impressive at both the high school and university level were the linkages teachers and professors made between using *A People's History* in their classrooms and their goals for an improved history education in general. As one high school teacher from Connecticut explained to Zinn, he found it thrilling that students were "pleased to read history that is so detailed and vivid after years of the pedantic prose they find so often in [conventional texts]." This teacher wrote:

> [I am] trying to teach my students that learning history isn't simply about facts and years, and timelines, and memorizing presidents. I'm teaching them that history is about people, about ordinary people doing extraordinary things that anyone—including any student in my room—is quite capable of. I want them to understand that the writing of history is affected by bias, by colonialism, by racism, and that there is no "one way" to look at history. I want them to be good critical readers and thinkers, and to learn how to do history, not just to read it. I want them to know that there are controversies, and let them examine all sides of these controversies and decide for themselves what they think.

These are just some of the objectives of my class. . . . I want you to know that you have been very influential on me both as a teacher and as a historian, and that your influence is very present in my class.[43]

The letters to Zinn written by high school and college teachers suggest some interesting differences as well as parallels in usage patterns of A People's History. Among the differences is that, because of its demanding reading level, in high schools Zinn's book seems to have been used most frequently in advanced courses, by honors and advanced placement classes. In contrast, college history department usage of A People's History seems to have occurred mostly at less elite institutions, especially community colleges. A community college instructor explained to Zinn, "With a large number [of students] who are poorly prepared for college-level work[,] the limitation I'm most frustrated with is knowing that I can't assign too much reading or ask the students to buy too many books. For that reason, being able to rely on one or two texts is very important."[44] While elite college and university history courses might require a standard textbook plus multiple other books, reliability as an anchor text made Zinn's book appealing for community college teachers.[45] Also appealing to community college teachers was the focus in A People's History on people of color and the working class, since these groups constitute a far larger share of the student population in community colleges than they do in elite colleges. This inclusive historical focus also made Zinn popular with teachers of second-chance and underserved high school students, who braved the problem that not all of their students were easily able to read at Zinn's level, since they found Zinn's perspectives on race and class so appealing to their students.

Some of the letters also overlapped in expressing to Zinn gratitude for providing an example of how to be a scholar, teacher, and activist simultaneously. For these teachers, Zinn comes off as a kindred spirit whose work demonstrated that the academic profession and teaching were compatible with political engagement. Thus, a professor who was director of graduate studies at a school in Colorado wrote to Zinn after he had heard him speak in person. "Thanks for being such an excellent role model for those of us who wish to be both scholars and activists. Your phrase 'clarity and passion' captures well the spirit of that dual enterprise."[46]

Also prominent among adults writing to Zinn were college students. Some had been assigned A People's History by a college professor, but many read the book on their own initiative. These students' letters to Zinn often included reflections on the poor history education they had received in school and how Zinn's book served as a powerful contrast now that they were in college. Some of these college students were already open to Zinn's radical perspective on American history, while others seemed shocked by content and analyses to which they had never been exposed before. Undergraduates and graduate students wrote to Zinn about how his work influenced projects they carried out at their universities, and some credited Zinn's book for their decision to study history or to become history teachers.

A common theme in this group of letters is that college students experienced a new interest in history, a subject many had been alienated from previously. A Columbia University college junior wrote Zinn in 2001 describing her history education: "For so many years, my parents and teachers sequestered me in an air bubble. In this imaginary world I could only see the U.S. government as honorable and righteous, [a] benefactor to the world at large. *A People's History of the United States* . . . rejuvenated my interest in American history, and inspired me to become involved in not just international human rights work (which had previously been my focus) but [also to] volunteer for national organizations." She thanked Zinn for giving her hope, even though she considered many things about the "state of the world" troubling. "Your writing keeps me from becoming despondent about the state of the world, and the political apathy of my friends, and fellow students. . . . I firmly believe it is only appropriate to thank someone whose work has truly played a major role in my life."[47]

Other students wrote that Zinn's narrative pushed them to finally engage in a critical assessment of the American past. A New Zealand college student thanked Zinn for teaching him "for the first time" to question historical narratives. "I recently finished reading your book *A People's History of the United States* (2nd ed.), following the reference to it in the movie 'Good Will Hunting.' . . . It has certainly forced me to rethink orthodox or mainstream accounts of history, and to look more critically at many aspects of history generally—along with more contemporary events." For this student, reading *A People's History* had been the inspiration for some of his own academic work. "[Your] book was one of the most thought provoking I have ever read, and has provided the inspiration for my law honors project, which relates to the philosophical vs. pragmatic origins of the U.S. Constitution. . . . In 'Good Will Hunting' your book was described as one that would blow your mind away. I must confess it certainly blew mine."[48]

Some college students wrote to Zinn after reading *A People's History* because of how it liberated them from the parochialism of their hometowns and their conservative schools. A college student from Diamond Springs, California, wrote Zinn about her struggles in high school as a progressive person in a largely conservative community. "I was embarrassed in high school to stand up for anything except the staunch conservative views doled out by 99 percent of the kids and teachers where I was raised—a small, mostly white, almost totally Republican community. I don't know why, but something in me just didn't agree with all that Hillary [Clinton] bashing." The student was concerned about what had been omitted from her history education.

> When, during my junior year in high school, I asked my history teacher about the internment of our Japanese-American citizens during World War II, she just sort of mumbled something to me about there being a page or two about it in my history book. (Mind you, before my junior year in high school, I had never even heard of this occurring, even though I have been a resident of California ever since I was born, and for all of the years I attended public schools. In addition, I have been taking American history courses since elementary school.) And I didn't know why my history book seemed to have glossed over it. . . . And in American Government, when we learned about affirmative action, the people made out to be the enemies of democracy were the big, bad minorities who were taking away rights from the poor. . . . These are the things that I learned, and this is the way that I learned them. . . . I became jaded and disinterested with history, sociology and the like for a while.

So for her, reading A People's History in college was a transformative experience: "I read the first chapter, . . . [and] I was shocked to learn about the way Columbus had treated the Native Americans. And here I had thought he was some big hero. . . . I was amazed and quite saddened to learn about the ways that people in power have utilized their money and resources to maintain that power throughout history. These people were not kings, not earls or dukes, but our own elected representatives, and owners of big businesses."[49]

Some college students were inspired after reading A People's History to engage with historical study more seriously, even motivating them to major in history. One student's letter referenced learning from Zinn that history was more than the "accomplishments of famous politicians and great men." "Reading [your] book," this student asserted, "I saw that history encompasses the story of ordinary people, how they have survived and persevered and organized for something." The novelty of this approach—which contrasted so dramatically with the top-down historical view in her high school classes—led her to emulate Zinn via her research in college. "[I was] in the process of formulating an honors thesis about a group of women in Seattle who demonstrated for rent control and lower food prices during the Great Depression, and came to realize that they had a stake . . . in working to change the system." She linked what she had read in A People's History to political and social activism, something other students wrote about in their letters to Zinn. "History to me is in part this story: how so-called ordinary people can work for change and how we can learn from them as we pursue our own activism. Thank you, Howard Zinn."[50]

Graduate students wrote to Zinn acknowledging that his work had influenced their own education trajectories. A doctoral candidate in African American studies wrote to Zinn, "Your book, *A People's History of the United States*, was the single most important text that sparked my desire to learn African American history. I was simply 'blown away' by your fantastic historical analysis. I learned things that shocked my senses and I have not been the same since (thank goodness)." He shared with Zinn text he had included in a fellowship application: "In college, I read Howard Zinn's *A People's History of the United States*. Zinn's work made me keenly aware of the shortcomings of my American history teachings and opened my eyes to a side of history [of] which I had almost no knowledge. Furthermore, it filled in large gaps of historiography created by ethnocentric scholarship that denied the integral part African Americans played in the creation of this nation."[51]

A doctoral student in history wrote to Zinn contrasting Zinn's activist example with the quiescent political stance of historians as a group: "As you know, the historical profession is on the whole quite conservative. Graduate students typically care more about making their cv's shine than making our workplaces, programs, and society more democratic—and less militaristic. The majority of history professors do not see themselves as historical actors or, in their public silence, as being complicit in maintaining the status quo. At times, it is depressing. . . . In many ways (my journey has been) partly inspired by your work as a scholar, activist, [and] public intellectual. For that, I thank you."[52] Similarly, a high school history teacher who had recently completed his history MA at William and Mary wrote to Zinn, "My graduate advisor's opinion notwithstanding, I really admire your work; I decided against PhD studies for now because I think the academy is way out of touch with the mass of the population. But your work, Mr. Zinn, is reaching people and bringing young minds to question what they have been taught about history."[53]

College student letters to Zinn often reflect great enthusiasm and a desire to have a personal connection with Zinn. This was true for students at community colleges as well as from more elite, private colleges and for both history majors and those with other majors. A Tufts University student wrote to Zinn after being assigned chapters of *A People's History* in a course called Social Movements in an "Experimental College" Peace Studies Department. "One of our assignments was 3 chapters from *A People's History*. . . . I read the entire book. I could not put it down. I gave it to all of my friends. And my parents. DO NOT STOP WRITING!" This student wanted to work for Zinn, asking whether Zinn had a job for him as a research assistant that summer.[54]

The college student letters and those from other adults to Zinn clear up one of the mysteries about *A People's History*: its emergence as a best seller in the conservative 1980s. Why would a leftist history of the United States sell more copies each year during the Reagan era, when the nation's political leadership had shifted so decisively to the right? The answer was that for many of the adults who wrote to Zinn, he was a kind of anti-Reagan—genuinely eloquent and learned, rather than acting from a script, and offering a critical perspective on capitalism, war, and race that opposed policies championed by the conservative president and his supporters. Zinn and his book kept alive the egalitarian ethos of 1960s social movements during the dark days of Reagan-Bush era of the 1980s and early 1990s, with their cuts in the safety net of social programs, dismantling of the New Deal order, soaring military budgets, counterrevolutionary wars, and indifference to the AIDS epidemic. These letters underscore what Anthony Arnove, who worked closely with Zinn on many projects, wrote about the role of *A People's History* in adult readers' political lives across the decades. Arnove saw the book as providing "sustenance to a progressive countercurrent that developed from the early 1980s," which he believed was a key reason why *A People's History* resonated so widely with adult readers both in the Reagan years and since.[55]

Though Americans after the 1960s have been portrayed by some historians and journalists as turning inward and retreating from civic life, the adult letters to Zinn in the 1980s provide powerful documentary evidence of continuing progressive political engagement.[56] The majority of the adults who wrote to Zinn were to different degrees politically engaged, which brought them to engage with Zinn, a scholar-activist whom they saw as informed, principled, and inspiring. Adults who wrote to Zinn after the Reagan years also aimed to connect with him around social and political issues that were of concern to them in and after the 1990s, especially the unending wars of the early twenty-first century of which Zinn was among the most prominent critics. Indeed, one of the reasons sales of *A People's History* increased in its second and third decade was because Zinn continued to be applicable to current issues in ways that adult readers found relevant, meaningful, and even remarkable.

In the late twentieth century and early twenty-first century, when Americans seemed to have lost touch with Martin Luther King Jr.'s democratic vision of a country free from racism, war, and poverty, Zinn's writing allowed countless readers to feel that they were not alone, that an eloquent and appealing scholar-activist affirmed their views. Thus, many of these letters show adults seeking connection with Zinn, whom they viewed as a like-minded ally. Many convey gratitude and a sense of relief, as if Zinn was a confidant, friend, political soul mate, even therapist—who shared and articulated their dissident view of the American past and present. For example, a man from Madison, Wisconsin, assumed that he and Zinn shared political perspectives, including on the "Bush-monster and his cronies." This letter writer made a link between George W. Bush's presidency and the history of resistance in the United States that Zinn documented. "It is crucial that people understand the cycles of history. Only the scale of what Bush is doing is new, the arrogance and hatred of our 'leaders' is old news in this country. . . . This nation was built on resistance and we must tap into that now and bring peace."[57]

Zinn's history embodied for many adults values and beliefs that resonated with them personally. To such readers *A People's History* offered clarity regarding their own thought. "Frankly," wrote a reader from Brooklyn,

> I've become one of your ardent admirers, and have read, or am in the midst of reading, just about every book of yours that's in print. . . . You see, I was born a Democrat, in Brooklyn, New York, and thus have regarded myself, all my life, as a genetic liberal. . . . But by the time I read your book, I had seen the demise of liberalism in this country, and didn't know how to re-focus my rage at the systemic injustices we live with. . . . I had written letters to the editors of various newspapers, laying blame on Mr. Clinton and his New Democrats, for example, for abandoning the core principles of the democratic party. What your book did for me was to help me realign my social and political philosophy and find a home in progressive thought. So thank you for your impact, and for helping me bridge the gap in my thinking. . . . There's an old saying that if a man is not a socialist at 20, he has no heart, and if he's not a conservative at 50, he has no brain. I would like to add that if he is not a progressive by the time he is 70, he has no soul."[58]

Similarly, a twenty-one-year-old man from Ohio emotionally shared his admiration for Zinn's "unbiased examination of the awful history of our government." "What I would give to meet you, kind sir! . . . [I have] nearly finished this monstrous epic on the making of the modern fascist America, and I must commend you. . . . As long as there is one man being stepped on for the benefit of any others, that one, many will find the strength to rise up. I am amassing my very own strength, sir, wrought in the fires of oppression, and it is with heartfelt enthusiasm that I greet you . . . and your history, knowing at last that I AM NOT ALONE."[59]

It was no accident that in dark and at times almost hopeless years for American leftists and liberals, Zinn seemed a beacon of hope, presenting resistance as a powerful theme in American history. After all, Zinn had written *A People's History* to "awaken a great consciousness of class conflict, racial injustice, sexual inequality, and national arrogance."[60] For this he received harsh criticism from non-radicals for reducing "historical analysis to political opinion."[61] But for Zinn, history's utility was linked with its capacity to motivate and inspire people to organize for change. To this end, he hoped to "bring to the light the hidden resistance of the people against the power of the establishment." People who appear to have no power, once they organize, Zinn expressed, have "a voice no government can suppress."[62] These ideas resonated with many adults who read A People's History. They passed it around to friends and family, distributed copies of chapters to students, and found perspectives offered in the book to be inspiring, a kind of inoculation against the greed, militarism, and indifference to racial and class inequity that ran rampant as America drifted rightward after the 1960s.

When we first began reading the admiring letters adults sent to Zinn, we were struck not only by their number but also by the way readers combined historical with political commentary. How, we wondered, could we separate out readers' admiring responses to A People's History from their responses to Zinn's role as a radical antiwar activist and political commentator in print, at the podium, and on alternative radio and even occasionally on television? It became evident that it was not possible or desirable to separate out responses to his different roles because both Zinn's readers and Zinn himself saw them as inextricably linked. The volume of letters from adults, addressing history, politics, and activism, stands as evidence that Zinn succeeded in his search for a usable past. The stories he told of America's history of resistance to war, racism, economic exploitation, and sexism fostered critical thought and political engagement among countless readers.

There is often an air of exhilaration in the letters from readers who credited Zinn's work with enabling them to recognize the roots of oppression in the American social order and the hostility and violence of its foreign policy. This was the mindset of a Connecticut man who compared his experience reading Zinn to escaping darkness: "I saw your talk at Eastern Connecticut [State University]. One of the students mentioned that he 'got depressed' when he read your 'People's History. . . .' You were saddened to hear that. Well, don't be sad. I think that young man had other problems because when I read your work, I feel just the opposite. As if a dark veil has been raised. I consider your writing to be a toolbox to be used to dismantle the lies of the ruling class/power elite and I thank you."[63]

The antiwar theme and evidence in A People's History brought some readers to make life-changing decisions, such as breaking with the U.S. military. This was the case with a veteran who e-mailed Zinn, "[Your books have been] part of my awakening politically. I read *People's History* when I was in the Navy and decided soon after that I couldn't be in the Navy anymore. Your book literally changed my life for the better. It helped me see through fog."[64]

There was such admiration and even love expressed in many letters and e-mails to Zinn from his adult readers that one can characterize it as a form of fan mail, especially in those that sound quite hyperbolic. But such correspondence offers powerful evidence that Zinn connected to his readers much more effectively than authors of other introductory works of American history, and it shows that they saw him not solely as an academic but also as someone with whom they felt a personal connection. It is unusual for academics to receive such letters as the one Zinn got from a New Yorker raving that *A People's History* was "a gem—a must read for every resident of the planet earth."[65] Or the one from a Texan who wrote Zinn that he had made "an important contribution to all mankind."[66] Or the one from a Massachusetts woman impressed by Zinn's eloquence and persona, having read *A People's History* and having attended a talk he gave. "To tell you the truth, I expected an old plump professor, hunched by years of teaching and writing, who (I hoped) would uplift somewhat my dismal outlook on life. . . . What I saw was a tall, thin, vibrant man, whose smile would put a sunflower to shame . . . as I listened, I said to myself, I would have given an arm and a leg to have had a history teacher like you."[67] Or from Ron Kovic, the author, antiwar activist, and Vietnam veteran: "How can words even begin to express what you have meant to our country and to the millions of people who have been touched by your teachings and your work. . . . You have truly made your life stand for something important."[68] Echoing such sentiments, an English teacher working at a middle school in Mexico e-mailed Zinn, "[I am] writing to let you know that, although I have never met you, I love you. You are a success Dr. Zinn, not because you are famous and/or wealthy. You're a big success because you tried, and continue to try, to make the world a better place." [69]

Some adults made personal connections in their letters between their political views and their lived experience, as when a retiree, a former member of the U.S. Air Force who participated in air raids when in combat (as Zinn had), wrote to Zinn: "I am now reading your *People's History of the United States* and have greatly appreciated your many articles and commentaries over the years and most recently those relating to the Iraq massacre." He lamented the napalm bombing he had carried out as "a crime."

I also flew with the Eighth and participated in two raids on Point de Grave (Royan). One to carry napalm and a second one to drop anti personnel bombs. . . . Those poor conscripts holed up there would have willingly surrendered.

Just after we dropped our bombs on the second mission we could see the French Landing craft, that had been circling the mother ships, start heading in. I don't know how many French men needlessly died, nor how many Germans, but we lost a few aircraft and crews as a result of collisions. Keep up the good work. It's guys like you who give me hope and faith in the human race.[70]

A Methodist pastor wrote to Zinn in 1995: "Back in 1992, a group of us, in counter celebration of Columbus' invasion, met each Wednesday . . . at 6:00 a.m. and read aloud and discussed, chapter by chapter, . . . *People's History of the United States*. . . . So much of your personal journey as an activist makes me think of my own, although my own activism has been more limited." But that activism, which he recounted, made him feel a personal connection to Zinn, who he knew was a historian whose view of the American past was influenced by his own role in the Black freedom movement in the South and in the movement against the Vietnam War. "I became involved in the civil rights movement in 1962," the pastor recalled, "when, in the first church I served I invited a new black family in the community to join our all-white church, after which all hell broke loose. I was in the March on Washington, marched in Selma the day after Bloody Sunday, was arrested for the first time while supporting women in a National Welfare Rights Organization march around the U.S. Capit[o]l. (I was tried with two white priests and we were acquitted by an all-black jury.) . . . I was arrested several times at the White House in re the Vietnam war, nuclear disarmament, South African apartheid, etc."[71]

Other adults described the role reading *A People's History* played in their understanding of how to engage politically as citizens moving forward. For example, one such reader, who found that reading *A People's History* was enlightening and "inspirational" ("an understatement"), wrote Zinn, "Without works such as yours, the rest of us would remain ignorant of our history and of our ability to challenge self-interested authority. . . . As one of the 'prison guards,' I too would like to work towards reclaiming our humanity."[72]

A significant number of adults wrote to Zinn that his political writings and activism had influenced their professional work. This was the case with a twenty-seven-year-old Chicano film director who, after completing his first film for public television, described how *A People's History* had inspired him:

History told by those who lived it rather than official history from the perspective of the powers of the day was what we were working toward (in our most recent project). It was in fact your book *A People's History of the United States* which gave much inspiration to produce Public Television from a different point of view than what tradition normally requires. Documentarians like historians are encouraged to use standards of objectivity and balance when it comes to the dialogue of the airwaves. This battle over context has been a great source of frustration for me. It has been good having you on the bookshelf, a voice of sanity and a confirmation that others have considered the same dilemmas I now face with PBS.[73]

Other adults wrote to Zinn about how reading *A People's History* had initiated for them personal reflection that led to a realignment of their political philosophy and politics. A Montana man described how reading the book had started his "journey to political consciousness." "I couldn't believe it," he wrote. "It seemed preposterous that the United States the grand and beautiful country of my birth could have done all of these terrible things. . . . Reading *A People's History of the United States* changed my life. Reading *You Can't Be Neutral on a Moving Train* changed it again. In [the] hours it took me to read your book[s] my entire perspective on life has changed. Now I can understand the incomparable power of people to change what is wrong with the world." This letter writer referred to a speech Zinn had given on *A People's History* in which he described "ours as a great quiz show culture. . . . A nation obsessed with trivia."

Reading his assigned high school "accepted reading," this man had been exposed to the "lists of how many killed here, how many manufactured here and the great omnipresent wonders of the capitalist system." "Your book," he wrote to Zinn, "may have shown me not just a little slice of truth but [also] for once a deeper vein of hopefulness. . . . Again[,] you have changed my life for the better, and I felt I should write to you, partly because I wanted to share my story, however small it may be, but mostly so I could thank you with all my being and soul for showing me the truth and for sharing a little part of your life.[74]

Some letter writers attributed to Zinn a newfound ability to think for themselves and thanked him for changing the way they "saw the world." A New Yorker e-mailed Zinn : "Your book . . . changed my life and the way I look at our country. It is filled with courage, sadness and love in a way that I never thought could be incorporated in a history book."[75] For this reader, Zinn's historical writing was innovative and inspiring. A Minnesota woman wrote Zinn, "[Reading *A People's History*] has been an eye-opener. . . . My historical world exploded with the information about the exploited and ignored. . . . Punching holes in the knowledge widely accepted by most Americans is a difficult task."[76] Similarly, a Nigerian American college student wrote to Zinn, "Your books . . . shaped my political ideologies. In the past I have not been interested in anything historical or political but your books have really made an impact on me so I even changed my major from business to political science and criminal justice. I just felt the need to thank you for opening the eyes of your readers, for us to not take things at face value but to carefully evaluate the reason why our government engages in various actions and conflicts."[77]

Some credited Zinn with contributing to dramatic "transformation" of their attitudes and views, saying that reading *A People's History* helped them become politically radicalized. A reader from California wrote,

> You, along with Sidney Lens and Jonathan Kozol, have had a profound in-
> fluence on my thoughts about and my views of the United States—so much
> so that I have become a confirmed socialist and now firmly believe there can
> be no social and economic justice in this country until we destroy corporate
> capitalism and dismantle the military-industrial-complex.... The transforma-
> tion of my attitudes and views is all the more remarkable, I believe, when one
> considers that I grew up believing the myths, lies and legends about the United
> States, attended the Military Academy at West Point and served 21 years in
> the army. I hope that you will continue to write such powerful and revealing
> books which are so necessary in a society which appears to be disintegrating.[78]

Adult letters to Zinn were so often politically charged because his writings about bringing "democracy alive" and writing history to empower people were a major departure from the conventions of academic historical discourse.[79] Zinn found it gratifying that *A People's History* helped bolster adult activism over the course of decades. A Kansas man wrote to him in 1996, "I just wanted to let you know that *People's History* changed my life. It was a turning point that made me turn to full time activism."[80] For readers, the connections Zinn made between history and activism in *A People's History* were powerful—especially in the book's final chapter (in its first edition), "The Coming Revolt of the Guards," where Zinn advocated for and even predicted a new wave of historically informed and trans-formative protest movements. Thus, a clinical psychologist wrote Zinn in April 2001 that this chapter was "perhaps the single most compelling [thing] . . . I have ever read." In this chapter Zinn defended his biases as a historian, while severely criticizing the "American system" for sustaining gross inequality of wealth and suppression of dissent. Zinn called for the transformation of society through tac-tics used in the past—"demonstrations, marches, civil disobedience, strikes and boycotts and general strikes; direct action to redistribute wealth, to reconstruct institutions" so that "our grandchildren, or our great grandchildren, might pos-sibly see a different and marvelous world." Reading this brought many adults to view Zinn as a role model with whom they wanted to correspond.[81]

Reading *A People's History* for many adults affirmed for them the power of their own voices, and some promised Zinn in their letters that they would use theirs to work for change. For example, a woman from New Mexico wrote to Zinn that reading *A People's History* helped her realize that a "lone voice does matter. . . . Even though I am a white woman who has enjoyed many privileges . . . I have also considered myself fairly progressive and leftist. Your brilliant, in-depth work has not only opened my eyes and heart to my privileges and blindness of what other people are not as privileged to enjoy, but also to the fact that my lone voice does matter. You have helped me to begin educating myself. I will never stay silent again. I promise."[82]

While many adults wrote to Zinn about the importance of political activism, some were at a loss as to how to proceed. A twenty-seven-year-old man from New York City e-mailed Zinn in 2004 expressing his desire to "make a difference . . . I just finished reading *A People's History of the United States* last night. . . . I subscribe to virtually all of what you say . . . but what confuses me most is how do I make a difference? I am climbing my way into the Upper Middle Class of America. . . . I know this country needs change—but is it possible for something this radical to occur (what you lightly proposed towards the end of the book?) What am I to do if I want to make a difference? . . . I can only hope to put some of my actions into helping this country to better itself any way possible."[83]

Others saw more clearly how they could participate in making progressive change and cited Zinn's work as inspiration for their political activities in and outside of their communities. A Virginian wrote Zinn, "As a teacher, youth worker, and parent of . . . three grown children, you truly have been an inspiration to me (going back to your anti-Vietnam work). . . . You have helped me become radical in the sense you and others have used the word: to get to the root cause of events. You have helped me to be able to pass some of what I have learned about being radical and an involved person to the young people I have worked with over the years. . . . You are ten years older than I am. I hope that I can be as involved and aware as you are if I make it another 10 years."[84]

At first glance, a reading of these politically charged letters might seem to confirm the fear among right-wing critics that Zinn was too dangerous to expose students to since his *People's History* promoted radicalization and affirmed leftist politics among adults. But Zinn's impact on history teaching and learning was far from identical inside and outside the classroom. The high school student letters and adult letters to Zinn indicate that we cannot universalize reader responses to Zinn since these varied according to the educational and social context, and depending on the letter writer's age, politics, and life experience. Judging by the political conversion experiences recounted by many adults in their letters, it seems that they, not Lepore's rebellious teenagers, responded most emotionally and impulsively to Zinn's book. A key difference was that high school students most often read *A People's History* under the guidance of their teachers, who presented the book in a comparative context, reading Zinn simultaneously with conventional textbooks. This meant students were less likely than adult readers to encounter Zinn as a soloist to gush over but instead were hearing a kind of duet and had to constantly consider how Zinn's voice compared—favorably and unfavorably—to that of more conventional historians.

Zinn also appealed to adult curiosity about the relationship between history books and political bias. As shown in chapter 1, *A People's History* explored whether it was possible or even desirable for historians to write objective history. Intrigued by such questions, many adult letters expressed gratitude to Zinn for being upfront with his biases while providing information they believed conventional textbooks and other histories ignored or misrepresented. Thus, a British reader wrote Zinn in response to *A People's History's* final chapter, "The Coming Revolt of the Guards," "Wow! That has to be one of the most powerful cases I have heard in support of polemical history. As you rightly stress, those who argue for 'balanced' history are merely offering an alternative bias."[85] Similarly, a Los Angeles attorney expressed appreciation for Zinn's "refreshing conception of a historian's role" and for not claiming "to be objective in the disingenuous sense of pretending to lack any social grounding or perspective derived from your own experience. . . . In fact, by acknowledging your biases and inclinations, you actually give the reader the feeling that you will do your best to *accurately* present the different viewpoints that you criticize." He contrasted Zinn's candor and sophistication on such issues with his own college education in history:

> My undergraduate degree from Harvard in 1988 was (nominally) in history, where that term—with no more than a token nod to historiography—was dryly defined as "recording of things said or done in the past." In contrast, I was pleased to encounter your description of history (roughly), "the present recounting of the past, done as an act of the present, by people of the present, and that affects the social structure of the present." I feel your definition provides a much more accurate statement of what history is truly about. Few histories are written to be documents recording the past; rather most histories are written with an eye towards influencing and shaping present behavior, by emphasizing selected precedential "lessons" from the past. Your candid recognition that history has a social effect on the present gives your books a dimension of relevancy.[86]

The adult letters to Zinn include vivid reactions to the pessimism-optimism tension in *A People's History*, with Zinn's indictment of American political and economic leaders versus his appreciation for resistance to oppressive acts of the power elite. More moderate readers had a tendency to respond critically to the indictment, which they sometimes found too sweeping and depressing, but most adult letter writers embraced Zinn's upbeat message about resistance.

Exemplifying the moderate response, a man in his sixties wrote from Italy, where his wife was studying on a Fulbright scholarship, "I've learned much from your history and am very glad that I read it. . . . But I felt defeated at the end. I have to ask: Do you really believe there were no good presidents? Not even one? Not even Roosevelt, whom my parents idolized because he gave desperate people such hope? Social Security alone, inadequate as it is especially in contrast to Western European social service systems, has made the difference between destitution and a tolerable life to elderly and disabled Americans."[87] Similarly, from Philadelphia came a message from a reader who experienced *A People's History* as a "breath of fresh air" but thought Zinn erred in failing to acknowledge a "progressive trend in history," that human society, based on lessons learned, does progress over time.[88]

Most readers who wrote to Zinn, however, had little reservation about his critical perspectives on American history. As an Albany, New York, writer put it,

> [I can] think more clearly after reading your books. Now I really understand what healthy skepticism means.
>
> Having the truth about U.S. history revealed to me has been both distressing and refreshing. In my case, the refreshing, liberating (". . . the truth will set you free") aspect has gotten the upper hand. But I can understand for many who have invested so much of their lives in the prevailing ideology, the truth may seem threatening. . . . I was raised in a conservative Evangelical Protestant home, the home of a pastor, and a young dunderheaded Republican. Only in the past couple of years have I begun to question the way things are in this country. Thanks to great truth tellers like you, Noam Chomsky, Barbara Ehrenreich, William Greider, etc. I have been encouraged to imagine a better world. Thank you for helping me awaken my conscience.[89]

Among adult letters to Zinn, more than a dozen came from prisons, attesting to the wide reach of *A People's History*. Zinn, a prison abolitionist who had published *Justice in Everyday Life: The Way It Really Works* (1974), a book sharply critical of incarceration, became aware of their cases and advocated on their behalf.[90] Some prisoners' letters spoke glowingly about what *A People's History* meant to them and fellow inmates. One recounted how the book was read, quoted, and debated:

> Dear Dr. Zinn, I have just received your letter to Prosecutor M——. Thank you for taking an interest in my case. You[r] letter holds great meaning for

me outside of its intended context. I am a great fan of your historical work *A People's History of the United States*. . . . In some respects your letter is much like a Michael Jackson fan receiving that famous glove. Except of course in this case a person from urban America rarely meets or hears from the people from whom *they* have learned so much. Your work . . . became the hottest and most often copied book in this institution. It was studied and discussed; it was used to resolve factual disputes. The question: Have you read the "Zinn book," at one point became the currency of social and political awareness if the answer was "yes" and a trip to the copy machine if the answer was "no." Your book has literally changed gang members into social and political activists. [91]

Some readers sent Zinn tender, idiosyncratic, and even eccentric expressions of appreciation for Zinn and his work. One included photos of his own child named for Zinn, Maxwell Zinn P——, explaining, "We continue to read your work and when Max gets old enough, I can assure you he will get his own copy of 'A People's History.'"[92] Zinn wrote back with delight, exclaiming, "[It is] such an honor to have you give Maxwell my name!"[93] Another included a photo depicting the tattoo of Zinn's profile she'd had inked on her stomach.[94] A chocolate company founder asked to use *A People's History* in a special chocolate gift box: "I want permission to use the entire 18th chapter from The People's History of the United States, 'The Impossible Victory: Vietnam,' for . . . [a] project [of] my company, [I]ntelligent [C]hocolates, producers of USDA certified organic artisan chocolate truffles."[95]

These examples indicate the warmth and admiration displayed by Zinn's loyal adult readership. The letters sent to Zinn attest that reading *A People's History* could make soldiers leave the military, convince dropouts to go back to school, and convert apolitical adults into radical activists. The book in many cases gave people what was for them a new way of looking at history and politics, while affirming that history was on their side.

Beyond the conceptual, political, and historical content of *A People's History*, Zinn was an extraordinarily engaging writer, the opposite of academics who produced jargon-filled and inaccessible tomes. Many adult letters commented on the quality of Zinn's writing, praising his reader-friendly style and lack of pretense. A New Jersey reader wrote, "What surprised me was not the book's content itself, fascinating though it is, but the fact that someone was saying in such a straightforward, comprehensive, and accessible way what so desperately needed to be said."[96] A middle school teacher wrote Zinn that his "scholarship and easy to read writing style" in *A People's History* made it a book he used as a "cornerstone reference" for his eighth-grade U.S. history course.[97] And a woman from California wrote Zinn, "You have a marvelous writing style. It is 'reader-friendly'—it never condescends or preaches."[98] Similarly, a college graduate who had been a history major wrote, "Most importantly to me, a layman, you are a very clear and entertaining writer, with a true story-telling ability. Your books were a pleasure to read."[99]

Zinn did not write like an academic in part because he did not care much about how academics saw his work, which was always intended for a broader readership. Though it may seem romantic to cast Zinn as "the people's historian," that was very much what he had in mind when he thought about his writing, as he wanted to reach those beyond the educated elite. He attributed this outlook not to any great insight or talent on his part but to his working-class roots and unconventional career trajectory. As he explained in an interview in 2003, "[When I wrote *A People's History*], a fundamental idea about my audience was in my head. I knew I was not writing for fellow scholars. That's my natural tendency anyway. After all, I hadn't gone [up] the academic ladder, right? I'd taken off ten years between high school and college—shipyards, Army, Air Force, knocked around. So I never learned the academic style. . . . I wanted to have some kind of spontaneity, a kind of easygoing style in my writing. And I wanted it to be readable not just for people with college education but any person who reads it."[100]

There is in the adult and high school student letters to Zinn much evidence that he succeeded in reaching readers of diverse ages and social backgrounds, from schools to prisons to the military. *A People's History*, which became a best seller in the Reagan era, continued for decades to increase its sales annually and outsold other introductory works of American history during Zinn's lifetime. But perhaps the most striking testament to Zinn's writing skill is contained in a long, handwritten letter that Jason, then an NYU graduate student, sent to Zinn in 1998. Jason had recently moved from Boston to New York, and after wearing out his welcome at the home of his girlfriend's parents he was without a home for several weeks. So, as he explained to Zinn,

> I decided to stay at the NYU library. . . . I always thought it would be neat to sleep among so many books and since the NYU library was open 24 hours it seemed like a good enough choice. So for three weeks I made the basement study room my home. To say the least it was not very comfortable, so I would read till I could not keep my eyes open anymore and fall asleep. One night I came to my bed/desk and left on it was a book named *You Can't Be Neutral on a Moving Train* by Howard Zinn. I opened it up simply because it was such a funny title for a book. . . . So I started reading . . . read and read and then the next night before the stacks closed got every single Howard Zinn book they had. So for the rest of my stay all night long each night I read your books. And the funny things is, after I discovered your books I did not even mind staying

at the library. In fact, I looked forward to reading all night. It may sound weird but from the moment I started reading *You Can't Be Neutral* I felt a certain connection with your writing. It felt like you had made sense of all my jumbled up thoughts that I could never verbalize very well. . . . You have really inspired me like no other. I have even decided to go to law school next year, so I can attempt to give a voice to people who otherwise might not have one (well actually, they have voices so maybe it's the ears of others that I need to work on). You have touched my life more than I can express in one letter, and for that I thank you.[101]

As this and other letters attest, Zinn's writing touched many lives, yielding an introductory work of history that was memorable at a time when most U.S. textbooks were forgettable.

Teachers

A People's Pedagogy

Even a quick glance at Howard Zinn's *People's History of the United States* reveals that he admired American dissidents, from the abolitionists of the 1830s to labor, civil rights, antiwar, and feminist activists of the twentieth century. And an equally brief look through Zinn's papers and speaking schedule attests that he had a special place in his heart for teachers who dared to make their history classrooms sites for rethinking the American past. Thus the story explored in this chapter is of the collaborative engagement between Zinn and innovative teachers across the United States, resulting in the development of curricula and pedagogies that aligned with their preferences for critical, meaningful history education. Telling this story involves examining Zinn's pedagogical ideas, which helped connect him to teacher-activists. His appreciation of the importance of pedagogy to student intellectual growth and political awareness, his dedication to revising history curricula, and his articulation of linkages between history education and activism made Zinn and teachers natural allies in the struggle for a more just society. The result was an array of collaborative efforts by teachers and Zinn that began in the 1980s and continued up until his death in 2010, through the work of the Zinn Education Project (ZEP) and other activities. This work lives on today through the history education curriculum of ZEP and the many teachers and teacher organizers Zinn inspired.

While Howard Zinn is best known for his published work as a historian, he was also a skillful teacher, political organizer, and orator, and for decades he used those talents to promote his dissenting views of the American past and present and the importance of pedagogical changes in history education. Zinn was among the most popular teachers at Boston University, where his classes were packed with hundreds of students. From the Vietnam War era through the early twenty-first century, Zinn crossed the country in speaking engagements, denouncing U.S. war-making and connecting America's crises to its history of inequality, racism, and violence.

After *A People's History* was published in 1980, Zinn's speaking engagements connected thousands of people with the historical perspective articulated in his book. In terms of education, the most important connections Zinn made as an author, teacher, and organizer in his national speaking tours was with like-minded high school teachers, especially those teacher-activists who were organizing grassroots efforts at educational reform. These teachers promoted history teaching beyond the textbook and combined student-centered pedagogy with a critique of American society and U.S. military interventions. Because of Zinn's broad vision of his role as a historian and activist and his interest in changing the way history was taught in the schools, he was interested in reaching beyond academia. Zinn connected directly and personally with key figures in teacher reform networks, forging working relationships and friendships with teacher-organizers from across the country, most notably Bill Bigelow, a founder of the teachers' magazine *Rethinking Schools*, and Deborah Menkart of the curriculum project Teaching for Change.

These teacher-organizers and reformers embraced *A People's History* and linked Zinn's work with their own democratic and inclusive approaches to historical teaching and learning, which Bigelow would dub "a people's pedagogy." They featured interviews with Zinn in their magazines, published his essays and speeches, taught *A People's History* in their classrooms, met with Zinn at workshops and during his speaking tours, and discussed joint educational ventures with him. The collaboration would develop into America's most popular online revisionist and radical history site, the Zinn Education Project, in 2008, a project that continues today.

Initially teachers were drawn to Zinn's work because of his approach to writing history, both in style and content it was conducive to stimulating classrooms with engaged students. Whether they were politically oriented or simply appreciated how *A People's History* served as a powerful contrast to official textbooks, these teachers understood that Zinn's book prodded students to confront questions of bias and interpretation that reside at the heart of the discipline. These asked what happened, who said so, and why—but also, of equal importance, what had been omitted. These questions support a wide range of pedagogical options, which innovative teachers encountering *A People's History* recognized immediately.

Pedagogy was important to Zinn, and his attentiveness to effective pedagogy, including his eagerness to create healthy debate while challenging traditional historical narratives, guided his writing of *A People's History*. Ten years after *A People's History* was published, Zinn, in an interview with *Rethinking Schools*, shared some of his thinking on history teaching and learning. He stressed that the value of the teaching of history in schools and colleges extended beyond the subject. "Students should be encouraged to go into history in order to come out of it, and should be discouraged from going into history and getting lost in it, as some historians do."[1] For Zinn, historical study in classrooms needed to be distinguished from the way the most narrow of conventional historians engage with history. Instead of getting lost in the past or in a sea of names, dates, and factoids, students should be encouraged to consider how history shapes the present. Critical thinking about history allows one to contextualize contemporary political and social conflicts and supports inquiry into a range of other questions, problems, and phenomena.

In this *Rethinking Schools* interview, Zinn stressed the need for teachers to explore with their students an inclusive approach to studying history. He echoed the ideal articulated explicitly in the most widely read chapter of *A People's History*, on Columbus and the legacy of conquest, in encouraging teachers to present history from the bottom up. He wanted students to understand that the past is more than "the memory of states," as Henry Kissinger once declared, but instead is shaped by a dynamic process impacted by mass movements and resistance to oppression, whose stories were neglected in most textbooks.[2]

Zinn suggested that teachers show students that history is not dead, that it is alive and pulsating through the present. In order to facilitate this critical understanding in classrooms, Zinn noted: "You can take any incident in American history and enrich it and find parallels with today. One important thing is not to concentrate on chronological order, but to go back and forth and find similarities and analogies."[3]

Zinn wanted his readers to engage deeply with history and to be changed by it. In *Experience and Education* (1938), philosopher John Dewey described learning as transformational to the individual student through authentic experiences and engagement with new material.[4] Zinn's writing embodies this notion of learning in that he believed that the study of history could and would awaken people from passivity and thereby change them.[5] Zinn believed effective teaching could bring history to life, with students experiencing history as meaningful, powerful, and relevant. He advised teachers to "ask students if anything in a particular historical event reminds them of something they read in the newspapers or see on television about the world today. When you press students to make connections, to abstract from the uniqueness of a particular historical event and find something it has in common with another event—then history becomes alive, not just past but present."[6]

So Zinn understood that students bring their own knowledge, perspectives, and questions to the study of history. He advised teachers to work with these perspectives and questions, not to shut them out. Questions that were relevant to adolescents bolstered strong history pedagogy. And controversial questions were to be welcomed, and dealt with openly:

> You must raise the controversial questions and ask students, "Was it right for us to take Mexican territory? Should we be proud of that; should we celebrate that?" History teachers often think they must avoid judgments of right and wrong because, after all, those are matters of subjective opinions, those are issues on which students will disagree and teachers will disagree. But it's the areas of disagreement that are the most important. Questions of right and wrong and justice are exactly the questions that should be raised all the time. When students are asked, "Is this right; is this wrong?" then it becomes interesting, then they can have a debate—especially if they learn that there's no simple, absolute, agreed-upon, universal answer. It's not like giving them multiple-choice questions where they are right or wrong. I think that's a tremendous advance in their understanding of what education is.[7]

Zinn's history pedagogy was informed by his commitment to highlighting for average citizens their own power and agency. Activist teachers were drawn to this predisposition, but teachers who were not overtly political also saw value in their students understanding that power resides beyond governments and that mass movements helped shape the past. Zinn believed that teachers should "address the problem that people have been miseducated to become dependent on government [and therefore think that citizen action means going to] vote every two years or four years." "That's where the history of social movements comes in," he told *Rethinking Schools*. "Teachers should spend time on Shays' Rebellion, on colonial rebellions, on the abolitionist movement, on the populist movement, on the labor movement, and so on, and make sure these social movements don't get lost in the overall story of presidents and Congresses and Supreme Courts. Emphasizing social and protest movements in the making of history gives students a feeling that they as citizens are the most important actors in history."[8]

Zinn understood that any history classroom, regardless of the age of the students, is replete with opinions, including those of the teacher. When asked about the role of teachers' personal perspectives in the classroom, he suggested that one way to "manage this tension" between teachers' bias and their role as professional educators was to make sure students understood that their views were as valid as those of their teachers. Zinn may have been considering college-level teaching here, but his views resonated with secondary teachers as well. Overall, he demonstrated a deep awareness of the power dynamics that teachers and students experienced in their classrooms:

The teacher, no matter how hard she or he tries, is the dominant figure in the classroom and has the power of authority and of grades. It's easy for the teacher to fall into the trap of bullying students into accepting one set of facts or ideas. It takes hard work and delicate dealings with students to overcome that. . . . The way I've tried to deal with that problem is to make it clear to the students that when we study history we are dealing with controversial issues with no one, absolute, god-like answer. And that I, as a teacher, have my opinion and they can have their opinions, and that I, as a teacher, will try to present as much information as I can but that I may leave out information. I try to make them understand that while there are experts on facts, on little things, on the big issues, on the controversies and the issues of right and wrong and justice, there are no experts, and their opinion is as good as mine.[9]

But Zinn did not remain neutral in the classroom. He did not think other teachers should either: "I don't simply lay history out on a platter and say, 'I don't care what you choose; they're both valid.' I let them know, 'No, I care what you choose; I don't think they're both valid. But you don't have to agree with me.' I want them to know that if people don't take a stand the world will remain unchanged, and who wants that?"[10]

Zinn considered moral and ethical issues alongside his pedagogy for history and advised teachers to do the same. He believed that simply presenting names and dates was insufficient, especially on such critical topics as the history of slavery and racism. "People have to be given the facts of slavery, the facts of racial segregation, the facts of government complicity in racial segregation, the facts of the fight for equality. But that is not enough." Zinn addressed the value of actively engaging with critical issues through diverse sources. In this way, he recommended that teachers move beyond the textbook, including his own: "Novels, poems, autobiographies, memoirs, the reminiscences of ex-slaves, the letters that slaves wrote, the writings of Frederick Douglass—I think they have to be introduced as much as possible. Students should learn the words of people themselves, to feel their anger, their indignation." In this way, Zinn hoped teachers would expose students to the full range of human experience, including the tragedies and accomplishments, the atrocities and the victories of the past, and to implement pedagogies allowing students to have experiences with sources that move them. "I think students need to be aroused emotionally on the issue of equality. They have to try to feel what it was like, to be a slave, to be jammed into slave ships, to be separated from your family."[11]

Zinn's pedagogical recommendations, along with *A People's History*, would come to be seen by many teachers as supporting "a people's pedagogy" in classrooms. This term was used by Bill Bigelow in the introduction to the teachers' guide *A People's History for the Classroom* (published in 2008 by Rethinking Schools), and it will be explored below.[12] Zinn was not a high school teacher, and so when it came to the specifics of secondary school unit, lesson, and activity design, he deferred to veteran teachers. Bigelow, who met Zinn at a teacher workshop and later collaborated with him on a number of projects, recounted in 2012, "[Zinn] was a great storyteller, he was funny, he was a wonderful lecturer, he was self-deprecating, he was brilliant. But Howard wasn't writing role plays or trying to invent different kinds of activities where his students or any students could experience this history in a different way. That was our job."[13]

Zinn understood that classroom teachers taught far longer hours than academics did and had a powerful knowledge base for understanding and teaching children and adolescents. Expressing his admiration for them, Zinn told a large audience of social studies teachers in 2008: "I always thought that middle school teachers and high school teachers are the most heroic people."[14] In this same speech he praised teachers for working harder than university faculty.

Demonstrating his lifelong respect, admiration, and support for classroom teachers, Zinn had collaborative relationships with many of them, distinguishing him from most other college-based historians. Zinn supported their initiatives, projects, and eventual movement for "a people's pedagogy" and "a people's history" in schools. These teachers, including Bigelow and Menkart, developed and implemented curricula and pedagogies that aligned with Zinn's preferences for engaging, critical, and meaningful history teaching and learning.

This approach was not invented by Zinn, as noted earlier. Zinn contributed to an already existing dialogue about history education in the schools that emerged in the early 1970s, influenced by 1960s social movements and critical pedagogy. This dialogue was promoted by grassroots teacher reform efforts that were under way well before Zinn began writing his alternative to conventional U.S. history textbooks. These projects supported "people's pedagogy" and people's history in schools before and after *A People's History* became popular with teachers.

Generations of teachers, including those who came to political consciousness in the Long 1960s, were bound by shared commitments to education reform and activism. The social and political movements of that period and subsequent ones served as catalysts for the emergence of teacher-led groups that sought to reform not only teaching and schools but also society itself. In the late 1970s and early 1980s, teachers in cities such as Portland (Oregon), Seattle, Minneapolis, and Milwaukee came together initially because of concerns they had about U.S. military interventions, the wars in Central America, and to oppose apartheid in

South Africa, but over time their commitments broadened to include other international and domestic issues. This teacher collaboration was informal at first but led to the development of organizations like Rethinking Schools, spurred partly by local concerns (in Milwaukee, in the case of Rethinking Schools).

One common thread connecting progressive and activist teachers to one another and eventually to Zinn was their interest in "critical pedagogy" that aimed to facilitate "democracy, equality, ecology, and peace."[15] This social change agenda defined the work of teacher-activists in the 1970s and 1980s, and *A People's History* proved, in the words of scholar-activist Ira Shor, to be "a remarkable tool" since it was "competent and comprehensive, situated in American society, and included the story of opposition."[16] The timing was perfect when *A People's History* came along, because teacher-activists had already been united by their search for relevant materials for classroom teaching that reflected their commitments.

Some teacher activism that supported people's pedagogy culminated in projects that involved Zinn and his work for the schools. These efforts began emerging in the 1970s with locally situated teacher-led groups, such as the Network of Educators' Committees on Central America, then moved to the founding of the national organizations Teaching for Change (TFC) and Rethinking Schools (RS) in the 1980s, and eventually led to the establishment of the Zinn Education Project (ZEP). All these endeavors are characterized by three core commitments shared by teacher-activists, Zinn, and the nonactivist teachers who used resources provided by TFC, RS and the ZEP: (1) creating authentic materials as alternatives to the textbook, (2) enacting a critical pedagogy foregrounding inquiry, and (3) promoting social justice in schools and society, including fighting racism.[17]

The teachers involved in curricular reform, who eventually developed Rethinking Schools, Teaching for Change, and the Zinn Education Project, were what education scholar Bill Evans termed "Relativist/Reformers," history educators emphasizing connections and relationships between the past and present, believing that knowledge of the past supports deeper understanding of people, events, and phenomena today. Relativist/Reformers believe that "every aspect of historiography is infected with misconceptions" and that objectivity in history is impossible. These teachers are predominantly social reformers since they hold a vision of a better world that shapes much of their professional practice.[18]

The Network of Educators' Committees on Central America (NECCA) sponsored Bigelow's early curricular work that led to the 1991 publication of *Rethinking Columbus* (which initially connected him to Zinn). NECCA evolved into Teaching for Change in 1989 and eventually moved to Washington, D.C., with

Menkart at the helm. The organization, as described on its website, "operates from the belief that schools can provide students the skills, knowledge and inspiration to be citizens and architects of a better world." The statement continues: "By drawing direct connections to real world issues, Teaching for Change encourages teachers and students to question and rethink the world inside and outside their classrooms, build a more equitable, multicultural society, and become active global citizens."[19]

Throughout the 1990s, Teaching for Change offered seminars on social justice topics to K–12 teachers and in 1998 published a collection of resources edited by Menkart and others, *Beyond Heroes and Holidays: A Practical Guide to K–12 Anti-Racist, Multicultural Education and Staff Development.*[20] In 1999, Teaching for Change ran workshops for teachers in the Washington, D.C., area on civil rights history curricula at Howard University. This eventually led to the award-winning teaching guide *Putting the Movement Back into Civil Rights Teaching*, also coedited by Menkart, in collaboration with the Poverty and Race Resource Action Council.[21]

Along with Portland, Milwaukee was a locus for teacher-led organizing in the 1970s and 1980s. Elementary school teacher Bob Peterson and other teacher-activists initially came together to improve education in their classrooms and schools and to help shape reform throughout the public school system. Peterson, who taught fourth and fifth grade for nearly thirty years, and who eventually became a founder of *Rethinking Schools*, described the organization as evolving from an informal teacher study group, along with some community activists who were grappling with how to apply a "progressive, left-leaning view of society to schools." "Having been a fan of book clubs and study circles ever since high school," Peterson remembered in 2011, "early in 1985 I got together with some teacher friends to read Henry Giroux's *Theory and Resistance in Education.* Giroux was one of several university educators writing about Paulo Freire and critical education theory."[22]

Over time the Milwaukee teachers, activists, and organizers came together as a group. Playing leading roles were Peterson's housemate David Levine; teachers Rita Tenorio, Cynthia Ellwood, and Peter Murrell; education historian Bob Lowe; Terry Meier, a local university instructor; and Tony Baez, an advocate of bilingual education. These educators were dismayed by what they perceived as negative and superficial education coverage in Milwaukee newspapers. Activated by their concerns, they hoped to put out "a publication . . . that dealt with educational issues in depth," Peterson wrote. Eventually they published a newspaper focusing on local policies in Milwaukee, while combining theory and practice: "Our perspective and articles would be grounded in teaching and organizing, and yet we would also print significant analytical articles. . . . It was Cynthia who came up with our name: Rethinking Schools. We realized that what we were really about was changing the institution of schools."[23]

These Milwaukee teacher-activists were not sure if they should call their publication a newspaper or a journal and did not know which format would best support a critique of public schools and promote antiracist, multicultural, critical education, and their interests in policy and teaching. Robert Lowe suggested to them that they publish rigorous pieces grounded in evidence, with the potential to "challenge and convince people who didn't already agree." After the first issue came out, in format more like a newspaper but in content more like a journal, *Rethinking Schools* received almost enough subscription dollars to fund the next issue. Within two and a half years the publication had over twenty thousand subscribers, including Milwaukee's superintendent of schools and mayor. Clearly the teacher-led movement was gaining momentum.[24]

Although *Rethinking Schools* was a publication first, it served to connect with teacher-activists and other teachers outside of Milwaukee—indicating a growing national movement for progressive educational change. So it made sense that eventually *Rethinking Schools* expanded its reach and became an organization. Peterson explained, "As we brought on additional writers and eventually editors from around the country, including Bill Bigelow and Linda Christensen from Portland, Oregon, and Stan Karp from New Jersey, we were able to provide quality, in-depth articles about teaching and policy issues outside of Milwaukee. We hired Mike Trokan, a longtime peace activist and organizer for the United Farm Workers, as business manager and rented a small office in the corner of the Milwaukee Peace Action Center."[25]

These teacher-activists had a broad vision: "*Rethinking Schools* believes that classrooms can be places of hope, where students and teachers gain glimpses of the kind of society we could live in and where students learn the academic and critical skills needed to make that vision a reality."[26] In accordance with Zinn's focus on "a people's history," *Rethinking Schools* embodied from its inception an approach to teaching and school change from the bottom up. Who better to be engaged in deep and systemic school and pedagogical change than teachers and activists on the ground, Peterson asked.[27]

Rethinking Schools and Teaching for Change were committed to democratic educational reform, but ultimately each organization had its own approach and purview. As Menkart put it, "*Rethinking Schools* has a lot of integrity as a journal. So, it's, I think, one of the best teacher journals. . . . If people subscribed to only one journal, it should be *Rethinking Schools*." Menkart distinguished the organizations by the degree to which each worked directly with teachers. "Teaching for

Change has been focused more on working directly with teachers in schools. . . . There's parent organizing and then we were [operating] the bookstore [in D.C.] . . . so it's more projects, whereas *Rethinking Schools* is specifically a journal and books."[28] Together they supported the work of teachers across the country, including the development of curricula supporting a people's pedagogy. Zinn became increasingly aware of the work of these teacher-led groups and eventually served as an advisor to some of their projects and publications. Overlap of aims and means culminated in 2008 when Bigelow, Menkart, Zinn, and others came together to launch the Zinn Education Project.

Zinn had a lifelong respect for and interest in K–12 education, and throughout his career he engaged with teachers in ways that enhanced his own understanding of history teaching and education in general as locations ripe with possibility for facilitating social change. The activist teacher with whom Zinn interacted most closely was Bigelow, who for decades worked to create and disseminate some of the most popular and powerful resources supporting people's pedagogy in schools. The two collaborated over a twenty-year period.

Bigelow elaborated on his educational methodology and philosophy in *A People's History for the Classroom* (for which he interviewed Zinn and in which he included two Zinn essays). For Bigelow, people's pedagogy engages students in actively analyzing and critiquing "traditional approaches to history—including their own textbooks."[29] Bigelow made a case for a pedagogy that supported the study of history from the bottom up. "A people's history requires a people's pedagogy to match," Bigelow wrote, and this included "strategies that illustrate how a people's history can be brought to life in the classroom."

> Laid out in neatly sequenced chapters, textbooks present social reality as if it were unfolding rather than being created by people. . . . Zinn proposes history as a series of choices and turning points—junctures at which ordinary people interpreted social conditions and took actions that made a difference. This is a powerful and hopeful insight that can not only help our students think about the present, but can empower them to act on it. What we think and how we act can make the world a better place. For teachers, our challenge is how to bring this insight alive in our classrooms—not just telling students this, but showing them.[30]

People's pedagogy is not passive but instead engages students in actively participating in experiencing and interpreting history. Bigelow described the merits of active learning in history classrooms, and specifically role plays, of which he developed many across decades that highlight the experiences of people often left out of standard textbooks. "Role plays are one teaching strategy that can bring history-making to life in the classroom," he wrote, because they require students to "imagine themselves in the circumstances of other individuals throughout history and to consider the choices that actual groups faced."[31]

People's pedagogy provides students with a participatory relationship to texts.[32] While a traditional history curriculum "treats students as word consumers," instructing them to read from textbooks and then to answer corresponding noncritical questions, people's pedagogy supports students as they strive to "talk back" to text, "to read for the silences and the neglected perspectives, to ask why certain choices were made (for example, why the text included no mention of the large numbers of Mexico war opponents), and to imagine what a more adequate treatment would be."[33]

Finally, a people's pedagogy highlights struggle for justice and equality, with these topics brought into the historical narrative far more than in most textbooks. This pedagogy stresses that U.S. history includes organized efforts to fight for the rights of disenfranchised groups as well as other humanitarian goals, something that many teachers believe is critical for their students to understand. People's pedagogy complicates the phrase "We the People." By including new voices in the narrative, a more nuanced and accurate American story can be told. History teachers, regardless of their political perspective or involvement with activism recognized (and still do) that this approach fosters quality history education, promoting civic engagement and a deeper understanding of the forces that have shaped the past and continue to influence society today.

The history of teacher activism and its connections with Zinn, *A People's History*, and people's pedagogy are illustrated in Bigelow's political and educational biography. Bigelow's life and work are exceptional due to his talent, dedication, and tenaciousness as a writer, curriculum designer, and activist. His story demonstrates how an idealistic teacher managed to have a national impact in working for better schools throughout his career.

Bigelow, who eventually became an editorial board member of *Rethinking Schools* and cofounder of the Zinn Education Project, already had a long history of activism when he became involved in reform efforts aimed at improving the teaching of history in schools. "I grew up in the [San Francisco] Bay Area. . . . There were [UC Berkeley student] demonstrations when I was in high school and [I began to realize] that . . . I was part of this culture. . . . And part of that was questioning the war in Vietnam. And so it was through that and the behavior of police . . . certainly People's Park and the Free Speech Movement before . . .

[these] were all a presence in my upbringing. And I just became more and more committed to critical politics."[34]

At Antioch College, from which Bigelow graduated in 1974, he was active in the antiwar and women's movements. His first educational project was in film, as part of the film collective headed by Julia Reichardt, whose early work culminated with *Union Maids* (1976), the Academy Award–nominated documentary on women workers in Chicago, based on the scholarship of Zinn's friends Staughton and Alice Lynd.

Through this film collective Bigelow got his first experience as an educator, in a historical project he helped create, which was "'a people's history of Dayton.' It centered on a ninety-minute slideshow of a radical history of Dayton [Ohio]. . . . There was a lot of teaching involved in that because we showed it in schools, we showed it in senior centers, wherever we could." Bigelow found this community history education work engaging and gratifying, paving the way for a teaching career. He says the project whetted his appetite for teaching, and so he did coursework to get certified as a teacher.[35]

Bigelow's first teaching job was at an alternative public school in Cincinnati. Here he and his colleagues were encouraged to develop relevant and engaging curricula. He recalls: "We could teach whatever we wanted, provided we [could] attract the students from the school to take the classes. . . . And really [we] just tried to figure out how do we teach about what matters. And so we taught a crime study class, we taught a class on capitalism, socialism and . . . one on neighborhood history."[36]

Bigelow and his young colleagues were enacting their own version of critical pedagogy, though they did not know at the time that other teachers were engaged in similar work across the country and that scholars were articulating theories that supported it. At this point, Bigelow and his peers had yet to become engaged in networks of teachers working for change. "So it was just the group of us trying to teach in a way that would excite kids, it would be in line with the things that we thought were important to teach about." And this came down to teaching their alternative school students to think critically in order to engage with their social and political reality. "None of us had really had education backgrounds. And so we just knew that changing the world was going to require young people thinking more critically."[37]

Bigelow would look back at his college coursework for teacher certification as having failed to provide exposure to the foundations of critical pedagogy or even to progressive education generally. For Bigelow, his experience in a school of education "did not particularly help" when it came to providing context, theory, and practices needed for working in schools as a teacher-activist with a social justice agenda. This came later on for Bigelow, in the mid-1980s, through engagement with works by Paulo Freire, the Brazilian educator and philosopher and leading advocate of critical pedagogy, and Ira Shor, a leading proponent of critical pedagogy in the United States, whose book on Freire helped introduce other American educators to his writings.[38] Bigelow also came together with other activist teachers, including a critical pedagogy inquiry group facilitated by Shor in Ohio in 1987, when Bigelow met Bob Peterson, who later helped found *Rethinking Schools*. Shor says of his work: "The foundational orientation of critical pedagogy is questioning the status quo. There are different ways you can question the status quo, but Freire positioned a certain political or ideological framework for questioning the status quo. The status quo was unequal, unjust, inhumane, even cruel, and that's why we questioned it, because we plant our feet in a dream of a better world."[39]

Bigelow had been teaching for just over ten years when he encountered the work of Freire and Shor and critical pedagogy as a framework supporting social justice in schools. "I didn't need somebody at that point to help me figure out how to write role plays or anything. But having Freire . . . address really bigger questions was the perfect thing right at that moment. And that's when I began reading Ira Shor and his conversations with Freire and then going back to Ira's earlier work."[40] Reading and engaging with Freire, Shor, and the writings of other education scholar-activists was done independently and not through affiliations with schools or universities. Shor described this group of activist teachers with whom he worked, which included Bigelow, as both going against the grain and without a home to study the foundations and practices of critical pedagogy. "The school systems and the universities that already exist will not teach it to us. In fact, they teach us the opposite. . . . There was no place in school where we could learn how to do this, and no place in the university. So we had to invent it ourselves, and then practice it wherever there was space available inside the school system and the universities."[41]

Bigelow and his peers were engaged, then, in a small but dynamic grassroots network independent of any university-based teacher education program. These teacher-activists valued the knowledge generated by their personal teaching experiences at least as much as the research generated by university-based scholars of education. Bigelow explains, "We realized that there was a hierarchy that we didn't want to accept." In the hierarchy, university-generated "knowledge" about teaching and learning was placed at the top, while the likes of curricula designed by and for teachers, field-tested and practical, were placed below. As Bigelow sums up, "The teaching that we were doing, and the thinking about teaching we were doing, and writing for that matter, we thought was more concrete and sharper than a lot of the stuff that we were seeing coming out of the university."[42]

Like Bigelow, many other teachers had been involved in or influenced by the peace, civil rights, feminist, and labor movements. Bigelow's initial work in teacher-led organizations took place at the end of the Carter presidency and with the escalation of covert wars in Central America by President Reagan in the early 1980s. Bigelow was among teachers who were alarmed by the bloody Contra War that Reagan secretly pushed in Nicaragua and the brutal death squads of the U.S.-backed regime in El Salvador. As Menkart explained, teachers were "both looking at U.S. foreign policy towards Central America, which nobody was taught about in schools in the U.S., and looking at the needs of refugee students coming here, who were in schools in large numbers. . . . . Teachers had no idea where they were coming from, or why they were here."[43]

In Portland, where Bigelow eventually lived and worked, teachers carried out their activism under the name of the Portland Central American Solidarity Committee, founded in 1979. In the 1980s like-minded teachers nationally organized the Network of Educators' Committees on Central America, which eventually was renamed the Network for Educators on the Americas but kept the same acronym, NECCA. Bigelow, who met Menkart through NECCA, described their agenda: "We wanted to teach about this war thing [U.S. involvement in Central America]. And . . . we wanted to support each other in that. And then we also wanted to connect with educators in Central America. And so we operated under the umbrella of the Portland Central American Solidarity Committee. Although I don't believe we [had] any formal tie, we certainly were all part of the same work along with people who were doing sanctuary work [the religious and political campaign in the U.S. to provide safe haven for Central American refugees fleeing its violent civil wars]."[44] Eventually, NECCA published resources for teachers, including a collection of materials for teaching about Nicaragua, *Inside the Volcano: A Curriculum on Nicaragua*, edited by Bigelow and Jeff Edmundson in 1990. Bigelow described the evolution: "[NECCA] collected a lot of the curriculum [work] that we had done around Nicaragua . . . that we were hoping to provide as a resource to teachers around the country, so that everyone didn't have to labor alone to create all the critical lessons to use with their students."[45]

Bigelow and the other teachers in NECCA were engaged primarily in curriculum development, creating school materials that addressed significant topics in the past and present, were critical of U.S. policies at home and abroad—especially U.S. involvement in Central America, and promoted social justice. "It was just our lives as teachers . . . as workers, as curriculum developers, as intellectuals, as people who cared about what was going on in the world." With the support of a few university-based radical scholars, including Shor and sociologist Jerry Lembcke, they began to develop alternative curricula on the likes of the Christopher Columbus "encounter" and labor history, and they sought to connect with other educators who were, in Bigelow's words, "thinking outside the textbook."[46]

Bigelow's most popular and influential curriculum guide, which became a best seller, *Rethinking Columbus: Teaching about the 500th Anniversary of Columbus's Arrival in the Americas*, copublished in 1992 by NECCA and Rethinking Schools, grew out of a popular set of *Rethinking Schools* articles written by Bigelow in the late 1980s, three years before the Columbus quincentenary.[47] These articles (and the teacher workshops they supported), along with Bigelow's involvement with NECCA, eventually led him to meet and befriend Zinn. As Bigelow explains, "It was NECCA, and in this instance the Network of Educators in the Americas, that was the sponsor of the Rethinking Columbus work that I was doing with teachers around the country. [That is] when I first connected with Howard."[48] NECCA's support had allowed Bigelow to take a year off from the classroom, facilitating teacher workshops from coast to coast to promote critical teaching about Christopher Columbus on the five hundredth anniversary of Columbus's first voyage to the Americas.

For Bigelow, this work was essential to history education reform since it would allow teachers to get to the heart of critical topics in U.S. history with their students, including race and empire. "[T]he 'discovery of America' is children's first curricular exposure to the encounter between two races. As such, a study of Columbus is really a study about us, how we think about each other, our country, and our relations with people around the world."[49] This national tour overlapped with Zinn's own speaking engagements in 1992, when he was in much demand because of his by then well-known indictment of Columbus in *A People's History*. It was at one of those events in Cambridge, Massachusetts, that Zinn and Bigelow first met.

Bigelow and Zinn came to value each other's work. Their writings on Columbus, their 1992 sessions promoting critical thinking and teaching about Columbus, and Native American protests that year had a lasting impact. They raised awareness about the need to interrogate myths—not only about Columbus but also about American history itself. As Bigelow recalls,

> I do think that Columbus was a shock to the historical heart, as it were, and created greater willingness to question more conventional history telling. So many people had never thought critically about the Columbus story, and so there was an openness—"If I was lied to about this, then what else?" In fact, as

I recall, Howard quoted a piece I wrote describing my student Rebecca, who had written in her "collective text" about other students' critiques: "Of course, the writers of the books probably think it's harmless enough—what does it matter who discovered America, really; and besides, it makes them feel good about America. But the thought that I have been lied to all my life about this, and who knows what else, really makes me angry." Of course, the anger can translate into a critical openness for a fuller story, or turn into cynicism: "they are all liars; I can't believe anyone about anything." So what educators do once they explode myths, is important.[50]

Not long after they connected during the Columbus quincentenary, Bigelow and Zinn were back in touch. In 1994 Bigelow wrote a letter to Zinn attesting to the dynamism of the teacher-activist network with which he was affiliated and its interest in promoting classroom use of Zinn's *A People's History of the United States.* "There is not a progressive teacher I know," Bigelow told Zinn, "who doesn't regularly consult *A People's History* and use pieces of it from time to time. I keep several copies around because I'm always giving them out." Bigelow's ambition to change history education in the schools both locally and nationally was evident as he opened his letter by reflecting back fondly on the teaching and speaking he and Zinn had done on Columbus across the country in 1992:

> Have you slowed down now that the Quincentenary hoopla has run its course? You must have been everywhere. I kept hearing from people who had gone to one of your talks, had heard you on the radio, or had read something or about you. I'm back in the classroom after my two years flying the friendly skies. . . . I enjoy being rooted again in a school community (though teaching is a lot more difficult than just two years ago), but I miss the regular contact with organizers and progressive teachers around the country. That boosted my confidence that we really can make a difference—that we *are* making a difference.

Bigelow sought in this letter to interest Zinn in an idea that he'd had for a while. Attesting to Zinn's ongoing contact with teacher-activists, Bigelow noted, "Bob Peterson at *Rethinking Schools* may have mentioned it to you when you were there [in Milwaukee] last year." Bigelow wrote:

> I'd like you to consider working on a new project with Rethinking Schools and me. Though I sometimes use chapters of *A People's History* with my students, the book is somewhat difficult for most high school students I've encountered. A high school history text/curriculum/reader that combines a running narrative with supplementary readings for students would be enormously useful

for teachers. As I imagine the book, it would be curricular, but would not be a curriculum like my labor curriculum [*The Power in Our Hands: A Curriculum on the History of Workers and Work in the United States* (1988)]. The book's narrative would be a somewhat simplified version of *A People's History*, but might also cover other topics of special interest to high school students, like the history of schooling, movements of young people, etc. The book would include source readings, songs, poems, interviews, timelines, examples of student writing, excerpts from novels and autobiographies—e.g., Martin Luther King Jr.'s Riverside Church speech laying out his reasons for opposing the Vietnam War, Wendy Rose's poetry . . . John Brown's interview after his capture at Harper's Ferry, Elizabeth Eckford's story of her first day trying to enter Little Rock's Central High . . . possibly contemporary interviews/articles about the *meaning* of history like Barbara Miner's interview with Suzan Shown Harjo that we included in Rethinking Columbus, as well as the excellent interview she did with you.

Bigelow hoped his proposed book would be bought by school districts for student use, although he foresaw that it would also "guide teachers in both the what *and* how of teaching history." "The overall aim would be to combine the strengths of *A People's History of the United States* and *Rethinking Columbus*, to establish an alternative "pole," and alternative vision of history/teaching/ learning. We've talked about the project at *Rethinking Schools* and everyone is extremely enthusiastic. I see this as a tremendous opportunity to get a radical perspective to a much wider audience than even *A People's History* has reached. Maybe that's overstating it, but I think this could be really important."[51]

Beyond the proposed book project itself, Bigelow's letter is significant in conveying a sense of momentum that radical and progressive history education reformers felt they were making in the wake of the national effort to rethink Columbus in 1992. And it was progress seen not only at the classroom level, where innovative teachers were experimenting with more critical history, but in print as well. Bigelow's discussion of potential publishers for the book project focused on the New Press, which was publishing a collection of teacher reform essays that had first appeared in *Rethinking Schools*. The New Press, Bigelow noted, had recently published James Loewen's *The Truth about Columbus*. "It is also publishing his provocative (if poorly titled) critique of U.S. History textbooks, *Lies My Teacher Told Me*."[52] The latter would become almost as big a best seller as *A People's History*. One of the nation's leading progressive publishers, the New Press would eventually publish a "People's History" book series, becoming an ally in popularizing the teaching-beyond-the-textbook ideals championed by Bigelow, *Rethinking Schools*, and Zinn. This grassroots educational reform movement, though still entailing a minority of teachers nationally, was having an impact.[53]

As noted, Bigelow and Zinn would eventually collaborate in the founding of the Zinn Education Project, launched in 2008, and Bigelow would himself publish *A People's History for the Classroom* (2008), the pedagogical companion to Zinn's work. This again attests to the close link between teacher reform efforts and Zinn. And even though in 1994 Zinn declined Bigelow's book idea, he took it seriously, found it intriguing, and was interested in finding ways to make *A People's History* more accessible for high school use—perhaps by abridging it.[54]

Zinn's letter to Andre Schiffrin of the New Press on Bigelow's book proposal conveys his respect for Bigelow and the teacher reform network with which he was associated. While most academic historians focused on their own work in academia, unaware that such networks of teacher-activists even existed, Zinn spoke of these teachers as colleagues, friends, and fellow activists. Of his admiration for Bigelow, *Rethinking Schools*, and their work challenging the traditional history curriculum, Zinn wrote to Schiffrin: "You may know Bill as that remarkably energetic and innovative West Coast high school teacher who, more than any other single person, is responsible for a dramatic change in the way the Columbus story is told in the nation's schools. . . . *Rethinking Schools*, a publication for teachers that comes out of Milwaukee, has become known to school teachers all over the country as an invaluable resource; its 1992 publication, *Rethinking Columbus*, was snapped up hungrily by schools all over the country and sold 200,000 copies. In short, both Bill and *Rethinking Schools* have an extremely impressive record, and I have great faith in them."[55]

Zinn's respect for Bigelow was reciprocated, and each recognized that though they worked in different realms they shared a common purpose. Bigelow explained how he saw their work aligning and also why Zinn appreciated him and other activist teachers. "Howard had an activist's heart, and he knew one when he saw one, and he knew that we did too, and that we were in it for the same thing, that he was not in it to try and win academic honors or just sell books . . . that we were doing it for the same reasons. And I think that Howard recognized that pretty much immediately."[56]

❧

Zinn's support of teacher-led efforts to reform history curricula and teaching would continue in the dawning Internet era. It was inevitable that the movement to challenge triumphalist history textbooks would develop a strong online presence and that Zinn would be involved. That presence received a major boost from William Holtzman, a former Boston University journalism student who had taken a course with Zinn and admired him. Holtzman had made a fortune marketing the smartphone predecessor Palm Pilot in the late 1990s, and after viewing the 2004 documentary about Zinn's life, *You Can't Be Neutral on a Moving Train*, he was inspired to act. Menkart says, "[He] had seen the scene of Howard . . . talking with students at a school in Chicago with copies of *A People's History* and . . . realized this is what he wanted to do with his . . . philanthropic endeavors." Holtzman contacted Menkart at Teaching for Change with an offer to make a donation so generous that initially she didn't believe it was genuine. "The call from Holtzman really was one of those that you [receive and] think, maybe this is a crank call." He wanted to give away four thousand copies of Zinn's book to schools along with the documentary film about Zinn. "Can you help me?" he asked Menkart. While Menkart and her colleagues were thrilled to have someone with means who was supportive, she was cautious. "We were very clear with him that you just can't give away the books . . . there'd have to be resources to go with it or else it's just going to become a shift from textbooks." What was needed, she believed, was a shift in pedagogy as well. "And he was open to that."[57]

In November 2007 Menkart and Bigelow cowrote a proposal to create the Zinn Education Project, and they shared it with Holtzman. They proposed a project that would promote awareness of Zinn's works and effective use of them: "We will reach both wide and deep . . . to promote and distribute Howard Zinn's work to middle and high schools across the country." They planned to offer teachers at no charge "*A People's History of the United States* (either full or abridged version), the DVD *You Can't Be Neutral on a Moving Train*, and an interactive teaching guide." The guide, they said, would include "a detailed essay on teaching *A People's History*, five or six interactive classroom-tested lessons, and a list of additional recommended resources." Their initial proposed budget to launch the project was $150,000, which included $86,000 for twenty-five hundred books and DVDs, the intent being to "interest teachers in the work of Howard Zinn and teaching *A People's History of the United States*." The film was included to aid busy teachers in accessing information about Zinn and his work: "[Teachers] will be more likely to find the time to view the film which will be an enticement to read the book and consider how to incorporate its approach in the classroom."[58]

Central to the project was the development of ancillary teaching materials. "The teaching guide, with excerpts from Zinn's texts, will ensure that teachers see and experience a direct application of Zinn's work in the classroom. The lessons are designed to reflect the participatory and critical nature of Zinn's presentation of history. Based on past experience in sharing these lessons, we know

that teachers and students will find them effective and will seek more of this cal-
iber. . . . The guide design will be attractive and user friendly—so both the length
and the layout will encourage the teacher to try out at least one of the lessons."[59]

Menkart and Bigelow thought it made sense to reach out to teachers familiar
with Teaching for Change and *Rethinking Schools*. "The outreach for this would
go to teachers already on the TFC and Rethinking Schools lists, and the teachers
who had received the complimentary packet as a result of the Zinn Education
Project campaign." To receive a class set of books, teachers would complete an
application in which they would describe how they planned to use *A People's
History* with their students. "We would ask that people apply only if they are in
a school where there would not be the funds to purchase a class set; so that the
sets can benefit schools and districts with the greatest need. . . . In exchange for
receiving the set, recipients would agree to share stories about student reactions
to the text and how they used the books, so that we can post these on a webpage
linked to Rethinking Schools and Teaching for Change."[60]

Holtzman enthusiastically e-mailed Zinn on December 11, 2007, about the
project's progress. "We're signed, sealed and fully funded. Not bad considering
my first email to you was October 15!"

> With a little luck, we will be reaching out to 10,000+ teachers and will distrib-
> ute 2,500+ teaching kits. I am not sure about the ripple effect because maybe
> we can have an impact on 20,000, 40,000, 60,000 students? Who knows, but
> we will give it our best shot. . . . You really don't need to thank me Howard
> . . . believe me, the pleasure is all mine. It's nice when you can honor someone
> who deserves to be honored. I am sure you feel the same way about the teach-
> ers who had a positive impact on your life.[61]

With the initial funds provided by Holtzman, and in collaboration with Zinn
who served as an active advisor, *Rethinking Schools* and Teaching for Change,
led by Bigelow and Menkart, launched the Zinn Education Project.

The project's reach and success were greatly enhanced by its strong online
presence. A user-friendly website was designed, along with the corresponding
Facebook page that provided frequent updates about newly developed teaching
materials and events, workshops and conferences, that supported and promoted
the work of the project. Initially the degree to which an online presence would
contribute to the project's success was not obvious to Menkart or Bigelow. Bigelow recalled,

> I laughed at this—that we were thinking from the start that we would have
> tens of thousands of teachers using our site. This was very much a make the

road by walking process. . . . Our first big "event" was the giveaway of 4,000 packets of 'A People's History . . . ,' You Can't Be Neutral (the film), and my A People's History for the Classroom. Then we gave away 800 copies of APH at the [National Council for the Social Studies annual conference] in 2008. . . We realized pretty quickly, as I recall, that mailing everything to people was not going to be cost-effective, and posting at the web made more sense.[62]

What began as a modest use of the Internet as an alternative to snail mail paved the way for a much more focused and effective effort at developing and disseminating educational resources online. A testament to the strong collaboration between activist teachers and Zinn in the early twenty-first century: the Zinn Education Project in 2020, twelve years after its founding, has more members and supporters on social media than does the National Council for the Social Studies, the largest U.S. organization devoted to social studies and history teaching and learning. Since its launch, tens of thousands of teachers from across the country have accessed materials from the project's website to implement people's pedagogy and people's history in their classrooms.

The popularity of the Zinn Education Project is, of course, inextricably linked with Zinn the historian. No other historian has had this kind of organic link to teachers, with a popular and growing website championing not just his books but also his approach to history. For countless teachers, Zinn was and remains "the people's historian." Teacher enthusiasm for A People's History and use of the book certainly contributed to its enduring popularity and sales. But the benefits flowed in both directions. Zinn's collaborative efforts aided teacher-reformers in bringing history to life.

The unique collaboration between teacher-activists such as Bigelow and Zinn, through the work of Rethinking Schools, Teaching for Change, and later the Zinn Education Project, resulted in changes to history teaching and learning in schools. Certainly this was the case among the growing teacher cohort connected with these organizations' resources.[63] More and more teachers aligned their curricula—in spirit, content, and approach—with A People's History of the United States. Although many of the teachers and groups discussed in this chapter started their work before the publication of A People's History, Zinn's history served to bolster their efforts and in many ways helped refine and sharpen their focus. It seems safe to conclude, then, that Zinn's enduring school presence, his book's usage in the classrooms of inventive teachers, was a consequence not only of his skill as a writer and historian but also due to ongoing support from teachers.

Retrospectives and Reviews

It would be an exaggeration to say that since its publication in 1980 *A People's History* has generated as much controversy as it has sales. But the intensity of Zinn's critics has sometimes made it seem that way. Zinn's book has been most angrily attacked by conservatives denouncing *A People's History* as "un-American" left-wing propaganda. In March 1986, for example, Accuracy in Academia (AIA), an organization policing academic radicalism, devoted its newsletter's lead article, "Hate-America History," to attacking Zinn's book as a tool for indoctrination that bred hatred for the United States. Another front-page story in the same issue attacked Virginia Tech professor Linda Arnold for assigning Zinn's book, urging that patriotic Americans complain to the Virginia Tech president that Arnold had her students read such subversive writings.[1] When AIA founder Reed Irvine phoned Arnold to object to her assigning *A People's History*, he asked her three times, "Don't you think the book should be burned?"[2] She told Irvine, "I'm against book burning," and she defended Zinn's work, crediting him with writing a book that held student interest, unlike most U.S. history textbooks, which her students found "deathly dull."[3]

Anti-Zinn fervor has remained intense in the twenty-first century, with some people urging that the book be banned. It was on the same grounds cited by AIA in 1986 that almost twenty-five years later Mitch Daniels, then governor of Indiana, took the occasion of Zinn's death in 2010, to explore covertly banning Zinn's supposedly un-American history from Indiana classrooms.[4] Two years later Zinn's book was banned from the schools in Tucson as part of the reaction against Mexican American studies.[5] And mean-spirited attacks have continued, with Mary Grabar's polemic *Debunking Howard Zinn: Exposing the Fake History that Turned a Generation against America* (2019) charging that *A People's History* was "designed to destroy Americans' patriotism and turn them into radical leftists" and claiming that Zinn "falsified American history to promote Communist revolution."[6] The lead blurb for Grabar's book, by David Horowitz, called *A People's History* "the Mein Kampf of the Hate America Left."[7] Such ideological attacks on *A People's History* reflect intolerance of dissent and promote the chauvinistic notion that a historical narrative highlighting the flaws in American politics and society is inherently un-American.

Though Zinn had died before the Daniels and Grabar attacks on *A People's History*, we know how he would likely have answered them. Zinn had rebutted the AIA "Hate-America History" article by pointing out that it "confused criticism of government with being anti-America." "[But] America is a society, it is the people," he had written. "Government is an artificial creation over society that makes decisions that may not be in the country's best interest." Far from demonizing America, Zinn said, his book celebrated "Americans who stood up with American ideals" and expressed "indignation at what the government has done to its own people and to other people in the world." Zinn wanted readers to come away from *A People's History* having learned "admiration and respect for those who went against [the oppressive acts of government and corporate leaders]."[8]

For Zinn, a key part of this controversy was about the paucity of pluralism and dissent in schools, an unattractive feature of public education that AIA sought to reinforce when it bashed *A People's History* for criticizing American capitalism and past business leaders such as Henry Ford. Zinn wrote, "Students have had [text]books [in which] they have learned about Ford [and others that AIA] has called heroes for 12 years [of their schooling]." He felt good, he said, giving students a chance to consider a different view. The goal of *A People's History* was "to present history and heroes who are ignored in traditional textbooks." "We disagree on who's a hero," he noted. "To me Ford was a man who used police and his army to beat up labor [organizers], workers, he is not my hero."[9]

There is no evidence that *A People's History* "turned a generation against America," as Grabar claims in her book's subtitle. Actually, there is much evidence from student and teacher writings—even beyond what is presented in chapters 3–5 of this book—about *A People's History* refuting this claim. In 1986, for example, students in a Memphis high school who read *A People's History* together with *Rise of the American Nation*—which their teacher termed "a very conservative and traditional text[book]"—wrote letters rebutting AIA's charge that Zinn's book fostered hatred of America.[10] One of these students wrote of finding that charge "ridiculous": "I loved America before I read Zinn's book and I still love it afterwards."[11] Traditional textbooks, according to a classmate, Holly H., bred a shallow form of patriotism, by stressing "[how] great America has always been." This she contrasted with *A People's History*, which enabled students to see the "mistakes" the United States had made historically: "Why put our heads in the sand and pretend these things never happened? . . . I have already read most of *A People's History of the United States*, and I don't hate America; I just understand the history of our country much better now."[12]

Criticism of *A People's History* has not been confined to self-identified conservative organizations, authors, and politicians. Judging by a History News Network (HNN) online vote conducted in 2012, a good number of American historians have scorn for *A People's History*. More than six hundred who participated in the HNN vote pronounced Zinn's history the second-least credible history book in print. Comments by participants in the HNN vote suggest this negative verdict reflects centrist and antiradical perspectives in the profession. Zinn's "viewing American history through a Marxist lens is a painful exercise in tortured reasoning," complained one critic, while another denounced *A People's History* as "absolutely atrocious agit-prop." Such comments led the *New York Times* to conclude in June 2012 that, with the anti-Zinn landslide, the Right had "scored an interim victory" among professional historians, though "the political direction of the country [was still] up for grabs" pending November's presidential vote."[13]

Criticism of Zinn has been so widespread and vociferous that Purdue University philosophy professor David Detmer published a book on such criticism, *Zinnophobia: The Battle Over History in Education, Politics, and Scholarship* (2018).[14] It was revelations about Mitch Daniels's censorship attempt against *A People's History* that prodded Detmer to undertake this detailed study of the attacks on Zinn's book, most of which he debunked as rooted in "groundless" claims.[15]

Detmer gave readers the opportunity to judge the merits of *A People's History* and its harshest critics by comparing their arguments. Our focus and aim in this chapter, however, differs from Detmer's in several respects. Our assessment of Zinn's book is informed not only by our own analysis as historians but also by our knowledge of how it has engaged students and other novice history learners. Academics—especially historians—reviewing the book understandably read it as experts in history but rarely considered how a history novice might respond differently to such an introductory work. Our assessment of *A People's History* is based in part on our analysis of hundreds of letters to Zinn from both high school students and history teachers, and this reader response and evidence of pedagogical usage were not available to the book's initial reviewers back in 1980. Most reviewers were interested in *A People's History* as history, but our interest is both historical and pedagogical.[16]

While Detmer's book analyzes and rebuts all of Zinn's major critics, including the most polemical and ideological, we will spend little time on polemics. This is not because we find them offensive or tedious—which some are—but because those who dismiss Zinn's book rather than engage with it substantively do not contribute meaningfully to a discussion of its true weaknesses and strengths. This contrasts with those who offered reasoned and evidence-based criticism of *A People's History*, including the historians we interviewed and corresponded with—who deepened our understanding of the book's problems, limitations, and strengths. Unlike Detmer's, our assessment of *A People's History* is centered not on published reviews but on how the forty-year-old book holds up today in the view of leading historians with whom we have consulted. We asked these scholars, each a specialist in a subfield of American history, to consider how Zinn's best-selling history looked in relation to contemporary historical scholarship as we entered the third decade of the twenty-first century.

In revised editions (1990, 1995, 1998, 2003) Zinn added chapters on the Reagan-Bush-Clinton years, with a final update to *A People's History* that went through the 2000 election and the rise of "the War on Terror." But the book's chapters on most of American history were necessarily grounded in scholarship that is now decades old. This does not mean the book is entirely out of date, since some scholarship holds up well over time, but the issue of what needs updating, in light of more recent scholarship that Zinn did not have access to over forty years ago, is one that readers and teachers should consider.

Given the book's length (over six hundred pages) and chronological coverage (the late fifteenth century though the turn of the twenty-first century), it will not be possible here to deal with all of *A People's History*. We explore Zinn's treatment of selected topics, from early Native American–white relations to the Vietnam War, in the hope that it will assist teachers and other readers in considering the book's content in relation to more recent historical scholarship.

Since this chapter will focus mostly on criticism, it is important to note that some reviews of *A People's History* were enthusiastic—much as the readers' reports had been (as we saw in chapter 1) for Cambridge University Press and Harper and Row. A *Library Journal* reviewer, for example, praised Zinn for writing "a brilliant and moving history of the American people from the point of view of those who have been exploited politically and economically and whose plight has been largely omitted from most histories. . . . The book is an excellent antidote to establishment history. Seldom have quotations been so effectively used: the stories of blacks, women, Indians, and poor laborers of all nationalities are told in their own words."[17] *A People's History* was a finalist for the American Book Award paperback history category in 1981, a rare honor for an introductory historical survey.[18]

The most hostile, polemical reviews of *A People's History* in 1980 came from antiradical historians and journalists. Harvard historian Oscar Handlin, a Nixon enthusiast and Vietnam War hawk, despised Zinn's antiwar politics and had a record of publishing intemperate reviews of books by radical historians. In 1962 Handlin blasted famed radical diplomatic historian William Appleman Williams's *Contours in American History* as a "total disaster. . . . an elaborate hoax . . . that parodies . . . the literary striving of unskilled freshmen."[19] Handlin's review of *A People's History* expressed outrage over its "idyllic" view of African American and Native American life and "the topsy-turvy quality" of Zinn's narrative, which dispensed with the traditional view of enlightened Europeans civilizing the Americas and led readers to believe instead that "it was [all] downhill" after "the destructive white strangers arrived." Handlin denounced *A People's History* as a "deranged . . . fairy tale."[20]

Handlin's review tells us more about his historical vision and its limitations than it does about Zinn's. Handlin opened it by declaring, "This is a book about Arawaks," as if it was absurd for an American history to center on Indigenous people. Handlin could not entertain seriously the idea that such people in the Americas or in Africa merited historical study in ways that foregrounded their views of the Europeans who conquered and enslaved them.[21] That he wrote such a belligerent review, and that the *American Scholar* published it, illustrates the discomfort among at least some senior scholars over the paradigm shift that Zinn's work (and the work of like-minded historians) represented.

Much as Zinn's critical treatment of race offended Handlin, the emphasis of *A People's History* on class conflict proved similarly offensive to Robert Zimmerman of the *San Diego Union* who published an anti-Zinn review in its pages. Zimmerman charged that Zinn had reduced American history to "simply the Marxist class struggle played out for 200 years in which 'the people' have been victimized by corrupt politicians and big business." Rather than discuss the evidence that *A People's History* offered on the significance of class conflict in American history, Zimmerman resorted to red-baiting, telling readers that "Howard Zinn's history reads like an entry from the Soviet Encyclopedia."[22] This review also illustrates the discomfort Zinn caused among nationalists as he replaced the traditional image of the United States as a land of opportunity, prosperity, and freedom with that of a nation whose capitalist system bred vast economic inequality and class conflict.

Fortunately for Zinn and his *People's History*, the *New York Times Book Review*, in contrast to the Handlin and Zimmerman polemics, ran a review that seriously and fair-mindedly engaged Zinn's arguments. That the book was reviewed at all by the *Times* was surprising since introductory books in history were rarely reviewed there, and books by leftists also tended back then to be ignored by the paper. It was a stroke of luck for Zinn that the review was assigned to Eric Foner, a brilliant historian who hailed from a prominent leftist family and was open to a radical historical narrative. Foner's trajectory as a historian in important respects resembled Zinn's: both had started out doing their Columbia dissertations on elected political leaders and then were influenced by the new social history—Zinn because of his oral history work on SNCC, Foner because of his contacts with radical historians E. P. Thompson and Eric Hobsbawm during his academic work in England—which was reflected in Foner's second book, on Thomas Paine and the American Revolution.[23] So Foner was not shocked by a book that looked at history from the bottom up. In fact, Foner would go on to serve as consulting editor for the American Social History Project *Who Built America?* textbook (1989), which, though less popular than *A People's History*, was among the largest collaborative labor history projects ever attempted. Foner was also an emerging public intellectual who wrote op-eds and articles intended to reach beyond academia, sharing with Zinn a desire to make history widely accessible.

Foner opened his *New York Times* review with a moving story illustrating the need for an introduction to American history that would broaden the focus beyond the political elite. Foner told of the anarchist Bartolomeo Vanzetti, in prison and awaiting execution in 1927, reading a U.S. history textbook and lamenting: "[It said] nothing . . . of the instinctive and intuitive aspirations of the poor, of the hardly articulated . . . souls of the humbles, except if I believe they are like the master." Foner noted that Vanzetti's comment still applied to U.S. history textbooks of the 1970s, which had failed to meaningfully incorporate into their narratives the new Black, women's, labor, and Native American histories. Foner credited Zinn with being "the first historian to attempt to survey all of American history from the perspective of this new [bottom-up] scholarship." He praised Zinn for making this history accessible, "writing with an enthusiasm rarely encountered in the leaden prose of academic history," offering a text that was "studded with telling quotations from labor leaders, war resisters, and fugitive slaves." In Zinn's book, Foner wrote, "there are vivid descriptions of events that are usually ignored, such as the great railroad strike of 1877."[24]

While praising these strengths of *A People's History*, Foner pointed to a number of weaknesses. He thought that Zinn's history reflected "a deeply pessimistic vision of the American experience." That even though *A People's History* highlighted resistance to oppression, it was always crushed or co-opted, and "the strikes and rebellions never appear to accomplish anything." He thought it problematic that "why such movements so often fail to achieve their goals is never adequately explained." Foner found Zinn so eager to document victimization of marginalized people that *A People's History* neglected to explore the uses such people made of power when they finally achieved a modicum of it via electoral politics, "as blacks did during Reconstruction." He also thought Zinn narrowed the roles of marginalized people into either "rebels . . . or victims," leading to a neglect of "less dramatic but more typical lives—people struggling to survive in difficult circumstances." Zinn, according to Foner, was weak in the realm of intellectual history, failing to "explore the ideologies of the various uprisings he details." In *A People's History*, Foner wrote, "rebellions are spontaneous responses to immediate conditions; the possibility that ordinary people may have complex political ideas is not considered."[25]

Foner's criticisms, though insightful, suggest a disconnect regarding the public's enthusiasm for Zinn's book (the millions of Americans who made the book a best seller). Why would so many people be drawn to a book that, as Foner argued, reflected a "deeply pessimistic vision of the American experience," in which struggles for social justice "never appear to accomplish anything"? The answer, in part, is that high school students and others did not read this introductory book in American history the way a professional historian such as Foner did.

When historians read about the great national railroad strike of 1877 in *A People's History*, they tend to see this as a demoralizing story of labor's defeat, not as an awe-inspiring struggle. This is because historians are so familiar with the strike Zinn describes. However, those for whom the story of this strike was new and unfamiliar, perceived Zinn's account as a moving tale of heroic struggle for workers' rights. All the more so because, unlike conventional textbooks that barely mentioned the strike, Zinn devoted seven action-packed pages to it, depicting it as one of the largest and most daring national labor uprisings in American history. While Zinn's narrative of the 1877 strike acknowledges defeat and that police and the National Guard were used to crush the workers' rebellion, he does not suggest the strike failed to accomplish anything. To the contrary, Zinn noted that "the railroads made some concessions, withdrew some wage cuts." The strike, he wrote, "taught many people of the hardships of others, and . . . led to congressional railroad regulation . . . [and] may have stimulated the business unionism of the American Federation of Labor as well as the national unity of labor proposed by the Knights of Labor, and the independent labor-farmer parties of the next two decades."[26]

Similarly, Zinn's chapter "The Socialist Challenge" devoted space to *successful* struggles for working-class rights—from the IWW's free speech fights to the election of Socialist Party candidates to local office, to the mill strike in Lawrence, Massachusetts.[27] Thus *A People's History* offered a vision of bottom-up social change that many readers saw as hopeful, in contrast to the pessimism that Foner perceived. Zinn's inclusion of extensive, powerful quotations from the most eloquent dissenters in American history added to the upbeat quality of his narrative.

Foner makes an important point in arguing that the failure of mass movements to achieve their goals "is never adequately explained" in *A People's History*. To explore this claim, we return to Zinn's depiction of the national railroad strike of 1877. Zinn does offer an explanation of the defeat: repression. He cites the deaths of more than one hundred people and the jailing of a thousand, concluding, "In 1877 . . . working people learned they were not united enough, not powerful enough to defeat the combination of private capital and government power."[28] But is this an adequate explanation? Why were workers not powerful enough to stop the government from deploying police and national guard against them? Zinn does not say. Yes, *A People's History* is an introductory work, and so one could argue that Zinn's brief conclusion was accurate and—for most high school students—adequate. Yet drilling down deeper here to explain the power dynamics and underlying social structure that yielded the defeat of the strike would have strengthened Zinn's discussion of its outcome.

Also ringing true is Foner's criticism of Zinn's tendency to view members of marginalized groups as "rebels . . . or victims," while devoting little attention to "less dramatic but more typical lives." But this was a function of the book's narrative structure and purpose. *A People's History* was—as indicated by its early working title, *Struggle for Democracy*—centered around the organizing of working people for their rights and social justice. This is a story of oppression and resistance, rather than a comprehensive social history of everyday life. To tell that story, Zinn almost had to place victims and rebels at center stage.

Foner is also correct that Zinn does not provide systemic analysis of "the ideologies of the various uprisings he details." But this does not mean, as Foner argues, that in *A People's History* "the possibility that ordinary people may have complex political ideas is not considered." As Foner himself acknowledged in his review, *A People's History* "is studded with telling quotations from labor leaders, war resisters, and fugitive slaves." Quotations of activists in protest movements ordinary people joined are also plentiful. So, if one considers these quotations alone, Zinn's book stands as an extensive documentary history of the dissident ideas if not ideologies of American working people.

The most weighty criticism Foner makes of Zinn's book concerns the problems "inherent" in its historical methodology, in "history from the bottom up." Foner praised this approach to history as a "necessary . . . corrective" to traditional histories that focus on the wealthy and powerful, but suggests that it is as limited in its own way as history from the top down. In traditional accounts, to take a single example, the Jacksonian era is portrayed as a time of democracy and reform, while Jackson's policy of Indian removal—a particularly shocking episode in America's home-grown holocaust—is ignored. Yet if previous historians disregarded the plight of the Cherokees, for Professor Zinn it is virtually the only aspect of the period that warrants attention. The result is still a partial view of Jacksonian America.[29]

Here Foner was calling for a new historical synthesis that brings together history from both the top down and the bottom up. Zinn was, in Foner's view, offering an additive approach that viewed the Cherokees and their victimization by Jackson in isolation from the rest of Jackson's policies and era, when he should instead have provided "an integrated account" that considered how those at the top and bottom of society are "shaped in large measure" by their relation to each other. Thus, "The strength of *A People's History*"—its pathbreaking shift of focus to the nonelite—"is also its weakness," Foner concluded. "Written to counter a prevailing tradition, it does not perhaps inevitably, transcend it. But open-minded readers will profit from Professor Zinn's account, and historians may well view it as a step toward a coherent new version of American history."[30]

This is a valid criticism and helps explain why some historians, including Foner, view Zinn as falling "toward the Manichean" and offering "an oversimplified narrative of the battle between the forces of light and darkness."[31] With Andrew Jackson, for example, Zinn, by introducing him through the lens of his most murderous, racist acts—his brutalization of Native Americans—demonizes him. This turns on its head the older, positive image of Jackson as representing democracy and the expansion in the Jacksonian era of voting rights and political participation to include the white working class.

Arguable as it is, such criticism misses an essential point about historiography. In the writing of a brief chapter in an introductory work of history, someone has to be center stage. In traditional textbooks, guided by the presidential synthesis, it is presidents who often occupy that spotlight, and the chapter covering the era of the Trail of Tears would be defined not by the tragedy of the Cherokees but by Andrew Jackson and the rise of (white male) "Jacksonian democracy." To work within that framework could easily lead, as it still does in even the best U.S. history textbooks today (including Foner's), to reducing the Trail of Tears to a sad but subordinate event in a democratic era.[32] That is why Michael Paul Rogin, in his pioneering revisionist work on Jackson, which Zinn drew on in *A People's History*, pushed the Native American tragedy to center stage even in the subtitle of his 1975 book *Fathers and Sons—Andrew Jackson and the Subjugation of the American Indian.* And it is why Zinn does not even mention Jackson in the title of his first chapter covering the years of his presidency, which Zinn chose to center on the fate of the Cherokees and Indian removal, "As Long as Grass Grows or Water Runs."[33]

A People's History does let readers know that there was more to Jackson's presidency than his Indian policy. Zinn criticizes U.S. history textbooks and historians of the Jacksonian era for addressing nearly everything about Jackson except his mistreatment of Native Americans:

> The leading books on the Jacksonian period, written by respected historians (*The Age of Jackson* by Arthur Schlesinger; *The Jacksonian Persuasion* by Marvin Meyers), do not mention Jackson's Indian policy, but there is much talk in them of tariffs, banking, political parties, political rhetoric. If you look through high school textbooks . . . in American history you will find Jackson the frontiersman, soldier, democrat, man of the people—not Jackson the slaveholder, land speculator, executioner of dissident soldiers, exterminator of Indians.[34]

Though Zinn's criticism of the traditional Jackson historiography and textbook hagiography here is persuasive, it does not negate the critical point Foner made about the narrow treatment of Jackson in *A People's History* and the benefits of integrating bottom-up and top-down history. Zinn could have enriched this narrative had he explored the relationship between Jackson's Indian policy and the rise of Jacksonian democracy. This was a missed opportunity to discuss the racially undemocratic mindset of the middle-class and working-class supporters of Jackson and the irony that rights expanded for white men were used to elect a president who represented the negation of democracy for Native Americans and African Americans.[35]

This leads us back to the criticism of Zinn discussed in chapter 1, from a Cambridge reader of his *People's History* book proposal, that Zinn tended to write off the two major political parties as twin pillars of the status quo, and so he devoted little attention to them. This tendency is visible in Zinn's discussion of Indian policy where he states that during Jackson's presidency "the two political parties . . . the Democrats and Whigs, . . . disagreed on banks and tariffs but not on issues crucial for . . . the Indians."[36] Actually Whigs, especially in the North, tended to oppose Indian removal.[37] *A People's History* quotes Theodore Frelinghuysen's powerful Senate speech on behalf of Native American rights: "We have crowded the tribes upon a few miserable acres on our southern frontier; it is all that is left to them of their once boundless forest; and still, like the horse-leech, our insatiated cupidity cries, give! give! . . . Sir . . . Do the obligations of justice change with the color of the skin?" But Zinn only identifies Frelinghuysen as a

New Jersey senator, without mentioning his prominence in the Whig Party, first in the Senate and then as its vice presidential candidate.[38] This connects with the recent scholarship of Daniel Walker Howe, the preeminent historian of the American Whig Party, who argued that Whig and northern regional revulsion for Jackson's lawlessness and Indian policy was so strong that it should lead us to discard the traditional historical construct of mid-1820s and 1830s America as being the "Jacksonian era."[39] Howe points to the closeness of congressional votes on key Jackson policies, including Indian removal, which as Zinn noted, barely passed in the U.S. House of Representatives by a vote of 102 to 97, as evidence that too many Americans dissented from Jacksonian policy for it to be seen as representative of them or their era.[40] Readers then, might want to read Howe as a useful update to Zinn and consider Howe's even more radical stance, rejecting the very idea of a Jacksonian era.

Zinn does go back to Jackson briefly, two chapters after his discussion of the fate of the Indians under him. This time Old Hickory makes a brief appearance in Zinn's chapter "The Other Civil War," on class warfare in industrializing America, with Jackson presented by Zinn as a phony, posing as a champion of the common man. Here Zinn is explicit about his view of the two-party system as a shell game designed to serve as a buffer from class conflict, distracting people from confronting real issues of social inequity. That system in Jackson's day (and since), in Zinn's words, gave people "a choice between two parties . . . allow[ing] them, in a period of rebellion, to choose the slightly more democratic one, [which] was an ingenious mode of control."[41]

For Zinn, the two-party system represented a trap for both Americans forced to choose leaders who had no genuine interest in true equality and for historians and textbook authors who allowed it to shape and distort their historical narratives. The two-party system elevated the importance of elections that had little meaning, took attention away from the class issues that really mattered, and made Americans think they should look to elected officials for leadership when in fact only dissident protest movements could bring real change. So, for Zinn, a people's history could be empowering to its readers only if it decentered electoral politics. As Zinn put it, explaining why he gave short shrift to Jackson: "The stories of the Anti-Renter movement and Dorr's Rebellion are not usually found in textbooks on United States history. In these books, given to millions of young Americans, there is little on class struggle in the nineteenth century. . . . Even where specialized books on the Jacksonian period deal with labor and economic issues they center on the presidency, and thus perpetuate the traditional dependency on heroic leaders rather than people's struggles."[42] There is a good deal of historical evidence to support Zinn's indictment of the two-party system (especially regarding its decades of evading action on slavery) and reason to agree that the presidential synthesis traditionally used in most textbooks crowds out social history and ordinary people. Still, this dismissive view of electoral politics leaves Zinn ill-equipped to probe the connections between class, race, and the U.S. political system, which is a different limitation than those he criticized in textbooks but a serious one all the same.

❦

Since Zinn's initial discussion of Jackson focused far more on Native Americans than on Jackson, and since *A People's History* devoted much more attention to Native American history than conventional U.S. history textbooks, it is important to see how an expert in Native American history views Zinn's treatment of that history. Unfortunately, and this is in itself a commentary on the state of the historical profession back in 1980, none of the reviewers of *A People's History* was a scholar of Native American history. So to attain such an assessment of Zinn's work, we consulted with James H. Merrell, the author of two Bancroft Prize-winning books, *The Indian's New World: Catawbas and Their Neighbors from European Contact through the Era of Removal* (1989) and *Into the American Woods: Negotiators on the Pennsylvania Frontier* (1999), as well as two seminal review essays on the failings of historians to write Native American history accurately and free from what historian Francis Jennings termed the cant of conquest.[43]

Merrell was favorably impressed with discussion of the Cherokees, the Trail of Tears, and Indian removal in *A People's History*. He credited Zinn with having mastered all the important historical works then available on the history of white-Indian conflict, including such major revisionist books as Rogin's on Jackson's Indian policy, Francis Jennings's paradigm-breaking history of early American expulsion of Indians, *The Invasion of America*, and the writings of Richard Drinnon, who as Merrell put it was "kind of the Francis Jennings of the early nineteenth century" in his work on violence in the West.[44]

Zinn's effective use of primary sources on the Cherokee experience was striking to Merrell: "He's got the Cherokee census of 1826 in here. [He offers] a remarkable amount of [revealing information]. So there's a granular level of detail here, but it's also sweeping. I don't know how he did it, frankly. Because he manages to show the ways in which the Cherokees were accommodating to white ways, and yet that only made them more resistant to surrendering their national identity and more effective at resisting it. It is really a terrific piece of work." Merrell was also taken with Zinn's perceptive account of white missionaries' relationship to Native Americans, especially since it was written back in the 1970s: "I honestly do not know how he did it . . . do you know how long he was working on this?"[45]

Merrell's sweeping, influential review essays have taken to task historians who specialize in early American history for uncritically adopting the loaded terminology and parochial mindset of European settlers in their accounts of the history of white-Indian interactions. Yet he was struck by how sensitive and sophisticated Zinn was about the language and euphemisms that historians traditionally used to discuss that history. Merrell noted that in *A People's History* Zinn wrote about the parochial and misleading terminology historians have used, "[such as] 'Indian removal,' as it had been politely called" (after which Zinn adds, "which is the point I have been making"). "[And] when Zinn wrote this," Merrell notes, "'ethnic cleansing' wasn't yet in the vocabulary, but right away he is aware that 'Indian removal' is a very antiseptic term for this [brutal expulsion of Native Americans from their land]." As if it was something neat or minor like "spot removal." Thus thanks to Zinn's critical reflection on this conventional term, the reader, according to Merrell, "is all of a sudden brought up short because you've been thinking 'Indian removal' is what it's called. And even at the time it was, but now the term's inadequacy is much more plain for all to see."[46]

Merrell was struck by the literary versatility Zinn displayed in his chapter on the Cherokees and Jackson. On the one hand, Zinn proved himself bold, as with his "willingness to take on Arthur Schlesinger Jr.," the eminent historian, for idealizing Jackson while ignoring his mistreatment of Native Americans. But on the other hand, Zinn displayed "restraint" to good effect, especially in the chapter's conclusion. As Merrell explains, "He ends the chapter with [Martin] Van Buren," Jackson's former vice president and successor as president, specifically an 1838 speech in which Van Buren told Congress that "the removal of the Cherokee Nation of Indians to their new homes west of the Mississippi . . . have had the happiest effects." On Zinn's ending with the quote, Merrell said, "I love the way, this is where I'm coming from too [in writing history] . . . you let them hang themselves. Let them speak and then set it up in a way that will let the reader see what your own point of view is." The effect is powerful. "It would have been easy for him to . . . add a couple of sentences [of his own views] there." But instead Zinn exercised authorial restraint, to devastating effect. Van Buren's statement needs no further commentary, it was so damning of both him and his predecessor. That chapter, Merrell found, "touches your head but also your heart." It leaves you angry about the mistreatment of the Cherokees while having you admire the Indians and their allies in battling "removal," clueing in readers "who had [previously had] no idea what these people [opposing Jackson] were up against."[47]

Some of the credit for the power of Zinn's narrative here and its enduring value, in Merrell's view, belongs to the strong scholarship that came out in the 1970s on Indian expulsion. Merrell thinks Zinn was wise to draw so heavily on

Rogin's work, saying, "I'm still an un-reconstructed Rogin fan. I still think that [Rogin's *Andrew Jackson and the Subjugation of the Indians*] is perhaps the best book on Indian removal." This is one reason Merrell finds Zinn's analysis of this history still valuable. "His take on Indian removal stands up very well. We know a great deal more [today] about the Cherokees than we did before and about the sophistication of their resistance. . . . So he would [have been] able to build [this up] even more. But I think he gets the basic structure of how sophisticated they were very much intact."[48]

Going beyond the Cherokees, Jackson, and the Trail of Tears to the larger history of white-Indian relations, Merrell thinks important recent trends in Native American historiography can serve as valuable updates to Zinn. Merrell's first suggested update bears a resemblance to Foner's point about *A People's History* being too narrowly focused on victims and rebels. Merrell and other historians of the Native American experience in the colonial era and early republic have over the past few decades stressed that white-Indian interaction was too complex to be understood simply in terms of violent conflict. As Merrell explains, "We've tended to focus on wars in American history in general, whether it's World War II or World War I or the Civil War. And so we tend to focus on Indian wars. But there were far more treaties between colonists and Indians in which they found a way to come together and not kill each other than there were wars between them."[49]

A key component of this recent scholarship is the concept, first articulated by historian Richard White, of a "middle ground" between white and Native American societies.[50] "This notion," as Merrell put it, "of people venturing from their own comfort zones out onto a middle ground where they had to . . . find ways of getting along . . . People have taken Richard's work and . . . said 'Oh, . . . everybody was happy and they got along on this middle ground.' And he says, 'No, it was a very violent place.' And part of being on the middle ground was what he called 'creative misunderstanding,' pretending that you understood the other person and not getting it at all, but getting it well enough to not bury a hatchet in their head."[51]

Merrell suggests that Zinn's account of the Native American experience would have been even more powerful if it had been less episodic, recognizing that Indians have always been an active historical force. "It would have been useful to find ways to weave Natives in throughout, and not just first contact with Europeans and removal and then in the west."[52] Merrell points to the Great Awakening, the mass religious revival of the eighteenth century, as an example of a movement involving Native Americans not traditionally linked to Indian history. This connects back to a key criticism that historian Michael Kammen raised about *A People's History* in 1980. Kammen saw Zinn's neglect of American religious history as a serious "sin of omission" since "religion has been a force that has been phenomenal rather than epiphenomenal in American life. . . . The Great Awakening, the single most consequential social movement between colonization and the American Revolution—and a movement fraught with egalitarian consequences—is not discussed."[53] This relates to Native American history because, as Merrell explains, Linford Fisher and other historians have shown, "there was an Indian Great Awakening."[54] Merrell notes that the awakening would have been an exciting story for Zinn to narrate because there was "a lot of strife" since most people thought revival leader George Whitefield and his followers were "crazy," in part because their movement's religious egalitarianism crossed gender, generational, and racial lines. "They're allowing women and children, and Negroes, as they put it, to stand up to exhort a populace, sometimes including Native Americans." "At the same time," Merrell added, "Natives were themselves leading revivals, some of those with elements of Christianity, some actually in opposition to it."[55]

The connection between religion and Native American resistance, Merrell points out, is embodied by the story of William Apess, a Pequot who was a Methodist minister in the 1820s and 1830s and author of the first American Indian autobiography. His writings and sermons were, according to Merrell, "quite brilliant." "He used Pilgrim sources to excoriate the Pilgrims for all the terrible things [colonists did] to Native Americans [in New England]." Merrell thought that Apess's story would have worked well in *A People's History* as "another way to show the continuing power of Native American activism."[56] Such sources as Apess's autobiography plus the new historiography discussed by Merrell should be used to update and supplement *A People's History* on the Native American experience.

Merrell credits Zinn for popularizing the work of a generation of historians from Jennings to Rogin who sought to get the United States to look more honestly and critically at the Native American experience: "I see them offering . . . a wake-up call to Americans, to say to both scholars and the public . . . our history is more complicated and more interesting and darker than you realized." But Merrell finds it "disappointing" how resistant Americans have been to this critical history. "What if the U.S. government had code-named Al Qaeda leader Osama Bin Laden not Geronimo but some other freedom fighter from America's past—say, George Washington? In this day and age, that you can [take the] label of a Native American leader who fought in defense of his people and tie it to a terrorist, or that you can call various parts of Afghanistan and Iraq 'Indian country' . . . just boggles the mind." Merrell finds that even today historians seem resistant to changing their discourse on Native American history: "You can't really have a conversation about where Native peoples belong in American history without realizing that we're speaking the same . . . language that those who slaughtered and removed Native Americans were speaking. No, we don't call them 'savages' anymore, or 'primitives,' or 'squaws.' . . . But our [incorrect] assumptions are still: 'Well, they didn't really grow crops, we had to teach them farming. . . .' It shouldn't be that hard to stop calling them settlers, without putting an adjective in front: *European* settlers, *Cherokee* settlers; to stop saying 'pre-contact,' as if the only encounters with strangers Native peoples had across millennia were with Europeans."[57]

In teaching undergraduates, Merrell is struck by the lack of critical Native American history that his students received in their secondary education. During a recent class, after a discussion of white-Indian relations in early America, one of his students asked, "Why didn't I learn any of this before we got here?" There was, Merrell could see, "a sense of 'we were robbed by our education.'" He thinks this is a key reason Zinn is "still popular" with students. "It's refreshing for them. It's more interesting. It's more exciting. It has a point of view and challenges what they've been told."[58]

∽

The other key topic in the history of race that has long been taught poorly in many high schools is slavery.[59] Zinn sought to change this, spotlighting slavery in his book, stressing the ugliness and brutality of racial slavery, plus Black resistance, arguing for the centrality of slavery and racism to the American experience. He did this by popularizing the pathbreaking scholarship of the 1960s and 1970s on slavery and the Black freedom struggle. Eric Foner, whose book on Lincoln and slavery won the Pulitzer Prize in history, discussed with us the chapter in *A People's History* titled "Slavery without Submission, Emancipation without Freedom." It was evident, Foner says, that Zinn "did come to master the existing literature" on slavery and offered insightful analysis and revealing primary sources on Civil War era Black soldiers and slaves running away [from plantations and farms]. "[I am] very impressed with the up-to-datedness of the other chapters too of that moment, of the works he was using. So [*A People's History*] did play a very valuable role in summarizing . . . the state of the literature [on slavery]." The strength of that literature, as Foner sees it, was extraordinary: "The [Herbert] Gutmans, [Eugene] Genoveses, the others—that work is . . . still being read, still important."[60]

Zinn's reading of the role of slavery in provoking the Civil War is, however, problematic. This is not to say it is wrong or uninformed by the relevant scholarship. In fact, Zinn's interpretation echoes Richard Hofstadter's classic critique of Lincoln on race and slavery in his book *The American Political Tradition* (1948).[61] Foner acknowledges that Zinn, in doubting that the moral issue of slavery played a major role in the origins of the Civil War, was presenting "a defensible position."[62] It was one that had other adherents among historians of his day but has been challenged powerfully by more recent historical scholarship, including Foner's *The Fiery Trial* (2011) and James Oakes's *Freedom National* (2014).[63] In *A People's History*, Zinn asserted that in the Civil War "the clash was not over slavery as a moral institution. . . . It was . . . a clash of elites. The northern elite wanted economic expansion—free land, free labor, a free market, a high protective tariff for manufacturers; a bank of the United States. The slave interests opposed all that."[64] But if Zinn was right, why would Lincoln risk civil war to prevent slavery's expansion to the west? And how do we explain Lincoln's behavior during the secession crisis—his unwillingness to compromise with the slave South as prior presidents had? As Foner explains, Lincoln "could [have] easily preserve[d] the Union by giving in to the South," dropping his opposition to slavery's westward expansion. "No problem. Just give them what they want. If you don't care about slavery, why not?"[65] These questions were not addressed in Zinn's cursory treatment of secession.

Zinn's view of the Civil War's origins not only underestimates Lincoln's moral antagonism against slavery but also misses how he stood up to the slave South. For example, Zinn asserts (as most textbooks do) that Lincoln's first inaugural address "was conciliatory towards the South and the seceded states." To support this view he cites Lincoln's claim that he did not intend to interfere "with the institution of slavery in the states where it exists." But Zinn overlooks the part of that inaugural address in which Lincoln—an ardent critic of the Dred Scott decision—defied that pro-slavery decision by advocating the protection of the due process rights of African Americans seized as fugitive slaves.[66] The Dred Scott decision had denied Blacks citizenship rights, yet there was Lincoln urging the protection of those very rights, right in front of pro-slavery Chief Justice Roger Taney, present at the inaugural, who had written that decision. This demonstration that the first president elected on an antislavery platform was going to defy the pro-slavery Supreme Court (and make the seizure of fugitive slaves more difficult) was certainly not conciliatory toward the southern slavocracy. And Zinn did not mention Lincoln's second inaugural address, which denounced slavery as a sin, depicted the Civil War as God's punishment for that sin, and cited slavery as the cause of the war. *A People's History* gives us Lincoln without the Gettysburg Address, unable to consider why in that speech, with the Civil War still going on, he heralded a "new birth of freedom."

Zinn's failure to acknowledge this moral dimension, the antislavery origins, of the Civil War, seems linked to his profound opposition to war in general. Zinn saw war as an immoral phenomenon and so was reluctant to recognize a moral dimension to any war. Thus in the World War II chapter of *A People's History* Zinn asserts, "Roosevelt was as much concerned to end oppression of the Jews as Lincoln was to end slavery during the Civil War; their priority in policy (whatever their personal compassion for victims of persecution) was not minority rights but national power. It was not Hitler's attacks on the Jews that brought the United States into World War II, any more than the enslavement of 4 million blacks brought Civil War in 1861."[67] This is, in Foner's view, "a nice literary device." "What does it mean to say the Civil War is not about slavery? It's certainly true [that the origin of] World War II was not about the Holocaust. The Holocaust took place, really after World War II began, and it wasn't the reason the United States entered the war. . . . But without slavery, no Civil War. No matter what you think the balance of causes were, and there were many of them, without slavery it's impossible to imagine that there would have been a Civil War."[68]

Foner recognizes that Zinn's take on the Civil War is linked to his stance "against all war," which he deems "a healthy point of view." "Zinn is very cynical about war, and he's cynical about the high-flying rhetoric used to justify war. . . . But my view of this is what Du Bois says . . . in *Black Reconstruction* . . . [that] 'war is murder, anarchy, injustice, but sometimes good comes from it.' That's the balance."[69] In contrast to Zinn, there is, Foner holds, "a tendency among what are called neo-abolitionist scholars to get into a gung ho view of the Civil War. I think that's not right. But on the other hand, to dismiss it as mindless slaughter with no point . . . , that the story of the Civil War is death, well, that's the story of every war, but it's not the whole story."[70]

Zinn's antiwar position also influenced the Reconstruction segment of his chapter "Slavery without Submission, Emancipation without Freedom." In his "emancipation without freedom" construct, the Civil War—even if one considers it as a moral struggle for freedom—ultimately failed to deliver the political and social equality needed to secure true freedom for Blacks.

Foner views Zinn's stress on Reconstruction's failure rather than its achievements as a reflection of the political atmosphere of the time Zinn was writing, when there was a loss of momentum in the struggle for racial equality after the collapse of "the Second Reconstruction" (the civil rights movement of the 1960s) and the drift of the nation rightward. *A People's History*, like every work of history, is, as Foner puts it, "a product of the moment it was written in." Zinn wrote in "a post–civil rights era moment when . . . you don't have Reagan yet, but you've had Nixon and the Supreme Court [abandoning the racial liberalism of the earlier Warren Court years]." "You're seeing the white backlash, you've seen the impulse of the movement kind of dissipating. And I think that's what is in-fluencing [Zinn]." Zinn sensed that in the first Reconstruction, as in the second, "you have these advances and then there's a retreat right after them."[71]

Zinn's treatment of Reconstruction was, according to Foner, also constrained by the fact that in the mid-1970s the historical scholarship on Black historical agency in the Reconstruction South "was still quite limited, underdeveloped actually." In the 1980s, when Foner was researching and writing his landmark synthesis on Reconstruction, he found such a paucity of grassroots studies that he had to do some himself.[72] So the Black history Zinn narrated on slavery and the Civil War era was much stronger and more evocative than the Reconstruc-tion section of the same chapter of A People's History in part because there was a much richer historical literature on slavery from which to draw. Foner explains, "[Zinn did not have] the literature on hand to develop what I would think would be a more complicated view of success and failure in Reconstruction, both to-gether." So in A People's History it is presented as "just a total failure."[73]

Foner gives additional evidence of how Zinn's "treatment of Reconstruction is quite limited."[74] For example, Zinn mentions that Black voting rights obtained during Reconstruction resulted in the election of two Black U.S. senators, twenty Black congressmen, and also Black state legislators. But this understates the po-litical revolution of this period when some two thousand African Americans held office in the South and thousands joined political organizations such as the Union League to assert their political rights.[75] And again because of the time in which Zinn was writing, he lacked access to studies that documented the impact that Reconstruction governments had on Black workers, as in South Carolina where the state government refused to bow to the pressure of white planters to suppress a strike by rice plantation workers.[76]

Zinn was too good a social historian to entirely miss the eagerness with which southern Blacks asserted and exercised their new freedoms during Rad-ical Reconstruction. So he drew on the work of historian Peter Kolchin on the way African Americans in Reconstruction Alabama "began immediately assert-ing their independence of whites, forming their own churches, becoming polit-ically active, strengthening their family ties, trying to educate their children."[77] Yet Zinn never confronted the contradiction between Kolchin's evidence of this emergence of Black freedom and his chapter's title and theme of "Emancipation without Freedom."

Instead Zinn, looking ahead to the tragic overthrow of Reconstruction, hedges on Black historical agency. While conceding that "southern blacks were determined to make the most of their freedom," Zinn stresses that this came "in spite of their lack of land and resources. . . . So long as the Negro remained dependent on privileged whites for work, for the necessities of life, his vote could be bought or taken away by threat of force. Thus, laws calling for equal treatment became meaningless."[78] But they did not become meaningless until Radical Reconstruction was overthrown, and so the question remains: what are we to make of the achievements of the Black political activism (and social assertiveness), the impressive expressions of Black historical agency and freedom in the Reconstruction era itself? This question would be illuminated brilliantly by Foner's Reconstruction scholarship, Leon Litwack's Pulitzer Prize–winning study, and others documenting the many ways Blacks defined and experimented with freedom in the Reconstruction era, as well as by the publications of the Freedmen and Southern Society Project.[79] But these came out too late for Zinn's book.

The meaning of the constitutional revolution represented by the Reconstruction amendments (the Thirteenth, Fourteenth, and Fifteenth Amendments) and its legacy for the twentieth-century civil rights movement—was overshadowed in *A People's History*. Zinn raced through the history of Reconstruction to get to its overthrow by southern white supremacists and abandonment by northern Republicans and the federal government.[80] He aptly stressed the tragedy of the overthrowing of Reconstruction governments, but the meaning and legacy of that first era of interracial democracy are not explored adequately. And so readers might want to contrast Zinn's image of failure with Foner's argument that Reconstruction was America's unfinished revolution—which, as Foner explains, "navigates between negative and positive, Reconstruction's attempted revolution on behalf of racial equality." "It's not failed, it's unfinished," he says.[81]

All this is not meant to suggest that *A People's History* should be disregarded by those studying or teaching the Civil War and Reconstruction. The point here is that historical research is a dynamic and ongoing process, and so Zinn's conclusions, shaped by the historical scholarship when he was writing in the 1970s and the politics of that time, must be interrogated in light of more recent scholarship. Nor should it be assumed that because Zinn's book is forty years old, his conclusions about the Reconstruction era are antiquated and not worth considering. Actually, in the opening decades of our own century—with the nation in retreat from the Voting Rights Act, affirmative action, and from other important legacies of the Black freedom movement—historians trended more toward Zinn's focus on Reconstruction's failures than Foner's more upbeat assessment of that era and its legacy. As Foner explains,

> [Zinn's construct of] emancipation without freedom . . . that's come back. I
> mean the current tendency in the study of that period is to downgrade the ex-

perience of freedom. And to say the same thing [as Zinn], racism was perma-
nent. "Yeah they passed these civil rights laws, Reconstruction amendments,
but they really didn't enforce them." My student Jim Downs's book argues that
formerly enslaved people had horrible health—lacked access to health care,
and were sick, diseased.[82] They're all dying of freedom. The other Downs,
Gregory (no relation) [recently published a book] on the failure of the army
[in the Reconstruction South] to actually protect [Black] people.[83] [There is] a
lot of literature now on [white supremacist] violence. So you're getting again
a picture of this period without a lot of progress or accomplishment. Carole
Emberton wrote a recent essay called "Unwriting the Freedom Narrative."[84]
So in a way his [Zinn's chapter] title ["Emancipation without Freedom"] is an-
ticipating something, but that's again a sign of where we are [in twenty-first-
century America: skeptical about racial progress].[85]

Foner sees in the Civil War and Reconstruction chapters of *A People's History* the strengths and limitations of Zinn's approach to American history. Zinn's
cynicism about reform, and Lincoln as the embodiment of that, leads him, in
Foner's view, to rely too heavily on the Hofstadter chapter on Lincoln in his
American Political Tradition (1948). Foner calls that chapter "a brilliant demo-
lition job" that underestimated Lincoln's antislavery commitment and ability to
change on the question of Black rights—to the point where Lincoln by 1865 had
publicly endorsed voting rights for literate Black men and African American
Union army soldiers.[86] Zinn follows Hofstadter in suggesting that since Lincoln
publicly had spoken up earlier in his political career against social equality between the races, this meant that he was not deeply opposed to slavery. But what
this position misses, as Foner explains, is that Lincoln "thinks about slavery
without thinking about race. We can't imagine that . . . To Lincoln slavery is an
intellectual issue, a political issue, an economic issue, it's a violation of fundamental rights. It's not a question of race." And although Zinn's quotation (picked
up from Hofstadter) of Lincoln opposing Black-white social equality in 1858 is
accurate, it is misleading. Yes, Lincoln did say then "I am not . . . in favor of
bringing about in any way the social and political equality of the white and black
races," but, as Foner notes,

> [Lincoln] actually says almost nothing about race his whole life. I'm not trying
> to make him into Martin Luther King Jr., but race is not important to his way
> of thinking. But we are so bogged down in it [our national obsession with
> race] that we can't imagine that. And that makes it very difficult to under-
> stand him. You . . . can piece together the quotes about Lincoln and race and
> you say, "oh, well, he said this," and then you realize there's like seven of them

[Lincoln quotes on race] his whole life. My old professor Jack Garraty once said, warning students, "A trend in your note cards is not necessarily a trend in history." You can throw things together, but actually the real point is [that] there's almost nothing there.[87]

What both Hofstadter and Zinn miss, as Foner points out, "[is that] you could genuinely hate slavery and be a racist at the same time"—and "Lincoln is a good example of that." Foner says that Lincoln's "personal view" was that "there should not be any slavery, and that's not the main point of the Civil War in the beginning, but without that personal view you're not going to get anywhere."[88] So there was complexity to Lincoln's thought that Zinn was apparently not interested in exploring. His bottom-up approach to history led him to peg the president as an obstacle to change, to emancipation, so he simply adopted Hofstadter's cynical reading of Lincoln. That reading was evidence based, so it is not illegitimate or entirely wrong, but it is at the very least debatable.

This brings us back to Foner's 1980 review of A People's History and what he was referring to when he urged a synthesis of bottom-up and top-down history. Foner recalls that he believed then, and does still, that A People's History represented a significant breakthrough in popular historical understanding "since 99 percent of the existing history was top-down."[89] That is why Foner had written that adding that bottom-up view "was a step toward a . . . coherent new vision" of American history.[90] But Foner also thinks that "you can't understand the historical situation only looking from the bottom up." To get that coherent new vision means including "all this material" from those beyond the elite, the likes of which Zinn had gathered, then combining it with "much better" coverage of the political elite, "the Jeffersons . . . the Lincolns, . . . the Roosevelts, and the others." Historians need to be "more sophisticated about analyzing them—but that wasn't what he [Zinn] was interested in."[91]

Foner thinks that Zinn's relative lack of interest in "electoral politics played a role in his limited coverage of the reforms implemented by Reconstruction governments and how Blacks used political power in them. By way of contrast, this use of political power is of great interest to Foner, who probes it with great care in his Reconstruction books. Foner speculates that this difference may be rooted in their different political orientations: "I came up through Marxism, and he's an anarchist. Political power is very important to me, whereas to him it's not, it's mass uprisings. . . . Zinn was interested in action and . . . in the people who are getting out there and fighting in the streets . . . not the pamphleteers [or reformers]."[92]

These flaws in Zinn's historical approach do not, as Foner well understands, negate the book's narrative power or its appeal. "Getting the voice of these [nonelite] people into the book is a wonderful thing and did really generate a lot of enthusiasm among student readers. And . . . the textbooks of the time were really boring. . . . *A People's History* grabs you, it absolutely grabs you, and it excited people. And a lot of people [still] read Zinn and just say 'God, I never knew all this.' . . . And this is a whole different vision of history . . . presented in an appealing way."[93]

The facet of Zinn's coverage of early American history that most infuriated antiradical critics, other than his takedown of Columbus, was his treatment of the Founders, the American Revolution they led, and the Constitution they wrote. Zinn critic Robert Zimmerman, suggested that "hardly a statue in a public square would survive Howard Zinn's sledgehammer." In Zinn's version of the American past, charged Zimmerman, "Ben Franklin and George Washington were colonial fat cats who engineered a so-called revolution to protect the interests of the propertied class."[94] Historian Joseph R. Conlin, who mocked *A People's History* as "a museum piece" from the 1960s, "like LSD on a sugar cube," accused Zinn of demonizing the Founders as a sinister "'elite,' . . . dedicated to inflicting misery." On Zinn's pages, wrote Conlin, "the leaders of the American Revolution" made "suckers of the thousands who did the fighting."[95]

Far removed from such antiradical sniping was the critical yet fair-minded review of Zinn's treatment of the Founders and the Revolution by Zinn biographer Martin Duberman. Though brief and centered on the Constitution, Duberman's analysis was both nuanced and insightful.[96] Duberman noted that Zinn was one of the few historians of his time whose view of the Constitution was heavily influenced by Charles Beard's classic debunking of the Founders, *An Economic Interpretation of the Constitution* (1913), which accused them of writing a document to serve their personal economic interests.[97] Zinn saw the Constitution as "a compromise between the slaveholding interests of the South and the moneyed interests of the North."[98] Duberman argued, "This basic statement isn't wrong but it does stand in need of considerable modification."[99] Even though the Founders had an elitist preference to "curtail direct democracy in favor of indirect republicanism (the Electoral College, the Supreme Court, and senatorial elections by states)," the participatory ethos of the Revolution led them to be responsive to the popular will of the free white male population. Thus, they opted for direct election in Congress's lower house and for constitutional conventions in each state. And when antifederalists bemoaned the Founders' failure to include a Bill of Rights in the Constitution, they responded by pledging to add a Bill of Rights after ratification—which they subsequently did.

Duberman challenged Zinn's Beardian economic interpretation of the struggle over the Constitution's ratification—as well as the document's genesis. "Some
debtors," Duberman explained,

> along with creditors, avidly favored the Constitution; the battle over ratifica-
> tion wasn't a simplistic struggle between those who had property and those
> who didn't, nor was it the creation of a cabal of creditors determined to col-
> lect monies owed them—which is pretty much Howard's position. Yet the
> Constitution *was* designed to set up a much stronger government than had
> previously existed, and a major reason was to protect property rights, includ-
> ing in slaves. But it wasn't the sole reason. Many patriots, well aware that the
> weakness of the preceding Articles of Confederation was likely to lead to the
> partition of states into a number of confederacies, and believing that the Revo-
> lution had been fought for the rights of man as well as property, felt it impera-
> tive to maintain the union intact as a standing example for people everywhere.
> The protection of property rights, in short, wasn't the sum and substance of
> the Constitution's design. Its adoption may have profited bondholders, but a
> description that reduces it to the wealthy consolidating their power leaves out
> a good deal. [100]

This critique is insightful and reflects a good deal of mainstream scholarship
on the Constitution and its ratification. What it misses, however, is how Zinn's
Beardian view of the Constitution works to provoke discussion and stimulate
reflection on the part of high school students and others with limited exposure
to historians' debates. While Duberman is right that Zinn's reading of the Constitution's origin is narrow, it does get students to think critically about class and
power in the early republic.

Despite the limitations of Zinn's chapters about the revolutionary era, their
critical stance on class, power, and the Constitution links them to some of the
best recent neoprogressive scholarship on the origins of the Constitution. As
Alan Taylor, the Pulitzer Prize–winning historian—and author of the 2017 book
American Revolutions: A Continental History, 1750–1804—notes, Zinn shared
with him (and two leading historians of the Constitution and its ratification,
Woody Holton and Terry Bouton), an understanding that a key attraction of the
Constitution to the Founders was that it served "as a way to limit the power of
the lower orders."[101] The difference was that Zinn, like Beard, "did tend to narrow down to the particular investment interests of the leading Federalists" their
yearning for a Constitution favoring the elite, "whereas more recent work [in-
cluding that of Holton, Bouton, and Taylor] has focused on their class identity
as framing [their elitist vision of the Constitution]."[102]

The strongest part of Zinn's economic interpretation of the Constitution concerns not the document's origins or ratification but its class bias. Even the Constitution's clause forbidding states from "impair[ing] the obligation of contract," argues Zinn, favors the wealthy. As he explains, "To protect everyone's contracts seems like an act of fairness, of equal treatment, until one considers that contracts between rich and poor, between employer and employee, landlord and tenant, creditor and debtor, generally favor the more powerful of the two parties. Thus, to protect these contracts is to put the great power of the government, its laws, courts, sheriffs, police, on the side of the privileged—and to do it not, as in premodern times, as an exercise of brute force against the weak but as a matter of law." [103] Zinn was fond of reminding people that "this much-touted Constitution . . . doesn't say anything about economic rights, at least for [working-class] people."[104]

Useful as it is, Duberman's focus on the Founders and the Constitution misses what was so unusual and innovative about Zinn's treatment of the American Revolution in *A People's History* compared to most textbooks of the time. After all, the center of gravity in Zinn's chapters on the Revolution was with the people, not the elite, and what Zinn brought to this historical narrative that seemed new to the public in 1980 was evidence from recent radical historical scholarship exploring what the Revolution looked like from the bottom up. This contrasted with his treatment of those at the top, whom Zinn was content to view through old iconoclastic historiography. Much as he did with Lincoln on slavery, drawing on Hofstadter from the 1940s, Zinn relied on an old muckraking account, Beard's, which dated back to 1913, when it came to the Founders and the Constitution.[105] So to get at the heart of Zinn's treatment of the American Revolution we need to explore his larger interpretation of its social dynamic and meaning.

The two chapters in *A People's History* on the American Revolution's origins, character, and consequences offer a provocative synthesis of what in the 1960s and 1970s was termed the "new social history." In these chapters Zinn uses Gary Nash's data on the growing socioeconomic inequality on the eve of the Revolution, Marvin Michael Kay's account of North Carolina's class-conscious white farmers' revolt to democratize local government, Dirk Hoerder's study of the class composition of Boston's revolutionary mobs, and Rhys Isaac's writing on class relations in Virginia. Zinn draws from John Shy on class tensions in the American military (where the poor did a disproportionate share of the fighting) and cites Jackson Turner Main on the wealthy 10 percent of America who owned nearly half the wealth of the country. He also relies on the likes of Rowland Berthoff and John Murrin on the Revolution's failure to radically change America's social structure, Staughton Lynd on the tenant uprisings in upstate New York, Edward Countryman on rural rebellions, and Francis Jennings on the Native American role in the Revolution.[106] In his synthesis of secondary sources Zinn presents colonial America as increasingly stratified, beset by class tensions and violence—a virtual cauldron of class conflict. "By 1760," Zinn writes, "there had been eighteen uprisings aimed at overthrowing colonial governments. There had also been six black rebellions from South Carolina to New York and forty riots of various origins.[107]

Though acknowledging that Americans from diverse social classes had grievances against the British imperialist regime, Zinn argues that the American elite saw mobilization against the empire as a way of defusing dangerous class tensions. This "possibility of directing much of the rebellious energy" of the American lower classes "against England and her local officials . . . was not a conspiracy, but an accumulation of tactical responses." Thus, in reading Zinn, the American Revolution comes across as less about liberty or national self-determination and more about capitalist hegemony and the consolidating of the American elite's dominance. "By creating a nation, a symbol, a legal unity called the United States . . . [this elite] could take over land, profits, and political power from favorites of the British Empire. In the process, they could hold back a number of potential rebellions and create a consensus of support for the rule of a new privileged leadership. . . . The Founding Fathers . . . created the most effective system of national control devised in modern times, and showed future generations of leaders the advantages of combining paternalism with command."[108] Zinn presented the Revolutionary War as a rich man's war and poor man's fight. The title of his chapter "Tyranny Is Tyranny" represents a slogan chanted in July 1776 by poor Bostonians rioting in a protest against the practice of the rich avoiding service in the Revolutionary army by paying for substitutes.[109]

Conservatives yearning for a filiopietistic reading of the Founders had good reason, then, to be upset at Zinn's treatment of the American Revolution. A People's History elevates class conflict above republican idealism about freedom and national liberation as the prime force igniting the birth of the United States. But attacking Zinn's interpretation as the act of a solo ideologue makes little sense since his narrative amalgamates critical scholarship by many leading historians. Alan Taylor points out, "[Zinn's argument about] the colonial elite re-directing populist anger at [the British] derives largely from Gary Nash's interpretation [in The Urban Crucible: Social Change, Political Consciousness and the Origins of the American Revolution (1979)]" and the work of Alfred F. Young, a leading historian of working-class protest in Revolutionary America. And it is an argument that Taylor draws on in his 2017 book on the Revolution.[110] Nash and Young, Taylor says, "make much of the significant shift in Boston after the Stamp Tax Riots when the Sam Adams leadership group managed to marginalize [radical protest leader] Ebenezer Mackintosh and then to narrow the focus of subsequent crowd actions [to the British and away from issues of social class and the colonial elite]."[111]

In *A People's History*, class is not the only lens through which Zinn examines this crucial period in American history. His discussion of race during the Revolutionary era is radical and important. Zinn stresses that the idealistic rhetoric of the Revolution about equality and self-determination excluded Native Americans. They were not considered equal and had no voice "in choosing those who would govern the American territories in which they lived." Nor could they "pursue happiness as they had pursued it for centuries before the white Europeans arrived." The victory of the patriot forces over the British promised nothing but misery for Indians. Zinn writes, "With the British out of the way [and with the dissolution of the Proclamation line of 1763 that had inhibited colonial expansion westward], the Americans could begin the inexorable process of pushing the Indians off their lands, killing them if they resisted. In short, as Francis Jennings puts it, the white Americans were fighting against British imperial control in the East, for their own imperialism in the West. . . . It helps to explain why most of the Indians fought for England during the Revolution."[112] Zinn follows the lead of Jennings's pathbreaking revisionist work on Native American history, agreeing with Jennings on "putting the Indian into the center of the American Revolution—after all, it was Indian land that everyone was fighting over."[113]

Turning to the Revolution's central document, the Declaration of Independence, Zinn notes that it omitted Indians and enslaved Africans from its "circle of united interest."[114] One of that document's grievances against King George was that he had incited slave rebellions and attacks from "merciless Indian savages." In language that calls to mind important twenty-first-century scholarship on the Declaration and the Revolution, such as Robert Parkinson's *The Common Cause*, Zinn writes:

> To say that the Declaration of Independence, even by its own language, was limited to life, liberty, and happiness for white males is not to denounce the makers and signers of the Declaration for holding the ideas expected of privileged males of the eighteenth century. Reformers and radicals, looking discontentedly at history, are often accused of expecting too much from a past political epoch—and sometimes they do. But the point of noting those outside

the arc of human rights in the Declaration is not, centuries late and pointlessly, to lay impossible moral burdens on that time. It is to try to understand the way in which the Declaration functioned to mobilize certain groups of Americans, ignoring others. Surely, inspirational language to create a secure consensus is still used, in our time, to cover up serious conflicts of interest in that consensus, and to cover up, also, the omission of large parts of the human race.[115]

Zinn offers an account of the Black role in the Revolution, showing that the pursuit of freedom could lead enslaved Africans to fight for either side—the British when they offered emancipation for service to the Crown, or the colonists, since "what the Revolution did," in Zinn's words, "was to create space and opportunity for blacks to begin making demands of white society." These demands Zinn documents with Black petitions for emancipation, the vote, and the right to testify in court, invoking the idealistic liberal rhetoric of the Declaration, seeing them as helping to seed the rise of gradual emancipation in the North. But this glimmer of progress did not offset the racial and class-based hierarchy and inequity that Zinn saw the Revolution and its Constitution securing: "The inferior position of blacks, the exclusion of Indians from the new society, the establishment of supremacy for the rich and powerful in the new nation—all this was already settled in the colonies by the time of the Revolution. With the English out of the way, it could now be put down on paper, solidified, regularized, made legitimate, by the Constitution"[116]

☞

Zinn also notes the gendered language of the Declaration, the phrase "all men are created equal," but thinks this "was probably not a deliberate attempt to make a statement about women." Instead he sees it as representing white male privilege: "Women were beyond consideration as worthy of inclusion. They were politically invisible. Though practical needs gave women a certain authority in the home, on the farm, or in occupations like midwifery, they were simply overlooked in any consideration of political rights, any notions of civic equality."[117] Zinn's awareness of gender inequality is also evidenced by his devoting the chapter after his two on the American Revolution to early American women's history: "The Intimately Oppressed." For its day, the inclusion of an entire chapter on women's history in an introductory survey of American history was a breakthrough.

Zinn's interest in women's history distinguished him from a large segment of the male-dominated New Left of the 1960s, which tended to be quite sexist. Zinn, even though associated with opposition to the Vietnam War, had been influenced in his youth by the 1930s Left, which was more egalitarian on gender. Zinn had been a teacher and mentor to female student activists at Spelman College, and he had published articles spotlighting their activism and written about them in some of his earlier books.[118] He dedicated his book on SNCC to Ella Baker, the brilliant Black freedom organizer whom he worked with as the only other middle-aged advisor serving on SNCC's board.[119] And when the Vietnam War ended—and with it his intense activism—the first major writing project Zinn completed was a play on the anarchist leader Emma Goldman.[120] Given this personal history, it is not surprising that Zinn made women's history a significant part of A People's History.

The historians who reviewed A People's History when it first came out were all men.[121] None had expertise in women's history or said much about Zinn's coverage of it. Nor have the book's more recent detractors focused on how women are depicted in A People's History. In order to assess Zinn's coverage of women's history we consulted with Bancroft Prize–winning historian Linda Gordon, author of Feminism Unfinished: A Short, Surprising History of American Women's Movements (2015). What we discovered after our discussion with Gordon is that Zinn's chapter on early American women's history, largely ignored by his critics, is arguably the weakest in the book. According to Gordon, there are fundamental flaws regarding chronology, contextualization, and conceptualization in this chapter.

Gordon's largest concern about Zinn's "The Intimately Oppressed" is that it "doesn't really have a chronology." So Zinn was "mixing things from very different points in time, and because of that it doesn't have much of a causal framework, what is causing these [changes in gender relations that he discussed]." For example, Zinn discusses "the cult of domesticity"—the ideal by which women were relegated to the home and served as guardians of its moral virtue—but absent chronology one cannot explain it. The rise of domesticity, according to Gordon, "happens because of industrialization. In pre-industrial society to speak of domesticity makes no sense because everybody is domestic, everybody is home, and work and home are completely one. But once men start going out to factories then you get a very different situation for women." There is a confusion here about the rise of domesticity in nineteenth-century America because Zinn was "taking things out of a chronological period and not filling in the context."[122]

Zinn made some mistakes on women's history that Gordon found "surprising" because they involved class issues Zinn was interested in and was "trying to incorporate . . . into his narrative." Here she cites Zinn's assertion that "women were being pulled out of the house and into industrial life, while at the same time there was pressure for women to stay home, where they were more easily controlled."[123] Zinn failed to grasp, Gordon says, "that the women being pulled out of the house and the women pressured to stay home are two different classes of women. Nobody is pressuring working-class women to stay home."[124]

Issues of class and chronology also got confused in the matter of women's dress. Zinn suggested that poor women were pressured into following middle-class and upper-class dress with regard to wearing corsets and petticoats.[125] But, as Gordon explains, "poor women were not wearing corsets and petticoats." And because Zinn provides no dates in this discussion and seems to have an urban bias, this, Gordon notes, "leads to something else that's missing, which is that . . . most Americans lived in the countryside until 1890. And most of those women were farmers. They were doing farm work . . . , taking care of animals, . . . growing vegetables. . . . the kind of work you do not wear corsets and petticoats for."[126]

Gordon suggests that readers supplement this Zinn chapter with more recent women's history work, such as that by Alice Kessler-Harris, that better gets at the intersection of class and gender.[127] The goal should be to develop an understanding of class differentiation, not overgeneralizing from one class to another when it comes to women's historical experience in the United States.

The later chapters in *A People's History* that deal with women and feminism in the twentieth century Gordon deems much stronger but not without problems. The first is that Zinn uncritically adopts the rhetoric of what Gordon terms "so-called radical feminists" whose discourse she thinks exaggerated the oppression of women. As an example of this, Gordon quotes Zinn calling the family a prison for women, "the most subtle and complex of prisons."[128] Gordon views this as a "wild exaggeration" because women have always had "considerable influence" in the family, and the prison metaphor obfuscates this and misses women's historical agency. Gordon points out, "While it's true that there were long periods in which there was nothing illegal about beating your wife . . . most men did not beat their wives. So you have to think about why is that? And part of what we know is that for most men the companionship of a woman was actually a very pleasurable thing." Gordon found that Zinn's account of second-wave feminism missed the distinction between two streams of the movement, liberal feminism and socialist feminism, so Zinn failed to address what Gordon sees as a "pretty strong socialist feminist stream."[129]

Zinn gave short shrift to the important court victories for women's rights in the 1970s. *A People's History* deals with *Roe v. Wade* but misses the legal revolution that began with the cases won by the ACLU Women's Rights Project, headed by Ruth Bader Ginsburg. These cases got the Supreme Court to begin applying the Fourteenth Amendment's equal protection clause to gender. Ginsburg only appears once in the later editions of *A People's History*, and that is as President

Bill Clinton's Supreme Court nominee, where Zinn used her appointment to the Supreme Court as evidence of Clinton's political "timidity." Here Ginsburg is characterized (unfavorably, for Zinn) as a moderate.[130] Linda Kerber's *No Constitutional Right to Be Ladies* (1999) ought to be consulted to go beyond Zinn in probing the legal front of the women's liberation struggle.[131]

A final problem Gordon sees with treatment of second-wave feminism in *A People's History* is that it misses the "intensity of the backlash" against feminism and the women's movement.[132] She thinks this is because Zinn, writing the book before the ascent of Reaganism and the right-wing juggernaut in American politics, had no way of knowing how furious, powerful, well financed, and enduring the conservative movement's crusade against feminism would be. So readers ought to supplement *A People's History* with works, like those by Marjorie J. Spruill and Donald T. Critchlow, on the New Right's antifeminist agitation against abortion rights, the Equal Rights Amendment, and the legacy of the women's movement.[133]

Along with these criticisms, Gordon offers praise for the documentary components of *A People's History* on woman's rights advocates. She "really love[s]" the long quotations Zinn provides from Sojourner Truth. Noting that Zinn does not include Truth's best-known "Ain't I A Woman" speech, she credits him for having "found far more interesting and more radically feminist statements from her."[134] Gordon tells of a colleague in women's history who continued to assign *A People's History* because her students loved Zinn's extensive quotes from eloquent dissident speeches in American history.

Despite problems in Zinn's treatment of women's history, he understood the importance of women and feminism in the larger story of American history. This was not the case with queer history. Zinn did not understand the importance of the LGBTQ experience in American history, and so he wrote nothing about it in the first edition of *A People's History*. Zinn's biographer, Martin Duberman, himself a pioneer in the writing of gay history, attributes this not to homophobia on Zinn's part but rather to his lack of familiarity with the LGBTQ experience. Zinn in the new 1995 edition of *A People's History* included an afterword apologizing for this oversight and added a brief section (three paragraphs) on the struggle for gay rights. Duberman writes that Zinn was one of the "few straight men of his generation, including those on the left, . . . who treated the plight of women and gay people as real and the movements to change attitudes about them with respect. Nor did he, like most of his compatriots, belittle their plight or treat them with condescension."[135] But in the 1980 edition of *A People's His-*

tory this did not result in any LGBTQ+ history, so it and new editions should be supplemented with pioneering gay U.S. histories by Jonathan Ned Katz, George Chauncey, Lillian Faderman, and more recent LGBTQ+ surveys.[136]

☞

In contrast to Zinn's uneven treatment of gender, but as in his coverage of dispossession of Indian lands, his discussion of pre–Civil War America's violent expansionism, its wars of aggression, was insightful. Zinn's historical work on early American empire building and war was some of his strongest, especially his chapter in *A People's History* on the Mexican War (1846–1848). Zinn's deep interest in the Mexican War contrasts dramatically with the spotty coverage of that war found in most U.S. history textbooks. Most dispense with the Mexican War in a page or so, but Zinn accorded it an entire chapter in *A People's History*, giving it the ironic and damning title, "We Take Nothing by Conquest, Thank God." Zinn devoted more space in *A People's History* to the Mexican War than he did to the Civil War, which was arguably a just war because it ended slavery. The Mexican War, on the other hand, was a blatantly unjust war aimed at stealing territory from Mexico (it ultimately halved the size of Mexico expanded U.S. territory by almost one quarter). Thus, it aligned better with Zinn's antiwar convictions and his agenda of using *A People's History* to indict American warmaking. The term Ulysses S. Grant, who served in the Mexican War, employed to describe this bloody U.S. dismemberment of Mexico was "wicked war," which was used as the title for Amy Greenberg's important book *A Wicked War: Polk, Clay, Lincoln, and the 1846 U.S. Invasion of Mexico* (2013). As a leading authority on the war, Greenberg shared her expertise with us in assessing Zinn's chapter on that conflict.

Greenberg had not read Zinn's chapter on the Mexican War before we asked her to. After reading the chapter she said that had she done so while she was working on *A Wicked War* it would have been "very helpful to me because a lot the stuff that he has is in there is not dissimilar to my take on the war." Greenberg is particularly impressed with Zinn's use of revealing memoirs of the war, noting, "I had thought I had discovered [Colonel] Ethan Allen Hitchcock myself." Zinn quotes Hitchcock at the start of his account, as a military witness and critic of how the United States provoked the war. She credits Zinn with offering "a lot of really good antiwar quotes" in the chapter. Zinn's narrative covers "some of the . . . remarkable things about the war, which most histories don't talk about at all, and in particular . . . all the civilians who were killed at the Battle of Vera Cruz and also the rapes by U.S. soldiers of Mexican women, . . . and the fact that the U.S. soldiers once they were there [in Mexico] didn't want to reenlist."[137]

Greenberg concurs with the central theme of Zinn's chapter, the "overall picture," "which is that [President James K.] Polk started the war with a lie, after putting the army in a position [in Mexican territory] where Mexico had to attack it, and that . . . there was a ton of enthusiasm for the war at the beginning, and then that enthusiasm among the soldiers depleted. That's all totally correct."[138] She is impressed with much of the analysis and detail in the chapter and sees it as better than most histories of the war written in Zinn's time or since.

Zinn's account of the war, however, is not flawless. Though most of the problems with it are, in Greenberg's view, minor, in that they did not impede its overall argument, she offers some corrections, alternative interpretations, and updates in light of more recent scholarship.[139] She finds that Zinn misunderstands the relationship between the regular U.S. Army troops and the volunteers in the war when he states, "Volunteers complained that the regulars were given special treatment."[140] In fact, the opposite was true; it was the volunteers who received special treatment. According to Greenberg, this was one reason the volunteers "were murdering and raping" Mexicans—"there was no discipline on the volunteers, at all . . . they were out of control. The regulars were treated horribly. . . . To be a regular in the army was about as low a position as you could have in the United States as a white man [in this era]." Greenberg does not see much evidence for Zinn's claim that "enlisted men complained the officers treated them as inferiors." Greenberg finds that Zinn makes too much of Colonel Hitchcock's claim that General Zachary Taylor supported the invasion of Mexico, saying Taylor's correspondence indicates a notable lack of enthusiasm. Greenberg also points out that the chapter's closing errs in stating that "Mexico surrendered." "Mexico did not surrender," she says. "The [Mexican] army surrendered, but the Mexican government did not surrender." Zinn did not "care about" or understand Mexico at "the government level of things," Greenberg thinks; his People's History focused on people as opposed to governments.[141]

Greenberg raises two interpretational issues concerning the home front that she thinks Zinn has wrong. Both are connected to the provocative and at times rigid framework that Zinn uses to examine American politics and class characteristics. As evident in his Jacksonian chapter, Zinn was scornful of the two-party system, viewing the parties as lacking substantial differences and so failing to offer voters genuine choice. Using this framework to assess responses to the Mexican War, Zinn stresses the shallowness of Whig Party opposition to the war, pointing out that though the Whigs in Congress criticized the war, they nonetheless voted to fund it. Greenberg believes that Zinn underestimates the depth and seriousness of Whig opposition to the war. She points out that Zinn's account of the initial congressional debate about the war's funding being limited to two hours fails to mention that those limits were imposed by the Polk administration, in the face of vehement objections from the Whigs, who were literally screaming in protest against the railroading of this legislation. Given the political culture of antebellum America, Greenberg sees Whig opposition to the war as quite impressive.[142]

Greenberg disagrees too with Zinn's class analysis of the war. Where Zinn depicts war fever as an elite phenomenon, she sees genuine enthusiasm for the war from the Democratic Party rank and file, which she links to racist anti-Mexican sentiment, leaving them "hell-bent on fighting Mexico and killing Mexicans." Zinn's idealization of the common people, especially workers, left him disinclined to probe this racist jingoism from below—to acknowledge, as Greenberg puts it, that "working people were pretty racist," but she also sees this as a function of the time in which he was writing, since much of the best historical writing on whiteness and working-class racism has come out after *A People's History* was published.[143]

On the connections between slavery and the Mexican War, Zinn does document abolitionist opposition to the war. That opposition was grounded in fears that this was a war initiated by a slaveholding president to expand the number of slave states, removing lands governed by an antislavery regime (Mexico had abolished slavery in 1829). But Zinn does not discuss how the conquest of additional territories would divide electoral politics in Washington, as the debate raged over whether slavery should be banned from those territories, a ban championed by Rep. David Wilmot of Pennsylvania but rejected by Congress when it voted down the Wilmot Proviso in 1846. There is nothing in Zinn's Mexican War chapter, then, on why, as Civil War historian James McPherson, puts it, a "war that almost destroyed the United States . . . in 1861 [was] in considerable part the consequence of what happened from 1846 to 1848."[144] Zinn failed to probe these connections between the Civil War's origins, the Mexican War, and slavery's emergence as a political and moral issue; his antiwar perspective led him to deny that slavery was the prime cause of the Civil War, as that might have made it seem a just war.

With regard to updating Zinn's Mexican War chapter, Greenberg believes that it should be supplemented by the recent work of Peter Guardino, whose illuminating book *The Dead March: A History of the Mexican American War* (2017) breaks much new ground on how the war was viewed by Mexicans and what they felt was at stake. Greenberg's own work takes us beyond Zinn in understanding why Polk's ambition to take more than half of Mexico was not realized. For example, Polk's own emissary, Nicholas Trist, had moral qualms about such ambitions and defied Polk in negotiating the peace treaty, which led to taking less territory from Mexico than Polk wanted. (The suggestion is that Zinn failed to acknowledge that not all expansionists were alike).[145] But Greenberg also unearthed new evidence on antiwar meetings, evidence that backs the argument in *A People's History* for a rise of extensive American opposition to this U.S. war of aggression.[146]

Even without these updates, Greenberg views Zinn's account of the war as valuable and engaging, finding it "incredible" that he devoted an entire chapter to it, a striking contrast to textbooks whose treatment of the war she finds so superficial as to be "ridiculous." Greenberg adds that she "would be thrilled" if a student, instead of learning almost nothing about the war from a textbook, read the Zinn chapter, brought it to her, and said "this is what happened in the U.S.-Mexican War, right?" "It would be: 'Oh, wow, you really know what was going on here.'" She concludes that despite Zinn's radical reputation and criticism of the war, the chapter overall offered a "totally balanced" account.[147]

⌀

Back in 1980 the business publication that gave *A People's History* the most attention was *Barron's* magazine. A *Barron's* review by Edward J. Walsh opened by red-baiting Zinn, terming him "a man of the far left whose thinking is attuned to that of the rulers of places, whose names begin, as does the title of his book, with the word 'People's,' as in the People's Republic of Vietnam." "Indeed," Walsh went on, "Zinn made two visits to North Vietnam during the late 'Sixties,' as the dust cover tells us, 'for the antiwar movement.'" Walsh implied that Zinn had to be a Communist or a Communist sympathizer, seeing "Zinn's book . . . [as] an attempt to indict capitalism and the notion of private property as the fundamental evils of American life." With "greedy businessmen" aligned with "power-mad politicians" not only oppressing U.S. workers but also fueling the military industrial complex and wars, "American capitalism" came across on Zinn's pages, according to Walsh, as "the principal source of oppression in the world."[148]

Almost a quarter-century later, in 2004, long after *A People's History* had become a best seller, historian Michael Kazin, the left-leaning editor of *Dissent*, wrote a review essay equally critical of Zinn's take on American capitalism. Kazin argued that Zinn had failed the American Left by writing a history of U.S. capitalism that was too simplistic to serve as a guide for those interested in organizing for social change. *A People's History*, he wrote, is "bad history, albeit gilded with virtuous intentions." "Zinn reduces the past to a Manichean fable and makes no serious attempt to address the biggest question a leftist can ask about U.S. history: why have most Americans accepted the legitimacy of the capitalist republic in which they live?" Kazin accused Zinn of writing a one-dimensional, defeatist account of American labor history in which "ordinary Americans seem to live only to fight the rich and haughty and, inevitably, to be fooled by them." These common people, Kazin wrote, "are like bobble-head dolls in work-shirts and overalls—ever sanguine about fighting the powers-that-be, always about to fall on their earnest faces."[149]

There are exaggerations in both these reviews. Contrary to Walsh, the author of A People's History was not a member of the Communist Party or a communist at all and was certainly closer to anarchism and pacifism than to the communist regime in Vietnam. And, contrary to Kazin, Zinn admired labor and labor movements far too much to patronize workers and treat them as if they were—in Kazin's condescending words—bobble-head dolls in work-shirts. A People's History is filled with eloquent quotations from labor organizers that highlight their intelligence and courage. Nonetheless, Walsh was correct that Zinn was immensely critical of capitalism. And Kazin was correct about Zinn lacking interest in explaining why workers supported capitalism. Zinn was far more focused on resistance to capitalism's inequities than exploring support for the system.

Since capitalist relations and labor history are so central to A People's History and its critics, we will focus on Zinn's treatment of both, drawing on our interview with historian Bryant Simon, author of important books on textile workers in the Jim Crow South, North Carolina poultry workers in the late twentieth-century era of union decline and business deregulation, and a corporate and consumer history of Starbucks.[150]

What impresses Simon the most about the capital-labor strife narrated in A People's History is "the ferociousness of the class politics." He says he is "struck . . . and even moved at times by the anger in the book," anger at "the injustice not just that these [resistance] stories haven't been told, but [also] that over and over again righteousness has been beaten down by a cabal of the unjust." Simon thinks this passionate narrative could bring labor history to life in the classroom: "I don't think . . . students are used to that sound and feel [especially in] . . . a textbook. I'm sure they're moved emotionally in the same way [Zinn] is by it." A People's History clearly has what Simon terms an "activist spirit."[151]

For Simon, what distinguishes Zinn's brand of labor history from his own, and from the conventions among professional historians, is its explicit moral positioning and its animated tone of advocacy. "The politics of [most] historical texts are clear, but in some way revealed in a kind of flatness of language," he says. "I don't think historians are pretending to be objective any more (. . . maybe some are), but this sense of outrage [sets Zinn apart]." The indignation Zinn expresses at capitalist injustice is much more explicit. Simon notes the contrast between Zinn's approach to writing and his own in his 2017 book *The Hamlet Fire*, which probed the history of a North Carolina poultry plant fire that killed twenty-five workers needlessly, due to the greed and negligence of the factory owner and government indifference. In his book, Simon says, he had been "in some ways . . . trying to mute this sense of outrage." "I mean I wanted people to be outraged but through the storytelling, not through the [authorial] anger that Zinn constantly brings to the text [in *A People's History*]. This sense of outrage. Maybe that's what we [academic historians] missed [in publishing historical narratives that failed to connect with the public]."[152]

Simon thinks Kazin's critique of *A People's History* was at best half right. He disagrees with Kazin's view that *A People's History* consistently oversimplifies workers' struggles for economic justice. "[Zinn] was pretty good about what working people do, broadly imagined," Simon says. "There's a kind of reclamation project that's going on that's cool. . . . That Kazin line [about bobble-head dolls in work shirts] flattens out what Zinn actually does, which is document these struggles, . . . the creativity and resources of working people, their persistent challenges to the dominance of capital in American life. I think by saying that [Zinn reduces workers to wooden-headed losers] he is flattening out that stuff and even the research [Zinn has] done to document these stories."[153]

It is true, Simon adds, that Zinn focuses almost exclusively on protest and struggle. "There's an arc . . . to the book . . . that change can't be made without struggle. The idea that power concedes nothing or rarely will. [Zinn] recognizes that and sees it as an important dynamic." The recalcitrance of management and its government allies is such a critical part of American labor history that Simon is surprised that any labor historian would "pretend that it isn't there [when] this might be what is exceptional to American labor history."[154]

At times, however, the moralism of Zinn's account of labor struggles and his impatience with elites oversimplify their interactions, in Simon's view. Zinn, he says, "sometimes turns to the passive voice about the opposition. There's a real active voice for working-class people, for dissent, for challenges to the reigning economic order. . . . [But] Zinn occasionally falls into [the mode of] analysis that Kazin described [and mocked], that working people are good . . . innocent, and virtuous, and those who control things are devious and bad . . . [with the latter rendered] . . . only one-dimensionally."[155]

Simon agrees that Zinn could have done more to explore the complexities of working-class consciousness and ideology, even though, as it stands, Zinn is engaging in telling labor history stories that are dramatic and unfamiliar to most readers. "There is all this kind of concrete [working-class] agency, and then they lose because they're manipulated into seeing themselves as white or something."

But on the other hand, "there are moments when the storytelling in *A People's History* is way more complicated and nuanced and [grounded in] more interesting research" than Kazin acknowledged. Valorizing the working class, "the people" as Zinn did in *A People's History*, also can be limiting in that it can impede any systemic, critical analysis of the working class's underside—its racist, nativist, and jingoist tendencies. All of which can be important in understanding the majority white world of blue-collar America, or, as Simon put it, taking "on the conundrums that began in the sixties . . . trying to figure out where the white working class is. I just read an interesting book about the poorer you are in America, the more patriotic you are. I think that kind of analysis Zinn doesn't have a lot of room for."[156]

Simon thinks Zinn's chapter centering on Gilded Age labor conflict is "great" in conveying the conditions of workers and their protests but that Zinn's "sense of class is pretty loose," reminiscent of Charles Beard. "There's haves and have nots. . . . He's clear about that. The haves are so often just sinister and nothing else. I can see why historians don't like that, but he's trying to do something different . . . A provocation." And that provocation is to get students to see anew: "Your past isn't what you think it is. In many ways, I'm gonna break that open." Kazin wouldn't even have readers, Simon says, if they hadn't read Zinn first. "[Zinn is] creating the terrain in which people can . . . raise questions about America and be angry about America. That to me is the contribution [of *A People's History*], which certainly should not be negated, even if he didn't get every last detail right."[157]

Citing Jefferson Cowie's classic study, *Stayin' Alive: The 1970s and the Last Days of the Working Class*, Simon reflected on its compelling argument that "what really disappeared" in America in the mid-seventies "was the ability to talk about class." Yet here we have Zinn in the late 1970s writing a book with its "insistence that class matters," which in Simon's view makes it seem "both dated and refreshing."[158] That it became a best seller and popular with students in an era of a collapsing labor movement and a culture in which talking about the working class was almost like "speaking a foreign language" (especially among youth growing up in postindustrial America) is from Simon's perspective little short of amazing. And in trying to figure out how this was even possible, Simon reflected on what would draw a young millennial female radical to *A People's History* despite its heavy reliance on a forgotten language of class:

> What she would see in the book . . . is its anger, its rejection of not just the Trumpian view of America but [also] mainstream politics of this kind of compulsory patriotism and celebration. . . . She would find . . . her way to the book because of its tone, and that tone is about anger. I think that's what makes the

book. . . . It's held together by Zinn's anger over injustice. . . . This is what Kazin misses. He's sort of pulling books off the shelf and saying "well, it doesn't match that, and so it's not good history." . . . Students would relate to its sense of anger, right, but that's why we read. We don't really read for content [alone], we read to be moved.[159]

The anger Simon alludes to does indeed seem a key part of the appeal of *A People's History*. With elaborate evidence and eloquence Zinn indicted inequality and the presence of poverty amid plenty that has always marked the American capitalist system, enabling readers to share his outrage over both this social injustice and see how resistant government and business have been to egalitarian movements seeking to right these wrongs. Today almost one in five American children are born into poverty, and U.S. wealth distribution is the most unequal in the developed world, with the top 5 percent owning two-thirds of America's wealth. So long as such poverty and inequality remain prominent features of the American social order, Zinn's dramatic accounts of historic workers' struggles will likely continue to resonate.[160]

There is another kind of anger associated with Zinn, and that is the anger of his conservative critics who seethe over what they see as his hatchet job on American capitalism, his refusal to acknowledge the enormous success and global appeal of the nation's engine of prosperity. And this takes us back to Kazin's complaint about the failure of *A People's History* to explain why most Americans accept the legitimacy of American capitalism. As mentioned, Kazin is correct, that with *A People's History* centered on protest there is little focus on exploring support of capitalism. This doesn't mean, however, that Zinn ignores the appeal of capitalism. Though he does not offer a systematic analysis of that appeal, Zinn suggests at several points in the book that the capacity of American capitalism to generate "enormous wealth" means that it "could create the richest ruling class in history, and still have enough for the middle classes to act as a buffer between the rich and the dispossessed."[161] Zinn even extends this argument to the working class and immigrants as well, when he notes, "The system was rich, productive, complex; it could give enough of a share of its riches to enough of the working class to create a protective shield between the bottom and top of the society. A study of immigrants in New York between 1905 and 1915 finds that 32 percent of Italians and Jews rose out of the manual class to higher levels (although not to much higher levels). . . . Enough Italians became construction workers, enough Jews became businessmen and professionals, to create a middle-class cushion for class conflict."[162] Admittedly, this is at best a kind of backhanded compliment, but it is an acknowledgement of American capitalism's success in building a middle class sufficiently well off to support the system. Amid all the Dickensian passages on social inequality and the dramatic stories about people's movement's challenging the inequity of capitalism, one can easily miss the occasional lines Zinn tosses out on the wealth and co-optive power of American capitalism. But the most prominent feature Zinn saw in capitalism was its inequity, so his account will always be objectionable to conservatives eager to cheer its triumphs.[163]

Zinn's account of the labor movement is weakest regarding the way that movement (and related mass movements in the United States in the 1930s) interacted with Franklin D. Roosevelt's administration to modify the capitalist system. Zinn echoes the New Left critique of New Deal timidity, stressing its failure to use the crisis of the Great Depression to transform the American socioeconomic system.[164] As Zinn puts it: "When the New Deal was over, capitalism remained intact. The rich still controlled the nation's wealth, as well as its laws, courts, police, newspapers, churches, colleges."[165] Even the Wagner Act (1935), a historic labor victory that finally gave unions the right to organize, free from violent employer harassment, enabling workers to hold democratic elections to unionize, and culminating in millions of workers winning union representation, was presented in A People's History as a clever means of co-opting labor militancy. Here Zinn argues that labor had been most effective when organizing spontaneous rebellions prior to union recognition.[166] But this leaves unexplained how workers viewed the labor movement gains won in the New Deal era, why workers voted overwhelmingly for FDR again and again, and why conservatives so bitterly denounced the New Deal as socialism and FDR as "a traitor to his [upper] class."[167]

Here again, Zinn's disdain for the two-party system and his impatience with liberal reform yielded a historical narrative that (as with his portrait of Lincoln) played down the impact of reformist political leaders. Grassroots CIO labor militants who staged the factory sit-down strikes that Zinn admired might not have won their historic battles had not New Deal liberal governors and the president himself refused to send in troops to quell them. Of course, FDR was not a socialist and had no intention of toppling capitalism, but under pressure from the labor movement and the Share Our Wealth movement, he helped erect what historians later dubbed the New Deal order, which, among other things, narrowed the gap between the middle class and the economic elite via progressive taxation. "So what happened to the rich?," asked economist Paul Krugman. "Basically the New Deal taxed away much, perhaps most of their income. No wonder FDR was viewed as a traitor to his class."[168] Such views examined side-by-side with Zinn's more skeptical conclusions about the New Deal and the labor movement of the 1930s can yield lively student debate about just how transformative both were.[169] This debate will be made all the more urgent since the New Deal order has been under siege, with progressive taxation, organized labor, and the social safety net in decline since the 1980s.[170]

&

In 2005 Howard Zinn appeared on cable television on comedian Jon Stewart's *The Daily Show*, and during that appearance he denounced the Iraq War. This elicited an angry letter to Zinn from a young man who claimed he was so outraged by Zinn's antiwar remarks that he had gone out and enlisted in the U.S. Army Reserve, which might lead to him being shipped out to the combat zone in Iraq. He wrote to Zinn:

> I ascertained, by hearing your comments, you believe that people that support the war in Iraq are generally ignorant, immoral, and naïve—that this war is only about oil. I suggest that next time you want to say such things you should be a man and say [it] to my face. You have my address, although I really don't think you would show up because you're a coward. You cover your fear with self-righteous indignation and pompous rhetoric. You have become obsolete and have no influence over anyone. You're a scared, weak, little old man.
>
> Lastly, I wonder how you arrived at the Jon Stewart show. Did you walk? I imagine you took a car. So I guess oil isn't so bad after all. I'm going to guess it might even heat your home. . . . If I die in the Middle East, I hope you will remember me, especially when you take a car to a T.V. studio and badmouth me and deem my values and me worthless. My Brooklyn friends would call that being a scumbag.[171]

Four days after receiving this letter, Zinn replied:

> Didn't your mother teach you to be polite, even if someone disagrees with you?
>
> You shouldn't throw around the word "coward" so easily. I flew combat missions as a bombardier in World War II. My two closest buddies were killed. I know something about wars, whether for good causes or bad. This is a bad cause, this war in Iraq. Do you know who is a coward? George Bush who evaded a war he believed in. Cheney, who did the same. Those who did not believe in the Vietnam war and refused to fight in it had the courage of their convictions. The veterans who came back from the war, often disabled, showed courage when they declared the war a monstrous evil because we were killing men, women, and children by the millions. For democracy? For liberty? Nonsense. To get a foothold in Southeast Asia. Do you believe the war in Iraq is for liberty or democracy? Those people in the White House have lied to the American people again and again.

You should study some history. I have spent my life since I got out of the war studying the history of the United States and its foreign policy. If you knew that history you would know how many times the American people have sent their kids to war on the basis of lies told to them by the political leaders of the country. Yes, it's oil that's at the heart of the war in Iraq. All you have to do is study a little of the history of the Middle East and you will see how true it is. I don't want you or any other young man or woman to die, or to lose an arm or a leg, thinking you are fighting for freedom, and you are really fighting for the oil corporations. When I hear a young person say "I'm fighting for my country" I feel sad. He or she is not fighting, killing, dying for the country, but for the government. There's a difference between the two.

I suggest two books for you to read: *Johnny Got His Gun*, by Dalton Trumbo, and *Born on the Fourth of July* by Ron Kovic (who went to Vietnam, innocent, like you, and came back from Vietnam paralyzed, and learning that it was not for democracy but for power politics). Read the history of the Vietnam war and see the parallels with today.

Remember, if you go to Iraq you will be going into a country where the people do not want you there. An unwelcome intruder. Our occupation has not brought democracy or liberty, only chaos and death. Study the photo of a little Iraqi girl weeping because her parents were shot to death by scared U.S. soldiers. Study the photo of blind GIs, the legless and armless GIs at Walter Reed hospital and ask: would George Bush give his eyes, his limbs?

Learn the meaning of real courage. The courage to refuse to be a victim of politicians' lies. True patriotism does not mean blindly supporting whatever your government does. It means supporting the ideals for which our country is supposed to stand.

I want you and other young people like you to learn from history, and to stay alive. If you want to help people in other countries, like Iraq, bring them food and medicine, not bombs and guns.

Howard Zinn, 490th Bomb Group. 8th Air Force[172]

There would be another round of letters exchanged between Zinn and this Iraq war volunteer,[173] but this first heated exchange tells us all we need to know about Howard Zinn and war. The author of *A People's History* passionately opposed U.S. military interventionism, whose democratic justifications he thought simply masked the corporate interests that led to such interventions. Zinn saw the history of U.S. war-making as constituting a usable past, that, if studied carefully and critically, could literally save lives. Having received the information and perspectives they needed to see the realities behind the war rhetoric of America's political leaders, some might oppose and refuse to fight in these wars. Zinn's own experiences as a World War II combat veteran helped shape his critical view of U.S. military interventionism. The fact that Zinn took the time to respond at such length to this young enlistee—and Zinn's second response to him was more than twice as long as this first letter—attests to how important questions of war, peace, and imperialism were to him. Clearly one of Zinn's prime goals in writing A People's History was to indict the U.S. government for the militarism and imperialism he believed had marred American history.

This exchange of letters is also revealing in the anger evident in Zinn's hawkish critic. Mainstream television shows rarely have guests speaking so critically and candidly about American war-making and the connections between war and capitalism. This helps explain why Zinn's young critic was so incensed. The same can be said of the American public school environment. The authors of U.S. history textbooks would never air such radical views indicting America's political leaders and richest corporations for fomenting unjust wars. Zinn's willingness to do so on national television, in speeches across the nation, and in A People's History made him an outlier. This is why in high school classes conservative students—as seen in their letters in chapter 4—responded more indignantly to Zinn on war than on any other issue. They had never before encountered a radical antiwar perspective in their textbooks.

The first thing to understand about A People's History on the wars of the twentieth century is that—whether writing about World War I, Vietnam, or even "the Good War," World War II—Zinn's aim was not a balanced history. To the contrary, Zinn wanted to indict these wars and warn readers (and activists in the present and future) about the hypocrisy, greed, and brutality that had been American war-making. If there are heroes in Zinn's wartime chapters, they are not on the battlefield but at home denouncing wars, championing democratic values threatened by American militarism.

To review Zinn's portrayal of twentieth-century U.S. war-making in A People's History, we spoke with a leading Vietnam War historian, Marilyn Young, now-deceased former president of the Society for Historians of American Foreign Relations. Young was the only historian we consulted who was personally close to Zinn. Our thinking was that since she was so familiar with his views on foreign policy and his antiwar activism, and had spoken with Zinn about A People's History when he was writing the book, she could offer some unique reflections on his discussion of Vietnam as well as his treatment of other wars. Although there was some overlap in their politics and critique of U.S. foreign policy, she was not as inclined toward pacifism as he was.

Young noted that World War II was so important to Zinn that he alluded to it even in the chapter on Columbus, where he linked the brutality of Columbus to the conquest-oriented mentality and lack of concern about mass casualties of enemies that led to Hiroshima. Many historians avoid making such connections, out of a concern about falling into presentism, a concern Zinn did not share. Young said that she and Zinn thought the charge of presentism was ludicrous:

> The whole point of studying history is to understand where we are and where we might be going. So presentism is always an aspect of it. It's never absent unless you're an antiquarian. A total antiquarian can be very happy and fruitfully occupied, essentially playing with him- or herself in the past, and that's fine. It's a nice way of making a living if you can get the work, and I have no objection to it. But once you engage in writing [history], once you're no longer an antiquarian, once you imagine you are really trying to get at truths about the past, then the present is always an aspect. . . . It's [even] an aspect in terms of the subject you chose.[174]

From Columbus through Vietnam, Zinn's view of how power was used in America offends conservatives, because, as Young put it, "Pardon me, but he shits all over the American myth. That's really what he does." And *A People's History* is saying "'So OK, let's really look at it. And it's ugly, man, it's really ugly.' And what's lovely about America, what he cherishes, is the capacity of ordinary people to resist." Young saw Zinn as challenging traditional textbook history's theme of progress:

> He's writing the history of the United States, which is supposed to be history that is incarnate in itself. It's always a fulfillment of its initial promise. What is the history of the United States? It's the way in which people of the United States strive to fulfill the values of the Founding Fathers. In other words, history is eliminated, in effect, because it's always about fulfillment. So everything is [going to get better]. "Oh, we're very bad to black people. Don't worry, that will be corrected [by the]. . . civil rights movement"—that kind of thing. And . . . [Zinn] says "No, I'm giving you a history of the United States. It's a history of resistance to what you take to be American values [the ones that lead to U.S. military aggression]. So the very thing you learn to cherish, I am saying [have] to be resisted in war." And that's such an extraordinary reversal.[175]

This can be seen in Zinn's chapter on World War I where the center of gravity is not the battlefields of Europe, where President Wilson waged a war ostensibly "to make the world safe for democracy," but the streets of the United States, where war resisters fought for free speech, freedom of the press, and freedom of assembly and against wartime repression. For Zinn, the genuine war for democracy was waged by activists against Wilson, his Espionage and Sedition Acts, and persecution of the war's critics.[176] Young praised Zinn's narrative of resistance as engaging and crucial, telling in gripping detail the story of the war's ramifications at home in much more depth than any textbook version. But she worried that in Zinn's chapter "the actual events of World War disappear into the account of the resistance . . . [so that] a kid reading the chapter would have no idea or a very vague idea of who was on whose side."[177]

The other problem with Zinn's World War I chapter is the way he seeks to root it (and all wars) in class conflict and the need to use nationalism as a tool to overcome it. To this end, Zinn argued that "American capitalism needed . . . periodic war . . . to create an artificial community of interest between rich and poor, supplanting the genuine community of interest among the poor that showed itself in sporadic movements. How conscious of this were individual entrepreneurs and statesmen? This is hard to know. But their actions, even if half-conscious, instinctive drives to survive, matched such a scheme. And in 1917 this demanded a national consensus for war."[178] Zinn offered no evidence, however, that class conflict—and the fear of it—was so strong in the United States that it precipitated the U.S. entry into the war in 1917.

Agree with it or not, *A People's History*'s World War II chapter is one of the most daring works of historical revisionism ever attempted in an introductory book in American history. It is also a deeply personal piece of historical writing, as Zinn interrogates and then jettisons the wartime patriotism of his youth bred by his own antifascist idealism. The question mark in his chapter title of World War II, "A People's War?," is not one that you will find in a standard history textbook. World War II is popularly depicted as "the Good War," since, as Zinn acknowledged, it was a war against "an enemy of unspeakable evil. Hitler's Germany was extending totalitarianism, racism, militarism, and overt aggressive warfare beyond what an already cynical world had experienced."[179]

Sounding an implicitly autobiographical note, Zinn observes early in the chapter that the tough questions about the Allied cause that "deserve thought" had not been raised during the war years because "the atmosphere was too dense with war fervor to permit them to be aired."

Did the governments conducting this war—England, the United States, the Soviet Union—represent something different, so that their victory would be a blow to imperialism, racism, totalitarianism, militarism in the world?

Would the behavior of the United States during the war—in military action abroad, in treatment of minorities at home—be in keeping with a "people's war?" Would the country's wartime policies respect the rights of ordinary people everywhere to life, liberty, and the pursuit of happiness? And would postwar America, in its policies at home and overseas, exemplify the values for which the war was supposed to have been fought?[180]

These questions enabled Zinn to explore thematically the underside of U.S. conduct in World War II at home (the internment of Japanese Americans, Jim Crowism, war profiteering, and the refusal to allow refugees in the United States) and abroad (the bombings of civilians in Dresden and Tokyo, the A-bomb incineration of Hiroshima and Nagasaki, and the lack of U.S. interest in rescuing millions of Jews who would perish in the Holocaust).

And the final question above about World War II's outcome enabled Zinn to include the Cold War in this same chapter, which, as Young points out, brings World War II "down a notch" by reminding readers that "the Good War" had a "not so great outcome"—the Cold War, which included a nuclear arms race that almost destroyed the planet.[181] Zinn criticized both sides of the Cold War, suggesting that it was illusory that World War II had killed fascism and noting that the victors emerging from that war preserved and embodied some of the worst and most dangerous features of fascism:

The fascist powers were destroyed.

But what about fascism—as idea, as reality? Were its essential elements—militarism, racism, imperialism—now gone? Or were they absorbed into the already poisoned bones of the victors? A. J. Muste, the revolutionary pacifist, had predicted in 1941: "The problem after a war is with the victor. He thinks he has just proved that war and violence pay. Who will now teach him a lesson?"

The victors . . . the Soviet Union and the United States . . . now went to work—without swastikas, goose-stepping, or officially declared racism, but under the cover of "socialism" on one side, and "democracy" on the other, to carve out their empires of influence . . . to build military machines far greater than the Fascist countries had built, to control the destinies of more countries than Hitler, Mussolini, and Japan had been able to do.[182]

Given the popularity of World War II as a just war ("that everybody [has] embraced ever since"), Young thought it took great writing skill to get a hearing for so critical a view. In this "very delicate territory," she believed, Zinn handled it "very, very well," as a central part of an "outstanding chapter."[183] Zinn mobilized the entire history of America's counterrevolutionary and imperialist activity to question whether the nation's posture in World War II as a guardian of freedom for weak countries was credible:

For the United States to step forward as a defender of helpless countries matched its image in American history high school textbooks, but not its record in world affairs. It had opposed the Haitian revolution for independence from France at the start of the nineteenth century. It had instigated a war with Mexico and taken half of that country. It had pretended to help Cuba win freedom from Spain, and then planted itself in Cuba. . . . It had seized Hawaii, Puerto Rico, Guam, and fought a brutal war to subjugate the Filipinos.[184]

And on and on for three more devastating paragraphs.[185]

Young also appreciated the way Zinn opens the chapter with the U.S. Communist Party (CP) flip-flop on World War II. First comes "the quote from its [the CP's] pre-patriotic phase," when it depicts World War II as imperialist, and then right after that Zinn shows the Communist Party reversing itself after Nazi Germany had invaded the Soviet Union, so it now championed the struggle against Hitler and his allies as a "people's war." This is, in Young's view, a clever way to raise questions about the legitimacy of the term "people's war."[186]

This is all part of the antiwar thread that winds throughout A People's History. The World War II chapter is vintage Zinn because, as Young put it, "he's relentlessly critical of everything that people are usually proud of . . . , thinking about empire and World War II, he's not willing to give it a pass." Young encountered Zinn's critical stance on the war in one of her conversations with him "in which I was saying 'Oh, come on, you can't say that World War II shouldn't have been fought. It wasn't Vietnam,' clinging to small elements of the Good War on my part. And he said 'if you think of how many [millions of] people died [in that war] it does raise the question of whether it should have been fought. And what about the possibility of resistance, which occurred in all the occupied countries as being the form of the undoing of the Third Reich, rather than the Battle of the Bulge or . . . bombing runs or whatever?'"[187]

Zinn did not have all the answers as he tried to imagine alternatives to U.S. intervention in World War II. This can be seen in a rare moment when Zinn came up empty on a World War II–related question, which occurred in a CSPAN interview in 2000 after the host asked him what he would have done had he been president when Pearl Harbor was bombed. Zinn replied:

That's the toughest question I've ever faced. . . . By then [December 7, 1941] it was too late, . . . but what do we do then? . . . People have asked me the question, "Well, what you would have done about Germany?" . . . the general question. . . . [But] you're the first one . . . who's asked me this very specific question. "What would you do if you were president on the day Pearl Harbor was attacked?" . . . And . . . with . . . the psychology I had then as a volunteer in the air force and so on, I'd say, "Well, of course, we're at war now, and we've gotta do all the things that war requires," and so on. . . . And now I think, "Well, what is the alternative to simply going in an all-out war which is going to result in enormous numbers of casualties? Is there any way of dealing with Japanese aggression in a way that is unique in world history?" . . . It's very hard for people to think this way 'cause once . . . a historical event has taken place a certain way, it is very hard to go back and imagine a different sequence of events. And once we have gone through World War II and won the war, and after dropping all those bombs . . . we can't imagine another scenario. And—and I confess I . . . haven't worked out an alternative scenario.[188]

Zinn's stumbling answer left him searching for alternatives to war, showing that his perspective—even if unrealistic—was grounded in a heartfelt desire to avoid the massive suffering and death that the war had wrought.

The aspect of Zinn's World War II chapter that evoked the most controversy among critics was its scathing account of the U.S. bombing of Hiroshima and Nagasaki. Zinn knew these atomic bombings were unnecessary to end the war and explored a number of explanations for the bombings, including intimidating the Soviet Union, so the bombings could come off as at least as much an opening salvo of the Cold War arms race as an action intended to end World War II. These arguments were neither new nor unique to Zinn and date back to Gar Alperovitz's book *Atomic Diplomacy* (1965) and even earlier to the critique of the bombings offered by British Nobel laureate in physics P. M. S. Blackett, both of whom Zinn quoted in his discussion of the bombing.

Zinn's summary of the revisionist critique of the bombing remains a useful introduction to this controversy but should be supplemented with more recent scholarship generated by President Truman's Potsdam diary and correspondence from the summer of 1945, which became available in the 1980s, as well as by the scholarly debate that ensued in 1995 on the fiftieth anniversary of the bombings. That debate was sparked by the censorship of an exhibit at the Smithsonian National Air and Space Museum on the Enola Gay and the bombing of Hiroshima (the censorship came in response to complaints by veterans and others hostile to a critical exploration of the bombing). The Truman papers, as historian Robert L. Messer aptly summarized in 1985, reveal "a cat-and-mouse game with the Soviets that might have had more to do with the bombing of Hiroshima and Nagasaki than the president ever publicly admitted."[189] On the other hand, most historians view such Cold War motivations as secondary to the desire to end the war.[190] And the newer scholarship attributes some of the blame for the bombing to the Japanese emperor and a militarist faction of the

Japanese regime stubbornly resisting surrender, even after recognizing the inevitability of military defeat.[191]

A powerful feature of Zinn's World War II chapter is the way he channels his own disillusionment with that war—as a veteran, a bombardier—into a compelling moral and historical case that a supposedly good war had normalized mass murder from the skies. This process had paved the way for the massive use of bombing by the United States in its next wars (Korea and Vietnam), in the Cold War era, with horrendous human costs, which was a key reason Zinn presented in the same chapter both World War II and the conflicts with the Soviet bloc that succeeded it.

Though in their day Zinn's critical conclusions about the bombings seemed radical, they have been recently echoed and even more carefully documented by John W. Dower, the Pulitzer Prize–winning historian of Japan and World War II. Dower showed that when the Nazis bombed civilians from the air in Spain and the Japanese did so in China during the 1930s, President Franklin Roosevelt condemned them as barbaric, but

> such moral outrage was short-lived . . . , and as World War II unfolded, it was England and the United States rather than the Axis powers that refined the theory, legitimization, and practice of firebombing densely populated areas. . . . At least 800,000 civilians, and possibly one million or more, were killed in the Anglo-American air raids in World War II. By the war's end, deliberately targeting men, women, and children in congested residential areas with "saturation" or "carpet" or "obliteration" bombing had been firmly established as strategically desirable and, certainly among the victorious Allied powers, morally acceptable.[192]

Dower, much like Zinn, sailing against the winds of public perception of World War II as the Good War, observed that "in its own way, the psychological and moral quantum leap from denouncing deliberate targeting of civilians as 'inhuman barbarism' (President Roosevelt's phrase in 1939) to embracing this as the very essence of realism by 1943, was as great as the technological leap from 'conventional' weapons of mass destruction to nuclear bombs. That it received less public attention—both at the time and subsequently—is not surprising: patriotic gore always trumps moral self-reflection."[193]

As a historian of Japan, Dower highlighted Japanese culpability for the tragedies of the war as Zinn—with his U.S. focus—had not. But Dower agrees with Zinn in seeing Hiroshima and Nagasaki as more than end points in the World War, since they, in Dower's words, symbolized "the onset of an epoch in which slaughter from the air became routine. More noncombatants were killed in

America's subsequent wars in Korea and Indochina than in the Allied bombing in World War II."[194]

On Vietnam, Zinn's chapter title "The Impossible Victory" and its opening paragraphs lay out his theme that the U.S. counterrevolutionary intervention there was doomed. A determined "nationalist revolutionary movement" refused to submit to the "maximum military effort, with everything short of atomic bombs" rained on it by the "wealthiest and most powerful nation in the history of the world." Zinn credited "the greatest antiwar movement the [United States] had ever experienced" for helping to bring the war to an end.[195] For Zinn, then, the almost unlimited U.S. military power had been defeated by two movements, that of the revolutionaries in Vietnam and the antiwar activists at home. Since Zinn's favorite subject was people's movements, it is not surprising that, as Young pointed out, Zinn "tells the story of the Vietnam War through the protests against it . . . which is not a bad way to do it at all, if you're talking about the impact on the United States, and this after all is *A People's History of the United States*. . . . It's a really U.S.-centered view of the Vietnam War, which is fine." Young also credited Zinn for resisting the temptation to give the antiwar movement—which they both were a part of—too much credit or exaggerate its efficacy, since he shows, as Young put it, the movement's "very slow buildup."[196]

Zinn's primary focus on the political war at home during Vietnam rather than the battle sites abroad means that, as Young explained, "the actual events of the war" come through only occasionally. She noted that this was a problem when he "talks about [the] Tet [offensive] in terms only of the NLF [National Liberation Front], and that's not accurate. And in general he leaves a vague relationship between Hanoi and the NLF because that's not really his subject matter."[197] But, to get the Vietnam side of the story in more detail one needs to supplement *A People's History* with either Young's *The Vietnam Wars* or other more recent accounts—including those by Nick Turse, Fredrik Logevall, Neil Sheehan, and Max Hastings—that have a stronger Southeast Asia focus.[198]

Though *A People's History* is best known for its coverage of the common people rather than the power elite—and the people's antiwar movement is often center stage in the Vietnam chapter—Young found Zinn's coverage of the war makers rich enough to generate an interesting discussion of U.S. political leaders' motivations for expanding, sustaining, and finally reconsidering the war. Young noted that overall in *A People's History* there is a materialist argument for U.S. military interventionism: "He's saying OK, this is capitalism. Capitalism will die if it doesn't grow. These are the directions in which it wishes to grow, and it's either foiled or not foiled." And, consistent with that, "[it's] not economic determinism by any means. On two occasions in the chapter he cites [material] resources, how we mustn't lose the resources of Southeast Asia." But later in the chapter, Young observed, "he [includes] a great quote by [John] McNaughton saying, 'What are we doing in this little pissant country? I mean we're going to lose not just America but the world if we keep bashing this little country.'"[199] So the economic resource argument falls away. "It wasn't Zinn's focus" in the Vietnam chapter, but Young suggested that teachers use it to "draw students into a discussion of that. How important was the resource argument? It was certainly there. . . . Why does it disappear? Why does the rationale for the war almost change year by year? So that it ends up being about itself. It ends up being about [U.S.] credibility and not about anything else." The idea being that "with Vietnam the material stakes are not high enough for the price paid. . . . Basically, that's the conclusion that he comes to, but you'd have to draw it out since he doesn't connect the dots, but any teacher can, and the material is inside the chapter."[200]

⌐

By the time Zinn wrote *A People's History* in the late 1970s, he had developed impressive expertise on the history of the Black freedom movement. Zinn was a participant in the Atlanta sit-in movement of the early 1960s, had written a landmark report for the Southern Regional Council on the Albany, Georgia, civil rights movement in 1962 (a report that Martin Luther King Jr. endorsed), was an organizer for the Mississippi Freedom Summer voter registration and Freedom Schools crusade in 1964, and had served as mentor to young African American women activists at Spelman and in SNCC, including his students. Zinn's years as a professor at Spelman, 1956–1963, when he lived on that historically Black campus, had opened his eyes to the importance of Black history and African American historians, novelists, journalists, and artists whose work illuminated that history.[201] As Zinn recalls in the afterword to the thirty-fifth anniversary edition of *A People's History*, "It was not until I joined the faculty of Spelman College . . . that I began to read the African American historians who never appeared on my reading list in graduate school (W. E. B. Du Bois, Rayford Logan, Lawrence Reddick, Horace Mann Bond, John Hope Franklin). Nowhere in my history education had I learned about the massacres of black people that took place again and again amid the silence of a national government pledged, by the Constitution, to protect equal rights for all.[202] Just as his Spelman years were ending, in 1964 Zinn would publish important works on race and the African American experience, *The Southern Mystique* and *SNCC: The New Abolitionists*. So one expects the chapter of *A People's History* on the freedom movement to be grounded in Zinn's years thinking about and working in the movement, which indeed it was. To help assess this chapter, we consulted with Wesley Hogan, author of *Many Minds, One Heart: SNCC's Dream for a New America* (2007), director of Duke University's Center for Documentary Studies, and a founder of the Student Nonviolent Coordinating (SNCC) Legacy Project, the leading oral history project on SNCC.[203]

As noted in chapter 1, before Zinn decided to write *A People's History* as a single volume he imagined it as a series including a full volume on Black history to be written by an African American expert (or at least a historian drawing heavily on Black voices and sources). Zinn stayed true to that vision, authoring a chapter rich in Black voices. He gives over to Black poets and novelists the opening five pages of the chapter on the history of racism and Black resistance. Hogan finds this opening of the chapter "magnificent." She thinks it "beautiful" the way Zinn introduced their voices.[204] Hogan especially admires the first line from this passage on the political significance of the arts for understanding Black America: "In a society of complex controls, both crude and refined, secret thoughts can be found in the arts, and in black society. Perhaps the blues . . . concealed anger; and the jazz, however joyous, portended rebellion. And then the poetry, the thoughts no longer so secret."[205]

Hogan is impressed that Zinn's chapter does what U.S. history textbooks did not dare to do during the Cold War: deal with the Communist Party's egalitarianism on race, which drew to the party leading radical Black intellectuals, such as Du Bois, and leftist Black politicians, such as Benjamin Davis, both of whom are mentioned in the chapter, as well as labor militants such as Angelo Herndon. Zinn's approach here anticipated the direction of later studies by leading historians of Black radical activism such as Robin D. G. Kelley.[206] Hogan appreciates Zinn's "inclusion of the Scottsboro [defendants] and how communism [and] anticommunism intersected with the Black freedom Struggle."[207]

In terms of updating Zinn regarding subsequent scholarship on such Black activism, Hogan suggests readers might study "the kind of debates people are now having about respectability politics. . . . Part of the debate is really thick in here and it would be great to include in that whole discussion of communism-anticommunism." So informed, Zinn might have explored "the role of class within the Black community and especially the way respectability politics played out in working-class [Black circles], in elite Black circles, [and] in middle-class Black circles."[208]

Zinn's civil rights movement chapter offers a gripping narrative of the Montgomery bus boycott, showing that it helped energize the freedom struggle in the 1950s and launched the young Martin Luther King Jr.'s career as a movement leader. However, this too needs to be updated, especially on the role of women. As Hogan notes, "there's no way he could have anticipated this when he was writing about Montgomery for *A People's History*," but, if you're going to update, it "a good place to begin is with Danielle McGuire's powerful insight . . . [that] what motivated so many people in getting involved in the civil rights movement, starting with Montgomery, was the sexual assault and rape of black women." That was what really motivated much of Rosa Parks's initial civil rights work, Hogan says, and "[got] her to that place where [as a veteran activist] she [was] willing to sit down [at the front of a bus]"—risking arrest and worse to protest racial discrimination. Beyond Montgomery, the role of women in the civil rights movement "generally could have been brought out more" in *A People's History*, Hogan says, though "[the] historiography wasn't quite there yet" when Zinn was writing. "But you think about all the stuff that's been done [recently by historians] on Rosa Parks, on the women's organizing that made the boycott possible; Zinn's chapter doesn't quite get that."[209]

On the question of nonviolence in the Black freedom movement, Zinn was correct to stress that principle in the work of Martin Luther King Jr. Recent scholarship, though, has revealed that despite its name, the Student Nonviolent Coordinating Committee, the key organization of the movement's student wing, from the start included organizers who were not pacifists. As Hogan says, it was "much more complex on the ground. SNCC people embedded in southern Black communities were quietly armed . . . even while people talked about stressing nonviolence to the general public. . . . SNCC people were staying at houses [in the Deep South] where there were reinforced walls and guns under mattresses and so forth." This was because white supremacist violence was such a deadly and immediate threat, and there was a tradition in southern Black communities of armed self-defense. Since Zinn did not explore these tensions and contradictions regarding nonviolence in the early Deep South organizing by SNCC, later books by Charles Cobb Jr. and Akinyele Omowale Umoja should be consulted to illuminate this complex history.[210]

Hogan also observes that while Zinn's indignation about the failure of the Justice Department to protect civil rights workers in the South was powerfully expressed in the chapter—"It's like, 'Department of Justice, do your effing job,'"—he did not do enough to explain the concept of federalism that limited such intervention. In this case Zinn understood that argument but simply rejected it as a weak excuse for federal cowardice in enforcing the law and standing up to segregationists. Hogan points out that despite such limitations, Department of Justice officials such as John Doar had been willing to show that they were monitoring civil rights violations, so that according to SNCC leader Bob Moses, when he was jailed in Mississippi for voter registration work, he called Doar at Justice, and Doar or his aides would take the call. This meant that, as Moses recalled, racist sheriffs could jail him, but they "could not throw away the key." In Moses's view, the Civil Rights Act of 1957 was not toothless (in the way Zinn's chapter implied) but had one tooth. "So Moses calls it a crawl space, that the 1957 Civil Rights Act basically create[d] this crawl space [via] which [SNCC could] start to go to Mississippi" and have at least an informal alignment with Justice Department officials that helped them operate in a very hostile environment, facing white supremacist terrorism.[211]

Similarly, though scathing on the lack of federal civil rights legislation, Zinn, as Hogan notes, failed to explain how the seniority system in Congress perpetuated this situation by empowering segregationist senators and House members. Since they were from the one-party South, these foes of the civil rights movement remained in office long-term and chaired influential committees—a situation hamstringing presidents even on the rare occasion that they were willing to champion such civil rights legislation. "So that needs to be inserted so students have a better sense of how the government actually works."[212]

Another recent finding by civil rights movement historians that Zinn missed was the role Black World War II veterans played in the freedom movement. Hogan thinks this was one impetus for the 1946 civil rights committee established by President Harry Truman. "The one thing Truman didn't admit in this committee but I think is really vital is . . . that the Black GIs came home after just fighting fascism to these stories of them being blinded and killed in the South. . . . Truman and the whole committee [knew] that." Further, "those GIs [were] a massive force for the civil rights movement. They [were] the elders who trained up all these young people; they [were] the people who organized with Ella Baker in the late forties and fifties, the network of [former] Black GIs in the South [including] Robert F. Williams, who organize[d] the self-defense patrols and [shot] back at the Klan."[213]

Zinn's anticapitalist perspective led him to be quite critical of Black capitalism. And while it is true that white politicians sometimes cynically talked up federal support for Black capitalism as a way of evading the need for civil rights and antipoverty work, Hogan finds that Zinn's discussion of Black capitalism lacks nuance. At times Black business leaders played an important role in the freedom struggle, and Black businesses symbolized a form of Black power and self-determination. On this issue she recommends that readers supplement Zinn with Nishani Frazier's *Harambee City: The Congress of Racial Equality in Cleveland and the Rise of Black Power Populism* (2017), "a great book that has a really complex breakdown of black capitalism . . . much more complexity than this [*A People's History*] has."[214]

On voting rights, Hogan notes Zinn's skepticism, when he depicts the ballot box as "a traditional cooling mechanism" used by the federal government to deter Black demands for substantive social change, a position she finds problematic in light of recent political history. This radical position needs to be reconsidered, according to Hogan, since it's "both true and not true, as we know from the huge voting rights struggle we're in right now, or just the debacle in Florida and 2000. . . . And I think he, like most [like-minded activists], and I include myself in there, up until fairly recently, and certainly up to his death in 2010; I was very sold on the [voting rights] progress narrative. And I think that's just not true, we've seen it massively contract." This suggests that as a strategy for progressive change, electoral politics is not a dead end, contrary to what Zinn at times seems to imply in his scathing criticisms of America's two-party system. Indeed, this may be why Zinn is sometimes quoted as saying that "if elections really counted, they'd be illegal," though there is no record of Zinn actually saying or writing this.[215]

As with Bryant Simon noting Zinn's use of the passive voice with labor's foes (and a kind of vagueness to that), Hogan finds in the civil rights movement chapter a lack of specificity at times in discussing the movement's opponents. For example, when Zinn writes that "the system was trying to contain the 'frightening explosiveness of the black upsurge,'"[216] Hogan asks, "Who's frightened? . . . Sometimes he goes into that general white people's voice."[217]

Hogan echoes Zinn's own concern (back when he wrote the initial book proposal for A People's History) that organizing a survey of U.S. history chronologically could impede deep analysis and truncate key historical themes. She thinks that because the civil rights movement chapter was primarily focused on the Long 1960s it would have been useful there to have offered a thematic argument that linked this era to earlier eras and expressions of Black resistance. "One thing I would add to the chapter . . . , is more about the idea of black self-determination as a theme that pulls all the way from the Underground Railroad through Reconstruction, through the 1930s, through the sixties and the civil rights movement, and then into now. . . . It's not about anti-white; it's not even really about protest, right? It's about, 'Can we have some say in the conditions of our lives?'"[218]

On protest itself, which was the main focus of Zinn's civil rights movement chapter, Hogan credits him with powerful writing. She especially admires the way he highlights the role of youth and even children in the movement, stressing that protest served as a political education for them. On this she points to Zinn's discussion of the Albany movement, where he writes that "as in all the demonstrations that would sweep over the South, little black children participated—a new generation was learning to act."[219] She finds this a very effective

way of sharing "that insight that young people themselves are really important civic actors, something that inspired high school students when they read
this."[220]

On some important aspects of the Black freedom struggle, "Or Does It Explode?" seems "prescient" to Hogan, strikingly prophetic of later developments,
such as the Black Lives Matter movement of the twenty-first century (that protests federal laws leading to mass incarceration of Black youth and state violence
against African Americans). Zinn writes critically of the provision Congress inserted into the Civil Rights Act of 1968 that seemed designed to criminalize militant Black community organizing, complete with a five-year prison sentence
for "anyone traveling interstate or using interstate facilities (including mail and
telephone)" to foment riots. This legislation exempted law enforcement officials, allowing them to violate people's rights if those officials were "engaged in
suppressing a riot or civil disturbance."[221] The chapter's section about structural
immobility, the lack of Black social mobility, also presages "a lot of the work on
economic democracy that's been showing up in the Black Lives Matter movement," observes Hogan.[222]

Zinn's realization that the Black freedom movement of the 1960s barely made
a dent on American institutional racism—in economics, law enforcement, and
education—is conveyed powerfully. His refusal to tell a triumphal story, his pessimism, gives the chapter's conclusion a realistic tone that continues to make
it relevant in the twenty-first century. As Hogan explains, Zinn addresses "the
miserable, inadequate schools." "He talks about the police and their role. He
talks about wealth inequality [and] legislators . . . not [being] accountable to
the people." He foresees "a lot of where the historiography [on the Black Freedom Struggle] would head." Hogan ultimately admires Zinn's concision: "I just
love his economy . . . his ability to move through so much stuff in such a short
chapter."[223]

Beyond the civil rights movement chapter, which Hogan views as having
great strengths and some weaknesses, she finds *A People's History* a uniquely
valuable introduction to the American experience. The book had an important
impact on her own work, first as a student, then as a historian, teacher, and political activist:

> This book for me as a young student . . . both an undergraduate and gradu-
> ate student[, was] such a milestone[,] to see bottom-up history as a positive
> thing. . . . I read this book outside the academy; I sought it out. It was such
> an important sort of North Star. And so, yes, I have problems with it. . . . But
> the big thing I would say, the overarching thing, was that it was a huge oasis
> in the desert. It was trying to imagine what history looks like from the point

of view of the bottom rail and what could organize people together. And I feel
. . . that it's still . . . a shining beacon . . . that gives us hope for actually building
organized power among people as a counterbalance to the military-industrial
complex and corporate power.[224]

≈

In presenting these nine historians' assessment of *A People's History*—and our
own—we make no claims about their typicality. All are in varying degrees left
of center and open to, or practitioners of, the new social history and the New
Left's critique of the U.S. role on the world stage, which Zinn's book popularized. Nonetheless, their candid and critical reading of chapters in *A People's
History* are worth reflecting on. The fact that these distinguished historians all
view Zinn's book—flawed as it is—as a serious work of history and a useful
introduction to the American past, some forty years after its publication, is
significant.

Zinn did, of course, have a left-wing bias and political agenda for his book—
to get Americans to think critically about their nation's history of class, race, and
gender oppression as well as its imperialist role on the world stage and to thus
be equipped to work to end these undemocratic features of the republic. The
way he sought to realize that agenda was to write a sweeping and critical history of the American experience since Columbus by synthesizing and making
accessible, to students and the broader reading public, some of the best radical
historical scholarship of the Long 1960s, one of America's greatest periods of
dissenting historiography. Zinn, as noted, also drew from the flawed iconoclastic works of great American historians from previous generations, most notably
Richard Hofstadter and Charles Beard. And he offered in 1980 what was then
arguably the richest collection of dissident speeches and other primary sources
on dissent ever presented in a popular introduction to American history.

The historians we consulted found weaknesses and strengths in *A People's
History*. Zinn's political perspective and approach to writing history tended
to give him great insight about and empathy with the oppressed. They are the
book's central characters, and Zinn brought them (and their struggles for a more
democratic America) to life in ways that have proven attractive and memorable
to masses of readers. At the same time, his political perspective and grassroots
resistance–oriented approach to history left him with little interest in explaining
workers' acquiescence with capitalism or in treating power elites with the empathy, sensitivity, and complexity needed to render them three-dimensionally. Nor
did he choose to explore productive relationships between protest movements
and reform politicians.[225] These flaws do nothing, however, to undermine the

book's narrative power. Portraying those in power as the nemeses of the people, in simple negative terms, made the stories all the more morally pure and dramatic.

Zinn, then, never chose to tackle the kind of synthesis of bottom-up and top-down history that Eric Foner advocated forty years ago when he reviewed *A People's History* for the *New York Times*. An irony in the marketing of Zinn's book is that the cover of several editions features Foner's quote: "Historians may well view it as a step toward a coherent new version of American history." But the quote omits Foner's central point: that for a coherent new version of America's past, historians would need to go beyond Zinn and sensitively probe the interaction between the elite and ordinary people, as Zinn had not.

This failure on Zinn's part should not obscure his achievement in introducing generations of readers to a more inclusive, egalitarian, and critical version of the American past than had been available to them when they were in school and reading dull textbook chapters on presidents, generals, and industrialists. By popularizing history from the bottom up, Zinn, as his friend and collaborator Anthony Arnove puts it, "fundamentally changed the way millions of people think about history with *A People's History of the United States*." The book's dramatic stories of people's movements struggling for social justice powerfully evoked, in Arnove's words, the "joy in the effort itself." As Arnove perceptively observes, Zinn, as a movement veteran, was especially qualified and able to offer an "appreciation of the bonds of solidarity, mutual affection, and creative expression that participation in social movements produced. The idea that *people* make history and can alter its course, that institutions have human origins and can be changed by humans, is truly subversive—and is a central reason this book has drawn the ire of so many censors and would-be censors."[226]

The oversights and flaws in *A People's History* are a reminder that it should not be seen as the definitive introduction to American history. But, as historian Timothy Patrick McCarthy aptly notes, while Zinn's book is not definitive, it has been transformative. It is "an opening salvo rather than the final word" on the "contributions of ordinary Americans who had been left out of more traditional histories."[227]

As an educational tool in high school classrooms especially, the one-sidedness of *A People's History* has actually made it all the more valuable and effective. In a nation and textbook world that were almost relentlessly pro-capitalist, reverential toward the military, avoiding confronting hard truths about racial, economic, and gender inequality, there came Zinn highlighting all these flaws unsparingly, with searing eloquence and sometimes red hot anger. Zinn was at war with the triumphalist narrative of American history and gave students not a synthesis or balanced narrative but rather a morally infused, bottom-up view that was radically different from the traditional view. The *Saturday Review* complained about this back in 1980: "Reciting his tale of villains and victims, Zinn admits his bias candidly, insisting that 'we need some counter force to avoid being crushed into submission.' But readers unwilling to approximate truth by splitting the difference between a standard textbook and an anti-textbook will find Zinn's narrative unsatisfying."[228] Unsatisfying? For that reviewer, perhaps yes. But for many teachers, students, and other readers— young and old—the task of comparing Zinn's "anti-textbook" with conventional textbook history was not irritating or unsatisfying. It was instead intellectually challenging and politically liberating—one of the more important reasons why it was then and remains today America's best-selling radical introduction to its history.

CHAPTER 8

On Stage and Screen

A People's History of the United States has proven enduringly popular with students, history teachers, and general readers, which is why the book sold more than three million copies by 2019.[1] But what is even more unusual for an introductory work of American history is that it has had a major impact on popular culture, as seen in movies, television, and theater. Zinn's version of the American past reached millions more people via movies and television than through bookstores selling *A People's History*. So if we want to understand Zinn's full effect on history teaching and learning, on popular conceptions of history, we need to move, as Zinn himself did, beyond the printed page to the world of cinema, television, and theater. Zinn's success in all these venues attests not only to the broad appeal of *A People's History* and his approach to American history but also to Zinn's perceptiveness about the importance of the mass media and the appeal of the performing arts.[2] The skill and eagerness he displayed in reaching millions of Americans by adapting his historical work for the big screen, television, and theater were unprecedented for a professional historian.

Zinn's impact on popular culture did not occur overnight. *A People's History* came out in 1980, and, while its sales increased annually, it was not until 1997 that Zinn's presence was noticed in Hollywood. *Good Will Hunting*, Academy Award nominee for best film of the year, referenced *A People's History* in one of its most memorable scenes.[3] This scene centers on a confrontation between Will Hunting, a brilliant and rebellious working-class twenty-year-old, played by Matt Damon (screenplay coauthor), and his therapist Sean Maguire, played by Robin Williams. Hunting has been given a suspended sentence for his role in a fight and is seeing the therapist on the order of a judge. Questioning whether the therapist has read all of the many books on his office shelves, and noting a U.S. history survey text among them, Hunting says: "If you want to read a real history book, read Howard Zinn's *A People's History of the United States*. That book will knock you on your ass." As Zinn put it in an interview in 2000, "[This was] a surprise to people who went to see the movie. . . . Here's a movie that recommends a book. That doesn't happen too often."[4]

It turns out that there is a backstory. Zinn told the interviewer: "[Damon's] mother [Nancy Carlsson-Paige] is a very good friend. . . . And when he was ten years old she gave Matt my book. His high school teacher in Cambridge [Massachusetts] used the book in class. Ben Affleck [who coauthored the screenplay for *Good Will Hunting*] also went to the same school; he read the book. So they both became fans of the book."[5] Carlsson-Paige would recall that, after *A People's History* came out in 1980, Zinn gave her a copy of the book, and she read it and then shared it with her sons Kyle and Matt by "read[ing] them the first chapter . . . the chapter that tells the story, the real true story, based on journals and documented evidence, of what Columbus and the Spaniards did to the Arawak Indians when they landed in the West Indies. It's an amazing and painful story, very unlike the myth that I had been taught and that most children in the U.S. are taught. . . . Matt [at ten years old] wanted me to read it to him several times, and then he began to read it himself. That chapter was important to him."[6] When she first read the script from *Good Will Hunting* and "saw that Matt and Ben had put a line in there including Howard Zinn and *A People's History*, I was thrilled to see it there. It made me happy. I felt that it was a way of paying tribute to somebody who'd been a really important influence in his life and somebody he really cares greatly for . . . and is close to."[7]

Zinn's challenge to the Columbus myth figures prominently in his second notice in American popular culture, via award-winning TV drama *The Sopranos*, a series focusing on fictional New Jersey Mafia boss Tony Soprano.[8] In the show's fourth season, in 2002, an episode opens with Tony's son AJ at breakfast reading aloud from a copy of *A People's History* assigned by his history teacher. "That is just one person's opinion, Anthony," his mother says. But AJ reads Zinn's quote from Columbus's log—"They would make fine servants. . . . With fifty men we could subjugate them and make them all do whatever we want"— and says, "That doesn't sound like a slave trader to you? . . . It's the truth. It's in my history book." Tony's response: "So you finally read a book, and it's bullshit." Tony grows irate and defends Columbus as a "brave Italian explorer," asserting, "In this house Christopher Columbus is a hero. End of story."[9] The clash prefigures a larger theme in the episode, as Tony's fellow gangsters will seek to violently disrupt an anti-Columbus rally held by Native Americans on Columbus Day. Unlike the *Good Will Hunting* reference, the appearance of Zinn's book in the *Sopranos* episode derives purely from the provocative nature of *A People's History*—and its inherent drama—as Zinn had no personal connections to those responsible for writing the script for the show.

These initial appearances on the big screen and television showed that Zinn was achieving a kind of popular recognition that no other historian had attained in his time. His *People's History* even crossed over into animation and comedy. In an episode of *The Simpsons*, cartoonist Matt Groening's hit animated comedy series, Lisa Simpson is pictured reading *A People's History*. And in a scene from *Broad City*, on Comedy Central TV, the character Ilana hides marijuana and a vibrator in a copy of *A People's History*.[10] Well past his death in 2010, *A People's History* was being used as a cultural marker, as in the feature film *Lady Bird* (2017).[11] The coming-of-age story centers on mother-daughter tensions and is set in the United States during the Iraq War. In one scene, the daughter sees a boy to whom she is attracted reading *A People's History of the United States*, symbolizing his dissident politics. After seeing him reading Zinn, she does too.

During the early twenty-first-century U.S. war in Iraq (and its counterpart in Afghanistan), Zinn crossed the country giving speeches that accorded perfectly with the antiwar theme of *A People's History*. He thus became an icon of the peace movement—and that rare if not singular octogenarian invited to speak at rock concerts. Pearl Jam's lead singer Eddie Vedder extended such invitations, and Zinn responded positively. Zinn confided to a friend that at one Pearl Jam concert he made what he jokingly termed "the best speech of my life. . . . It was three words long: 'End the war.'"[12]

These breakthroughs into popular culture enabled Zinn's book to reach way beyond academia and high schools, and beyond avid general readers and activists too. But they barely scratch the surface in conveying the way Zinn connected to popular culture. One could argue that Zinn's most weighty and enduring contribution to American popular culture came not from mentions in movies or TV but in the way he helped initiate projects aimed at teaching dissident U.S. history to mass audiences via live theater and then via documentary film.

The first such project began in 2003 almost by accident in connection with a public event sponsored by HarperCollins, the publisher of *A People's History of the United States*, to commemorate the book's millionth copy sold. The publisher suggested to Zinn that this event be an academic conference in which leading historians reflected on the significance of *A People's History*. Zinn rejected this idea, opting instead for dramatic readings of dissident speeches and writings from the American past, drawing on and beyond sources cited in the book.[13] "There are juicy possibilities in the book for actors" Zinn explained to his editor at Harper. "Not my words but the passages I quote in the book [from dissenting historical figures]."[14] "A distinguished cast of actors and writers" did historical readings at the *People's History* commemoration at the 92nd Street Y in Manhattan in February 2003, including James Earl Jones reading Frederick Douglass, "Marisa Tomei reading the reminiscences of a New England mill girl, Danny Glover reading the protest of a Black Georgia legislator being expelled after the Civil War, Kurt Vonnegut reading Mark Twain opposing the Philippine War and Eugene Debs opposing World War I, Alice Walker reading Mississippi sharecropper [and civil rights organizer] Fannie Lou Hamer, and others reading the words of Christopher Columbus, John Brown, Helen Keller, [participants in] a House Un-American Activities interrogation, Malcolm X, a Gulf War resister, [and] a family member of a victim of the September 11 Twin Towers attack."[15] Zinn had rejected an academic event in favor of making the commemoration "something meaningful" to those beyond the historical profession and doing it in a way that aimed to be "artful" and "inspiring."[16]

The response to these readings was so enthusiastic—"the audience was electrified by it," according to one participant[17]—that Zinn gathered the texts of all twenty-seven of the readings for a brief book published by HarperCollins, so as to encourage theater companies, as well as high schools and colleges, to stage their own readings of "this highly charged material."[18] The positive response to the New York City commemoration and its format led Zinn to repeat it and adapt it as theater and as a documentary film. In doing so he was connected to many other leading progressive actors and figures from Hollywood and Broadway, and a whole new way of popularizing grassroots history came into being.[19]

None of this would have happened had Zinn been a conventional academic historian. Such a historian would likely have jumped at the opportunity to have one's work be the subject of a scholarly conference. But Zinn did not view academics as his primary audience. Nor did he care much about what academic historians would have to say about his book. He was more interested in reaching beyond the elite, bringing people's history to the people. Zinn's egalitarianism was such a powerful part of his politics and persona that he opted not to celebrate himself and his work but rather to honor the dissident voices of the American past. As Zinn explained to Anthony Arnove, who helped organize the dramatic readings at the New York commemoration, he felt that the success of his book was due more to these people who themselves had made history than to him as the narrator of that history.

Zinn, as Arnove put it, had "the experience over the years of readers of *A People's History of the United States* saying to him [that] what they found compelling [in the book]" was its historical quotations. Readers would say, "[I'd] never read these words of Sojourner Truth or Frederick Douglass, or Eugene Debs, or David Walker. And why hadn't I?" This, in Arnove's view, left Zinn with "an understanding that it wasn't his words or interpretations" that made *A People's History* so revelatory to readers. Rather, "it was that he's shone a light on the history of the people who had actually been the voices of these movements and struggles."[20] So focusing on these voices seemed to Zinn the most appropriate way to commemorate his book's popularity.

Zinn's idea for this dramatic reading was consistent with his long-standing interest in literature and theater (as well as the arts in general). His history courses always drew heavily on novels, poetry, short stories, plays, and protest music, and so did *A People's History*.[21] Zinn's first major writing project after the Vietnam War ended in the 1970s had been his play on Emma Goldman, which would be produced and published, and he would follow up with two other plays, most notably *Marx in SoHo*.[22] In Arnove's words, Zinn's theatrical experience enabled him to see that the dramatic words of dissidents in American history "were the most powerful elements of the book to bring to life" and that "there would be a way to do it with musicians, and actors, and poets that would be dramatic, and exciting, and enticing, and inspiring." This also connected with his years of organizing as a civil rights and antiwar activist, which, as Arnove noted, "left Howard with a sense of political flair. He knew how to reach people and how to excite audiences."[23]

Over the years, Zinn had drawn close to prominent writers such as novelist Kurt Vonnegut, a fellow World War II veteran who shared his disillusionment with war, and novelist and poet Alice Walker, his former student, who shared his radical politics and activism against racism and war.[24] So Zinn's inviting writers to participate in the readings, along with actors and actresses, was also true to his own history. Zinn, a great admirer of folk and protest music—he had played Woody Guthrie records in his U.S. history classes and hosted Joan Baez's visit to Spelman College—wanted such music along with the readings. So he invited Patti Smith to play at the commemoration. Smith, in accepting the invitation (she would play her song "People Have the Power") explained that she had been introduced to *A People's History* by consumer advocate Ralph Nader and quipped that as a reader of Zinn's book she was now "one in a million."[25]

The focus on documents of dissent at the *People's History* commemoration (and in theater events that would follow) grew out of a primary source project that Zinn had been interested in for years. He had long wanted to publish a major collection of dissident documents as a companion to *A People's History* but had never been able to convince HarperCollins to get behind this project.[26] By the time of that *People's History* commemoration in 2003, Zinn had been working for several years on such a volume with another publisher (Seven Stories Press).[27] Given Zinn's age (he was in his late seventies when he began working on this collection) and his hectic schedule, he decided not to do this book solo but rather to work on it collaboratively with a writer, activist, and editor, Anthony Arnove—who had worked closely with Zinn in getting his play *Marx in SoHo* published and produced.[28] This collaboration between Zinn and Arnove led in 2004 to the publication of *Voices of a People's History of the United States*, which brought into print over two hundred documents (more than six hundred pages) of words from dissident Americans from Columbus's time through the turn of the twenty-first century. Most of the documents that served as the basis of the readings at the 2003 *People's History* commemorative event and the subsequent theatrical events and film were included in *Voices of a People's History*.[29]

Zinn opens his introduction to *Voices of a People's History* by putting at center stage those who made history from below via their resistance to oppression. "Readers of my book *A People's History of the United States*," he begins, "almost always point to the wealth of quoted material in it—the words of fugitive slaves, Native Americans, farmers and factory workers, dissenters and dissidents of all kinds. These readers are struck, I must reluctantly admit, more by the words of the people I quote than by my own running commentary on the history of the nation." To back this up, Zinn offers moving quotations from such historical figures as Native American leader Powhatan, the Black scientist Benjamin Banneker, white southern abolitionist Sara Grimke, transcendentalist Henry David Thoreau (protesting the Mexican War), and escapee from slavery Jermain Wesley Loguen (denouncing the Fugitive Slave Act).[30]

While one can question whether the quoted historical material was more influential with readers of *A People's History* than Zinn's own words, it was much more powerful and engaging than the very limited expressions of political dissent heard in mainstream American culture.[31] As Zinn astutely observes in the introduction to *Voices of a People's History*, what is "common to all these voices" gathered in the collection "is that they have mostly been shut out of the orthodox histories, the major media, the standard textbooks, the controlled culture."[32] This is because conventional discourse by elites—"presidents and generals and other 'important people'"—was center stage, while dissident oratory was neglected. This was a key reason that Zinn's brilliant initiative, his organizing famed actors and writers to read the words of dissent gathered in *Voices of a People's History*, would prove so enormously popular. As Arnove points out, Zinn "realized that there's something very powerful about encountering voices that come out of social movements. And that social movements can produce great works of literature and art."[33] Amid a mass media establishment that tended to ignore the history of radical dissent, that too often trivialized history, and an electoral system that reduced political expression to superficial sound bites and slanderous attack ads, Zinn and Arnove would bring first to the stage and then to film a dazzling array of meaningful and moving dissident oratory and mem-oir—offering an oasis of critical, radical political thought in an America that seemed barren of both.

The 2003 commemorative event at the 92nd Street Y in Manhattan embodied the egalitarian spirit of *A People's History* not only in its focus on the voices of dissidents and resistance but also in the democratic process Zinn and his fellow producers of this event used in organizing it. According to Arnove, the process used to develop the program with actors, musicians, and writers evolved in ways that made it "work very collaboratively. So it's not as if we came up with a script and then we said to James Earl Jones, 'Here's what you're reading.' We said to James Earl Jones, 'We'd really love you to read. We'd love for you to read Fred-erick Douglass.' And then it's a conversation. And then with every actor it's a conversation not just about what they read but [also] the edits of what they read, and sometimes the actor or musician has a suggestion or someone they want to read that we hadn't considered."[34] And so changes in the program as well as the book *Voices of a People's History* came out of this consulting process.

Arnove found it "great to see how Howard worked with people. Howard had ideas about what he thought would work. But it was understood that [it had] to be something that the person was passionate about reading and performing. . . . Also, because we collaborate with them, they do get to say, 'I'd really love to read something by a woman about this.' Or 'I'm really passionate about these issues, can we find it?' And often with musicians, they'll have songs that they really want to do." This collaborative approach helped attract the talented actors who would make the history come alive in their readings at the commemoration. So did Zinn's reputation as a writer and his long history of antiwar and civil rights organizing, which made it easy to recruit great talent. As Arnove recalled, "we went up to people who identified themselves in some way to Howard, over the years. A correspondence? They had done an event together? The person had written to Howard and said, 'I love your work.' Or 'you inspired me.' There were people we knew to be admirers and readers and engaged with Howard's work. . . . So Howard had connections . . . with politically engaged actors and musicians."[35]

Even with all this talent and a script grounded in some of the great dissident oratory of American history, there was no guarantee that the readings would make for a successful theatrical experience. After all, the people most famil-iar with such documents were historians, and even in their classrooms it was a challenge to arouse interest in primary sources. Add to this the bare-bones way the readings were done, "with no production value, no blocking, no sets, no cos-tumes . . . just a music stand, microphone, and reading," and it is little wonder that, as Arnove recalled, "we weren't even sure it would work, to be perfectly honest."[36]

But it did work. "The audience was fun, the actors were fun," and there was, as Arnove observed, "something transcendent about that event. And [it] made us aware that this really worked as a forum. The way that history . . . really spoke to the present." The result was that instead of just being a production for that one special occasion, commemorating the millionth copy of *A People's History* being sold, the dissident readings became a continuing theatrical event. This transpired not only because of the audience reaction and Zinn's and Arnove's being so impressed with the way the reading brought history to life but also because of the way the performers in the first reading responded. According to Arnove, "The actors having done it, and the musicians having done it, wanted to do it again." And they also had suggestions about adding other actors and musicians to the cast: "'Oh, have you thought of this person?' Or . . . 'I know this person who would love to do it.' Or 'I was in a play with them.' Or a movie. Or 'I toured with them.'"[37]

Another reason the readings became theatrical events put on across the country is that they were, with their strongly dissident political content, such a contrast to the normal work most actors did. Zinn and Arnove realized that very talented actors and actresses wanted to be politically engaged in their work, but, as Arnove put it, "[they ordinarily] don't have the luxury of it because the parts aren't being written. The roles aren't there. They have to do the roles that they can get in order to work in the field."[38]

So what Zinn and Arnove were doing when they put on *Voices of a People's History* theatrical events had a distinctive, almost unique quality, combining acting skill, political engagement, and a sense of history. "Howard," in Arnove's words, offered these actors "an opportunity to read things they were passionate about and that are dramatic, and that are powerful. And in front of a live audience that's engaged. Sometimes [film] actors are literally acting on green screens where the person who's in the scene with them in a movie isn't even there. . . . A very alienating process. But to get to do a live event? And with an appreciative audience? And read these words? That's why actors in particular really love the experience of doing that."[39] This is what actress Vanessa Martinez had in mind as she raved about the "fantastic time" she had in her *Voices of a People's History* performance, contrasting the typical role she played that only allowed her to "spit out fiction" as opposed to taking on the voices of dissenting historical figures, which she termed "the most empowering thing that I have ever done."[40]

The cast of readers expanded as the program's reputation soared; it became a magnet for politically engaged writers and actors. Arnove compared it to Bob Dylan's Rolling Thunder tour, as it grew and grew and had some of the feel of a social movement. "[There were new] people who were coming along. People who were bringing in other people. And we even had [actors and writers] . . . seek us out because they'd seen it or heard about it, and they were fans of Howard's. So over the years there's just been a process of self-identification, and then personal connections to other artists who have taken part in the shows."[41] Zinn said,

> [There was] a feeling of exultation all around as we began performing this in front of a live audience because these audiences of a thousand people each were so enthusiastic . . . greeting the readings and the actors with genuine exultation, and this . . . [had] an effect on the actors themselves. Well, the actors had come to this project knowing the book and wanting to do it, and then experiencing the reaction of the audience, and listening to one another, because actors are often sparked by one another and what they do. So that the result was . . . a very gratifying one for everyone. So much so that when we were finally finished . . . people were talking about going on and on with it and staying together as a group, which, of course, is virtually impossible to do with people who are busy and working on movies and working on stage plays. But that was the spirit.[42]

Indeed, after a 2005 *Voices of a People's History* performance, actress Marisa Tomei wrote Arnove of the "amazing response," saying "it keeps coming in." "One person wanted to do monthly readings in a space, are you guys open to doing that?"[43] Actor David Strathairn wrote Zinn that the *Voices* performance had been "great theatre, . . . true theatre" and that it had been a real privilege to be a part of it. He praised Zinn as "the first person who[se] writing I read that pulled back the curtain on history."[44]

Zinn was right about the audience (and cast) enthusiasm for *Voices of a People's History*, but the question remains: why were they so enthusiastic? Brian Jones, an actor (and historian) who performed in many of the *Voices* events, and so had many occasions to observe audience members and discuss their reactions, offered some insightful observations. Jones sees politics, community, education, and celebrity all playing a role in the audiences' enthusiastic response. In the political realm, it was exhilarating for progressive audiences to witness contemporary issues they cared about so passionately—war, racism, sexism, poverty, and other social inequality—raised with such eloquence by the historical figures depicted on stage and to be reminded that Americans had battled courageously, and at times triumphantly, against such ills. *Voices* provided, in Jones's view, a political forum treasured by people who lacked one. Some of the readings surfaced such a spirit of solidarity that one could feel as if one was attending a political rally, reminding people that there were liked-minded progressives. Along with the artistry of the actors, it was affirming to see famous actors one had watched and admired on stage and screen (in nonpolitical roles) articulating visions of equality that audience members shared.

There was also an educational process, Jones noted, initiated by the readings, a discovering of historical figures who audience members had never heard of, being quoted on stage raising issues and denouncing forms of oppression that the audience cared deeply about. "A typical reaction was 'Did this really happen?'" There was a shock of recognition coupled with "a feeling of inspiration" as people found themselves moved by these eloquent radical voices from the American past and wanting suddenly to know more about them. And there were also speeches by figures the audience members knew well, such as Martin Luther King Jr., addressing issues like war, which many had not known he spoke on, and with such great eloquence—and this too was exhilarating. Jones also emphasized that the structuring of the readings was done artfully, with minimal but crucial historical introductions setting the context, and the readings ordered so that that one related to and led to the next. This added drama seamlessly, making the show work so well on both an emotional and intellectual level.[45]

Audience enthusiasm also was connected to how unique *Voices* was with regard to its radical politics, historical sensibility, and form. With *Voices of a People's History* theatrical events (and later as a film, *The People Speak*), Zinn was in the early twenty-first century doing in popular venues something parallel to what he had done back in 1980 in publishing *A People's History of the United States*. Whereas in *A People's History* Zinn was opening students, teachers, and general readers to a whole new world of dissent and a history of grassroots social movements that had been neglected by textbooks, with his theatrical productions of *Voices of a People's History* he was opening up theater to radical history one would rarely, if ever, see on Broadway. In both cases Zinn showed a keen awareness that because radicalism was considered politically incorrect or too controversial by American cultural institutions, its rich history had been largely ignored. And Zinn had the foresight to suspect that a mass audience might be receptive to, even eager for, such history both in print and in theaters.

There was also a striking parallel between *A People's History* in print and *Voices of a People's History* on stage in that in both venues Zinn opted for a minimalist approach. Just as *A People's History* was that rare introductory history that included no photos, maps, or other graphics, *Voices of a People's History* included no scenery, no costumes, no frills. In both cases the singular focus on dissident expression was offered in an unadorned way that served to highlight that the words (and the reality they represented) were what was so distinctive and worthy of engagement.

Zinn's awareness of the shortcomings of American popular culture, its traditional neglect and indifference to radical, critical history of the United States, was not a new development. This was a long-standing concern of his. He had been thinking in these terms since at least the late 1970s when the TV drama *Roots* shocked America with its candid depiction of slavery's cruelty. For Zinn the significance of this TV series rested in part with how rarely such critical history founds its way to any of the mass media. As Zinn explained,

> *Roots*, by reaching millions of people through television, actually gave people, especially whites, but even Black people who didn't know their own history very well, for the first time . . . historical consciousness about slavery and what it meant. Because history textbooks for a long time treated slavery in such a way that you could never get the full picture of the brutality of slavery and what it did to people. So *Roots* was a rare example of when the media did something important with history. But . . . for the most part, that kind of historical understanding is missing from the media.[46]

So, with *Voices of a People's History*, Zinn had the chance to challenge American cultural institutions in a way that *Roots* had done. But Zinn had firsthand experience with the reluctance of corporate entertainment leaders to engage with radical history. In 1999 the Fox network optioned *A People's History* for a historical television series it was planning. This was initiated by a Fox vice president who had read *A People's History* in college and thought it would work well in such a series. Knowing—from *Good Will Hunting*—the connection with Matt Damon and Ben Affleck, Fox brought them into the project along with Chris Moore, who had produced *Good Will Hunting*. The idea was for the three of them and Zinn to serve as coproducers of a TV adaptation, and the star power of Damon and Affleck was likely a key reason for the network's interest. As Zinn explained, Fox "fooled around with it for a couple of years" but never made the series. Zinn speculated that aside from that one vice president "probably none of them knew the book." Zinn joked, "My theory is that finally Rupert Murdoch [the archconservative head of Fox] read the book . . . and they dropped the project. I doubt it. He probably hasn't read a book for years."[47]

The next stop was HBO, which went for Affleck's pitch that the network air docudramas based on historic events covered in *A People's History*. The project got a bit farther than it had at Fox. HBO, upon the suggestion of Zinn, Damon, Affleck, and Moore, hired three prominent writers: John Sayles to write a script on the girls and women of the Lowell mills, Howard Fast on the American Revolution, and Paul Laverty on Columbus and Bartolomé de Las Casas. As Zinn recalled, "They wrote the scripts. HBO turned them down. And that was the end of the project."[48] Arnove attributes HBO's abandonment of the series to a leadership shake-up that caused some financial belt-tightening and a reluctance to take on such new projects.[49]

After this second turndown it seemed clear that no movie studio or network was going to fund the production of a movie or TV series based on *A People's History*. This was concerning to Zinn's collaborators on this project, not only because of their commitment to having *A People's History* brought to the screen but also because, as Arnove put it, "Howard [in his eighties] wasn't getting any younger."[50] Moore, an experienced Hollywood producer, realized that if the film was going to be made he was going to have to come up with the financing. As he explained in 2008,

> We've been working on trying to bring Howard's book *A People's History of the United States* to the screen rather than a bookstore near you . . . [since] about '98, so it's almost ten years now. . . . [Zinn's] message would probably not get out if it wasn't for a smaller production company like ourselves that believed in it. It's not something a mainstream studio would probably take on in this earlier stage. But it's hard as a person . . . to hear the readings in the day, in the night, to read this book and not respond to it. It's certainly very honest, very truthful. It's a different side of history that we're not used to hearing. And . . . we feel very compelled as people who believe in telling the truth and believe in this message, that it should be out there, it should be viewed by the mainstream public.[51]

Moore also realized that the best way forward was to drop the docudrama approach that HBO and Fox had seemed to prefer. So Moore said to Zinn, "Well, wait a second. You're doing these live [*Voices of a People's History*] events. You've got these actors, you've got these musicians. People love these events. Maybe this is the way to make the film."[52] So in this way the theatrical events merged with the film project, which would now center on bringing to the screen the readings of dissident historical sources that had so engaged theater audiences. As part of this shift, Arnove, who had been coproducing those theatrical readings, was brought in as a codirector of the film, along with Zinn and Moore, and as coproducer, along with Matt Damon, Josh Brolin, Moore, and Zinn.

Raising the funds, some $2.5 million, to make the film was not easy, but Moore's persistence and Damon's own resources helped make it possible.[53] For his part, Zinn was, as he explained in 2008, thrilled with this new direction of the film project. He much preferred that the film center on the reading of dissident speeches and writings instead of historical docudrama. As Zinn noted, now the film would be strictly nonfiction:

> This is real. What was envisioned before by Fox and HBO were feature films based on [historic] incident[s]—which, when you think about it, is a very difficult thing to do. I am happier with the present situation because . . . when you start to fictionalize history, you are in great danger of moving away from what the historian intended to do. You are caught up in the story, the drama, you sensationalize it, distort it. And so here, where I have final say over the script, I feel very confident that what will come out will reflect my view of American history. Which means what will come out will be an in-your face [laughs] radical history in which we feature dissenters and troublemakers and visionaries and socialists and anarchists, and if television is put off by that, well that's too bad. It'll be on DVD. But right now they are editing the material and preparing to show it at the Berlin Film Festival. . . . To put it in Hollywoodese terms—"It's a go." [54]

Perhaps most amazing of all, the History Channel agreed to broadcast this film, which would be titled *The People Speak*. The History Channel would seem the most unlikely venue for a film by Howard Zinn since its focus has been almost exclusively on history from the top down, on generals, presidents, and wars. But fortunately for Zinn and the whole *People Speak* team, the director of history programming when they approached the History Channel was Nancy Dubuc, a dynamic young executive who was interested in broadening the channel's viewership, rebranding, and reaching beyond its older, white male demographic.[55] In December 2009 the History Channel broadcast *The People Speak* to a national audience of some nine million viewers.[56] It reached more than three times the readership of *A People's History*, and in that sense it was Zinn's greatest success in popularizing history from the bottom up.

These numbers were quite meaningful to Zinn, who realized the limited reach of even a best-selling book like *A People's History*. Thus when asked in a press conference for *The People Speak* why it was important to move beyond print and bring the voices of *A People's History* to the world of film, Zinn replied:

> Despite the large sales of the book . . . compared to the fate of history books in general . . . when you compare a million or two million readers of the book to ten million people watching a television program or twenty million people going to the movies there are huge numbers of people out there who, unfortunately don't read books. And so the thought was to bring the message and the information of the book to a public which was not going to buy the book

or buy any book. And so, yes to widen the readership for this book, and especially . . . to reach a lot of young people. Because young people have grown up in a visual culture where they, I think, read less books and see more television and movies. And I think the book has a special message . . . a special appeal to young people who are looking for something to stimulate them and to ignite feelings of idealism that I think young people naturally have. So that was the intent, to reach a wider public.[57]

Zinn's ability to draw a large audience was linked to the appeal that he had for popular musicians as well as actors, who proved eager to join the cast. Arnove, who worked closely with the performers in both the theatrical events and the film sees this appeal as connected to the artistic sensibility in *A People's History* itself. So that even before they met Zinn, musicians and actors knew he valued the arts and saw them as a very important form of expression with vast political implications. As Arnove explains, "If you look at the book, Howard talks about the arts. He talks about jazz musicians. He talks about painters. So he has a sense throughout of the role of culture and the artists' culture, and the role that artists and writers in particular can play in social movements. I mean he himself has a story about [radical folksinger Woody Guthrie, and] how he began to learn about aspects of labor history [most notably the Ludlow Massacre] from listening to Guthrie's songs. So that infuses *A People's History*. And artists and musicians really catch on to that." Indeed, the Guthrie connection, on top of Zinn's inclusive approach to history, engagement with the arts, and his long history of activism helps to explain why Bob Dylan, Bruce Springsteen, and other leading recording artists with a history of political engagement would agree to perform in the film. In it both Dylan and Springsteen cover Guthrie songs. The chance to work on the project and meet Zinn was, as Arnove put it, "huge for people [in the arts]." "When we filmed Bruce Springsteen for the film you would think it would be that Howard was there being a fan of Bruce Springsteen. But in reality Bruce was there being a fan of Howard. And it was even like that with Bob Dylan."[58]

Springsteen is a striking example of how deeply musicians who were engaged politically connected with Zinn, how meaningful they found his historical work, and how happy and even eager they were to perform for *The People Speak*. Back in 2007 Springsteen had told *Rolling Stone* magazine, "*A People's History of the United States* had an enormous impact on me. . . . It gave me a sense of myself in the context of this huge American experience and empowered me to feel that in my small way, I had something to say, I could do something. It made me feel a part of history, and gave me life as a participant."[59] And after *The People Speak* film crew and producers, including Zinn, came to Springsteen's home to film his singing Woody Guthrie's "This Land Is Your Land" and his own "The Ghost of Tom Joad," Springsteen sent Josh Brolin—the actor who had set up this filming—a note thanking him "for making my childhood dream come true in spending the day with Howard Zinn."[60]

Arnove also credits the accessibility of *A People's History* for making it a favorite among musicians and others in the arts and helping incline them to assist in converting the book into a theater and film project. *A People's History*, Arnove explains, is "something you can read that's intellectual and has ideas without being intimidating or [leaving you feeling] you have to go to the university and study history in order to be able to read it and engage in and understand it. And so a musician on a tour bus, a lot of these musicians read going from city to city. So it's something they can read, that they're welcomed into. It's well-written. So they appreciate that. It's reader-friendly. It's something that doesn't talk down. It's something that people who might have gone a different route, into art school or drama school or even just bypassed college, as a lot of musicians and actors do, can still engage with very seriously, very intellectually."[61]

Zinn's goal politically for the movie was identical with that in *A People's History* itself, which was to empower people by inspiring them to believe that they, like the protesters he was spotlighting, could make a difference via their activism. He cited his "old filing cabinet full of the letters that people" sent him after reading *A People's History* and his hope that the movie would have the same effect as the book had—as described in those letters—that it would "make people who see it . . . feel that they will want to do something, that they can do something, that it'll be meaningful . . . to do something, that their kids will be proud of them for doing something."[62] He thought that collectively the readings of these dissenting voices from the American past spoke to the present in that "what they were saying to us today is think for yourself. Don't believe what the people up there [in power] tell you. Live your own life. Think your own ideas. And don't depend on saviors. . . . Don't depend on leaders to do what needs to be done. Because whenever the government has done anything to bring about change, it's done so only because it's been pushed by social movements, by ordinary people organizing."[63]

Zinn also hoped that the film, by acquainting viewers with eloquent dissidents of the American past, could serve as a powerful antidote to despair, the hopelessness of those concerned deeply about social problems but pessimistic about prospects of change. Speaking with great sensitivity about such politically induced depression, Zinn observed, "I get letters from people who say, 'I have been in despair.' And when I get a letter like that, I know that letter writer is speaking for millions and millions of people in this country who are in despair.

And they're in despair about the world, or despair about our society . . . about AIDS and disease and war." Zinn hoped the film would give such people "a glimmer of hope" by

> [exposing them to] some piece of history that suggested "Hey, there were people in the past who have been feeling the same way." And at a certain point, people who felt that way, they had to act. The spur to action spread, and it soon involved numbers of people, and then something in the world changed. And so if people can read something, see something that goes against the feeling of frustration and sadness and despair, and makes them feel hopeful and alive again, aside from what it might accomplish in the larger society, in terms of creating a social movement, what it may accomplish for individual people is a very important thing.[64]

Although the media often mocks Hollywood celebrities who take progressive political positions, stereotyping them as shallow and faddish, the prominent actors and musicians (and writers) who were a part of *The People Speak* actually had quite principled reasons for supporting this film project. They were all familiar and impressed with Zinn's inclusive approach to history, having read and been influenced by his *People's History of the United States*. The interviews cast members gave in connection with the film attest to the book's broad reach and to its influence. Acclaimed performers such as Bruce Springsteen and actor Danny Glover shared Zinn's belief that knowledge of America's dissident past could be empowering and inspiring, that it could lead to critical thought, engaged citizenry, political awareness, and activism.

Glover, who gave voice to the words of Langston Hughes, John Lewis, Martin Luther King Jr., and Henry McNeal Turner in *The People Speak*, saw Zinn's work as providing "an opportunity to look at history from a different kind of vantage point," centering on "people struggling for justice." Glover has a long history of progressive activism, dating back to his student days in the late 1960s, when he participated in the Third World student strike at San Francisco State College. A speech Glover gave in 2003 against the Iraq War is published in *Voices of a People's History*. Glover saw *The People Speak* readings' focus on protest as embodying the admonition by Frederick Douglass that power concedes nothing without a demand. And the film showed "the demand and the changes that have happened with the civil rights movement, the abolitionist movement, the [woman's] suffrage movement, women's liberation, the movement of workers . . . for collective bargaining." Glover hoped the film would teach that "these voices are part of our collective memory." He wanted "people to be empowered by the voices," enabled to see that "as Howard has said about change coming from . . . mobilizing and organizing . . . the only way we become architects of our own rescue."[65] Glover had learned of Zinn's work decades earlier via the Pacifica public radio network. He viewed Zinn as "one of the great human beings of our time . . . not simply an academic historian [but also] an activist, not [just] in the business of chronicling history . . . [but] one of the active participants in making history." Few academics are in this category other than Zinn and Noam Chomsky, he said. Glover hoped the film would reach young people, and that they "would listen to the voice of Howard Zinn, who is past eighty years old, . . . find their own voice, the same kind of resonance, [and realize] that the most important role that they can play in their lives . . . outside of being a parent is to be a citizen, an active citizen."[66]

Jasmine Guy, who in the film did the reading of Marian Wright Edelman and Alice Walker (both students of Zinn at Spelman), Abbey Lincoln, and Sylvia Woods, admired both Zinn and the women whose words she brought to life in *The People Speak*. She thought Zinn provided an important corrective to the superficial way African American history is too often taught.

> The way we have learned our American history has been blotchy to me. For Black America, we go from slavery to the civil rights movement, and we leave out a lot of information and a lot of important people who fought for equality and freedom way before the sixties. A lot . . . happened between those two periods. We also had a wonderful philosophical adventure during the Harlem Renaissance period, and there are many voices of the everyday [person] that I think we just never learned about. I love that Howard Zinn brought to light these brilliant people, these people who put their careers and their lives on the line to speak out for what they knew was right. They are our heroes, and our kids need to know about them as well, and need to know what they were saying.[67]

Guy found the words she was reading inspirational, from jazz singer Abbey Lincoln's objections to the way that Black women were demeaned and stereotyped to Children's Defense Fund founder Marian Wright Edelman's complaint about how the United States prioritized military spending while neglecting the needs of impoverished children. And labor organizer Sylvia Woods's description of how as a child at school she was sent to the principal's office for refusing to sing the Star Spangled Banner because "if this is the land of the free . . . how come she can't do what the white kids do?" Giving voice to these eloquent women was so "amazing," Guy exclaimed in advance of a performance filmed for *The People Speak* "I've been excited for two days. I haven't had any sleep."[68]

For poet Martín Espada, who read five pieces in *The People Speak*, including the words of César Chávez, Tecumseh, and Leonard Peltier, the film as well as Zinn's *A People's History* related to his own past as a working-class Puerto Rican from Brooklyn.

> My history, my experience, has been defined by what we call race and what we call class in this country. In fact, race and class have built walls around my life, and I've spent my whole life pulling down those walls, one stone at a time. . . . I read *A People's History of the United States* many years ago, and I felt as if finally someone in the world was holding a mirror up to my face . . . that I was visible for the first time in many ways. . . . That I was seeing, reading a history that spoke directly to my experiences, to the experiences of my family, my community, and more than that, of course. What *A People's History of the United States* teaches is our relationship to everyone else in the country; [it] . . . gave me a way to learn about myself . . . [and] about all the people at all places past and present that I was connected to as a fellow human being.[69]

Espada was drawn to *The People Speak* by his friendship with Zinn and admiration for Zinn's writing, oratory, and activism. He thought Zinn a "visionary" who embodied "great moral and personal and political clarity."

> When you read *A People's History of the United States*, when you listen to Howard Zinn give a lecture, or even when you spend time with him, you benefit from that tremendous clarity, his understanding of a world where there is hope in spite of everything we know about humanity, or, better put, because of everything we know about the history of humanity. Howard Zinn makes me believe it is possible to change the world. He makes me utilize something that I think of as my political imagination. And, in fact, I would say that indirectly Howard Zinn has inspired many of my poems.[70]

In an interview Espada gave in connection with the film, he illustrated the way Zinn's sense of "hope and political imagination" influenced his own, influenced his poetry, by reading from his poem "Imagine the Angels of Bread" (the title poem from his American Book Award–winning collection), which he believed embodied Zinn's vision:

> This is the year that squatters evict landlords,
> gazing like admirals from the rail
> of the roofdeck
> or levitating hands in praise
> of steam in the shower;
> this is the year

that shawled refugees deport judges,
who stare at the floor
and their swollen feet
as files are stamped
with their destination;
this is the year that police revolvers,
stove-hot, blister the fingers
of raging cops,
and nightsticks splinter
in their palms;
this is the year
that darkskinned men
lynched a century ago
return to sip coffee quietly
with the apologizing descendants
of their executioners.

This is the year that those
who swim the border's undertow
and shiver in boxcars
are greeted with trumpets and drums
at the first railroad crossing
on the other side. . . .[71]

Prior to the film, Kerry Washington had done *Voices of a People's History* readings in New York, Los Angeles, and New Mexico. She traced her involvement in the project to her affection for Zinn and his role in shaping her understanding of history:

I was already in my twenties when I read *A People's History*, but it had a profound influence on my life. Howard Zinn is such an important and brave contributor to our society. He has worked tirelessly to ensure that every voice is heard in the narrative of our shared history as a nation. It was jarring for me to learn how much history, particularly the history of marginalized people, was not being taught. The way Howard breathes life into these stories is important and powerful. Collaborating with him in this creative way is really such an honor. I'm grateful I've had this opportunity to learn from him and to work alongside him. And I will be forever grateful for his existence and his vital contributions.[72]

Viggo Mortensen read the Bartolomé de Las Casas account of Columbus's crimes in *The People Speak,* and it was Mortensen's initiative that led to its reading in the original Spanish in addition to English. He also read Smedley Butler's indictment of U.S. imperialism. Mortensen had been a longtime admirer of Zinn's, having read both his historical works and political speeches. Mortensen recalled that when he first read *A People's History of the United States* it was "a revelation": "Many of the persons in that book . . . I was familiar with, and some of the speeches, some of the statements I knew part or all of . . . , but seeing them all together it was really illuminating, and it was an inspiration to read them. And *Voices of a People's History of the United States* was a unique book for me. I went out and bought as many as I could and gave them to all my friends and family." Mortensen linked his respect for Zinn to the way Zinn "constantly reminds . . . [the reader] that it is a government of the people, by the people, for the people. Very few historians, social commentators, certainly politicians really adhere to that; they go on the defensive or fudge it."[73]

Mortensen was especially impressed with the contemporary relevance of Zinn's account of the Vietnam War. Though this disastrous war was engineered by the U.S. political elite, and critics of the war had been right, back then the reigning orthodoxy was that "unless you are in government you lack the expertise to criticize the war and so ought to keep your mouth shut." Here Zinn's history showed that outside critics were wiser than the so-called experts. This, Mortensen thought, was an important lesson because especially "the mainstream media makes one feel that people like me and others that are on stage for this event—actors, singers, performers, certainly any kind of celebrity, whether you are a ballplayer, singer, actor, any person with a public profile, you really ought to shut your mouth. You see that in the press a lot. So what is this dumb actor talking about? What does he know?"[74]

As to his hopes for *The People Speak,* Mortensen spoke about it inspiring political thought and action. "If this works out, it will engage people, not only inform people. It will inspire people to see the country as potentially much more diverse, much more interesting, much greater in the sum of its parts. The truth about yourself, the truth about your country, especially including all the bad parts, can be an inspiration, can motivate a person to work toward a more just society. And that can best be undergirded by independent and critical thinking. Hopefully they'll read Howard Zinn. Hopefully they'll think for themselves. The whole purpose of introducing someone to Howard Zinn, whether it be this DVD, whether it be his books, isn't so they can say 'Oh, I read Howard Zinn, I know some stuff.' It's to encourage a person to think for themselves. That's what Howard Zinn's given me. He's helped me think for myself. He's helped me say

'Wait a minute. I'm going to check the sources on this. I'm going to see if there's another version of this.'"[75]

There was, of course, awareness among those working on *The People Speak* project that the version of history it presented was much more radical and critical than traditional U.S. history textbook triumphalism. But they thought this a plus, an inducement for greater engagement with the nation's history and for reflection on the meaning of America. Singer John Legend, who performed Marvin Gaye's "What's Going On" and read an antiwar speech by Muhammad Ali in the film, thought, "Some people will be really educated by seeing what we talk about in this project. I think for a lot of young people particularly, history doesn't seem relevant to them. And the United States has a sense of amnesia . . . about our past. And . . . kind of brushes over the injustices of the past and acts like they never happened. But I think it's helpful and informative to learn more about the history of the country and some of the inhumane things we've done, in order to make us a better country. We need to know about those things so we don't repeat history. . . . I think Zinn's [view is] an important perspective to have. . . . Here's the story of America from the mouths and eyes of the people that usually don't get to tell their story. . . . [A break from the norm in which] the winner gets to tell the history and gets to frame how history is told."[76]

David Strathairn, who read Eugene Debs and John Brown in *The People Speak*, expressed the hope that those unfamiliar with the critical material covered in the film would "not be despairing, not be kind of crushed by the enormity of the contrariness," by the way it contrasted with "history that most of us have been taught from the normal history books." He hoped that instead viewers would be open to learning from this "what *People's History of the United States* is teaching, sharing, and showing." Strathairn acknowledged that the clash between these two versions of the American past took those new to it to "a contrary and very flinty place."

> It's a place of friction. And it can cause a lot of confusing and unsettling [thoughts] if your myths of your country . . . your race, if those things you have been taught are being challenged. . . . But I would hope that people would come away from hearing something further illuminating, come away fuller, and not so "Oh, my God, I've been lied to, I've been duped, I've been hoodwinked in my education." I hope they would come away with the energy to, the urge to, explore from this moment on anything from a 360-degree approach because there's always two sides to every story. And the story we've been taught, the story that we have learned, . . . we've been taught it for certain reasons. But when you discover the other side of that story, it doesn't necessarily wipe the . . . [existing] one off the slate. It just informs it. And it just makes

you more aware of the way things work and how things have worked and why things are the way they are.[77]

Chris Moore acknowledged that making a film with so critical a take on American history involved political risk, which could be seen in the difficulty in getting it financed. But he also knew that a film that spoke to America about issues it cared about could yield a large national audience—as had been the case with Michael Moore's *Fahrenheit 911*, a scathing film on the Bush administration and its Iraq War, back in 2004, which was the highest-grossing documentary ever made. Still, when asked at a 2008 press conference for *The People Speak* whether he felt any trepidation about filming "the most radical version of American history the mass of Americans will have ever seen," Moore admitted he did: "There's definitely some trepidation." Contrary to the stereotypes about Hollywood liberalism, Moore said, "We're also so divided that you go into a room, or you make a phone call to somebody you've known for five years, you've done two projects with, and you have no idea what their politics are, actually. People are afraid to talk about it. That's why I'm so respectful of all these performers who want to come up here and stand here, not only in front of you now, but on stage." They wanted to be a part of a film reflecting Zinn's dissenting view of the American past. Moore noted that political tensions could even be felt by "people in the crew . . . in local bars, [where] somebody said 'Are you here for the Zinn thing? You bunch of commie bastards.'"[78]

But such tensions and obstacles seemed worth taking on and overcoming, in Moore's view, if the film got people to think about history more critically and to begin a dialogue about it. He hoped *The People Speak* would extend to all of American history the kind of rethinking evident in that scene in *The Sopranos* where Zinn's book provoked an argument about Columbus. In Moore's eyes, that was "a very emblematic pop culture scene of what makes this book important; it [made] people talk for the first time." And, rather than being a boring or preachy history lesson, it taught but was still "a very funny scene." Moore recalls "[AJ is] in the kitchen . . . reading passages [from *A People's History*] to his mom about Columbus. . . . Tony walks in . . ., and you get that great Tony Soprano moment where he looks and says [something like], 'He was a great Italian . . . , he's a hero, and in this house Columbus will always be a hero.'" AJ's mom is really listening to him, but his dad's mind is closed. "The point is: that's what happens in a lot of homes across the country . . . that some people, . . . like [Tony Soprano], want the world to be a certain way, and they don't want to think about [historical accounts that challenge their assumptions], and they don't want to read about it. They just want, 'It's Columbus Day. We celebrate because he discovered America, woo-woo.'"[79]

Moore thought there would be many such moments in *The People Speak* and that Americans would have the opportunity to rethink their assumptions about the nation's past and the way it is celebrated. As an example, he pointed to the memorable Frederick Douglass oratory in the film. "I love the Fourth of July speech [of] Frederick Douglass . . . where he talks about"—and here he paraphrases from memory—"'It's great you invited me to come here and be the speaker at your [celebration]. . . but I don't know [what] you're celebrating. You know, Fourth of July is independence for you [whites], but it wasn't independence for me. And there's a whole lot of people who are still not independent in it.'" For Moore this was one "those sobering moments" when people, including himself, were prodded to see beyond their "happy little lives" and think about the "bad spots" in the American experience and what might be done to move America toward a more democratic future.[80]

Moore admitted that it was a challenge finding viewers for a film that combined education with entertainment. He thought he would count it "a big success" if it encouraged viewers to learn more about Zinn's book, about their own history and what's going on in the world, and then spread its message that "democracy is not a spectator sport." He also thought that Zinn was "very successful and famous" among leftists but had not really entered the consciousness of a majority in mainstream America, and he hoped the film would help change that. He hoped it would show America that if we all looked at history and lived "a little more like Howard," then "we'd all be humanized a bit . . . [and] maybe [realize] it's OK to not make as much money, to make sure that everybody else is all right."[81]

When *The People Speak* aired on the History Channel in December 2009, it garnered positive reviews across the country, even from reviewers uncomfortable with the politics that framed it. Mary McNamara, the *Los Angeles Times* reviewer, for example, noted that "class division is a drumbeat throughout 'The People Speak,' which is a primer of liberal ideology with a decided bent toward socialism; no one's reading a few rousing passages of Ayn Rand's for instance. . . . Concepts such as patriotism . . . and national security are portrayed as the whip and cattle prod used by the power elite. Even World War II is cast as a false model for American military domination."[82] Nonetheless, McNamara praised the film for offering a "[valuable] reminder that no president, no Congress, no government ever solved a problem or righted an injustice until prodded into action by protest." She also praised the performances: "Without exception, [they] are thrilling." But she noted, "It is the authors, not the actors, who are the stars here. For a nation grown accustomed to weepy personal confession, to the cynical invective of political commentators on both the right and the left, and the carefully worded rhetoric of politicians, the eloquence, force, and bluntness of people such as Susan B. Anthony, Frederick Douglass, César Chávez and Malcolm X are a shock to the system and a welcome reminder that when real change comes it is neither gentle nor deferential."[83]

A positive review even came from the History News Network (HNN), which had often run articles by historians who harshly criticized Zinn *People's History*. The HNN reviewer, Brian Trautman, praised the way the film's reading of speeches, "charter documents, letters, diaries, [and] journal entries" breathed life into these and other historical primary sources, bringing "to the screen the actions and effects of dissent, civil disobedience, and agitation for equality and justice." "*The People Speak*," he said, "tells of the extraordinary and courageous acts of everyday people, many of whom were thrust into leadership roles, . . . who were responsible for facilitating an end to slavery and Jim Crow, to war and the genocide of Native Americans; [who] built labor unions, . . . advanced women's rights, . . . and defended the gay community." The film, Trautman said, "inspires contemporary civic engagement to create real and meaningful change."[84]

Trautman questioned why celebrities "were invited to tell the remarkable stories of average Americans." But he realized that this was an effective way to draw a mass audience. He praised the "rousing performances" in the film "by today's most talented and accomplished actors, poets, and musical artists."[85]

Zinn's remarks in *The People Speak* provided structure, placing war, imperialism, racism, class conflict, sexism, and the struggles for justice and equality at the heart of the American experience, but center stage was mostly reserved for the words of dissenting Americans. And the film was successful, drawing nine million viewers; one would have to look far and wide to find a historian who would dismiss that. In view of this success, the right-wing press didn't have much to say about *The People Speak*.[86] *Newsweek*, though, raised an important question about it. "[Could this] new documentary help historian Howard Zinn break through into the mainstream?" The reviewer suggested that unless the film changed things, Zinn's work would "continue to languish in cult status." "Being bold was never an issue for Zinn: he's been protesting wars since he returned home from World War II. Yet mainstream acceptance has eluded him, thanks in part to a perspective so leftist that even many of the longtime Boston University professor's outspoken Hollywood supporters appear moderate by comparison." *Newsweek* perceptively recognized a central goal of *The People Speak* when it asked: "Can a celebrity-heavy documentary about the untold stories of American history have a real impact on the way Americans view both their country and their right as free citizens to organize in protest when they disagree with official policies?"[87]

Though not pretending to have definitive answers to questions about Zinn, radical history, and mainstream America, *Newsweek* noted Zinn's growing influence:

> Assembled from clips of more than 60 live stage adaptations since 2003, *The People Speak* is part of a larger movement to bring the unsung heroes of American history, and Zinn, broader recognition. Interest in Zinn's work has been growing—though it remains largely a favorite of liberals and academics, *A People's History* has sold more than 1 million copies since 2000, as many as it had sold in the two decades before that—and led to the formation of Voices, a nonprofit arts, education, and social justice organization, in 2007. The History Channel is also producing 24 short films based on *The People Speak* for educational use in schools around the country in conjunction with existing resources, such as the abridged textbook, *A Young People's History of the United States*.

Newsweek quoted coproducer Matt Damon: "To be on History [the History Channel] is huge . . . because it's such a compelling presentation and it can reach so many people who would not have heard of the book, and hopefully get people thinking critically about the history they're being told, and about their own role in shaping their country." "With *The People Speak*," concluded *Newsweek*, "it looks like Howard Zinn may finally get his close-up. As for the term 'radical,' Zinn doesn't mind it. 'After all,' he says, 'peace is a radical idea. But it's an idea whose time has come.'"[88]

The questions raised by *Newsweek* about the film's impact cannot be answered definitively without large-scale empirical studies of the ways masses of viewers responded to it, and such studies do not exist. The same is true of assessing with certainty whether the film's ambitious goals—popularizing Zinn's dissident view of the American past and fostering civic engagement—have been realized. Certainly getting the film produced by the likes of Matt Damon and Josh Brolin, enacted by leading actors, musicians, and writers, and reviewed so positively are all impressive. And getting the film aired on the History Channel, reaching millions, is evidence of impacting the American mainstream. Since that viewership (nine million) nearly tripled the already sizable readership of Zinn's *People's History of the United States*, it is impossible to argue that the film was only seen by leftists and admirers of Zinn's book. The film did reach mainstream America, and this exposure was significant, but, again, we have no way of knowing how many of viewers came away convinced by its bottom-up approach to history and its critical take on war, capitalism, and inequality.

One must bear in mind that the viewership of *The People Speak* never approached that of the most popular of mainstream, non-radical historical documentaries on television. Those of Ken Burns on the Civil War and on the history of baseball drew forty million and forty-five million viewers respectively when they first aired on PBS. Nor did *The People Speak* match the viewership of Michael Moore's documentary *Fahrenheit 911*, which drew sixteen million to nineteen million viewers to movie theaters.[89] But none of these more popular films were surveying as large a chunk of American history via readings of dissident speeches and other primary sources. That *The People Speak* drew millions of viewers to voluntarily learn about this history seems a remarkable achievement.

The People Speak aired on TV in 2009, but its popularization of voices of historical dissidence continues. It sparked international interest and emulation, as in England where Academy Award–winning actor Colin Firth, after seeing and loving a performance of *Voices of a People's History* in New York, collaborated with Anthony Arnove on a series of theatrical events featuring readings from the book.[90] As in the United States, a film version followed that looked at history from the bottom up (in this case English history), featuring Firth and other eminent British actors, including Ian McKellen, Vanessa Redgrave, and Ben Kingsley. The film was aired on History UK TV in October 2010. Unlike in the United States, where books—*A People's History* and *Voices of a People's History*—led to theatrical and film versions, in England a book followed: *The People Speak: Voices That Changed Britain* (2012). There has also been an Australian version of *The People Speak*, produced by Foxtel and aired on Australia's History Channel in 2012, which was inspired by the American version and licensed by its creators but produced independently. And in the United States, the History Channel has aired segments of the American version of *The People Speak* in schools from coast to coast.[91]

Major U.S. theatrical events with prominent actors reading *Voices of a People's History* have continued, as have smaller community productions, supported by the nonprofit Voices of a People's History.[92] But perhaps the most significant ongoing part of the nonprofit organization's work is its efforts to impact the next generation in schools. Voices of a People's History has worked with U.S. high school students and teachers, and students have participated in public readings of selections from the documents gathered in *Voices of a People's History* and shown in *The People Speak*. The idea was to involve prominent actors and actresses in this work too. Before and after production of *The People Speak*, its actors have been a part of efforts to involve teachers and students in school readings. For example, Kerry Washington recalled that one of her favorite live performances of *Voices of a People's History* was in New Mexico: "[After] we did this powerful performance [we] went to a local high school to do a reading with the students. It was unforgettable to watch the kids breathe so much life into the stories . . . speaking these truths."[93]

Similarly, in 2012, three years after *The People Speak* aired on the History Channel, its cast members Matt Damon and rapper Lupe Fiasco engaged with the work of supporting such student and community productions of these historical reading events, designed to foster education and civic engagement. At Team Englewood Community Academy, a high school in the far southeast side of Chicago—one of the city's poorest communities—ten sophomores worked with adults from the community on such a production, via the curriculum generated by the Voices of a People's History organization. In support of this work, Damon and Lupe Fiasco traveled to Chicago (the rapper's hometown) to do a fund-raiser, came to the school to speak to the students, and attended the students' performance. Local hip-hop poet and educator Kevin Coval—who also founded the teen poetry festival Louder Than a Bomb—helped to launch this Chicago Voices of a People's History project. He said that the goal was "expanding the notion of what literature is: a canon for the people, of the people." As part of the project, the students were asked to "respond to speeches by Sojourner Truth, Frederick Douglass, and others with their own text in their own words." Hearing the talks by Damon and Lupe Fiasco, and having them watch their reading, thrilled the students, as seventeen-year-old student Jerome Wade explained: "It touches me that you guys would come here and do work like this. . . . The first thing [about Englewood] that comes to your mind is gangs, but it isn't only that. You may not have . . . funds, but everyone has a voice."[94]

Among the most enduring Voices of a People's History collaborations with schools are those in New York City, which continue to this day. The most high-profile of these involves students from Maxine Greene High School in Manhattan, since it culminates in annual performances at Lincoln Center for the Performing Arts. This program is overseen by actor and historian Brian Jones, who is also a board member of the Voices of a People's History Foundation. Jones, who worked with Zinn as the star of the initial production of Zinn's play *Marx in SoHo*, along with other actors, visits Maxine Greene High School twice each month to work with the students on their production. The way the project works is that each student is responsible, by semester's end, for reading a three-minute selection from *Voices of a People's History* in the class's public performance. The students get to choose the document they want to read. Then they research its historical context, select the passage from their document, and discuss what it means to them. The learning that occurs involves not only history but also cultivating oratorical skills. Students learn how to speak clearly, slowly, and confidently, making eye contact, but also the historical significance of their lines, so that they can be delivered with conviction. There is also a civic engagement aspect to this work since the documents are all about the ways that ordinary Americans have resisted oppression, which students learn about as they research their reading and learn more than what initially drew them to it. A student often comes to realize, as Jones says, "there's even more going on here, [things] I didn't even see before."[95]

Jones sees this work as reviving "the lost art of recitation." Years ago high school students would memorize and recite great speeches, such as Lincoln's Gettysburg Address or the words of other famed leaders. And there is, as Jones put it, "great value in putting those words in your mouth. . . . It becomes part of your intellectual equipment. You can borrow from it. You can reach for it [or quote it] when you need it." What the Voices project does in a similar way is give students mastery and ownership of great words from the American past, only in this case the words are from protesters often ignored in the traditional curriculum, such as enslaved people, Indigenous people, or others that Zinn was calling to our attention. So it is both historically illuminating and often personally and politically empowering, showing students that supposedly powerless people can make history.[96]

Among the most striking insights Jones has gained from his years of working with students on Voices of a People's History is that pedagogically the primary source research and theatrical work Zinn inspired was in its own way even more valuable in the classroom than *A People's History* itself. With *A People's History* Zinn was opening the door to a more critical way to see American history and a bottom-up perspective that students found stimulating. But there he was still the storyteller. With *Voices of a People's History*, Zinn was moving out of that role and giving it to students, along with documents from which they were to start exploring this history. And while the Voices collection of documents facilitated the use of primary sources, the theatrical component added a special motivation to "think through very carefully" the historical meaning and contemporary resonance of the words because at the semester's end "the students were going to have the authentic feedback experience of being up on a stage, giving these speeches to a public audience."[97] In this sense, Zinn had taken, as Jones sees it, what traditionally has been "the nerdiest and most boring" part of history classes, reading primary source documents, and made it an exciting individual and community activity.

∽

Whether viewed separately or together, Zinn's initiatives in the realm of popular culture, in theater, film, and in schools, are impressive. He had managed—with considerable help from talented writers, actors, musicians, and producers—to place his own words and the words of dissenting Americans, radicals, and "troublemakers" in front of masses of Americans on film, on TV, and in live theater. And because these efforts foregrounded history makers in their own words, in front of his own, in *Voices of a People's History* and *The People Speak* he had managed to reach millions of Americans. This without sparking a backlash from the Far Right and without the finger wagging from the historical profession that he had encountered in reaction to his *People's History of the United States*, even though his film reached many more Americans than had his book. And on top of all this, the *Voices* work is still resonating in schools today and in theaters both in the United States and internationally. Remarkably, all this innovative popular culture work came when Zinn was in the final decade of his life. As effective as Zinn was as a civil right and antiwar organizer in his forties and as a best-selling author in his fifties, there are grounds for arguing that he had his greatest impact on Americans in the last decade of his life, in his eighties. He "went Hollywood," perhaps, but in the most egalitarian of ways—using movies, theater, and TV as educational tools. Zinn, in this last chapter of his career as people's historian, had managed to mobilize movie stars and stage actors, rock stars and rappers, pop singers and poets, to popularize radical history in the twenty-first century.

ACKNOWLEDGMENTS

We would both like to acknowledge the staff of NYU's Tamiment Library whose brilliant archival work making Howard Zinn papers available made this book possible. Tamiment archivists, including Tim Natfali, Tim Johnson, Mike Koncewicz, Shannon O'Neil, and the late Michael Nash, were all wonderfully helpful. Robby's friend and colleague the late Marilyn Young played an important role in bringing the Zinn papers to NYU, and the archive and this book would not exist had not Myla Kabat-Zinn been so generous in donating her father's papers. Sonia and Robby are grateful to Myla for sharing with us other correspondence of her father that illuminated the origins and impact of *A People's History of the United States* and for sharing her keen insights about that book and her father's history. Bill Bigelow and Deborah Menkart were generous with their time, and we are grateful to them for sharing their knowledge of the history and ongoing work of the Zinn Education Project. We also thank Bill Patterson for sharing his memories of the pioneering work he did in teaching high school with *A People's History* and Rebecca Mayer and Alison Hallett for writing us about their experiences in those memorable classes.

Anthony Arnove's generosity with his time and files on his collaborative work with Howard Zinn on *The People Speak* film were essential to the research and writing of chapter 8. We are deeply grateful to him and to all those who took the time to do the interviews that he shared on that film project, including actors Jasmine Guy, Danny Glover, Viggo Mortensen, Kerry Washington, and David Strathairn, poet Martin Espada, producer Chris Williams, and singer John Legend. It was inspiring to hear these talented artists speaking with such eloquence on the value of making history accessible on stage and film. Historian and actor Brian Jones played an important role in our understanding Zinn's work on stage and the school theater program he helped to establish.

We are grateful to the historians who shared their insights on the strengths and limitations of *A People's History*, including Eric Foner, James Merrell, Linda Gordon, Bryant Simon, Amy Greenberg, Wesley Hogan, Alan Taylor, Paul Buhle, Robin D. G. Kelley, and the late Marilyn Young. We are also grateful to Ira Shor for his insightful comments on activist teachers as they were influenced by critical pedagogy. The fine work of Zinn biographer Martin Duberman was also of assistance in assessing Zinn's historical perspective. We are grateful to Robby's old friend John Inscoe of the University of Georgia for providing wise advice on trimming a very fat manuscript, and to Chris Dodge for his brilliant copyediting. Our thanks to *Reviews in American History* for permission to use material from Robby's article, "The Second Worst Book in Print? Re-thinking A People's History of the United States" (June 2014), and to the History News Network for permission to use material from his online article "Will Trump's Last Battle Be against Howard Zinn (and America's History Teachers)?," HNN, Nov. 20, 2020.

The great patience and support displayed by Mick Gusinde-Duffy of the University of Georgia Press are much appreciated and proved pivotal to the completion of this book.

Perhaps now more than ever, Howard Zinn's comments on American society, equality, and justice summon us to consider our role in reform and social change. Working on this book, Sonia Murrow found this to be true, and most especially when it comes to the inequality of access to educational opportunity faced by many young people in this country. She is so grateful to many friends, students, and colleagues who talked with her about these and other themes, which inevitably helped shape this book. She is also thankful for the support she received from the PSC-CUNY Research Foundation of the City University of New York, which made it possible for her to devote time to this project.

Sonia thanks her family, especially her devoted parents, Hope Griswold Murrow and Daniel Murrow, whose lifelong dedication to social justice and the field of mental health informs her work and life. And finally, Lev and Talia, her children, were exceptionally understanding and patient while she worked on this book, and on a daily basis they provide her with abundant inspiration and love. She thanks them from the bottom of her heart. This book is dedicated to them.

Robby thanks his wife Rebecca Hyman, son Daniel Hyman-Cohen, and Lucia Hsiao for helping this book along in ways too numerous to count, making it possible for him to keep productive and reasonably sane through the insane time of pandemic and Trumpism. Goes to show that love can be more powerful than physical or political maladies.

The co-dedication of this book is to Tom Hayden, whose life, work, and friendship Robby cherishes, and whose memory is present whenever he reflects on the history and democratic legacy of the 1960s. In remembering Tom, the words that come to mind—along with the opening of the Port Huron Statement—are those that Ted Kennedy used to eulogize his brother Bobby (whom Tom so admired): "A good and decent man who saw wrong and tried to right it, saw suffering and tried to heal it, saw war and tried to stop it."

NOTES

INTRODUCTION

1. Zinn saw his historical scholarship as part of a dissenting tradition of radical history writing that exposed the abuses of the power elite and illuminated the processes of egalitarian, democratic social change. For his thoughts on the meaning and implications of radical history, see Howard Zinn, "What Is Radical History?," History Is a Weapon, https://www.historyisaweapon.com/defcon1/zinnwhatisradicalhistory.html.

2. Howard Zinn, Dana Frank, and Robin D. G. Kelley, *Three Strikes: Miners, Musicians, Salesgirls, and the Fighting Spirit of Labor's Last Century* (Boston: Beacon Press, 2001).

3. Robin D. G. Kelley, e-mail to Robert Cohen, Sept. 21, 2019, copy in authors' possession.

4. Howard Zinn, *A People's History of the United States* (New York: HarperCollins, 35th anniversary ed., 2015), 23.

5. Todd Gitlin, *The Twilight of Common Dreams: Why America Is Wracked by Culture Wars* (New York: Metropolitan Books, 1995), 126.

6. Larry Cuban, *Teaching History Then and Now: A Story of Stability and Change in Schools* (Cambridge, Mass.: Harvard Education Press, 2016).

7. David Tyack and Larry Cuban, *Tinkering toward Utopia: A Century of School Reform* (Cambridge, Mass: Harvard University Press, 1997).

8. Howard Zinn, adapted by Rebecca Stefoff, *A Young People's History of the United States: Columbus to the War on Terror* (New York: Seven Stories Press, 2007).

9. Dan Simon, e-mail to Robert Cohen, Nov. 11, 2019, copy in authors' possession; Deborah Menkart, e-mail to Robert Cohen, Nov. 11, 2019, copy in authors' possession.

10. Martin Espada, "Another Bomb Threat in Tucson," in Martin Espada, *Zapata's Disciple* (Evanston: Northwestern University Press, 2016), ix–xxix.

11. Barbara Aria, "History in the Making," *Time Out New York*, Feb. 2003, 20, Howard Zinn Papers, Tamiment Library, New York University (hereafter Zinn Papers).

12. Howard Zinn, *Failure to Quit: Reflections of an Optimistic Historian* (Monroe, Maine: Common Courage Press, 1993), 127–129.

13. Simon to Cohen, Nov. 11, 2019.

14. *The People Speak* (2008), directed by Howard Zinn, Anthony Arnove, and Chris Moore.

15. Eric Foner, e-mail to Robert Cohen, Dec. 13, 2019, copy in authors' possession.

16. Steven Levitsky and Daniel Ziblatt, *How Democracies Die* (New York: Broadway Books, 2019).

17. Brad Plumer, "Full Transcript of Donald's Trump's Acceptance Speech at the RNC," *Vox*, July 22, 2016, https://www.vox.com/2016/7/21/12253426 /donald-trump-acceptance-speech-transcript-republican-nomination-transcript.

18. Robert Cohen, "Martin Luther King. Jr. Understood What Trump Does Not," History News Network, Oct. 30, 2018.

19. See "Trump: 'I Love the Poorly Educated,'" *Daily Beast*, Apr. 13, 2017, https://web .archive.org/web/20200810152242/https://www.thedailybeast.com/trump-i-love-the -poorly-educated. A similar pattern of avoidance can be seen with regard to LGBTQ history. Only five states (California, New Jersey, Illinois, Colorado, and Oregon) currently mandate the teaching of LGBTQ history in their public schools.

20. Howard Zinn with Ray Suarez, *Truth Has a Power of Its Own: Conversations about "A People's History"* (New York: New Press, 2019), 200–202.

21. James Baldwin, "A Talk to Teachers," *Saturday Review*, Dec. 21, 1963, in James Baldwin, *Baldwin: Collected Essays*, edited by Toni Morrison (New York: Library of America, 1998), 686.

22. This quote and all the Trump quotations below are from his speech at the White House Conference on American history, Sept. 17, 2020, https://www.whitehouse.gov /briefings-statements/remarks-president-trump-white-house-conference-american -history. After Trump had denounced Zinn as a propagandist, historians widely panned the report of the 1776 Commission that came out of Trump's White House Conference on American History as right-wing propaganda. Historians said it obscured the significance of slavery in American history, falsely characterized progressivism as anti-democratic (alongside fascism), and ignored the past century of critical historical scholarship on these and other central topics in the American experience. See "'A Hack Job,' 'Outright Lies': Trump Commission's '1776 Report' Outrages Historians," *Washington Post*, Jan. 20, 2021.

CHAPTER 1. ORIGINS AND APPEAL

1. The sales figures were reported by Harper Collins and cited in Myla Kabat-Zinn, e-mail to Robert Cohen, Jan. 3, 2020, copy in authors' possession. The 3,328,552 total, as of 2019, represents steady sales, since total sales had been 2.5 million as of 2015, as cited by Anthony Arnove, introduction to Howard Zinn, *A People's History of the United States*, 35th anniversary ed. (New York: Harper-Perennial, 2015), xviii.

2. Annual sales had gone up from 16,000 in 1982 to 44,000 in 1991 (with total sales by June 1991 of 260,000 books, plus 30,000 of the 1984 abridged version of the book, *The Twentieth Century: A People's History*). See Howard Zinn to Rick Balkin, March 10, 1992, Zinn Papers. Sales reached the one million mark in 2002.

3. *The People Speak* interview with Howard Zinn, January 8, 2008, Boston, transcript

in authors' possession, courtesy of Anthony Arnove; Hugh Van Dusen, e-mail to Robert Cohen and Marilyn Young, Oct. 3, 2012, copy in authors' possession.

4. Howard Zinn, foreword and series preface, in Ray Raphael, *A People's History of the American Revolution: How Common People Shaped the Fight For Independence* (New York: New Press, 2001), xi, xiii–xiv; Diane Wachtel to Howard Zinn, Aug. 25, 2000; Howard Zinn to Diane Wachtel, Sept. 10, 2000, both in Zinn Papers.

5. Martin Duberman, *Howard Zinn: A Life on the Left* (New York: New Press, 2012), 310.

6. See chapters 3–4 for documentation of how an innovative high school history teacher used Zinn's book for decades to challenge textbooks and promote historical debate among his students.

7. Bill Bigelow, telephone interview with Robert Cohen, Nov. 28, 2012, transcript in authors' possession. On the origins of the Zinn Education Project, see Rethinking Schools and Teaching for Change, "Zinn Education, Submitted to William Holtzman," Nov. 28, 2007, Zinn Papers.

8. Duberman, *Howard Zinn*, 235.

9. *The People Speak*, interview with Howard Zinn

10. Hugh Van Dusen to Howard Zinn, Oct. 24, 1991, Zinn Papers.

11. "Speaking of History" ad, Harper Perennial, [Oct. 1991], Zinn Papers. *The Twentieth Century* volume referred to in the ad is an abridged version of *A People's History* that consisted of the larger book's chapters on that century.

12. There is a poetic quality to this argument, in that it implies that millions of readers influenced by the protest movements (and their precursors), whose stories Zinn narrated in *A People's History*, had made his book their own and had embraced democratic history, because, like Zinn, they valued peace and social justice and saw knowledge of the history of such struggles as a key to social progress in the present and future.

13. On Zinn's civil rights activism in the Deep South, see Howard Zinn, *You Can't Be Neutral on a Moving Train: A Personal History of Our Time* (Boston: Beacon Press, 2002), 15–84; Robert Cohen, *Howard Zinn's Southern Diary: Civil Rights, Sit-Ins, and Black Women's Student Activism* (Athens: University of Georgia Press, 2018); Duberman, *Howard Zinn*, 29–128. On Zinn's antiwar activism in the Vietnam era, see Zinn, *You Can't Be Neutral*, 103–162; Duberman, Howard Zinn, *Howard Zinn*, 129–154.

14. *The People Speak*, interview with Howard Zinn.

15. C-Span *Book Notes*, interview with Howard Zinn by Brian Lamb, March 12, 2000.

16. Ibid.

17. *The People Speak*, interview with Howard Zinn.

18. Howard Zinn, *LaGuardia in Congress* (Ithaca: Cornell University Press, 2010).

19. Howard Zinn, *SNCC: The New Abolitionists* (Boston: South End Press, 2002).

20. Zinn, *You Can't Be Neutral on a Moving Train*, 58; Cohen, *Howard Zinn's Southern Diary*, 8, 95.

21. Tapes and transcripts of these interviews are in Zinn Papers.

22. Zinn used "Growing Up Class-Conscious" as the title of the chapter in his mem-

oir about his working-class youth and his political baptism in the Depression decade. See Zinn, *You Can't Be Neutral*, 163–182.

23. Duberman, *Howard Zinn*, 23–25; Cohen, *Howard Zinn's Southern Diary*, 16, 243n64; Zinn, *You Can't Be Neutral*, 172–173.

24. Duberman, *Howard Zinn*, 22; Howard Zinn, "The Colorado Coal Strike, 1913–14," in Howard Zinn, Dana Frank, and Robin D. G. Kelley, *Three Strikes: Miners, Musicians, Salesgirls, and the Fighting Spirit of Labor's Last Century* (Boston: Beacon Press, 2001), 7–55; Howard Zinn, *Failure to Quit: Reflections of an Optimistic Historian* (Monroe, Maine: Common Courage Press, 1993), 30–36. In April 1914 the Ludlow Massacre occurred amid violent conflict between National Guard troops and striking coal miners employed in the Rockefeller-owned Colorado Coal and Fuel Company in Ludlow, Colorado. After a ten-hour gun battle that left seven strikers and a boy dead, the National Guard burned the miners' tent village. Two mothers and eleven children died in that fire. Guthrie released his protest song "The Ludlow Massacre" in 1946. See Scott Martelle, *Blood Passion: The Ludlow Massacre and Class War in the American West* (New Brunswick: Rutgers University Press, 2007) 2; Thomas G. Andrews, *Killing for Coal: America's Deadliest Labor War* (Cambridge, Mass.: Harvard University Press, 2008), 1–6.

25. Zinn, *You Can't Be Neutral*, 165.

26. Cohen, *Howard Zinn's Southern Diary*.

27. Howard Zinn, *Vietnam: The Logic of Withdrawal* (1967; repr., Boston: South End Press, 2002).

28. Zinn, *You Can't Be Neutral*, 127–134.

29. Duberman, *Howard Zinn*, 175–179.

30. Zinn, *You Can't Be Neutral*, 93–94; Howard Zinn, *The Bomb* (San Francisco: City Lights Press, 2010), 65–87.

31. Zinn was deeply troubled about the massive loss of life and suffering inflicted by the U.S. military on a city of "civilians, . . . old people, school children" in Hiroshima, when he read John Hersey's graphic book on the consequences of its atomic bombing. This led Zinn, as a fellow at Harvard's Center for East Asian Studies in 1960, to research the bombing and publish a critical article, "A Mess of Death and Documents." See Zinn, *You Can't Be Neutral*, 95–96; Zinn, *The Bomb*, 17–64.

32. Howard Zinn, introduction to Howard Zinn and Anthony Arnove, *Voices of a People's History of the United States*, 10th anniversary ed. (New York: Seven Stories Press, 2014), 27. Zinn noted in the preface to the play he wrote (in 1975) on Emma Goldman that he had never heard of the famed American anarchist until he met her biographer Richard Drinnon at a conference in the early 1960s. "It struck me," Zinn noted, "that in all my work in American history, whether in undergraduate or graduate school, her name had never come up." Howard Zinn, *Three Plays: The Political Theater of Howard Zinn—Emma, Marx in SoHo, Daughter of Venus* (Boston: Beacon Press, 2010), 3.

33. Zinn, introduction to Zinn and Arnove, *Voices of a People's History*, 28.

34. Ibid.

35. C-Span *Book Notes*, interview with Howard Zinn.

36. Howard Zinn to Daniel Okrent, May 1, 1972, "Proposal for 'A People's History of the United States: In Celebration of the 200th Anniversary of the Declaration of Independence,'" copy in authors' possession, courtesy of Myla Kabat-Zinn.

37. Ibid.; Zinn had used the term "people's history" in April 1972, a month before sending this people's history books series proposal to Knopf, when he wrote the introduction for *Harvey Wasserman's History of the United States* (New York: Harper and Row, 1972) (see p. v). Zinn termed Wasserman's book "a beautiful example of people's history" that highlighted social inequality, racism, sexism, war, and the inspiring people's movements opposing those evils—movements that kept alive "the spirit of resistance and unity against arbitrary power."

38. Zinn to Okrent, "Proposal." In Zinn's introduction to Wasserman's book, as in his series proposal to Knopf, Zinn stressed the need for accessibility: "What is 'people's history' and why do we need it? To begin with we would expect a people's history to be written in such a way that we can all understand it. Free of that pretentious vocabulary which the professional scholar uses to disguise the ordinariness of his ideas." Zinn, introduction, Wasserman, *History of the United States*, v.

39. Zinn to Okrent, "Proposal."

40. Ibid.

41. Ibid.

42. Cohen, *Howard Zinn's Southern Diary*, 10–11, 16–17.

43. Zinn thought that class analysis was crucial to any people's history of the United States, "that behind the politics, the wars, the diplomacy stressed in conventional histories of this country there is something more basic, something the political scientist Harold Laswell once described as 'who gets what and why?'" Zinn introduction to Wasserman, *History of the United States*, v).

44. Zinn to Okrent, May 1, 1972, "Proposal"; "Prison abolitionist": Howard Zinn, *Justice in Everyday Life: The Way It Really Works* (Boston: South End Press, 2002).

45. Zinn to Okrent, May 1, 1972, "Proposal."

46. Ibid.

47. Howard Zinn, *A People's History of the United States*, 514–524.

48. Ibid., 443–446.

49. Zinn to Okrent, "Proposal".

50. Ibid. Note, however, that Zinn in his book proposal did use the word "synthesis," depicting his proposed book as a "one-volume synthesis held together by a unified interpretation of the American past and a strong, provocative point of view." But judging from the body of the proposal he was not referring here to an attempt to synthesize a top-down and bottom-up view of the American past. Howard Zinn, "Struggle for Democracy: A People's History of the United States (prospectus)", [1977], Zinn Papers.

51. Zinn to Okrent, "Proposal." GIs testified in these Winter Soldier hearings (organized by antiwar activists) in Detroit in 1971, calling attention to war crimes committed by U.S. troops Vietnam. See Vietnam Veterans Against the War Collective, *Winter*

Soldiers, documentary film (1972); Ron Carver, David Cortright, and Barbara Doherty, eds. *Waging Peace in Vietnam: U.S. Soldiers and Veterans Who Opposed the War* (New York: New York University Press, 2019).

52. *The People Speak* press conference, Jan. 9, 2008, Boston, transcript in authors' possession, courtesy of Anthony Arnove.

53. Howard Zinn, *Albany: A Study in National Responsibility* (Atlanta: Southern Regional Council, 1962).

54. Zinn, *You Can't Be Neutral*, 103–162.

55. C-Span *Book Notes*, interview with Howard Zinn.

56. Zinn, "Struggle for Democracy" (prospectus).

57. Ibid.

58. The high school textbook of the 1970s that came closest to resembling Zinn's proposed people's history, in its critical view of American history and the dissident politics of its authors, was *As It Happened: A History of the United States* (New York: McGraw Hill, 1975). The lead author, historian Charles G. Sellers, was, like Zinn, a civil rights movement veteran (Sellers had been a Freedom Rider and antiwar activist). Two of Sellers's coauthors, Henry Mayer and Alexander Saxton, would produce major revisionist works on the history of race in America. *As It Happened* broke with the coverage model of most textbooks, exploring key themes and problems in American history in depth, using an inquiry approach centered around provocative, contradictory primary sources. The anti-textbook failed commercially, however, because it used a textbook format (and textbook publisher) but was too radical to be adopted widely by school systems. So *As It Happened* never made it to a second edition.

59. Jesse Lemisch, "Jack Tar in the Streets: Merchant Seamen in the Politics of Revolutionary America, *William and Mary Quarterly*, July 1968, 371–407; Jesse Lemisch, "The American Revolutions Seen from the Bottom Up," in Barton Bernstein, ed., *Towards a New Past: Dissenting Essays in American History* (New York: Vintage, 1969), 3–45; Jesse Lemisch, *Toward a Democratic History* (Ann Arbor, Mich.: Radical Education Project, 1967); Jesse Lemisch, "The American Revolution Bicentennial and the Papers of Great White Men: A Preliminary Critique of Current Documentary Programs and Some Alternative Proposals, AHA (American Historical Association) Newsletter, Nov. 1971, 7–21; Staughton Lynd, *Class Conflict, Slavery, and the Constitution* (Indianapolis: Bobbs-Merrill, 1967); Alfred F. Young, *The Democratic Republicans of New York, 1763–1797* (Chapel Hill: University of North Carolina Press, 1967); Alfred F. Young, ed., *The American Revolution: Explorations in the History of American Radicalism* (DeKalb, Ill.: Northeastern University Press, 1976).

60. See A. A. M van der Linden, *A Revolt against Liberalism: American Radical Historians, 1959–1976* (Amsterdam: Rodopi, 1996), Peter Novick, *That Noble Dream: The "Objectivity Question" and the American Historical Profession* (New York: Cambridge University Press, 1988), 414–572; Jon Weiner, "Radical Historians and the Crisis in American History," *Journal of American History*, Sept. 1989, 399–433; "Looking Back: Radical Historians Get Growing Following, Dispute 'Myths' of the Past," *Wall Street Journal*, Oct. 19, 1971.

61. See also E. P. Thompson, "History from Below," *Times Literary Supplement*, April 7, 1966.

62. Despite the many references Zinn made to the radical historians he drew on in *A People's History*, some readers have wrongly assumed that he invented grass roots radical history (history from the bottom up). In addition to knowing about such scholarship, Zinn had contributed to it, through his book *SNCC: The New Abolitionists* (1964), his history of the student wing of the Black freedom movement, and through his essays published in such early collections of the new social history as Alfred F. Young, ed., *Dissent: Explorations in the History of American Radicalism* (DeKalb: Northern University Press, 1968), and Martin Duberman, ed. *The Anti-Slavery Vanguard: New Essays on the Abolitionists* (Princeton: Princeton University Press, 1965). For *A People's History*, Zinn would choose not to use footnotes, hoping to make it more accessible to general readers. Nonetheless, he would credit by name many historians whose scholarship he drew on, and he included them in the book's bibliography. In the first edition, however, Zinn neglected to cite historian Edward Countryman for his work on land rioters in early America. After Countryman complained to Zinn that his ideas and wording had been used without crediting him, Zinn apologized and pledged to credit Countryman in future editions, which he did in both the text and the bibliography. Despite this slip, there is no pattern of plagiarism in *A People's History*. Indeed, Michael Kammen, the Pulitzer Prize–winning historian, complained (in his *Washington Post* review of *A People's History*), "Zinn's gravest error of commission is too include *too many* tedious quotations from radical historians. . . . So much attention to historians, historiography, and historical polemic leaves precious little space for the substance of history. Thus Phillip Foner, a radical historian, is cited nine times while Thomas Jefferson is mentioned only eight." Michael Kammen, "How the Other Half Lived," *Washington Post*, March 23, 1980, emphasis added. On the Countryman correspondence with Zinn, see Edward Countryman to Howard Zinn, Feb. 24, 1989, and Howard Zinn to Edward Countryman, Feb. 28, 1989, both in Zinn Papers. In the revised version of *A People's History*, Zinn credited Countryman for his "pioneering work on rural rebellion" (63).

63. Zinn, "Struggle for Democracy" (prospectus).

64. Zinn, introduction to Wasserman, *History of the United States*, ix.

65. Ibid.

66. Zinn, "Struggle for Democracy" (prospectus).

67. Howard Zinn, "Slavery Without Submission, Emancipation without Freedom," chapter 9 in *A People's History of the United States*; Zinn, "A People's War?," chapter 16 in *A People's History of the United States*.

68. Zinn, *A People's History of the United States*, 23.

69. Zinn, "Struggle for Democracy"(prospectus).

70. Ibid.; Zinn, *A People's History of the United States*, 7–11.

71. Zinn, "Struggle for Democracy" (prospectus).

72. Zinn, *A People's History of the United States*, 10.

73. Zinn, "Struggle for Democracy" (prospectus).

74. Ibid.

75. Ibid.

76. Ibid.

77. Howard Zinn, foreword to Ray Raphael, *A People's History of the American Revolution*, xi.

78. Zinn, "Struggle for Democracy" (prospectus).

79. Ibid.

80. Reader C, review of Howard Zinn's proposal for a one-volume *People's History of the United States* for Cambridge University Press, Zinn Papers.

81. Reader A, review of Howard Zinn's proposal for a one-volume *People's History of the United States* for Cambridge University Press, Zinn Papers.

82. Reader B, review of Howard Zinn's proposal for a one-volume *People's History of the United States* for Cambridge University Press, Zinn Papers.

83. Ibid.

84. Cynthia Merman, telephone interview with Robert Cohen, Oct. 5, 2012, notes in authors' possession.

85. Robert C. Twombly, reader's report on Howard Zinn, *A People's History of the United States* for Harper and Row, Zinn Papers.

86. Ibid.

87. George Kirschner, reader's report on Howard Zinn, *A People's History of the United States* for Harper and Row, Zinn Papers.

88. Ibid.

89. Cynthia Merman to Howard Zinn, March 7, 1979, Zinn Papers.

90. Kirschner, reader's report.

91. C-Span *Book Notes*, interview with Howard Zinn.

92. Ibid. One of the striking things about this public backlash against Zinn's popularization of a critical view of Columbus is how it contrasted with the reaction of leading historians of the age of exploration, for whom such criticism of Columbus seemed neither new nor shocking. David B. Quinn, who wrote the foreword to the 1983 edition of Samuel Eliot Morison's classic, admiring biography of Columbus that Zinn sharply criticized in *A People's History*, took Morison to task for failing to be sufficiently critical of Columbus—and in doing so cited a scholarly study that dated back to 1966. Quinn wrote, "Columbus cannot be detached from the imperialist exploitation of his discoveries and he must be made to take some share of responsibility for the brutal exploitation of the islands and mainlands he found. His greed for gold, his approval of slavery, his willingness to exploit to death the native societies he encountered (though he was not the worst of the conquistadores in these respects) cast a shadow over his achievements that cannot be passed over now as lightly as it was by Morison in 1942 or even in 1974. Carl Ortwin Sauer in *The Early Spanish Main* (Berkeley and Los Angeles: Univ. of California Press, 1966) laid a heavy burden of responsibility for the cruel, early stage of Spanish imperialism on Columbus's shoulders, and it is hard to disregard that charge. . . . [Columbus was] a man who, away from the sea, may have been sensitive and proud as Morison described him, but who was also often alien to common humanity." David B. Quinn, foreword to Samuel Eliot Morison, *Admiral of the Ocean Sea: A Life of Christopher Columbus* (Boston: Northeastern University Press, 1983), xviiii–xix. For

a brilliant transnational account of the rise of the Columbus myth, see Michel-Rolph Trouillot, *Silencing the Past: Power and the Production of History* (Boston: Beacon Press, 1995), 108–40.

93. Zinn, *A People's History of the United States*, 7.

94. Ibid., 7–9.

95. Ibid., 10.

96. Howard Zinn to Cynthia Merman, Oct. 4, 1978, Zinn Papers.

97. Zinn, *A People's History of the United States*, 10.

98. Cohen, *Howard Zinn's Southern Diary*, 16.

99. Zinn, *You Can't Be Neutral*, 58.

100. Duberman, *Howard Zinn*, 160–165.

101. These and all the other sales figures below on Zinn's books in the 1960s are from "Some Information on My Past Writings," in Zinn, "Struggle for Democracy" (prospectus).

102. Abraham Fortas, *Concerning Dissent and Civil Disobedience* (New York: New American Library, 1968).

103. Timothy Patrick McCarthy, ed., *The Indispensable Zinn: The Essential Writings of the "People's Historian"* (New York: New Press, 2012), xxii–xxiii.

104. Zinn and Arnove, *Voices of a People's History*, 27.

105. Heather J. Boeresma to Howard Zinn, Sept. 19, 2001, Zinn Papers.

106. Hugh G. Schaeffer to Zinn, [n.d.], Zinn Papers.

107. Lisa Krug, e-mail to Zinn, Nov. 1, 2006, Zinn Papers.

108. McCarthy, *The Indispensable Zinn*, xxi.

109. Angelica Marquez to Howard Zinn, Oct. 2, 2006, copy in authors' possession, courtesy of Myla Kabat-Zinn.

110. Joe Levy, "Interview with Bruce Springsteen," *Rolling Stone*, Nov. 15, 2007, 177.

111. Duberman, *Howard Zinn*, 285–318.

112. "Characteristic optimism": Stephen Bird, Adam Silver, and Joshua C. Yesnowitz, *Agitation with a Smile: Howard Zinn's Legacies and the Future of Activism* (Boulder, Colo.: Paradigm, 2013), 12–14; Howard Zinn, *Failure to Quit: Reflections of An Optimistic Historian* (Monroe, Maine: Common Courage Press, 1993).

113. Jesse Kindig, e-mail to Howard Zinn, Anthony Arnove, and Brenda Coughlin, Jan. 21, 2005, Zinn Papers.

114. Robert Cohen and Sonia Murrow, "Who's Afraid of Radical History? Mitch Daniels's Covert War on Howard Zinn's *People's History of the United States*," *Nation*, Aug. 5, 2013, https://www.thenation.com/article/archive/whos-afraid-radical-history.

CHAPTER 2. BEFORE *A PEOPLE'S HISTORY*

1. George H. Gallup Jr., "How Many American's Know U.S. History, Part 1," *Gallup News*, Oct. 21, 2003; Mark C. Schug, "Why Kids Don't Like Social Studies," *Proceedings of the Annual Meeting of the National Council for the Social Studies*, Nov. 1982, 1–26.

2. Frances FitzGerald, *America Revised: History Schoolbooks in the Twentieth Cen-*

tury (New York: Random House, 1980); Jean Anyon, "Ideology and United States History Textbooks," *Harvard Educational Review* 49, no. 3 (1979): 361–386.

3. James W. Loewen, *Lies My Teacher Told Me: Everything Your American History Textbook Got Wrong* (New York: New Press, 2008), 1–4.

4. See Thomas Bender, "Wholes and Parts: The Need for Synthesis in American History," *Journal of American History* 73 (1986): 120–136.

5. FitzGerald, *America Revised*, 96–104.

6. Larry Cuban, *Teaching History Then and Now: A Story of Stability and Change in Schools* (Cambridge, Mass.: Harvard Education Press, 2016).

7. Ibid.; Michael W. Apple and Linda K. Christian-Smith, *The Politics of the Textbook* (New York: Routledge, 2017), 2.

8. David B. Tyack and Larry Cuban, *Tinkering toward Utopia: A Century of Public School Reform* (Cambridge, Mass.: Harvard University Press, 1995), 7, 8.

9. Larry Cuban, "Reforms that Stick: How Schools Change," *Larry Cuban on School Reform and Classroom Practice*, Aug. 30, 2016, https://larrycuban.wordpress.com/2016/08/30/school-reforms-that-stick-the-center-and-periphery.

10. Tyack and Cuban, *Tinkering toward Utopia*, 8.

11. Gary B. Nash, Charlotte Antoinette Crabtree, and Ross E. Dunn, *History on Trial: Culture Wars and the Teaching of the Past* (New York: Vintage Press, 2000), 26.

12. Ibid., 72.

13. FitzGerald, *America Revised*, 96–102.

14. Jean Anyon, "Ideology and United States History Textbooks," 363, 383.

15. Ibid., 384, 369.

16. Ibid., 369–370.

17. Ibid., 375, 377.

18. Ibid., 373–374.

19. Ibid., 382–384.

20. Ibid., 385. Nevertheless, Anyon concluded her class analysis of textbooks with some optimism, suggesting that if curricula and textbooks aim to shape social attitudes in one direction, then they can aim to shape attitudes in other directions as well, such as promoting justice and equality.

21. FitzGerald, *America Revised*, 127, 139.

22. Roger Clark, Jeffrey Allard, and Timothy Mahoney, "How Much of the Sky? Women in American High School History Textbooks from the 1960s, 1980s and 1990s," *Social Education* 68, no. 1 (2004): 57–63.

23. Jennifer S. Macleod and Sandra T. Silverman, *"You Won't Do": What Textbooks on U.S. Government Teach High School Girls, with Sexism in Textbooks: An Annotated Source List of 150+ Studies and Remedies* (Pittsburgh: Know, Inc., 1973), 2–3.

24. Myra Sadker and David Sadker, *Failing at Fairness: How America's Schools Cheat Girls* (New York: Simon and Schuster, 2010).

25. FitzGerald, *America Revised*, 97.

26. See Catherine Cornbleth and Dexter Waugh, *The Great Speckled Bird* (New York: St. Martin Press, 1995); James A. Banks, "Approaches to Multicultural Curriculum Reform," *Multicultural Education: Issues and Perspectives* 4 (2001), 225–246.

27. Cornbleth and Waugh, *The Great Speckled Bird*, 35–36, 13. Most U.S. history textbooks were following a hoary and parochial historiographical tradition (critiqued in Nathan Huggins's pathbreaking essay) replicating and reinforcing America's "master narrative"—inherited from the Founders—that focused on the capacious and expanding freedom of whites while marginalizing slavery and the longevity of Black unfreedom. So that even when slavery was mentioned it was treated as an aberration that did nothing to change the lofty freedom narrative. See Nathan Huggins, "The Deforming Mirror of Truth: Slavery and the Master Narrative of American History," *Radical History Review*, Winter 1991, 25–48.

28. Cornbleth and Waugh, *The Great Speckled Bird*, 37.

29. Ibid., 35, 38–39.

30. Most high school textbook authors seemed unaware that their nationalist assumptions distorted the history they wrote. The great British historian Eric Hobsbawm was among the most eloquent critics of such nationalist writing, pointing out that it rendered such historians "mythmakers rather than serious students of the past." Quoted in Richard J. Evans, *Eric Hobsbawm: A Life in History* (London: Abacus, 2020), 553. See also E. J. Hobsbawm, *Nations and Nationalism since 1780* (Cambridge, UK: Cambridge University Press, 1990), 12–13.

31. Thomas B. Fordham Institute, *The Mad, Mad World of Textbook Adoption* (Washington, D.C.: Fordham Institute, 2004), 1–77.

32. On the persistence of such regionalism, see "Two States, Eight Textbooks, Two American Stories," *New York Times*, Jan. 12, 2020.

33. John Walton Caughey, John Hope Franklin, and Ernest R. May, *Land of the Free: A History of the United States* (New York: Benzinger Bros., 1966).

34. Joseph Moreau, *Schoolbook Nation: Conflicts over American History Textbooks from the Civil War to the Present* (Ann Arbor: University of Michigan Press, 2010), 301, 303.

35. Ibid., 304, 305–306.

36. Caughey, Franklin and May, *Land of the Free*, 12.

37. Moreau, *Schoolbook Nation*, 267–268.

38. FitzGerald, *America Revised*, 38–39.

39. Apple and Christian-Smith, *Politics of the Textbook*, 10.

40. Stephanie Simon, *Politico*, "Bad Grades for Texas Textbooks," Sept. 10, 2014, https://www.politico.com/story/2014/09/texas-textbooks-criticism-110809.

41. FitzGerald, *America Revised*, 29–30.

42. Ibid., 100–102.

43. Ibid.

44. William J. Bennett, "From 'To Reclaim a Legacy,'" *American Education* (1985), in *Debating the Canon: A Reader from Addison to Nafisi*, ed. Lee Morrissey (New York: Palgrave Macmillan, 2005), 111–116.

45. Diane Ravitch and Chester E. Finn Jr., *What Do Our 17-Year-Olds Know? A Report on the First National Assessment of History and Literature* (New York: Harper and Row, 1987), 226–229.

46. Fitzgerald, *America Revised*, 101–102; Cameron McCarthy, "Multicultural

Education, Minority Identities, Textbooks, and the Challenge of Curriculum Reform," *Journal of Education* 2 (1990): 121–124.

47. Lawrence Cremin, *Popular Education and Its Discontents* (New York: Harper Collins, 1989), 117.

48. See Arthur M. Schlesinger, *The Disuniting of America: Reflections on a Multicultural Society* (New York: W. W. Norton, 1998); Diane Ravitch, "Multiculturalism: E Pluribus Plures," *American Scholar* 59, no. 3 (1990): 337–354; and Catherine Cornbleth, "Controlling Curriculum Knowledge: Multicultural Politics and Policymaking," *Journal of Curriculum Studies* 27, no. 2 (1995): 165–185.

49. "2014 U.S. History Assessment," National Assessment of Educational Progress, 2014, https://www.nationsreportcard.gov/hgc_2014/#history.

50. Cuban, *Teaching History Then and Now*, 70.

51. *A Nation at Risk* was a 1983 report by the National Commission on Excellence in Education, commissioned by President Ronald Reagan. The report aimed to convince Americans of the failures of American education. History education was not central to the report (math and science were), but the report argued that American history education was deficient and needed reform to support a national identity and shared values around economic and global concerns. David Pierpont Gardner et al., *A Nation at Risk: The Imperative for Educational Reform: A Report to the Nation and the Secretary of Education, United States Department of Education* (Washington, D.C.: National Commission on Excellence in Education, 1983).

52. Cuban, *Teaching History Then and Now*, 70.

53. Bethany L. Rogers, "Teaching and Social Reform in the 1960s: Lessons from National Teacher Corps Oral Histories," *Oral History Review*, 35, no. 1 (2008): 39.

54. John Hale, *The Freedom Schools: Student Activists in the Mississippi Civil Rights Movement* (New York: Columbia University Press, 2016), 37–67.

55. See, for example, David L. Angus and Jeffrey Mirel, *The Failed Promise of the American High School, 1890–1995* (New York: Teachers College Press, 1999); and Herbert M. Kliebard, *Forging the American Curriculum: Essays in Curriculum History and Theory* (New York: Routledge, 2018).

56. Larry Cuban, "History Content and Teaching: A Historic Struggle," *Larry Cuban on School Reform and Classroom Practice,* January 5, 2014, https://larrycuban .wordpress.com/2014/01/05/history-content-and-teaching-a-historic-struggle/.

57. Cuban, *Teaching History Then and Now*, 93–94.

58. See, for example, Teaching History, National History Education Clearinghouse, https://teachinghistory.org/.

59. Cuban, *Teaching History Then and Now*, 93.

60. Organizations that supported these efforts include Educators for Social Responsibility, Facing History and Ourselves, the Zinn Education Project, Rethinking Schools, and Teaching for Change.

61. See Ronald W. Evans, "Teacher Conceptions of History," *Theory and Research in Social Education* 17, no. 3 (1989), 210–240.

62. Zinn underscored the importance of assigning point of view to historians in the

pages of *A People's History*: "The historian's distortion is more than technical, it is ideological; it is released into a world of contending interests, where any chosen emphasis supports (whether the historian means to or not) some kind of interest, whether economic or political or racial or national or sexual" (8).

63. Loewen, *Lies My Teacher Told Me*, xi.

64. A History of US, Joy Hakim's ten-volume book series, published in 1995, was also popular, but it was written mostly for middle school students.

65. James W. Loewen, *Lies My Teacher Told Me: Everything Your American History Textbook Got Wrong* (New York: New Press, 2018), xxii and cover.

66. Samuel S. Wineburg, Daisy Martin, and Chauncey Monte-Sano, *Reading Like a Historian: Teaching Literacy in Middle and High School History Classrooms* (New York: Teachers College Press, 2012), xi.

67. Stanford History Education Group, https://sheg.stanford.edu/.

68. Sam Wineburg, Daisy Martin, and Chauncey Monte-Sano, *Reading Like a Historian: Teaching Literacy in the Middle and High School Classroom* (New York: Teachers College Press, 2012), 128.

69. Ibid., 124–142.

CHAPTER 3. IN HIGH SCHOOL CLASSROOMS

1. Rich Lowry, "Mitch Daniels Takes Issue with Howard Zinn's So-called History," *Oregonian*, July 29, 2013; Robert Cohen and Sonia Murrow, "Who's Afraid of Radical History? Mitch Daniels's Covert War on Howard Zinn's *A People's History of the United States*," *Nation*, Aug. 5, 2013, https://www.thenation.com/article/archive/whos-afraid-radical-history.

2. On effective history pedagogy, see David R. Olson, "On the Language and Authority of Textbooks," *Journal of Communication* 30, no. 1 (1980): 186–196; Sam Wineburg, *Historical Thinking and Other Unnatural Acts: Charting the Future of Teaching the Past* (Philadelphia: Temple University Press, 2001); Bruce A. VanSledright, "What Does It Mean to Think Historically. . . and How Do You Teach It," *Social Education*, 68, no. 3 (2004): 230–233; Mimi Lee, "Promoting Historical Thinking Using the Explicit Reasoning Text," *Journal of Social Studies Research* 37, no. 1 (2013): 33–45; and Bruce A. VanSledright, *Assessing Historical Thinking and Understanding: Innovative Designs for New Standards* (New York: Routledge, 2013).

3. See, for example, Sam Wineburg, "Undue Certainty: Where Howard Zinn's *People's History of the United States* Falls Short," *America Educator*, Winter 2012–2013, 27–34.

4. Bill Bigelow, telephone interview with Robert Cohen, Oct. 28, 2012, transcript in authors' possession.

5. Laura Bennett to Zinn Education Project, Teaching Outside the Textbook Essay Contest, 2007, courtesy of Deborah Menkart, copy in authors' possession.

6. Michael Presser, Teaching Outside the Textbook Essay Contest, 2007, courtesy of Deborah Menkart, copy in authors' possession.

7. Laura Vantine to Howard Zinn, Sept. 12, 1980, Zinn Papers.

8. Ben Honoroff to Howard Zinn, Jan. 31, 2000, Zinn Papers.

9. Presser, Teaching Outside the Textbook Essay Contest.

10. For examples of scholarship on student learning done without the kind of direct statements from students found in the Patterson student letters, see Michael Pressley and Peter Afflerbach, *Verbal Protocols of Reading: The Nature of Constructively Responsive Reading* (New York: Routledge, 1995); Bruce A. VanSledright, "Confronting History's Interpretive Paradox while Teaching Fifth Graders to Investigate the Past," *American Educational Research Journal* 9, no. 1 (2002): 1089–1115; Jane Bolgatz and Kevin Colleary, "What Color Was Joan of Arc's Hair? Developing Critical Literacy through Historical Thinking Skills," *Counterpoints* 326 (2008), 119–131.

11. Zinn's letters to Patterson seem not to have been saved and are not in Zinn Papers.

12. Bill Patterson to Howard Zinn, Aug. 16, 1989, Zinn Papers.

13. Bill Patterson to Howard Zinn, Jan. 25, 1999, Zinn Papers.

14. Bill Patterson to Howard Zinn, Sept. 2, 1987, Zinn Papers.

15. Ibid.

16. David Kobrin, *Beyond the Textbook: Teaching History Using Documents and Primary Sources* (Portsmouth, N.H.: Heinemann, 1996), 15.

17. John Dewey, *How We think* (1910; repr., Mineola, N.Y.: Dover Publications, 1997), 11.

18. Ibid.; Barton and Levstik, *Teaching History for the Common Good*, 197.

19. Bill Patterson to Howard Zinn, Sept. 2, 1987, Zinn Papers.

20. Bill Patterson to Howard Zinn, June 11, 1991, Zinn Papers.

21. Bill Patterson to Howard Zinn, Jan. 25, 1999, Zinn Papers.

22. Ibid.

23. Unless otherwise indicated, all quotes are attributed to Bill Patterson, Oct. 1 and 10, 2013, telephone interviews with Robert Cohen, transcript in authors' possession.

24. See Lee Shulman, "Knowledge and Teaching: Foundations of the New Reform," *Harvard Educational Review* 57, no. 1 (1987): 1–23.

25. Bill Bigelow, *A People's History for the Classroom* (Milwaukee: Rethinking Schools, 2008), 1.

26. Peter Filene and Peter Wood, "Textbooks and Teaching: A Reintroduction," *Journal of American History* 84, no. 4 (1998): 1407.

27. See Peter N. Stearns, *Meaning over Memory: Recasting the Teaching of Culture and History* (Chapel Hill: University of North Carolina Press, 1994); David Neuman, "Training Teachers to Think Historically: Applying Recent Research to Professional Development," *History Teacher* 45, no. 3 (2012): 384.

28. Bill Patterson to Howard Zinn, June 11, 1991, Zinn Papers.

29. Bill Patterson telephone interview with Cohen.

30. Patterson telephone interview with Cohen.

31. This inclination to play devil's advocate was important because some students proved so enthused about encountering a new and different way of looking at the past that they were initially as uncritical of Zinn as they had formerly been of their text-

book. Indeed, the letters reflect that despite Patterson's pushing back on this, some students nonetheless were so admiring of Zinn that they adopted the posture of Zinn fans who regarded him as the sole and heroic truth teller about American history.

32. Patterson telephone interview with Cohen.

33. Thomas Holt, *Thinking Historically* (New York: College Entrance Examination Board, 1990), 27.

34. Linda Levstik and Keith Barton, *Researching History Education: Theory, Method, and Context* (New York: Routledge, 2008), 191–192.

35. See Lee S. Shulman, "Knowledge and Teaching: Foundations of the New Reform," *Harvard Educational Review*, 57, no. 1 (1987): 1–23; Keith C. Barton and Linda S. Levstik, "Why Don't More History Teachers Engage Students in Interpretation?," *Social Education* 67, no. 6(2003): 358.

36. Edward H. Carr, *What Is History?* (New York: Random House, 1961), 23.

37. The exact quote from the 1966 song "For What It's Worth," by Buffalo Springfield: "There's something happening here. What it is ain't exactly clear" (Atco Records).

38. The letters from Bill Patterson's students quoted in this chapter and those reprinted in chapter 4 are all from the correspondence files, series II, TAM. 542, in Zinn Papers, comprising the letters Zinn received from the 1980s through the turn of the twenty-first century.

39. Robert Cohen, "When Assessing Zinn, Listen to the Voice of Teachers and Students," *History News Network*, Jan. 7, 2013, https://historynewsnetwork.org/article/149974.

40. Howard Zinn, *A People's History of the United States* (New York: Harper & Row, 1980), 10.

41. David C. King et al., *Addison-Wesley United States History*, presidential ed. (Boston: Addison-Wesley, 1986).

42. VanSledright, "What Does It Mean to Think Historically?", 230.

43. On student learning, see Dan A. Porat, "It's Not Written Here, but This Is What Happened: Students' Cultural Comprehension of Textbook Narratives on the Israeli-Arab Conflict," *American Educational Research Journal* 41, no. 4 (2004): 963–996.

44. On textbook neglect of debate, see A. Crismore, "*The Rhetoric of Textbooks: Metadiscourse,*" *Journal of Curriculum Studies* 16 (1984): 279–296; D. R. Olson, "On the Language and Authority of Textbooks," *Journal of Communication* 30 (1980), 186–196.

45. Patterson, telephone interview with Cohen.

46. Gary Kornblith and Carol Lasser, eds., "Teaching the American History Survey at the Opening of the Twenty-First Century: A Round Table Discussion," *Journal of American History* 87 (March 2001), 1409–1441.

47. Zinn, *A People's History of the United States*, 9–11.

48. On meta-discourse, see Crismore, "The Rhetoric of Textbooks," 4.

49. Matt to Zinn, letters from Bill Patterson's classes to Zinn, Zinn papers.

50. Howard Zinn, *Postwar America, 1945–1971* (Boston: South End Press, 2002).

51. Patterson, telephone interview with Cohen.

52. For one such analysis of 1960s radical history revisionism, see Peter Novick, *That*

Noble Dream: The "Objectivity" Question and the American Historical Profession (New York: Cambridge University Press, 1998), 415–468.

53. Howard Zinn, *Failure to Quit: Reflections of an Optimistic Historian* (Monroe, Maine: Common Courage Press, 1993), 127.

54. VanSledright, "What Does It Mean to Think Historically," 231.

55. See James W. Loewen, *Teaching What Really Happened: How to Avoid the Tyranny of Textbooks and Get Students Excited about Doing History* (New York: Teachers College Press, 2009).

56. Holt, *Thinking Historically*, 1.

57. "2014 U.S. History Assessment," National Assessment of Educational Progress, 2014, https://www.nationsreportcard.gov/hgc_2014/#history.

58. Laura J. Dull and Sonia E. Murrow, "Is Dialogic Questioning Possible in Social Studies Classrooms?" *Theory and Research in Social Education* 36, no. 4 (2008), 391–412.

59. Zinn Education Project Facebook, https://www.facebook.com/ZinnEducationProject.

CHAPTER 4. "DEAR MR. ZINN"

1. To ensure confidentiality, the letters were edited to delete any information that might reveal its author's identity (ellipses indicate these omissions, and in a few cases the omissions of ungrammatical clauses that obscure a student's ideas).

2. Michael Paul Rogin, *Fathers and Children: Andrew Jackson and the Subjugation of the American Indian* (New York: Knopf, 1975).

3. Renee C. Romano, "Hamilton: A New American Civic Myth," in Renee C. Romano and Claire Bond Potter, eds., *Historians on Hamilton: How a Blockbuster Musical Is Re-Staging America's Past* (New Brunswick: Rutgers University Press, 2018), 300.

4. Ibid.

5. Howard Zinn, Mike Konopacki, and Paul Buhle, *A People's History of American Empire: The American Empire Project, a Graphic Adaptation* (New York: Metropolitan Books, 2008), ix.

6. David C. King, et al., *Addison-Wesley United States History*, presidential ed. (Menlo Park, Calif.: Addison Wesley, 1986).

7. Ibid, 13–15.

8. Zinn, *A People's History of the United States*, 1–22. This does not mean the students' discussion of history was 100 percent accurate. As relative novices, some students, including several whose letters appear in this chapter, made historical errors. For example, several indicate that Zinn called Columbus a rapist, but Zinn did not charge Columbus with that crime. Nor did Las Casas, quoted in Zinn's book, though Las Casas did charge (*A People's History*, 8) that Spanish conquerors raped Indigenous women. Similarly, one of the student letter writers erred in conflating the story of Val-

ley Forge with that of mutinies in New Jersey. Zinn had written that it was Congress, not George Washington, that had "ignored the common soldier, who was not getting paid, who was suffering in the cold, dying of sickness, watching the civilian profiteers get rich." *A People's History of the United States*, 81.

9. King et al., *Addison-Wesley United States History*, 246.

10. Zinn, *A People's History of the United States*, 149–169.

11. Since these letters originated as the culminating activity of high school history classes—albeit a voluntary and extra-credit one, readers should consider whether this in any way biased the letters.

12. Alison Hallet, e-mail to Robert Cohen, April 15, 2018, and Rebeca Mayer, e-mail to Robert Cohen, June 13, 2018, copies in authors' possession.

13. Robert Cohen, "When Assessing Zinn, Listen to the Voices of Teachers and Students," *History News Network*, Jan. 7, 2013, https://historynewsnetwork.org /article/149974.

14. Mayer e-mail to Cohen, June 13, 2018.

15. Mayer's classmate, Alison Hallet, was equally effusive as she looked back on her classes with Patterson that made use of Zinn's book: "As one of Bill Patterson's students in the 1990s, I clearly remember his use of Zinn as an educational tool. At that time in my life, it was critically influential to be exposed to the idea that textbooks represented a point of view, rather than a definitive accounting of history" (Hallet to Cohen, April 15, 2018).

CHAPTER 5. NOT JUST FOR KIDS

1. Jill Lepore, "Zinn's History," *New Yorker*, Feb. 3, 2010, https://www.newyorker.com /books/page-turner/zinns-history.

2. Hugh Van Dusen to Rick Balkin, Jan. 12, 1994, Zinn Papers.

3. Steve Furey to Howard Zinn, Dec. 5, 2002, Zinn Papers.

4. Elizabeth (last name omitted) to Howard Zinn, July 1, 2001, Zinn Papers.

5. Trevor Maloney to Howard Zinn, Dec. 27, 1996, Zinn Papers.

6. Bruno Familia, e-mail to Howard Zinn, April 21, 2004, Zinn Papers.

7. Laurie McKibben to Howard Zinn, Feb. 24, 2003, Zinn Papers.

8. Ibid.

9. Jonathan Blitstein to Howard Zinn, Nov. 5, 2003, Zinn Papers.

10. Matthew Crisp to Howard Zinn, Feb. 18, 2004, Zinn Papers.

11. Adam R. Gross to Howard Zinn, Jan. 31, 2000, Zinn Papers.

12. Benjamin Mason to Howard Zinn, Dec. 4, 2000, Zinn Papers.

13. Kai Matsumiya to Howard Zinn, May 8, 2000, Zinn Papers.

14. Emily Meinert to Howard Zinn, Aug. 3, 2005, Zinn Papers.

15. Maxwell Aley to Howard Zinn, Sept. 29, 2003, Zinn Papers.

16. Tom Morgan to Howard Zinn, May 26, 1994, Zinn Papers. The reference to chapter 21 in Morgan's letter was to the (overly) optimistic chapter in the book's first edition,

"Revolt of the Guards," predicting that the middle and professional classes would unite with the lower classes in a progressive revolt.

17. Igor Markstein to Howard Zinn, July 7, 1993, Zinn Papers.

18. Emily Rader to Howard Zinn, Jan. 12,2000, Zinn Papers.

19. *Campus Report*, March 1986, Zinn Papers.

20. Peter Shaw to Howard Zinn, June 4, 2001, Zinn Papers.

21. Emily Meinert to Howard Zinn, Aug. 3, 2005, Zinn Papers.

22. Daniel Joseph Boorstin, Brooks Mather Kelley and Ruth Frankel Boorstin, *A History of the United States* (New York: Prentice Hall, 2002).

23. Tom Anderson to Howard Zinn, Mar. 5, 2000, Zinn Papers.

24. Larry Schweikart and Michael Allen, *A Patriot's History of the United States: From Columbus's Great Discovery to the War on Terror* (New York: Sentinel Press, 2004).

25. Liz Dwyer to Howard Zinn, April 22, 2005, Zinn Papers.

26. Mary Ellen Cardella to Howard Zinn, n.d., Zinn Papers.

27. Jo Ann Carlotto to Howard Zinn, June 20, 2007, Zinn Papers.

28. Thomas Doyle to Howard Zinn, July 14, 1994, Feb. 9, 1996, and Feb. 18, 1998, Zinn Papers.

29. Doyle to Howard Zinn, Feb. 9, 1996, Zinn Papers.

30. Doyle to Howard Zinn, Feb. 18, 1998.

31. Ted Neitzke to Howard Zinn, Aug. 29, 2000, Zinn Papers.

32. Royce Disbrow to Howard Zinn, Feb. 21, 1989, Zinn Papers.

33. Roxanne Dunbar-Ortiz, *An Indigenous Peoples' History of the United States* (Boston: Beacon Press, 2014).

34. Roxanne Dunbar Ortiz to Howard Zinn, Oct. 9, 1981, Zinn Papers.

35. Marilyn Frankenstein to Howard Zinn, April 28, 1982; France H. Conroy to Howard Zinn, Feb. 28, 1982; M. J. Ogden to Howard Zinn, Jan. 8, 2004, and Feb. 17, 2008; Frank Salzano, e-mail to Howard Zinn, Feb. 26, 2006, Michael A. Schwartz to Howard Zinn, Jan. 29, 2007, all in Zinn Papers.

36. Howard Zinn, *A People's History of the United States*, 35th anniversary ed. (New York: HarperCollins, 2015), 256, 684.

37. Peter Shaw to Howard Zinn, March 25, 2001, Zinn Papers.

38. Howard Zinn and Anthony Arnove, *Voices of a People's History of the United States*, 10th anniversary ed. (New York: Seven Stories Press, 2014), 24.

39. Rachel Bradshar to Howard Zinn, Oct. 7, 2009, Zinn Papers.

40. Michael Jordan to Howard Zinn, Sept. 21, 1992, Zinn Papers.

41. Tom Anderson, e-mail to Howard Zinn, March 5, 2000, Zinn Papers.

42. M. J. Ogden to Howard Zinn, Jan. 8, 2004, Zinn Papers.

43. Kevin Brodie to Howard Zinn, Sept. 29, 1998, Zinn Papers.

44. Emily Rader to Howard Zinn, Jan. 12, 2000, Zinn Papers.

45. Note, however, that at elite colleges and universities *A People's History* was assigned outside history departments, especially in writing, education, and social work courses.

46. George Cheney to Howard Zinn, Nov. 12, 1992, Zinn Papers.

47. Columbia University student (name illegible) to Howard Zinn, Oct. 29, 2001, Zinn Papers.

48. Ben Mackey to Howard Zinn, July 12, 2001, Zinn Papers.

49. Heather Woodford to Howard Zinn, 2000, Zinn Papers. Hillary Clinton as First Lady was promoting national health care reform loathed by many conservatives.

50. Erin Gettling to Howard Zinn, 2000, Zinn Papers.

51. Joseph Fitzgerald to Howard Zinn, April 17, 2001, Zinn Papers.

52. John Baranski to Howard Zinn, May 1, 2002, Zinn Papers.

53. Tom Anderson to Howard Zinn, March 5, 2000, Zinn Papers.

54. Dan Kaplan to Howard Zinn, no date, Zinn Papers.

55. Anthony Arnove, introduction to Zinn, *A People's History of the United States*, 35th anniversary ed., xix.

56. Michael S. Foley, *Front Porch Politics: The Forgotten Heyday of American Activism in the 1970s and 1980s* (New York: Macmillan, 2013), 3.

57. Matt Early to Howard Zinn, Feb. 25, 2003, Zinn Papers.

58. Meyer Pincus to Howard Zinn, Aug. 18, 2000, Zinn Papers.

59. Joey Thompson to Howard Zinn, July 5, 2001, Zinn Papers.

60. Zinn and Arnove, *Voices of a People's History*, 28.

61. David Greenberg, "Agit-Prof: Howard Zinn's Influential Mutilations of American History," *New Republic*, March 19, 2013, https://newrepublic.com/article/112574 /howard-zinns-influential-mutilations-american-history.

62. Zinn and Arnove, *Voices of a People's History*, 28.

63. Bob Englehart to Howard Zinn, May 2, 2000, Zinn Papers.

64. Scott Satterwhite, e-mail to Howard Zinn, Feb. 21, 2004, Zinn Papers.

65. Bob Saymaker to Howard Zinn, Feb. 25, 1994, Zinn Papers.

66. Albert Benson to Howard Zinn, May 6, 1993, Zinn Papers.

67. Mildred Martinez to Howard Zinn, Oct. 18, 1994, Zinn Papers.

68. Ron Kovic to Howard Zinn, Oct. 28, 1994, Zinn Papers.

69. Dana Trombely to Howard Zinn, April 14, 2008, Zinn Papers.

70. Frank Durgin to Howard Zinn, April 20, 2003, Zinn Papers.

71. Harry C. Kiely to Howard Zinn, March 2, 1995, Zinn Papers.

72. William B. Davis to Howard Zinn, Nov. 27, 2001, Zinn Papers. The "prison guards" reference comes from the chapter in *A People's History*, "The Coming Revolt of the Guards," in which Zinn explains that the "prisoners of the system will continue to rebel, as before" but that the "new fact of our era is the chance that they may be joined by the guards." This, for Zinn, would take us down the path of social change, to a "different and marvelous world" (478).

73. John Valadez to Howard Zinn, Oct. 28, 1993, Zinn Papers.

74. Daniel Bernofsky to Howard Zinn, 2000, Zinn Papers.

75. Jerome Thelia to Howard Zinn, July 20, 2004, Zinn Papers.

76. Emily Meinert to Howard Zinn, Aug. 3, 2005, Zinn Papers.

77. College student (name illegible) to Howard Zinn, Nov. 22, 1999, Zinn Papers.

78. Norman E. Dunlap to Howard Zinn, July 29, 1989, Zinn Papers.

79. Zinn and Arnove, *Voices of a People's History*, 24.

80. Bill May to Howard Zinn, March 13, 1996, Zinn Papers.

81. Zinn, *A People's History of the United States*, 35th anniversary ed., 581–582.

82. Laura Nesbit to Howard Zinn, July 14, 2003, Zinn Papers.

83. Josh Konetzni, e-mail to Howard Zinn, July 19, 2004, Zinn Papers.

84. Bob Trip to Howard Zinn, n.d., Zinn Papers.

85. British reader (name illegible) to Howard Zinn, Zinn Papers.

86. Abraham Meltzer to Howard Zinn, Feb. 16, 1993, Zinn Papers.

87. Neill S. Rosenfeld to Howard Zinn, July 18, 2004, Zinn Papers.

88. Steve Halpern to Howard Zinn, Oct. 27, 1995, Zinn Papers.

89. Daniel Schreffler to Howard Zinn, May 12, 1993, Zinn Papers.

90. Howard Zinn, *Justice in Everyday life: The Way It Really Works* (New York: William Morrow, 1974).

91. Hugh R. Lyons to Howard Zinn, Oct. 26, 1992, Zinn Papers.

92. Doug Parsons to Howard Zinn, Jan. 5, 2005, Zinn Papers.

93. Howard Zinn to Doug Parsons, April 5, 2004, Zinn Papers.

94. Autumn Konrad to Howard Zinn, Jan. 15, 2010, Zinn Papers.

95. Stuart Doblin to Howard Zinn, Sept. 10, 2002, Zinn Papers.

96. Zelko Cipris to Howard Zinn, Oct. 9, 1994, Zinn Papers.

97. Michael Jordan to Howard Zinn, Sept. 21, 1992, Zinn Papers.

98. Michiele D'Angelo to Howard Zinn, Feb. 2, 2000, Zinn Papers.

99. Abraham Meltzer to Howard Zinn, Feb. 16, 1993, Zinn Papers.

100. "Nat Segalof Interview with Howard Zinn," *Audio Book Today*, July 28, 2003.

101. Jason F. to Howard Zinn, Oct. 7, 1998, Zinn Papers.

CHAPTER 6. TEACHERS

1. Barbara Miner, "Why Students Should Study History: An Interview with Howard Zinn," in Wayne Au, Bill Bigelow, Stan Karp, eds., *Rethinking Our Classrooms: Teaching for Equity and Justice*, vol. 1 (Milwaukee: Rethinking Schools, 1994), 179–181.

2. Henry Kissinger, *A World Restored: Metternich, Castlereagh, and the Problems of Peace, 1812–22* (Gloucester, Mass.: Peter Smith, 1973).

3. Miner, "Why Students Should Study History."

4. John Dewey, "Experience and Education," *Educational Forum*, 50, no. 3, (1986), 241–252.

5. Felisa Tibbitts and Michael Kuelker, "Howard Zinn: A Conversation about Education and Activism," *Fourth R* 15, no.1 (Winter 2005), 4–7.

6. Ibid. Some leading historians criticize the way Zinn used the present to shape his teaching (and writing) about the past. The late Michael Kammen, of Cornell University, in a review of Duberman's biography of Zinn, wrote, "[Zinn's] work is unabashedly guilty of what less partisan historians denigrate as the 'Whig fallacy,' namely, seeing the past in light of present concerns. . . . By failing to recognize the pastness of the past,

to appreciate it in its own terms, the Whig cannot appreciate the radically different alternatives the past presents to the present." Michael Kammen, "The Insubordinate Historian: The Life and Legacy of Howard Zinn," *Los Angeles Review of Books*, Nov. 29, 2012. This amounts to charging Zinn with presentism. Such criticism exemplifies the split between historians wary of presentism in historical study and high school teachers (and Zinn) who incorporate presentism into their teaching as the "motivation" that will get young students to become engaged with the material and to see it as relevant to the present and to their lives. (Presentism is, for example, embedded in the standard New York City public school lesson plan format in its "motivation" segment—designed to motivate student historical learning by connecting the past to the present.)

7. Miner, "Why Students Should Study History," 180.

8. Ibid.

9. Ibid., 180–181.

10. Ibid., 181.

11. Ibid.

12. Bill Bigelow, *A People's History for the Classroom* (Milwaukee: Rethinking Schools, 2008).

13. Bill Bigelow, telephone interview with Robert Cohen, Nov. 28, 2012, notes in authors' possession.

14. Howard Zinn, keynote speech at National Council for the Social Studies 88th Annual National Conference, Houston, Nov. 16, 2008. A video of the speech can be found on the Zinn Education Project's website: https://www.zinnedproject.org /posts/8567.

15. Ira Shor, telephone interview with Sonia Murrow, Aug. 2, 2019, notes in authors' possession. Zinn's critique of history education was rooted in a larger critique of American schooling and how he viewed the role of education in a democratic society. See Howard Zinn and Donaldo Macedo, *Howard Zinn on Democratic Education* (New York: Routledge, 2016); and Howard Zinn and Donaldo Macedo. "Schools and the Manufacture of Mass Deception: A Dialogue," *Counterpoints* 422 (2012), 120–143.

16. Shor interview.

17. Ibid.

18. Ronald W. Evans, "Educational Ideologies and the Teaching of History," in *Teaching and Learning in History*, ed. Gaea Leinhardt, Isabel L. Beck, and Catherine Stainton (Hillsdale, N.J.: L. Erlbaum, 1994), 189.

19. "What We Do: Our Mission," Teaching for Change, https://www.teachingforchange.org/about/what-we-do.

20. Enid Lee, Deborah Menkart, and Margo Okazawa-Rey, *Beyond Heroes and Holidays: A Practical Guide to K–12 Anti-Racist, Multicultural Education and Staff Development* (Washington, D.C.: Network of Educators on the Americas, 1997).

21. Deborah Menkart, Alana D. Murray, and Jenice L. View, *Putting the Movement Back into Civil Rights Teaching* (Washington, D.C.: Teaching for Change, 2004).

22. Bob Peterson, "The Birth of Rethinking Schools," *Rethinking Schools*, Fall 2011, https://www.rethinkingschools.org/articles/the-birth-of-rethinking-schools. Henry A.

Giroux's book referenced is *Theory and Resistance in Education: Towards a Pedagogy for the Opposition* (Westport, Conn., Greenwood, 2001).

23. Peterson, "The Birth of Rethinking Schools."

24. Ibid.

25. Ibid.

26. "Our History," Rethinking Schools, https://rethinkingschools.org/about-rethinking-schools/our-history.

27. Peterson, "The Birth of Rethinking Schools."

28. Deborah Menkart, telephone interview with Robert Cohen, Nov. 4, 2012, notes in authors' possession.

29. Bigelow, *A People's History for the Classroom*, 4.

30. Ibid., 3.

31. Ibid. Many of the role plays Bigelow developed for teachers are based on topics from Zinn, *A People's History of the United States*.

32. Ibid., 4.

33. Ibid., 5.

34. Bigelow interview with Cohen.

35. Ibid.

36. Ibid.

37. Ibid.

38. See Ira Shor, *Freire for the Classroom: A Sourcebook for Liberatory Teaching* (Portsmouth, N.H.: Heinemann, 1987).

39. Shor interview with Murrow.

40. Ira Shor, *Critical Teaching and Everyday* Life (Chicago: University of Chicago Press, 1980).

41. Shor interview with Murrow.

42. Bigelow interview with Cohen.

43. Menkart interview with Cohen.

44. Bigelow interview with Cohen.

45. Ibid.

46. Ibid.

47. Bill Bigelow, *Rethinking Columbus: Teaching about the 500th Anniversary of Columbus's Arrival in America* (Milwaukee: Rethinking Schools, 1991).

48. Bigelow interview with Cohen.

49. "Bill Bigelow's Statement," *Progressive*, Jan. 26, 2012, https://progressive.org/dispatches/bill-bigelow-s-statement.

50. Bill Bigelow, e-mail to Robert Cohen, Nov. 10, 2019, copy in authors' possession.

51. Bill Bigelow to Howard Zinn, Jan. 31, 1994, Zinn Papers.

52. Bigelow to Zinn, Jan. 31, 1994. The Loewen titles are *The Truth about Columbus: A Subversively True Poster Book for a Dubiously Celebratory Occasion* (New York: New Press, 1992); and *Lies My Teacher Told Me: Everything Your American History Textbook Got Wrong* (New York: New Press, 2008).

53. New Press, https://thenewpress.com/.

54. Zinn wrote to both his agent and New Press publisher Andre Schiffrin indicating that he was pondering Bigelow's proposal and asking if New Press would be interested. Zinn's agent Rick Balkin responded, "Bill has a very nifty idea." But the book would likely be difficult to market. "[In the school world] this would be hard to place: a lefty high school text is probably still controversial, [since] H.S. [high school] publishers are generally reactionary." Balkin thought that such a book would have more potential if it was geared not to schools, with their conservative text adoption traditions, but to a "Y.A. [young adult] trade publisher." "Downplay the curricula paraphernalia," he wrote. "Teachers will know what to do with it. As a Y.A. book parents can buy it, and [high schools and junior high schools] will hear about it, and use it if they want." This may be why Zinn, after hearing from his agent, told Schiffrin, "I think I would simplify Bigelow's proposal, produce an abridged version without all the extra material he proposes (then it could be marketed as a trade book for a general audience as well), and put all the extras in an accompanying teachers guide." Howard Zinn, e-mail to Andre Schiffrin, May 6, 1994, Zinn Papers.

55. Howard Zinn, e-mail to Andre Schiffrin, May 6, 1994.

56. Bigelow interview with Cohen.

57. Menkart interview with Cohen.

58. Deborah Menkart and Bill Bigelow, "Zinn Education Project Memo, Submitted to William Holtzman," Nov. 28, 2007.

59. Ibid.

60. Ibid.

61. William Holtzman, e-mail to Howard Zinn, Dec. 11, 2007, Zinn Papers.

62. Bill Bigelow, e-mail to Robert Cohen, Nov. 24, 2019, in authors' possession.

63. Though the ranks of the founders of the Teaching for Change and Rethinking Schools initiatives were limited in racial diversity initially, their work would attract progressive teachers of color who became prominent organizers and authors in this teacher reform movement. Teachers of color have been critical actors in bringing people's pedagogy to the schools and have edited Rethinking Schools publications. A recent volume for teachers, *Teaching for Black Lives* (2018) was coedited by Dyan Watson, social studies program coordinator at Lewis and Clark College in Portland, Oregon. Watson taught social studies at Sunset High School in Beaverton, Oregon, where she offered the first African American history course in the school. Another of the book's three coeditors, Jesse Hagopian, teaches Ethnic Studies at Garfield High School in Seattle, where he is also an adviser to the Black Student Union. An activist and writer as well as a teacher, Hagopian was a leader of a 2013 boycott of the Measures of Academic Progress test, which began when his school staff unanimously agreed to not administer the test, after which the boycott spread to several other schools in Seattle. Dyan Watson, Jesse Hagopian, and Wayne Au, eds., *Teaching for Black Lives* (Milwaukee, Wis.: Rethinking Schools, 2018). For Hagopian's essay on the boycott and the national push against high-stakes testing, see Jesse Hagopian, "After We Scrapped the MAP," in *Voices of a People's History of the United States*, edited by Howard Zinn and Anthony Arnove (New York: Seven Stories Press, 2004), 650–51.

CHAPTER 7. RETROSPECTIVES AND REVIEWS

1. "Virginia Tech Professor Defends Zinn," *Campus Report* (Accuracy in Academia), March 1986.

2. Jon Weiner, "Reed Irvine Rides the Paper Tiger," *Nation*, April 5, 1986, 479.

3. Ibid., "Virginia Tech Professor Defends Zinn."

4. Robert Cohen and Sonia Murrow, "Who's Afraid of Radical History? Mitch Daniels's Covert War on Howard Zinn's *A People's History of the United States*," *Nation*, Aug. 5, 2013, https://www.thenation.com/article/archive/whos-afraid-radical-history.

5. Martin Espada, *Zapata's Disciples* (Evanston: Northwestern University Press, 2016), xiii.

6. Mary Grabar, *Debunking Howard Zinn: Exposing the Fake History that Turned a Generation against America* (Washington, D.C.: Regnery Publishing, 2019), 61, 250. Grabar's charge that Zinn sought to "promote Communist revolution" in is grounded in the false assumption that Zinn believed such a revolution was desirable and possible in the United States. Zinn's writings indicate that he held no such beliefs when he was writing *A People's History* or even decades earlier. For example, in 1969, in an essay on Marxism and the New Left, Zinn argued against the notion that "the traditional Marxian ideal" of the overthrow of capitalism by an "an organized class conscious proletariat" was tenable in modern America. At a time when some in the militant wing of the New Left flirted with the idea of armed revolution, Zinn held that "the overwhelming power of the state will permit only tactics that fall short of violent revolution." Howard Zinn, "Marxism and the New Left," in *Dissent: Explorations in the History of American Radicalism*, ed. Alfred F. Young (DeKalb: Northern Illinois University Press, 1968), 365, 369. As far back as the 1940s, Zinn's critical view of communism and the Soviet Union had been influenced by radicals disillusioned with both, such as Arthur Koestler. See Zinn, *You Can't Be Neutral of a Moving Train*, 178.

7. Grabar, *Debunking Howard Zinn*, back of jacket.

8. "Zinn Fends Off AIA Written Attack: Defends His 'Different' Textbook," *Boston University Daily Free Press*, March 14, 1986.

9. Ibid.

10. Linda G. Lyle, To Whom It May Concern, April 14, 1986, Zinn Papers.

11. Michelle Jordan, To Whom It May Concern, April 14, 1986, Zinn Papers.

12. Holly Hickman, To Sir, April 13, 1986, Zinn Papers. See also Amy Canestrari, To Whom It May Concern, April 14, 1986, Zinn Papers.

13. Jennifer Schuessler, "And the Worst Book of History Is . . . ," *New York Times*, July 16, 2012.

14. David Detmer, *Zinnophobia: The Battle over History in Education, Politics, and Scholarship* (Winchester, UK: Zero Books, 2018).

15. Ibid., 1–5.

16. Even the best histories of the American historical profession neglect the profession's impact on schools, pedagogy, and the world beyond academia. For example, Peter Novick's brilliant account of the profession's engagement with the "objectivity ques-

tion" makes no mention of *A People's History*, though it popularized among teachers and the public a skeptical view of objective history. See Novick, *That Noble Dream: The "Objectivity Question" and the American Historical Profession* (New York: Cambridge University Press, 1988).

17. James Levin, review of *A People's History of the United States*, *Library Journal*, Jan. 1, 1980, 101.

18. "Nominees for American Book Awards Announced," *New York Times*, March 6, 1981.

19. Oscar Handlin, review of *Contours of American History*, *Mississippi Valley Historical Review*, March 3, 1962, 743–744.

20. Oscar Handlin, "Arawaks," *American Scholar*, Autumn 1980, 546, 548.

21. Ibid., 546, 550.

22. Robert Zimmerman, "Black, White and Red All Over," *San Diego Union* [circa 1980], Zinn Papers.

23. Eric Foner interview with Robert Cohen and Sonia Murrow, March 14, 2018, New York City, transcript in authors' possession; Eric Foner, *Tom Paine and Revolutionary America* (New York: Oxford University Press, 1976).

24. Eric Foner, "Majority Report," *New York Times Book Review*, March 2, 1980, 10.

25. Ibid., 10, 31.

26. Howard Zinn, *A People's History of the United States*, 35th anniversary ed. (New York: Harper Collins, 2015), 251.

27. Ibid., 332, 340, 335–337.

28. Ibid., 251.

29. Foner, "Majority Report," 31.

30. Ibid.

31. Eric Foner, "Zinn's Critical History," *Nation*, Feb. 4, 2010, https://www.thenation .com/article/society/zinns-critical-history/ .

32. Eric Foner, *Give Me Liberty: An American History*, 5th ed. (New York: Norton, 2017) 347–349, 367–377.

33. Zinn, *A People's History of the United States*, 125–148.

34. Ibid., 130.

35. Failing to address the critical role of racism among Jackson supporters, Zinn portrays their enthusiasm for Old Hickory in class terms: "Some white working people saw Jackson as their hero, because he opposed the rich man's bank." Zinn, *A People's History of the United States*, 130. See also David Roediger, *The Wages of Whiteness: Race and the Making of the American Working Class* (New York: Routledge, 2007).

36. Zinn, *A People's History of the United States*, 130.

37. "Voting on Indian affairs" in the two-party system "proved to be the most consistent predictor of partisan affiliation." Daniel Walker Howe, *What Hath God Wrought: The Transformation of America, 1815–1848* (New York: Oxford University Press, 2007), 357. See also Fred S. Rolater, "The American Indian and the Origins of the Second American Party System," *Wisconsin Magazine of History* 76 (1993), 180–201.

38. Zinn, *A People's History of the United States*, 138.

39. Howe, *What Hath God Wrought*; Daniel Walker Howe, *The Political Culture of American Whigs* (Chicago: University of Chicago Press, 1984); Daniel Walker Howe, "Goodbye to the 'Age of Jackson'?" *New York Review of Books*, May 28, 2009.

40. Zinn, *A People's History of the United States*, 138.

41. Ibid., 216–217.

42. Ibid., 216.

43. James H. Merrell, "Second Thoughts on Colonial Historians and American Indians," *William and Mary Quarterly*, July 2012, 451–512; James H. Merrell, "Some Thoughts on Colonial Historians and American Indians," *William and Mary Quarterly*, Jan. 1989, 94–119.

44. James H. Merrell interview with Robert Cohen and Sonia Murrow, April 25, 2018, Poughkeepsie, New York, transcript in authors' possession.

45. Ibid.

46. Ibid.

47. Ibid.

48. Ibid.

49. Ibid.

50. Richard White, *The Middle Ground: Indians, Empires, and Republics in the Great Lakes Region, 1650–1815* (New York: Cambridge University Press, 1991).

51. Merrell interview.

52. Ibid.

53. Michael Kammen, "How the Other Half Lived," *Washington Post Book World*, March 23, 1980.

54. Linford Fisher, *The Indian Great Awakening: Religion and the Shaping of Native Cultures in Early America* (New York: Oxford University Press, 2014).

55. Merrell interview.

56. Ibid.

57. Merrell interview.

58. Ibid.

59. Joe Helm, "Teaching America's Truth," *Washington Post*, Aug. 28, 2019.

60. Foner interview.

61. Richard Hofstadter, *The American Political Tradition and the Men Who Made It* (New York: Knopf, 1948), 119–174.

62. Foner interview.

63. Eric Foner, *The Fiery Trial: Abraham Lincoln and Slavery* (New York: Norton, 2011); James Oakes, *Freedom National: The Destruction of Slavery in the United States, 1861–1865* (New York: Norton, 2014).

64. Zinn, *A People's History of the United States*, 188–189.

65. Foner interview.

66. Oakes, *Freedom National*, 75–78.

67. Zinn, *A People's History of the United States*, 410.

68. Foner interview.

69. Ibid.

70. Ibid.; Drew Faust, *The Republic of Suffering: Death and the American Civil War* (New York: Vintage. 2008).

71. Foner interview.

72. Eric Foner, *Reconstruction: America's Unfinished Revolution* (New York: Norton, 1988), which won the Bancroft Prize.

73. Foner interview.

74. Ibid.

75. Eric Foner, *Freedom's Lawmakers: A Directory of Black Officeholders during Reconstruction* (Baton Rouge: Louisiana State University Press, 1996).

76. Eric Foner, *Nothing but Freedom: Emancipation and Its Legacy* (Baton Rouge: Louisiana State University Press, 1983), 74–110.

77. Zinn, *A People's History of the United States*, 199.

78. Ibid., 199, 203.

79. Foner, *Reconstruction*; Leon F. Litwack, *Been in the Storm So Long: The Aftermath of Slavery* (New York: Knopf, 1979); Ira Berlin, Barbara J. Fields, Steven F. Miller, and Leslie Rowland, eds., *Free at Last: A Documentary History of Slavery, Freedom, and the Civil War* (New York: New Press, 1992); Ira Berlin, Barbara J. Fields, Steven F. Miller, and Leslie Rowland, *Slaves No More: Three Essays on Emancipation and the Civil War* (New York: Cambridge University Press, 1992).

80. See Eric Foner, *The Second Founding: How the Civil War and Reconstruction Remade the Constitution* (New York: Norton, 2019).

81. Foner interview.

82. Jim Downs, *Sick from Freedom: African American Illness and Suffering during the Civil War and Reconstruction* (New York: Oxford University Press, 2012).

83. Gregory Downs, *After Appomattox: Military Occupation and the Ends of War* (Cambridge, Mass.: Harvard University Press, 2015).

84. Carole Emberton, "Unwriting the Freedom Narrative: A Review Essay," *Journal of Southern History*, May 2016, 377–394.

85. Foner interview.

86. Ibid. Lincoln's endorsement of voting rights for Black army veterans and literate Black men in his April 11, 1865, speech infuriated John Wilkes Booth—who was in the audience. Booth "turned angrily to his companion" and said "that means nigger citizenship. . . Now, by God, I'll run him through. This is the last speech he will ever make." And it was. Booth assassinated the president four days later, on April 15. Louis R. Masur, *Lincoln's Last Speech: Wartime Reconstruction and the Crisis of Reunion* (New York: Oxford University Press, 2015), 3–4.

87. Zinn, *A People's History*, 188; Foner interview.

88. Foner interview.

89. Ibid.

90. Foner, "Majority Report," 31.

91. Foner interview.

92. Ibid.

93. Ibid.

94. Zimmerman, "Black, White and Red All Over."

95. Joseph Conlin review of *A People's History of the United States*, *Wisconsin Magazine of History*, Winter 1980–81, 139.

96. Martin Duberman, *Howard Zinn: A Life on the Left* (New York: New Press, 2012), 229–231.

97. Zinn's admiration for Beard was unaffected by the extensive historical work challenging Beard's economic interpretation of the Constitution. Zinn credited Beard with trying "to dispel the fog of romantic nonsense spread through our school system in which the Founding Fathers who drafted the Constitution were depicted as selfless patriots" when they were in fact "masters of slaves, owners of property, and holders of bonds, whose economic interests . . . made them want a strong, conservative government that would prevent rebellion by the propertyless." Howard Zinn, introduction to Harvey Wasserman, *History of the United States* (New York: Harper and Row, 1972), v.

98. Zinn, *A People's History of the United States*, 98.

99. Duberman, *Howard Zinn*, 230.

100. Ibid., 231.

101. Alan Taylor, e-mail to Robert Cohen, Sept. 30, 2019. See Woody Holton, *Unruly Americans and the Origins of the American Constitution* (New York: Hill and Wang, 2008); and Terry Bouton, *Taming Democracy: "The People," the Founders, and the Troubled Ending of the American Revolution* (New York: Oxford University Press, 2009).

102. Taylor e-mail.

103. Zinn, *A People's History of the United States*, 100.

104. Howard Zinn, *Failure to Quit: Reflections of an Optimistic Historian* (Monroe, Maine: Common Courage Press, 1993), 70.

105. Zinn's fondness for Beard is echoed in the recent work of historian Richard B. Drake, who finds Beard's writings insightful on the connections between economics, U.S. foreign policy, and imperialism. See Richard B. Drake, *The Return of the Master Historian of American Imperialism* (Ithaca: Cornell University Press, 2018), 1–6.

106. Zinn, *A People's History of the United States*, 60, 63, 64, 66, 68, 77–80, 83–85, 87–88.

107. Zinn, *A People's History of the United States*, 59.

108. Ibid.

109. Ibid., 75.

110. Taylor e-mail; Taylor, *American Revolutions: A Continental History, 1750–1804* (New York: Norton, 2017), 97. On the continuities between Zinn's view of the American Revolution and more recent scholarship on the Revolution, see Alfred. F Young, Gary B. Nash, and Ray Raphael, eds., *Revolutionary Founders: Rebels, Radicals, and Reformers in the Making of the Nation* (New York: Vintage, 2012).

111. Taylor e-mail.

112. Zinn, *A People's History of the United States*, 86.

113. Ibid., 88. On the way Jennings's and Zinn's emphasis on racist expansionism still resonates in recent scholarship on the American Revolution, see Alan Taylor, "Expand or Die: The Revolution's New Empire," *William and Mary Quarterly* 74, no. 4 (Oct.

2017): 619–632; Serena R. Zabin, "Conclusion: Writing to and from the Revolution," *William and Mary Quarterly* 74, no. 4 (Oct. 2017): 753–764.

114. Zinn, *A People's History of the United States*, 72.

115. Ibid., 73. Parkinson suggests that the author Declaration of Independence's authors were not ignoring Native American and enslaved Africans but were "othering" them, rendering them, via exclusion and demonization, a source of nationalist opposition and mobilization during the Revolution. See Parkinson, "Exclusion at the Founding: The Declaration of Independence," in *Revolutionary Moments: Reading Revolutionary Texts*, ed. Rachel Hammersley (London: Bloomsbury Press, 2015), 53–60. See also Robert F. Parkinson, *The Common Cause: Creating Race and Nation in the American Revolution* (Chapel Hill: University of North Carolina Press, 2016).

116. Zinn, *A People's History of the United States*, 88, 89.

117. Ibid., 73.

118. Robert Cohen, *Howard Zinn's Southern Diary: Civil Rights, Sit-Ins, and Black Women's Student Activism* (Athens: University of Georgia Press, 2018), 1–75.

119. Zinn, *SNCC: The New Abolitionists*.

120. Howard Zinn, "Emma," in *Three Plays: The Political Theater of Howard Zinn—Emma, Marx in SoHo, Daughter of Venus* (Boston: Beacon Press, 2010), 3–102.

121. Note, however, that from outside the historical profession came an insightful review of *A People's History* by a prominent female scholar, Jean Anyon, an education professor. See Jean Anyon, "Issues and Voices from the Past: Whose History in American Classrooms? An Essay Review of *A People's History of the United States*," *Journal of Education*, Summer 1980, 67–74. Anyon pronounced Zinn's book "vital and valuable" (72–73) but did not focus on his treatment of women's history.

122. Linda Gordon, interview with Robert Cohen, May 21, 2019, New York City, transcript in authors' possession.

123. Zinn, *A People's History of the United States*, 112.

124. Gordon interview.

125. Zinn, *A People's History of the United States*, 112.

126. Gordon interview.

127. Alice Kessler-Harris, *Women Have Always Worked: A Concise History* (Champaign: University of Illinois Press, 2018).

128. Zinn, *A People's History of the United States*, 504, 514.

129. Gordon interview.

130. Zinn, *A People's History of the United States*, 645.

131. Linda Kerber, *No Constitutional Right to Be Ladies* (New York: Hill and Wang, 1999).

132. Gordon interview.

133. Marjorie J. Spruill, *Divided We Stand: The Battle over Women's Rights That Polarized American Politics* (Bloomsbury: New York, 2018); Donald T. Critchlow, *Phyllis Schlafly and Grassroots Conservatism: A Woman's Crusade* (Princeton: Princeton University Press, 2018).

134. Gordon interview.

135. Duberman, *Howard Zinn*, 228.

136. Jonathan Ned Katz, ed. *Gay American History: Lesbians and Gay Men in the USA* (New York: Plume, 1992); George Chauncey, *Why Marriage? The Historical Background That Shaped Today's Debate about Gay Equality* (Basic Books: 2004); Lillian Faderman, *Odd Girls and Twilight Lovers: A History of Lesbian Life in Twentieth-Century America* (New York: Columbia University Press, 1991); Don Romesburg, ed. *The Routledge History of Queer America* (New York: Routledge, 2019).

137. Amy Greenberg, telephone interview with Robert Cohen, Sept. 18, 2019, notes in authors' possession.

138. Ibid.

139. Ibid.

140. Zinn, *A People's History of the United States*, 161.

141. Greenberg interview.

142. Ibid.

143. Ibid.

144. James McPherson, "The Wicked War," *New York Review of Books*, Feb. 17, 2013.

145. Amy S. Greenberg, *A Wicked War: Polk, Clay, Lincoln, and the 1846 U.S. Invasion of Mexico* (New York: Knopf, 2012), 174–175, 206–207, 218–222, 238–240, 256–260.

146. Ibid., 129, 153, 188–199, 236. One other error in Zinn's discussion of the antiwar movement was his description of a conversation between jailed antiwar tax refuser Henry David Thoreau and Ralph Waldo Emerson—who thought antiwar protest "futile." Zinn, repeating a popular story, has Emerson visiting Thoreau in jail and asking him "what are you doing in there?" To which Thoreau is said to have replied, "What are you doing out there?" (*A People's History*, 156). But according to historian Lewis Perry, this conversation "almost certainly never occurred. Neither man recorded it. Thoreau was not in jail long enough to converse with visitors." Lewis Perry, *Civil Disobedience: An American Tradition* (New Haven: Yale University Press, 2013), 94–95.

147. Greenberg interview.

148. Edward J. Walsh, "Balancing the Books," *Barron's*, March 24, 1980.

149. Michael Kazin, "Howard Zinn's History Lessons," *Dissent*, Spring 2004, https://www.dissentmagazine.org/article/howard-zinns-history-lessons. .

150. Bryant Simon, *The Fabric of Defeat: South Carolina Millhands, 1910–1948* (Chapel Hill: University of North Carolina Press, 1998); Bryant Simon, *The Hamlet Fire: A Tragic Story of Cheap Food, Cheap Government, and Cheap Lives* (New York: New Press, 2017); Bryant Simon, *Everything but the Coffee: Learning About America From Starbucks* (Berkeley: University of California Press, 2010).

151. Bryant Simon, telephone interview with Robert Cohen, July 12, 2019, notes in authors' possession.

152. Ibid.

153. Ibid.

154. Ibid.

155. Ibid.

156. Ibid.

157. Ibid.

158. Simon interview. See Jefferson Cowie, *Stayin' Alive: The 1970s and the Last Days of the Working Class* (New York: New Press, 2010).

159. Simon interview.

160. Zinn believed that "the issue of class conflict" that "ran through" *A People's History*, helped account "for the fact that the book has been so popular. . . . It speaks to what people are already thinking and feeling [as reflected] over the years [in the] many polls where they ask, do you believe this country is run for the rich? Over-whelmingly, people say yes." Barbara Aria, "History in the Making," *Timeout New York*, Feb. 2013, 20.

161. Zinn, *A People's History of the United States*, 84.

162. Ibid., 349.

163. When attacked by a right-wing organization for his anticapitalism in *A People's History*, Zinn replied, "American capitalism has been a failure. Having so many home-less people and poor is a failure, and with this system there's an enormous amount of waste." "Zinn Fends Off AIA Written Attack," *Daily Free Press* (Boston University), March 14, 1986.

164. See, for example, Barton Bernstein, "The New Deal: The Conservative Achieve-ments of Liberal Reform," in *Toward a New Past: Dissenting Essays in American His-tory*, ed. Barton Bernstein (New York: Vintage Books, 1969), 263–288.

165. Zinn, *A People's History of the United States*, 403.

166. Ibid., 402.

167. Black workers in the Jim Crow South, barred from voting in general elections, could vote in union elections, a rare democratic right in an antidemocratic society. So dismissing the Wagner Act as an instrument of corporate control, as Zinn does, misses the meaningful right it accorded to such workers. See Robert Rodgers Korstad, *Civil Rights Unionism: Tobacco Workers and the Struggle for Democracy in the Mid-Twentieth Century South* (Chapel Hill: University of North Carolina Press, 2003). Zinn's eager-ness to indict the New Deal's record on labor led him to underestimate the impact of the March on Washington Movement (which runs against Zinn's usual tendency to celebrate people's movements). This African American protest movement, led by A. Philip Randolph, in its demand for an end to racial discrimination in the defense industries, pressured FDR to issue the first executive order in support of black rights since Reconstruction, establishing the Fair Employment Practices Committee (FEPC) to stop racial discrimination in those industries. Zinn was dismissive of the FEPC as having "changed little" since it "had no enforcement powers." Zinn, *A People's History of the United States*, 404. While the FEPC could have been far more effective, it did have some notable successes, even in the Jim Crow South. In Birmingham, Alabama, Black organizers secured FEPC intervention, "guaranteeing the hiring of seventeen thousand black workers." Sara Rzeszutek Haviland, *James and Esther Cooper Jackson: Love and Courage in the Black Freedom Movement* (Lexington: University Press of Kentucky, 2015), 64. And in the North, the FEPC, by providing Black workers the right for the first time to "file complaints" against racist employers, "improved morale." John Morton

Blum, *V Was for Victory: Politics and American Culture during World War II* (New York: Harcourt, 1976), 196. See also Merl E. Reed, *Seedtime for the Modern Civil Rights Movement: The President's Committee on Fair Employment, 1941–1946* (Baton Rouge: Louisiana State University Press, 1991).

168. This progressive taxation raised the top income tax rate from 24 to 63 percent during Roosevelt's first term and up to 79 percent in his second, and it would later peak at 91 percent. A similar hike in the estate tax from 20 to 77 percent led to a long-term decline in the concentration of wealth so that the richest 0.1 percent of Americans' share of the nation's wealth fell from 20 percent in 1929 to close to 10 percent by the 1950s. Paul Krugman, *The Conscience of a Liberal* (New York: Norton, 2007), 47–48.

169. One could similarly debate Zinn's conclusions about the New Deal and Black America. Zinn stressed New Deal failures to assist Blacks economically during the Great Depression and FDR's cowardice in refusing to support federal anti-lynching legislation. Zinn, *A People's History of the United States*, 404–405. But Zinn failed to mention, let alone explain, why in 1936 African Americans for the first time overwhelmingly abandoned the Republican Party, the party of Lincoln, to vote to reelect FDR. Nor did he cover the way FDR's court appointments transformed a reactionary Supreme Court into a more liberal court, resulting in major civil rights victories—including *Smith v. Allwright* (1944), which chipped away at southern voting rights violations by outlawing white primaries, and *Gaines v. Canada* (1939), in which the court for the first time ordered a segregated university to admit an African American student. See Harvard Sitkoff, *A New Deal for Blacks: The Emergence of Civil Rights as a National Issue* (New York: Oxford University Press, 2008).

170. See Jefferson Cowie, *The Great Exception: The New Deal and the Limits of American Politics* (Princeton: Princeton University Press, 2017).

171. Anthony H. to Howard Zinn, March 22, 2005, Zinn Papers.

172. Howard Zinn to Anthony H., March 26, 2005, Zinn Papers.

173. Anthony H. to Howard Zinn, July 4, 2005; Howard Zinn to Anthony H., July 17, 2005, both in Zinn Papers.

174. Marilyn Young, interview with Robert Cohen, Dec. 17, 2015, New York City, transcript in authors' possession.

175. Ibid.

176. Zinn, *A People's History of the United States*, 359–376.

177. Young interview.

178. Zinn, *A People's History of the United States*, 363-364.

179. Ibid., 407.

180. Ibid., 408.

181. Young interview.

182. Zinn, *A People's History of the United States*, 424.

183. Young interview.

184. Zinn, *A People's History of the United States*, 408.

185. Ibid., 408–409.

186. Young interview.

187. Ibid.

188. C-Span *Book Notes*, interview with Howard Zinn by Brian Lamb, March 12, 2000.

189. Robert L. Messer, "New Evidence on Truman's Decision," *Bulletin of Atomic Scientists*, Aug. 1985, 50.

190. Michael J. Hogan, ed., *Hiroshima in History and Memory* (New York: Cambridge University Press, 1996) 1–36.

191. Ibid., 80–115.

192. John W. Dower, *Cultures of War* (New York: Norton, 2010), 160–161.

193. Ibid., 195.

194. Ibid., 232.

195. Zinn, *A People's History of the United States*, 469.

196. Young interview.

197. Ibid.

198. Marilyn Young, *The Vietnam Wars: 1945–1990* (New York: Harper Perennial, 1991); Nick Turse, *Kill Everything That Moves: The Real American War in Vietnam* (New York: Picador, 2013); Frederik Logevall, *Choosing War: The Lost Chance for Peace and the Escalation of the Vietnam War* (Berkeley: University of California Press, 2001), Frederik Logevall, *Embers of War: The Fall of an Empire and the Making of America's Vietnam* (New York: Random House, 2013); Neil Sheehan, *A Bright Shining Lie: John Paul Vann and America in Vietnam* (New York: Vintage, 1989); Max Hastings, *Vietnam: An Epic Tragedy, 1945–1975* (New York: HarperCollins, 2018).

199. A McNaughton memo is quoted by Zinn giving such a warning, but not with the colorful LBJ phrasing Young described. See Zinn, *A People's History of the United, States*, 499.

200. Young interview.

201. Cohen, *Howard Zinn's Southern Diary*.

202. Zinn, *A People's History of the United States*, 686.

203. Wesley Hogan, *Many Minds, One Heart: SNCC's Dream for a New America* (Chapel Hill: University of North Carolina Press, 2009).

204. Wesley Hogan, telephone interview with Robert Cohen, July 11, 2019, transcript in authors' possession.

205. Zinn, *A People's History of the United States*, 443–444.

206. Robin D. G. Kelley, *Hammer and Hoe: Alabama Communists during the Great Depression* (Chapel Hill: University of North Carolina Press, 1990). There is, however, an important history concerning Black disillusionment with the Communist Party that Zinn does not address in *A People's History*. For example, Bayard Rustin's break with the CP came when the party pressured him not to work against racial discrimination in the armed forces during World War II, subordinating the struggle against racism to the Soviet Union's desire for unity in the war effort. See Stephen Drury Smith and Catherine Ellis, ed., *Free All Along: The Robert Penn Warren Civil Rights Interviews* (New York: New Press, 2019), 303.

207. Hogan interview.

208. Ibid. On "respectability politics," see Evelyn Brooks Higginbotham, *Righteous Discontent: The Women's Movement in the Black Baptist Church, 1880–1920* (Cambridge, Mass.: Harvard University Press, 1993), 150–184.

209. Hogan interview. See Danielle L. McGuire, *At the Dark End of the Street: Black Women, Rape, and Resistance—a New History of the Civil Rights Movement from Rosa Parks to the Rise of Black Power* (New York: Vintage, 2011). See also Jean Theoharis, *The Rebellious Life of Mrs. Rosa Parks* (Boston: Beacon Press, 2015).

210. Hogan interview. See Charles Cobb Jr., *This Non-Violent Stuff'll Get You Killed: How Guns Made the Civil Rights Movement Possible* (New York: Basic Books, 2014); Akinyele Omowale Umoja, *We Will Shoot Back: Armed Resistance in the Mississippi Freedom Movement* (New York: New York University Press, 2014).

211. Hogan interview.

212. Ibid.

213. Ibid. See Timothy Tyson, *Radio Free Dixie: Robert F. Williams and the Roots of Black Power* (Chapel Hill: University of North Carolina Press, 2001).

214. Hogan interview.

215. Ibid. Regarding "if elections really counted," that quote has also been attributed to Mark Twain and Emma Goldman, but neither of them is the source of that quote either, though Goldman's critique of women's suffrage comes close to echoing that idea. Zinn's skepticism on voting as means of securing major social change can be seen, for example, in a 2008 article where he argued, "Voting is easy and marginally useful, but is a poor substitute for democracy, which requires direct action by concerned citizens." Howard Zinn, "Election Madness," *Progressive*, April 8, 2008, https://progressive.org /magazine/election-madness-Zinn.

216. Zinn, *A People's History of the United States*, 465.

217. Hogan interview.

218. Ibid.

219. Zinn, *A People's History of the United States*, 454.

220. Hogan interview; Wesley Hogan, *On the Freedom Side: How Five Decades of Youth Activists Have Remixed American History* (Chapel Hill: University of North Carolina Press, 2019).

221. Zinn, *A People's History of the United States*, 461; Hogan interview.

222. Hogan interview.

223. Ibid.

224. Ibid.

225. See Sean Wilentz, *The Politicians and the Egalitarians: The Hidden History of American Politics* (New York: Norton, 2017).

226. Anthony Arnove, introduction to the Zinn, *A People's History of the United States*, 35th edition, xiii, xvii.

227. Timothy Patrick McCarthy, ed., *The Indispensable Zinn: The Essential Writings of the "People's Historian"* (New York: New Press, 2012), xxiii.

228. "Books in Brief," Luther Spoehr review of Zinn, *A People's History of the United States*, *Saturday Review*, Feb. 2, 1980, 37.

CHAPTER 8. ON STAGE AND SCREEN

1. Myla Kabat-Zinn, e-mail to Robert Cohen, Jan. 3, 2020, copy in authors' possession.

2. Howard Zinn, *Artists in a Time of War* (New York: Seven Stories Press, 2003).

3. Matt Damon and Ben Affleck won the Academy Award for best original screenplay in *Good Will Hunting,* and Robin Williams won the Academy Award for best supporting actor.

4. C-Span *Book Notes,* interview with Howard Zinn by Brian Lamb, March 12, 2000.

5. Ibid.

6. Nancy Carlsson Paige, interview for *The People Speak,* Jan. 8–9, 2008, Boston, courtesy of Anthony Arnove.

7. Ibid.

8. *The Sopranos* won twenty-one Emmy Awards and five Golden Globes.

9. In the scene, AJ's mother also explains to Tony that AJ's history teacher said that "if Columbus was alive today he would go on trial for crimes against humanity like Milošević." She also tries to defend Columbus by citing the fact that George Washington was a slaveholder.

10. TPM, "Dear TV, Feb. 19, 2015, http://talkingpointsmemo.com/.

11. Written and directed by Greta Gerwig.

12. Anthony Arnove, introduction to *Howard Zinn Speaks: Collected Speeches 1963–2009* (Chicago: Haymarket Books, 2012), vii.

13. Howard Zinn, "Obama Is Going to Need Demonstrations and Protests to Do the Right Thing," AlterNet, March 12, 2009; Howard Zinn, ed., *The People Speak: American Voices, Some Famous, Some Little Known: Dramatic Readings Celebrating the Enduring Spirit of Dissent* (New York: HarperCollins, 2004), ix–x. Anthony Arnove believes that had the idea of doing dramatic historical readings not occurred to Zinn for the millionth copy celebration at the 92nd Street Y in 2003, it would almost certainly have occurred to him the following year in connection with book events for their *Voices of a People's History of the United States* (New York: Seven Stories Press, 2004), which offered more than two hundred documents from which such readings could be drawn. Anthony Arnove, telephone interview with Robert Cohen, Jan. 17, 2020, notes in authors' possession.

14. Howard Zinn, e-mail to Hugh Van Dusen, May 10, 2002, Zinn Papers.

15. "Howard Zinn Talks with Op-ed News about *The People Speak,*" *Op-ed News,* Dec. 15, 2009; Zinn, *The People Speak,* ix–x; Voices of the American People: A Celebration of the Millionth Copy of Howard Zinn's A People's History of the United States, program handed out at New York City event, Feb. 23, 2003, Zinn Papers.

16. "Howard Zinn Talks with Op-ed News."

17. Brian Jones, telephone interview with Robert Cohen, Oct. 5, 2019, notes in author's possession.

18. Zinn, *The People Speak,* x.

19. By 2007 *Voices of a People's History* had been performed more than forty times

"in front of more than 22,000 people." Three years later the total number of performances had more than doubled, which included not only theaters but also high schools and churches. *The People Speak*, hosted by Howard Zinn, [2007], program handed out at event, Zinn Papers; "Anthony Arnove Reflects on Making THE PEOPLE SPEAK with Howard Zinn," Op-ed News, Feb. 14, 2010.

20. Anthony Arnove, interview with Robert Cohen and Sonia Murrow, May 21, 2019, New York City, transcript in authors' possession.

21. Robert Cohen, *Howard Zinn's Southern Diary: Civil Rights, Sit-Ins, and Black Women's Student Activism* (Athens: University of Georgia Press, 2018), 17, 107–108, 117–119, 121, 131, 146.

22. Howard Zinn, *Three Plays: The Political Theater of Howard Zinn—Emma, Marx in SoHo, Daughter of Venus* (Boston: Beacon Press, 2010).

23. Arnove interview with Cohen and Murrow.

24. See Howard Zinn, memorial tribute to Kurt Vonnegut, [2007], Zinn Papers; Alice Walker, "What Nurtured My Outrage, Really?," in Cohen, *Howard Zinn's Southern Diary*, ix–xiii.

25. Patti Smith, e-mail to Howard Zinn, Dec. 29, 2002, Zinn Papers.

26. Arnove interview with Cohen and Murrow.

27. Though Zinn had long been interested in this documents project, his busy schedule had led him to shelve it for a while. A conversation with Seven Stories Press publisher Dan Simon and Anthony Arnove helped revive the project, which would be completed as a coauthored work with Arnove. Arnove interview with Cohen, Jan. 17, 2020.

28. Arnove interview with Cohen and Murrow. Arnove's interest in history had been inspired by his reading of *A People's History*. See Arnove, introduction to Howard Zinn, *A People's History of the United States*, 35th anniversary edition (New York: Harper-Perennial, 2015), xiv; Arnove, introduction to *Howard Zinn Speaks*, vii–xi. Arnove, like others inspired by Zinn, went on to do important historical and political work. See his critique *The Iraq War: The Logic of Withdrawal* (New York, Metropolitan Books, 2007), modeled in its political clarity and brevity (and subtitle) on Zinn's *Vietnam: The Logic of Withdrawal* (1967; repr., Chicago: Haymarket Books 2014). Zinn wrote the foreword for Arnove's book on Iraq. Arnove also was a producer for *Dirty Wars* (2013), an Academy Award-nominated documentary on the U.S. "War on Terror." He has also collaborated with Zinn on a book of interviews, *Howard Zinn, Terrorism and War* (New York: Seven Stories Press, 2002), edited *The Essential Chomsky* (New York: New Press, 2008), and coedited with Colin Firth a British document collection, *The People Speak; Democracy Is Not a Spectator Sport* (Edinburgh: Cornergate Books, 2012). For a discussion of the origins of the Zinn-Arnove collaboration on *Voices of a People's History* by its publisher, see Dan Simon's memorial tribute to Zinn, "Goodbye Howard, Good Bye," [2010], copy in authors' possession, courtesy of Anthony Arnove.

29. Howard Zinn and Anthony Arnove, *Voices of a People's History* (New York: Seven Stories Press, 2004).

30. Ibid., 23.

31. It is true that Zinn and many readers of *A People's History* admired the dissident oratory and other protest documents quoted in his best-selling book. But there are grounds for questioning whether—as he claimed—readers were "struck more" by those people he quoted than by his "own running commentary on the history of the nation." After all, *Voices of a People's History of the United States*, his and Arnove's book of dissenting voices from the American past, offered far more extensive excerpts as well as complete documents, yet it has not been the best seller that *A People's History* has been, which suggests that Zinn's "commentary" is, after all, central to the cogency and popularity of *A People's History*. Yet it is also true that when these words were moved from the printed page to theater and film, Zinn was absolutely right that those dissident voices, brought to life by talented actors, proved even more popular than *A People's History*.

32. Zinn and Arnove, *Voices of a People's History*, 24.

33. Arnove interview with Cohen and Murrow; *The People Speak*, hosted by Howard Zinn.

34. Arnove interview with Cohen and Murrow; Howard Zinn to James Earl Jones [circa fall 2002], Zinn Papers.

35. Arnove interview with Cohen and Murrow.

36. Ibid.

37. Ibid.

38. Ibid.

39. Ibid.

40. Vanessa Martinez, e-mail to Anthony Arnove, Oct. 6, 2005, Zinn Papers.

41. Arnove interview with Cohen and Murrow.

42. Howard Zinn interview, *The People Speak* interviews, Jan. 8–9, 2008, Boston, transcript in authors' possession, courtesy of Anthony Arnove.

43. Marisa Tomei, e-mail to Anthony Arnove, Oct. 12, 2005, Zinn Papers.

44. David Strathairn to Zinn [n.d.], Zinn Papers.

45. Brian Jones interview. The readings were grouped in four segments: race, class, war, and women. See *The People Speak*, hosted by Howard Zinn.

46. "Interview with Howard Zinn," *Spare Change News*, June 28–July 11, 2001.

47. Robert Birnbaum, "Howard Zinn on *A People's History of the American Empire*," *Identity Theory*, Oct. 1, 2008, http://identitytheory.com/howard-zinn-a-peoples-history-american-empire.

48. Ibid.

49. Arnove interview with Cohen, Jan. 17, 2020.

50. Arnove interview with Cohen and Murrow.

51. Chris Moore interview, *The People Speak* interviews, Jan. 8–9, 2008, Boston, transcript in authors' possession; *The People Speak* press conference, Jan. 8–9, 2008, transcripts in authors' possession. It was easier to make a low-budget film connected to Zinn, which Deb Ellis and Dennis Mueller did when in 2004 they completed their documentary about Zinn, *You Can't Be Neutral on a Moving Train*, based on his Zinn's autobiography of the same title. The film was narrated by Matt Damon.

52. Arnove interview with Cohen and Murrow.

53. Chris Moore, e-mail to Howard Zinn, Jan. 24, 2008; Chris Moore, e-mail to Matt Damon, Jan. 24, 2008, both in Zinn Papers.

54. Birnbaum, "Zinn on *A People's History of the American Empire*."

55. Arnove interview with Cohen, Jan. 17, 2020. Dubuc was also an alum of Boston University, where Zinn had been a very popular professor for many years.

56. Martin Duberman, *Howard Zinn: A Life on the Left* (New York: New Press, 2012), 310.

57. Howard Zinn remarks at *The People Speak* press conference, Jan. 8–9, 2008, Boston, transcript in authors' possession.

58. Arnove interview with Cohen and Murrow.

59. "Bruce Springsteen Raves about Howard Zinn," Voices of a People's History, Nov. 15, 2007, https://peopleshistory.us/news/bruce-springsteen. These remarks by Springsteen about Zinn appeared initially as a sidebar to Joe Levy's interview with Springsteen in the Nov. 1, 2007, issue of *Rolling Stone*.

60. Josh Brolin remarks at *The People Speak* press conference, Jan. 8–9, 2008, Boston, transcript in authors' possession.

61. Arnove interview with Cohen and Murrow.

62. Zinn remarks at *The People Speak* press conference, Jan. 8–9, 2008.

63. Howard Zinn interview, *Bill Moyers Journal*, Dec. 11, 2009.

64. Zinn remarks at *The People Speak* press conference.

65. Danny Glover interview, *The People Speak* interviews, and Glover remarks at *The People Speak* press conference, Jan. 8–9, 2008, Boston, courtesy of Anthony Arnove, transcript in authors' possession.

66. Glover interview.

67. Jasmine Guy interview, *The People Speak* interviews, Jan. 8–9, 2008, Boston, courtesy of Anthony Arnove, transcript in authors' possession.

68. Ibid.

69. Martín Espada interview, *The People Speak* interviews, Jan. 8–9, 2008, Boston, courtesy of Anthony Arnove, transcript in authors' possession.

70. Ibid.

71. Ibid.

72. Kerry Washington interview, *The People Speak* interviews, Jan. 8–9, 2008, Boston, courtesy of Anthony Arnove, transcript in authors' possession.

73. Viggo Mortensen interview, *The People Speak* interviews, Jan. 8–9, 2008, Boston, courtesy of Anthony Arnove, transcript in authors' possession.

74. Ibid.

75. Ibid.

76. John Legend interview, *The People Speak* interviews, Jan. 8–9, 2008, Boston, courtesy of Anthony Arnove, transcript in authors' possession.

77. David Strathairn interview, *The People Speak* interviews, Jan. 8–9, 2008, Boston, courtesy of Anthony Arnove, transcript in authors' possession.

78. Chris Moore remarks at *The People Speak* press conference, Jan. 8–9, 2008, Boston, transcript in authors' possession.

79. Chris Moore interview.

80. Ibid.

81. Ibid.

82. Mary McNamara, "The People Speak," *Los Angeles Times*, Dec. 12, 2009.

83. Ibid. The *New York Times* review was also positive. See Brian Stelter, "New Boss, Same as the Old Boss: Howard Zinn Traces Social Change," *New York Times*, Dec, 12, 2009. See also Matthew Gilbert, "Stars Bring to Life the Words of the People," *Boston Globe*, Dec. 12, 2009.

84. Brian J. Trautman, "Howard Zinn on TV: A Review," *History News Network*, Dec. 9, 2009, https://historynewsnetwork.org/article/121261.

85. Ibid.

86. This is not to say that there were no right-wing critics of the film. On one such critic and a rebuttal to him, see Brian Jones, "Who's Afraid of the Big, Bad Zinn?," Socialistworker.org, Dec. 16, 2009, https://socialistworker.org/2009/12/16 /whos-afraid-of-zinn.

87. Kristi York Wooten, "Will Howard Zinn Get Broad Acclaim with New Film?," *Newsweek*, Dec. 10, 2009, https://www.newsweek.com /will-howard-zinn-get-broad-acclaim-new-film-75677.

88. Ibid.

89. These estimates of the viewership for Moore's film are based on the movie industry formula for converting gross earnings to total viewers—this formula was generously provided by theater owner Derek Hyman.

90. Colin Firth, e-mail to Howard Zinn, Nov. 16, 2008, Zinn Papers.

91. Arnove interview with Cohen, Jan. 17, 2020.

92. Arnove interview with Cohen and Murrow; Jones interview.

93. Washington interview.

94. "Empowerment in the Classroom," *Yes*, Feb 9, 2012 (Chicago), clipping, courtesy of Anthony Arnove.

95. Jones interview. On this student learning and identification with the historical figures whose words they read, see the student statements in Seven Stories Institute People's History Broadcast/Podcast Project, e-mail, cc'ed to Zinn, May 9, 2006, Zinn Papers.

96. Jones interview.

97. Ibid.

INDEX

abolitionism, 18, 158, 161, 196, 212, 243, 253

Abu-Jamal, Mumia, 130

Accuracy in Academia, 44, 140, 179

activist teachers, 4, 65; collaborate with Zinn, 158, 159, 167–168, 175–178; create school reform organizations, 164–166

Adams, Samuel, 205

Affleck, Ben, 239, 248, 303n3

Afghanistan war, 6, 43, 193, 240

African American studies, 46, 144

African Americans, 30, 46, 52, 113, 123, 206; citizenship and, 195; enslavement of, 196; New Deal and, 300n169; Reconstruction and, 197, 198, 200. *See also* Black history; Black Lives Matter; Black political activism; civil rights movement; slavery

ahistoricism, 55

Ali, Muhammad, 258

Alien and Sedition Act, 20

Allen, Michael, 136

Alperovitz, Gar, 226

American Civil Liberties Union Women's Rights Project, 208

American exceptionalism, 2, 59, 129, 135

American expansionism, 46, 210

American Federation of Labor (AFL), 49, 185

American Historical Association, 39

American Revolution, 11, 184, 193, 201, 249; historiography, 26, 202, 204; Zinn's treatment of, 137, 203, 204, 205, 206

Americanism, 10

Americanization movement, 57

anarchism, 27, 214

Anthony, Susan B., 59, 261

anticommunism, 230

antifascist idealism, 99, 223

antilabor efforts, 8, 18

antiquarianism, 18

Anti-Renter movement, 189

anti-Semitism, 114; Holocaust, 112, 196, 224

antislavery politics, 195, 196, 199, 212

antiwar movement, 14, 15, 39, 50, 78, 213, 228. *See also* World War II; Zinn, Howard: Vietnam War activism

Anyon, Jean, 48, 49–50, 59, 278n20, 297n121

apartheid, 149, 163

Apess, William, 193

Apple, Michael, 54

Arawaks, 28, 37, 81, 87, 113, 183, 239

Arnold, Linda, 179

Arnove, Anthony, 7, 304n27; collaboration with Colin Firth on British *Voices* book, theater events, and film, 263; on impact of *A People's History*, 236; *The People Speak* film and, 249, 251–252; *Voices of a People's History* (ed. with Zinn), 43; on Zinn's *People's History* theater events, 243–246; on Zinn's popularity in Reagan era, 145; on Zinn's relationships with performing artists, 241, 242

Articles of Confederation, 202

authoritarianism, 8

Bacon's Rebellion, 20

Baez, Joan, 242

Baez, Tony, 165

Bailey, Thomas, 31

Baker, Ella, 207, 232

Baldwin, James, 9, 10

Banks, James, 51

Banneker, Benjamin, 243

Beard, Charles, 201, 202, 203, 216, 235, 296n105; Zinn's admiration of, 296n97

Bennett, Gwendolyn, 22

Bennett, William, 56

Bernstein, Barton, 26

Berthoff, Rowland, 203
Beyond Heroes and Holidays (ed. Menkart), 165
Bigelow, Bill, 171, 290n29; Network of Educators' Committees on Central America, 171, 172; "people's pedagogy," 159, 160, 163, 167–168; *Rethinking Schools*, 78, 159, 164–166, 173, 174, 178; social activism, 169, 171; Zinn Education Project, 64, 167–170, 176–178. *See also* activist teachers; Zinn Education Project
—works of: *People's History for the Classroom*, 175, 291n54; *Rethinking Columbus*, 172, 173
Bill of Rights, 201
Bin Laden, Osama, 193
Black capitalism, 232
Black experience, 20, 22
Black freedom movement. *See* civil rights movement
Black history, 13, 18, 26, 197, 229, 230
Black Lives Matter (BLM), 2, 10, 234
Black political activism, 198, 230, 242
Black veterans, 232
Blackett, P. M. S., 226
Blacks. *See* African Americans
Blassingame, John W., 26
Bloody Sunday, 149
Boorstin, Daniel, 136, 137, 139
Bouton, Terry, 202
Brecht, Bertolt, 30
Broad City (TV show), 240
Brolin, Josh, 7, 249, 252, 262
Brown, John, 174, 241, 258
Buhle, Paul, 97
Bureau of Indian Affairs, 55
Burns, Ken, 263
Bush, George H. W., 145, 182
Bush, George W., 43, 44, 146, 219, 220, 259
Butler, Smedley, 257

California State Board of Education, 53
Camus, Albert, 37, 38, 85
capitalism, 18, 21, 58, 66, 85, 92, 150, 204; Black, 232; challenges to 49, 63, 145, 151, 180, 213; connections to war, 221, 223, 228, 262; folklore/myths of, 16, 29, 30; inequities of, 2, 16, 50, 65, 262; reverence for, 24, 40,

129, 135, 139, 183, 217–218, 236; students' criticism of Zinn's negative view of, 86–87; workers' acquiescence to, 48, 235; Zinn on, as failure in United States, 299n163
Carnegie, Andrew, 48, 86
Carr, E. H., 76
Carter, Jimmy, 171
Caughey, John Walton, 53, 54
censorship, 44, 68, 69, 181, 226, 236
Chauncey, George, 210
Chàvez, César, 255, 261
Cheney, Dick, 219
Cheney, Lynne, 57
Cherokees, 28, 81, 187–188, 190–192, 194
Chicago Voices of a People's History, 264
Chomsky, Noam, 44, 154, 254
Christensen, Linda, 166
Christian-Smith, Linda, 54
Civil Rights Act (1957), 232
Civil Rights Act (1964), 57
Civil Rights Act (1968), 234
civil rights movement, 22, 230–233, 253, 254; Bloody Sunday, 149; Freedom Rides, 15, 274n58; Freedom Schools, 229; impact on Zinn, 14, 15, 24, 198, 229; institutional racism and, 234; marches, 149, 151, 299n167; Mississippi Freedom Summer, 24, 58, 229; Montgomery bus boycott, 230, 231; as Second Reconstruction, 196, 198; sit-ins, 15, 229; Southern Regional Council, 24, 229; Spelman College students and, 17, 207. *See also* Black political activism; King, Martin Luther, Jr.; Student Nonviolent Coordinating Committee
Civil War, 194–196, 198, 199, 200, 210, 212
class warfare, 49, 189
classism, 12, 63, 136
Clinton, William Jefferson, 209
Cobb, Charles, Jr., 231
Cold War, 26, 28, 57, 91, 115, 224, 226, 227, 230
colonialism, 1, 20, 140, 205; neocolonialism, 21
color line (Du Bois), 2, 28
Columbus, Christopher, 132, 138, 257; genocidal conquest, 2, 36, 37, 105; "New World" Arrival Anniversary, 13, 149, 172–173; quest for gold, 36, 104, 116, 127; rape, 122, 125, 127, 284–285n8; *Rethinking Columbus*,

172, 173; slavery, 2, 37, 75, 104, 106, 113, 125; treatment of Native Americans, 143, 187, 239, 276–277n92, 303n9. *See also* Morison, Samuel Eliot; *People's History, A*: Columbus chapter

Commager, Henry Steele, 31

Common Core State Standards, 61, 76, 92

communalism, 14

communism, 16, 116, 230, 292n6

Confederate statues, 2, 53

Conlin, Joseph R., 201

conservatives, 29, 74, 111, 145, 146, 209; attacks on *A People's History*, 6, 44, 88, 96, 179–181; among historians, 31, 48, 144; Horowitz, 44, 179; Limbaugh, 44; Murdoch, 248; *National Review*, 44; schools and, 4, 6, 48, 56, 63, 87, 180; among students, 96, 97, 98, 142–143. *See also* history textbooks

Cornbleth, Catherine, 51, 52, 279n27

Countryman, Edward, 204, 275n62

Coval, Kevin, 264

Cowie, Jefferson, 216

Cremin, Lawrence, 56

Critchlow, Donald T., 209

critical pedagogy, 163, 164, 169–170

critical thinking/engagement, 59, fostered by teachers using *A People's History*, 9, 10, 62, 64, 70, 72, 95, 172, 253, provoked by *The People Speak*, 257–258

Crockett, Davy, 59, 115

Cruz, Ted, 73

Cuba, 1, 23, 61, 81, 114, 225

Cuban, Larry, 4, 47, 57–59, 60, 62

Cuban Missile Crisis, 61

Cullen, Countee, 22

Damon, Matt, 7, 43, 238, 239, 264; adapting *People's History* for television, 248, 249, 262

Daniels, Mitch, 44, 63, 76–77, 179, 180, 181

Davis, Benjamin, 230

Debs, Eugene, 241, 258

Declaration of Independence, 19, 205–206, 297n115

Declarations of Independence (Zinn), 43, 131

Delillo, Don, 130

democratic idealism, 7, 86

Democrats, 24, 29, 146, 188, 212; Johnson, 24, 57, 66; Kennedy, 24, 62; Truman, 226, 232. *See also* Roosevelt, Franklin D.

Detmer, David, 181

Dewey, John, 68, 160

disability rights, 3, 138

Disobedience and Democracy (Zinn), 39

Doar, John, 231, 232

Doctorow, E. L., 20

Dominican intervention, 20

Dominican Republic, 36

Dorr Rebellion, 189

Douglass, Frederick, 7, 162, 240, 244, 253, 260, 264

Dower, John W., 227

Downs, Gregory, 199

Downs, Jim, 199

Doyle, Thomas, 137

Dred Scott decision, 195

Drinnon, Richard, 190

Du Bois, W. E. B., 2, 26, 27, 28, 196, 229, 230

Duberman, Martin, 201, 202, 203, 209–210

Dubuc, Nancy, 250, 306n55

Dunbar, Paul Laurence, 22

Dunbar-Ortiz, Roxanne, 138

Dylan, Bob, 7, 246, 251

Eckford, Elizabeth, 174

economic inequality, 217

Edelman, Marian Wright, 254

Edmundson, Jeff, 171

education federalism, 53

education scholarship, 51, 54, 58, 81, 164, 170

educational reform, 47–48; Elementary and Secondary Education Act (1965), 54, 57; National Defense Education Act (1958), 57; teacher-initiated, 42, 59, 78, 159, 163, 172, 174. *See also* multicultural education / multiculturalism

egalitarianism, 28, 96, 193, 230, 241

Eisenhower, Dwight D., 25

Electoral College, 201

electoral politics, 32, 185, 189, 200, 212, 233

Elementary and Secondary Education Act (1965), 54, 57

elitism, 13, 22, 38

Ellis, Deb, 43, 305n51

Ellsberg, Daniel, 17

Ellwood, Cynthia, 165
Emberton, Carole, 199
Equal Rights Amendment, 209
Erikson, Erik, 129
Espada, Martín, 7, 254, 255, 256
ethnic studies, 5
Eurocentrism, 20, 51
Evans, Bill, 164

Faderman, Lillian, 210
fascism, 16, 224, 232, 270
Fast, Howard, 130, 249
Federal Bureau of Investigation, 24
federalism, 231
feminism, 51, 208, 209
Fiasco, Lupe, 264
Fifteenth Amendment, 198
Finn, Chester E., Jr., 56
Firth, Colin, 130, 263
Fisher, Linford, 193
FitzGerald, Frances, 48, 55, 59
folk music, 21, 22
folklore, 16, 22
Fonda, Jane, 130
Foner, Eric, 8, 236; *New York Times* review of
    A People's History, 184–187; on Zinn on Re-
    construction, 197–200; on Zinn on slavery
    and Civil War, 194–196
Ford, Henry, 180
Fortas, Abe, 18, 39
Foucault, Michel, 21
Founding Fathers, 59, 74, 201, 202, 203, 204,
    222, 279n27, 296n97
Fourteenth Amendment, 198, 208
Franklin, Benjamin, 201
Franklin, John Hope, 53, 229
Frazier, Nishani, 232
Freedom Rides, 15, 274n58
Freedom Schools, 229
Freire, Paulo, 42, 165, 170
Frelinghuysen, Theodore, 188
Fugitive Slave Act, 243

Garraty, Jack, 200
Gaye, Marvin, 258
Genovese, Eugene, 194
George III, 205

Geronimo, 193
Gilded Age, 68, 86, 216
Gilman, Charlotte Perkins, 27
Ginsburg, Ruth Bader, 208, 209
Giroux, Henry, 165
Gitlin, Todd, 2
Glover, Danny, 7, 240, 253–254
Goldman, Emma, 7, 18, 27, 207, 242, 272n32,
    302n215
Good Will Hunting (film), 43, 142, 238, 239,
    248, 303n3
Gordon, Linda, 207, 208, 209
Grabar, Mary, 179, 180
Grant, Ulysses S., 210
Great Awakening, 192, 193
Greenberg, Amy, 210, 211–213
Grimke, Sara, 243
Group on Advanced Leadership (GOAL), 54
Guardino, Peter, 212
Gulf of Tonkin incident, 66
Gulf War, 241
Guthrie, Woody, 16, 40, 242, 251–252, 272n24
Gutman, Herbert, 26, 194
Guy, Jasmine, 254

Haiti, 36, 121, 225
Hamer, Fannie Lou, 241
Handlin, Oscar, 183
Harding, Vincent, 20
Harjo, Susan Shown, 174
Harper's Ferry, 174
Harrisburg trial, 20
Hastings, Max, 228
Herndon, Angelo, 230, 231
heroism, 91
Hiroshima bombing, 2, 227–228; influence on
    Zinn's antiwar perspective, 17, 222, 272n31;
    student rebuttal to Zinn's critique of, 111;
    Zinn's critical history of, 37, 91, 224, 226, 227
Hirsch, E. D., 57
historical relativism, 81, 83
historical revisionism, 223
Historical Thinking Project, 61
History Channel, 11, 43, 250, 260, 262, 263, 264
history education: activism and, 67, 78, 139,
    158, 163, 168; conservative versus progres-
    sive, 56–58; failures of, 3, 6, 8, 42, 60, 65–66;

history of, 3, 70; online efforts, 5, 42; standardized tests and, 78, 92; student/teacher critiques of, 100, 101, 132, 135, 140, 142, 172–173. *See also* history textbooks; *People's History, A*: impact on history education

History News Network (HNN), 181, 261

history textbooks, 63, 187; adoption politics, 8, 53, 135–136, 291n54; "common culture" approach, 56, 59, 279n27; conservatism/conventionality of, 6, 56, 66, 82, 100, 113; inadequacies of, 6, 31, 40, 48, 51, 60; reform efforts, 53, 60; unpopularity of, 34, 42, 46, 75, 135, 157, 179

—unrepresented/underrepresented topics: class, 49, 184, 188, 194, 230; gender, 55–56; race, 55, 190; wars, 58, 68, 210, 221. *See also* history education

Hitchcock, Ethan Allen, 210, 211

Hitler, Adolf, 218

Hobsbawm, Eric, 184, 279n30

Hoerder, Dirk, 203

Hofstadter, Richard, 195, 199–200, 203, 235; Zinn's admiration of, 24, 29

Hogan, Wesley, 230, 231, 232, 233–235

Hollywood liberalism, 259

Holocaust, 112, 196, 224

Holton, Woody, 202

Holtzman, William, 175–176, 177

Homestead Strike (1892), 49

Honoroff, Ben, 66

Horowitz, David, 44, 179

House Un-American Activities Committee, 241

Howe, Daniel Walker, 189, 293n37

Hughes, Langston, 7, 22, 253

immigrants/immigration, 13, 41, 48, 51–52, 58, 137, 217

Indian removal, 8, 112, 187, 190, 192; debated by Whigs and Democrats, 188–189; Zinn's critique of, as antiseptic term, 191

Indian Wars, 68

indirect republicanism, 201

individualism, 50, 56

Industrial Workers of the World, 49

industrialism, 49, 81

industrialization, 48, 49, 189, 207

Iraq war, 43, 44, 148, 219–220, 240, 253, 259

Irvine, Reed, 179

Isaac, Rhys, 203

Jackson, Andrew, 74, 138, 293n35; as slaveholder, 95, 119, 188; student responses to Zinn's depiction of, 108, 110, 115, 122, 125; Zinn's critical history of treatment of Native Americans by, 96, 187, 188, 190–192; Zinn's critique of veneration of, as democratic hero, 188

Jackson, Michael, 155

Jacksonians, 29, 86, 118, 187–189, 211, 293n35

Jefferson, Thomas, 113, 115, 200, 275n62

Jennings, Francis, 26, 190, 193, 204, 205

Jim Crow, 8, 39, 214, 224, 261, 299–300n167

jingoism, 212

Johnson, Lyndon B., 24, 57, 66

Johnson, Samuel, 77

Jones, Brian, 246, 247, 264–265

Jones, James Earl, 240, 244

Justice in Everyday Life (Zinn), 154

Kammen, Michael, 192, 193, 275n62

Karp, Stan, 166

Katz, Jonathan Ned, 210

Kay, Marvin Michael, 203

Kazin, Michael, 213, 214, 215–216, 217

Keller, Helen, 133, 241

Kelley, Robin D. G., 1, 2, 230

Kennedy, John F., 24, 62

Kennedy, Ted, 268

Kerber, Linda, 209

Kessler-Harris, Alice, 208

Killens, John Oliver, 20

King, Martin Luther, Jr., 145, 229, 230–231, 247, 253; in textbooks, 55; Zinn's Albany report and, 24

King, Stephen, 125

Kingsley, Ben, 263

Kirschner, George, 34–35

Kissinger, Henry, 50, 160

Klein, Naomi, 130

Knights of Labor, 185

Kolchin, Peter, 197

Korean War, 227

Kovic, Ron, 130, 148, 220

Kozol, Jonathan, 130, 151
Krugman, Paul, 218

labor history/historians, 1, 26, 46, 50, 172; debating quality of coverage of, in *A People's History*, 214–215; Zinn's engagement with, 16, 19, 184, 251
labor movement, 15, 161, 171, 185–186, 214, 216, 218; American Federation of Labor, 49, 185; antilabor efforts, 8, 18; biographical roots of Zinn's support for, 16, 40; Homestead Strike, 49; Industrial Workers of the World, 49; Knights of Labor, 185; labor-farmer parties, 185, low wages, 23, 49, 185; Pullman Strike, 49; railroad strike, 49, 184, 185, 186; textbook distortions of, 48–49
labor-farmer parties, 185
Lady Bird, 240
Las Casas, Bartolomé, 249, 257, 284–285n8
Latinx rights, 41, 138
Laverty, Paul, 249
Legend, John, 7, 258
Lembcke, Jerry, 172
Lemisch, Jesse, 26, 274n58
Lens, Sidney, 151
Lepore, Jill, 129, 130, 135, 152
Lerner, Gerda, 26
Levertov, Denise, 22
Levine, David, 165
Levine, Lawrence W., 26
Lewis, John, 253
LGBTQ movement, 14, 209
LGBTQ studies, 46
liberal feminism, 208
liberals, 29, 140, 259, 260, 262; Zinn's critique of, 24, 146, 206, 208, 218, 300n169
Limbaugh, Rush, 44
Lincoln, Abbey, 254
Lincoln, Abraham, 59, 203, 218, 265, 295n86; Zinn's critical depiction of, 194–195, 199–200
Litwack, Leon, 198
Loewen, James, 55, 56, 60–61, 174
Logevall, Fredrik, 228
Loguen, Jermain Wesley, 243
London, Jack, 27

Long 1960s, 2, 3, 15, 17, 31, 41, 65, 163, 233, 235
low wages, 23, 49, 185
Lowe, Robert, 165, 166
Ludlow Massacre (1914), 16, 18, 40, 132, 251, 272n24
Lynd, Alice, 169
Lynd, Staughton, 19, 26, 39, 169, 204

Mackintosh, Ebenezer, 205
Macleod, Jennifer, 51
Maddox, Robert James, 26
Main, Jackson Turner, 203
Malcolm X, 241, 261
Manifest Destiny, 134
March on Washington, 149, 299n167
Martin, Daisy, 61
Martinez, Vanessa, 245
Marx in Soho (Zinn), 242, 243, 264
Marxism, 200, 292n6
Maxine Greene High School, 264
May, Ernest R., 53
Mayer, Rebecca, 100, 102
McCarthy, Joseph, 107
McCarthy, Timothy Patrick, 41, 236
McCarthyism, 8
McGuire, Danielle, 231
McKay, Claude, 22
McKellen, Ian, 263
McKinley, William, 104, 105
McNamara, Mary, 260
McNaughton, John, 229
McPherson, James, 212
Meier, Terry, 165
memorization, 110, 265; excessive emphasis in conventional history classes, 46, 101, 119; teachers seeking to go beyond, 60, 64, 82, 137, 140
Menkart, Deborah, 5, 159, 163; *Beyond Heroes and Holidays* (ed.), 165; Teaching for Change and, 165, 166, 167; Zinn Education Project's founding and, 176–178. *See also* activist teachers; Zinn Education Project
Merrell, James H., 190, 191, 193–194
Messer, Robert L., 226
Mexican War, 68, 75, 83, 86, 118; student dis-

sent from Zinn's scathing view of, 98, 109; Zinn's treatment of, 99, 210–211, 212, 213

Mexico, 1, 2, 75, 114, 119, 138, 148, 168, 210–213, 225

Meyers, Marvin, 188

middle class, 30, 49, 63, 101, 188, 217–218, 230

military industrial complex, 25, 151, 213, 235

Miner, Barbara, 174

minstrel shows, 22

Mississippi Freedom Summer, 24, 58, 229

Monroe Doctrine, 20

Monte-Sano, Chauncey, 61

Montgomery bus boycott, 230, 231

Moore, Chris, 248, 249, 259–260, 305n51, 307n89

Moore, Michael, 259, 263

Moreira Alves, Márcio, 20

Morison, Samuel Eliot, 28, 31, 37, 38, 80, 93, 105, 276–277n92

Morrison, Toni, 52

Mortensen, Viggo, 7, 130, 257, 258

Moses, Bob, 231, 232

Moyers, Bill, 130

Mueller, Denis, 43, 305n51

multicultural education / multiculturalism, 5, 20, 56, 57, 165; additive approach, 22, 28, 51, 52–53, 55, 187; revisionist approach, 1, 51, 52, 139; transformative approach, 51, 52, 53

Murdoch, Rupert, 248

Murrell, Peter, 165

Murrin, John, 203

My Lai massacre, 10, 98, 123

Nader, Ralph, 130, 242

Nagasaki bombing, 2, 17, 87, 91, 111, 224, 226, 227

Nash, Gary B., 48, 203, 204–205

"Nation at Risk, A" (1983), 57, 280n51

National Assessment of Educational Progress (NAEP), 56, 92

National Association for the Advancement of Colored People (NAACP), 54, 55

National Council for the Social Studies (NCSS), 55, 178

National Defense Education Act (1958), 57

National History Education Clearinghouse, 61

National Liberation Front (NLF), 228

National Review, 44

National Teacher Corps, 58

National Welfare Rights Organization, 149

nationalism, 20, 21, 24, 76, 77, 223

Native Americans: activism, 18, 115, 193, 239; during American Revolution, 204, 205; Apess, 193; Bureau of Indian Affairs, 55; history, 26, 52, 184, 193–194; Indian Wars, 68; mistreatment of, 86, 97, 261, 297n115; Trail of Tears, 187, 192. See also Arawaks; Cherokees; Indian removal; Jackson, Andrew: Zinn's critical history of treatment of Native Americans by

nativism, 5

Navasky, Victor, 130

neocolonialism, 21

Network of Educators' Committees on Central America (NECCA), 164, 171, 172

New Deal: collapse of, 8, 145; critiques of, 218, 299–300n167, 300n169

New Left historians, 26, 47, 76, 206, 218, 235; impact initially confined to academia, 42, 46; scholarship's influence on Zinn, 14, 17, 275n62

Nineteenth Amendment, 50

Nixon, Richard M., 24, 50, 183, 196

Oakes, James, 195

Okrent, Daniel, 19, 273n38

pacifism, 214, 221

Paige, Nancy Carlsson, 239

Paine, Thomas, 184

Parkinson, Robert, 205, 297n115

Parks, Rosa, 231

parochialism, 142

paternalism, 204

patriotism, 10, 86, 216, 222, 260; as hindrance to critical historical thought, 53, 87, 96–97, 98, 179–180, 220; motivates student questions about Zinn's historical assumptions and arguments, 91, 111; yields misleading, nationalistic textbook narratives, 53, 83, 133, 179, 180, 223, 260

Patterson, Bill, 73, 136, 285n15; correspondence with Zinn, 67, 68–69, 94, 282n11;

Patterson, Bill (*continued*)
  critical pedagogy, 67–68, 69–73, 75–84, 87,
  97–99, 102; parental responses to Zinn,
  69, 74; *People's History* assignment, 62–63,
  65, 67–68, 71–75, 81, 92–93, 99; student
  letters to Zinn, 64, 67, 74–75, 81, 85–95, 98,
  100–115, 122, 137, 282–283n31
Peltier, Leonard, 255
Pentagon Papers, 17, 20, 22
People Speak, The (film), 11, 43, 247; attracts
  distinguished cast, 252–255; cast members'
  views of significance of, 255–260; diffi-
  culties in getting TV network support for,
  248–249; evolution from theater project,
  249–250; reviews and impact after broadcast on History Channel, 261–263; school
  theater projects sparked by, 264–267, 303–
  304n19; Zinn's view of educational value
  and political meaning of, 250–253
*People Speak: Voices That Changed Britain,
  The* (book), 263
People's History, A (Zinn): accessibility, 2, 3,
  43, 155–156; adult readers, 129–135, 148–151,
  153–157; attempts to ban, 179–180; as
  bottom-up history, 22, 25, 29, 84, 185–186,
  200, 203; classroom assignments, 179,
  180–181; commemoration of publication,
  242, 244; as companion/comparative text,
  64, 68, 70, 72; dramatic reading of, 240,
  242; impact on history education, 3, 4–6,
  13, 37, 41, 42–43, 44, 47, 62; need for, 59, 60;
  origins of, 3, 19, 20–23, 25, 26–32, 39–40;
  popular culture impacts, 4, 43, 238–266;
  popularity, 1–2, 11–13, 41, 46, 238, 262;
  public criticism of, 3, 4, 31, 33–35, 63, 64,
  179–182; in public schools, 11; sales, 11, 238;
  student reactions, 86, 101, 115, 118, 142–144,
  152–153; view of historian's role, 8–9
—Columbus chapter, 98, 120, 122, 160, 201,
  222, 235, 259; challenge to form and substance of conventional textbooks, 28, 35–36;
  echoing scholarship of Age of Exploration,
  276n92; parent's ire over teacher assigning,
  36; used by teachers to debate standard
  textbook account, 68, 74, 82, 86, 88
—criticism as: Beardian economic determinism, 201–202, 216; demonizing white
  settlers and capitalists, 183, 213, 215; failing
  to explain workers' support for capitalism,
  213–214; "hate America" history, 179–180;
  melodramatic reading for immature
  teens, 129–130; misreading role of class in
  nineteenth-century U.S. women's history,
  207–208; neglecting electoral politics and
  underestimating reformist political leaders, 199, 200–201, 211–212, 218; neglecting
  LGBTQ history, 209–210; pessimistic reading of American history, 184; valorizing
  workers, ignoring their racism and jingoism, 212, 216
—Native Americans, 18, 40, 97, 138, 143, 172;
  perspective on European invasion, 20,
  30; twenty-first-century Native American
  student's response to *A People's History* 41;
  Zinn's treatment of, criticized and praised,
  182, 183, 184, 192
People's History for the Classroom (Bigelow),
  163, 167, 175, 178
People's History series (New Press), 11, 19
people's pedagogy, 62, 159, 163, 164, 167, 168,
  178, 291n63
Peterson, Bob, 165, 166, 170, 173
Philippines, 1, 2, 23, 104, 105, 123
pluralism, 30, 180
police violence, 10
Polk, James K., 211, 213
poor working conditions, 49
Portland Central American Solidarity Committee, 171
Powell, Adam Clayton, Jr., 54
Powhatan, 243
presentism, 37, 39, 222, 288–289n6
Presser, Michael, 66
prison rights movement, 3, 14, 21–22, 154–155,
  208, 234, 287n72
Progressive Era, 68, 84
progressivism, 270
protest music, 7, 242
Pullman Strike (1894), 49

racial segregation, 15, 18, 58, 162
racism, 12, 36, 47, 63, 65, 92; as American
  foundation, 1, 2, 52–53, 140, 212; experiences of, 83, 194; institutionalized, 55,

234; in school curricula, 58, 66, 136, 164; Zinn's connections with and inspiration from struggles against, 15, 17, 18, 39; Zinn's view on prominence in American history, 28, 224. *See also* racial segregation; slavery

Rafferty, Max, 53
railroad strike (1877), 49, 184, 185, 186
Rand, Ayn, 260
Ravitch, Diane, 56, 57
Reagan, Ronald W., 11, 53, 56, 156, 280n51; draws opposition from progressive teachers, 42, 65, 132, 145, 171; as Great Communicator, 2; shift of American politics rightward unforeseen by Zinn, 30, 209
Reaganism, 42, 209
realism, 227
Reconstruction, 28, 48, 53, 138, 185; Zinn's treatment of, 196–199, 200
Redgrave, Vanessa, 263
regionalism, 53
Reichardt, Julia, 169
republican idealism, 204
Republicans, 29, 198; Bush, George H. W., 145, 182; McKinley, 104, 105; Roosevelt, Theodore, 23, 49. *See also* Bush, George W.; Lincoln, Abraham; Nixon, Richard M.; Reagan, Ronald W.; Trump, Donald J.
Rethinking Columbus (Bigelow), 172, 173
Rethinking Schools (1986), 65, 159–161, 163–168, 170, 172–178, 291n63
revisionist multiculturalism, 51, 52
Robbins, Tim, 130
Roe v. Wade, 208
Rogers, Bethany, 58
Rogin, Michael Paul, 187, 190, 192
Romano, Renee, 96, 97
Roosevelt, Franklin Delano, 154, 196, 200, 218, 227, 300n168
Roosevelt, Theodore, 23, 49
Roots (TV miniseries), 248
Rose, Wendy, 174
Rosenberg, Ethel, 20
Rosenberg, Julius, 20
Rough Riders, 23

Sadker, David, 51
Sadker, Myra, 51
Salinger, J. D., 129
Sarandon, Susan, 130
Sayles, John, 248
Schell, Jonathan, 20
Schiffrin, Andre, 175, 291n54
Schlesinger, Arthur, Jr., 57, 188, 191
school boards, 4, 48, 51, 52, 56, 84
school districts, 4, 7, 11, 53, 54, 59, 64, 68, 130, 174
Schweikart, Larry, 136
second-wave feminism, 51, 208, 209
Seeger, Pete, 130
Seixas, Peter, 61
Sellers, Charles, 50, 274n58
sensationism, 19
sexism, 2, 58, 65, 66, 136, 147; struggle against, 27, 52, 58, 246, 261; textbooks reinforce, 50–51, 136
Share Our Wealth movement, 218
Shays' Rebellion, 161
Sheehan, Neil, 228
Shor, Ira, 164, 170, 172
Shy, John, 203
Silverman, Sandra, 51
Simon, Bryant, 214, 215, 216–217, 233
Simon, Dan, 5, 6, 214–217, 304n27
Simpsons, The (TV show), 240
1619 Project, 10
slavery, 27, 188, 243, 254; as American foundation, 2, 8, 10, 37, 97, 194, 297n115; American Revolution and, 206; Constitution and, 201, 202; Dred Scott decision, 195; Fugitive Slave Act, 243; fugitives, 184, 186, 194, 195, 243; historiography of, 26, 53, 197, 203; Mexican War connections, 210, 212; obscured by Trump's aborted 1776 Commission, 270n22; rebellions, 204, 205; in school curricula, 54, 194, 265; television's neglect of, 248; view of history of enslaved, 81, 85, 104, 113, 119, 183; Zinn's treatment of, 28, 162, 190, 194–196, 197, 199–200, 203. *See also* abolitionism; antislavery policy; Columbus, Christopher; slavery; Jackson, Andrew
Smith, Patti, 242

SNCC: The New Abolitionists (Zinn), 15, 39, 229, 275n62

social history/historians, 184, 197, 203; inspired by 1960s mass democratic protest movements, 14; pre-Zinn disconnect between textbooks and new, 46, 48, 76; as transforming American historiography and shaping *A People's History*, 25–26, 203, 275n62; weakness in neglecting power elite and interaction with nonelite, 186–187; Zinn as popularizer of, 33, 42, 47, 84, 92, 235

social inequality, 2, 16, 189, 218, 246, 273n37

socialism, 27, 49, 116, 185, 218, 260

socialist feminism, 208

socialist movement, 40

Socialist Party of America, 49, 185

Sopranos, The (TV show), 239, 259, 303n8

Southern Historical Association, 38

Southern Regional Council, 24, 229

Southern Society Project, 198

Spanish colonialism, 36, 276–277n92, 284–285n8

Spanish-American War, 81, 87, 111

Springsteen, Bruce, 7, 41, 251–252, 253, 306n59

Spruill, Marjorie J., 209

Stamp Tax Riots, 205

standardized testing, 9, 42, 65, 67, 78

Stanford History Education Group (SHEG), 61, 62

Star Spangled Banner, 253

Steinbeck, John, 20

Stewart, Jon, 43, 219

Stone, Oliver, 130

Strathairn, David, 246, 258–259

Student Nonviolent Coordinating Committee (SNCC), 15, 39, 229–230, 275n62

supply-side economics, 65

Swados, Henry, 19

Taney, Roger, 195

Taylor, Alan, 202, 204, 205

Taylor, Zachary, 211

teacher activism, 164, 168–169, 171, 173

teacher reform movement, 4, 159, 163, 174, 175, 178, 291n63

Teaching for Change (1989), 65, 159, 164–165, 166, 176, 177–178, 291n63

Team Englewood Community Academy, 264

Tecumseh, 255

Tenorio, Rita, 165

Terkel, Studs, 19

terrorism, 6, 65

Tet offensive, 228

Thatcher, Margaret, 65

Thirteenth Amendment, 198

Thompson, E. P., 26, 184, 275n61

tokenism, 46

Tomei, Marisa, 7, 240, 246

totalitarianism, 223

Trail of Tears, 187, 192

Trautman, Brian, 261

tribalism, 102

Trist, Nicholas, 212

triumphalism, 258

Trokan, Mike, 166

Truman, Harry S., 226, 232

Trumbo, Dalton, 220

Trump, Donald J., 8, 10, 102, 216, 268, 270n22

Trumpism, 268

Truth, Sojourner, 209, 241, 264

Tubman, Harriet, 133

Tuchman, Barbara, 19

Turner, Henry McNeal, 253

Turse, Nick, 228

Twain, Mark, 27, 241, 302n215

Twombly, Robert C., 33–34, 36, 38

two-party system, 23, 40, 189, 218, 233, 293n37

Tyack, David, 47, 59

Umoja, Akinyele Omowale, 231

Underground Railroad, 233

Union League, 197

unionism, 185

United Civil Rights Council (UCRS), 53

U.S. Constitution: Bill of Rights, 201; Fifteenth Amendment, 198; Fourteenth Amendment, 198, 208; origins, 142, 201, 203, 206, 229, 296n97; ratification of, 201, 202; slavery, 28, 81; Thirteenth Amendment, 198

U.S. Department of Justice, 231, 232

U.S. expansionism, 46, 75, 83, 97, 205, 210, 213

U.S. foreign policy, 50, 58, 62, 66, 87, 171; nationalist myths and, 97

U.S. imperialism, 3, 36, 47, 221, 257; 1960s generation's interest in critical history of, 12, 14, 18; teachers' use of *A People's History* to question, 66, 87; Zinn's interest in viewing from perspective of those whose nations experienced, 20, 22, 31, 220; Zinn's multigenerational lens on, 17, 18, 296n105

U.S. militarism, 2, 61, 63, 65, 147; teachers' interest in provoking student debate about, 66, 92; Zinn and New Left critique of, 14, 35, 220–221, 228; Zinn denounces during antiwar speaking tours, 43; Zinn's interest in depicting in People's History book series, 20, 22–23

U.S. Supreme Court, 18, 161, 195, 196, 201, 208–209, 300n169; Dred Scot decision, 198; Ginsburg, 208, 209; Taney, 195

Van Buren, Martin, 191

Van Dusen, Hugh, 11, 12, 13, 130

VanSledright, Bruce, 81

Vantine, Laura, 66

Vanzetti, Bartolomeo, 184

Vedder, Eddie, 44, 240

Vietnam (Zinn), 39, 304n28

Vietnam War, 68, 127, 132, 182, 257; anticommunism and, 24, 99, 213, 214; atrocities of, 2, 37, 98, 227; conclusion of, 50, 207, 242; criticism of, 17, 18, 24, 39, 88, 149, 152, 158, 174, 206, 219; disillusionment with, 25, 26, 168; Gulf of Tonkin incident, 66; as imperialism, 87, 106; My Lai massacre, 10, 98, 123; National Liberation Front, 228; students dissenting from Zinn's view of, 87, 104, 111; Tet offensive, 228; textbook distortion of, 66; U.S. soldiers, 23, 120, 220, 273–274n51; Zinn on impact of, on American politics, 228; Zinn's opposition to and impact of, on *A People's History*, 17, 20; Zinn's *Vietnam*, 39, 304n28

Voices of a People's History (ed. Zinn and Arnove), 5–6, 43, 243–250, 256–257, 263–266, 272n32, 303n13, 303–304n19, 305n31

Voices of a People's History Foundation, 264

Vonnegut, Kurt, 241, 242

voting rights, 15, 24, 187, 197, 199, 233, 295n86, 300n169

Voting Rights Act (1965), 198

Wade, Jerome, 264

Wagner Act (1935), 218

Walker, Alice, 241, 242, 254

Walker, David, 241

Walker, George, 22

Walker, Margaret, 22

Wall Street Journal, 44

Walsh, Edward J., 213

War on Poverty, 57

Washington, George, 193, 201

Washington, Kerry, 7, 256, 263–264

Watergate, 25, 132

Waugh, Dexter, 51, 52, 279n27

Whigs, 29, 188, 211–212

White, Richard, 192

white nationalism, 8

white supremacist terrorism, 232

white supremacy, 5, 248, 250, 253, 255–256

Whitefield, George, 193

Williams, Bert, 22

Williams, Robert F., 232

Williams, Robin, 238, 303n3

Williams, William Appleman, 183

Wilmot, David, 212

Wilmot Proviso, 212

Wilson, Woodrow, 222, 223

Wineburg, Sam, 61

women's history, 15, 50, 206–207, 208, 209, 297n121

women's movement, 14, 169, 209

women's rights, 40, 208, 261. *See also* Equal Rights Amendment

women's studies, 46

Woods, Sylvia, 254

working class, 1, 50, 138, 187, 230, 255; anticapitalist rebellions, 2, 30, 49, 185–186; historiography/history of, 13, 26, 204–205; racism of, 188, 212; Zinn's roots in, 16, 17; Zinn's treatment of, 16, 33, 40, 48–49, 66, 141, 208, 215–216, 217

World War I, 222–223

World War II, 28, 68, 127, 192, 242, 260; as antifascist, 99, 224; Black soldiers, 232, 301n206;

World War II (*continued*)
 Japanese internment, 83, 87, 98, 103–105,
 143, 224; Jewish oppression, 196; U.S.-Soviet
 relations, 57, 91, 224, 226; Zinn's experi-
 ences, 2, 17, 88, 120, 134, 219, 221, 261; Zinn's
 treatment of, 221, 222, 223, 225–228. *See also*
 Hiroshima bombing; Nagasaki bombing
Wright, Frank Lloyd, 33
Wright, Richard, 22
Wynter, Sylvia, 52

You Can't Be Neutral on a Moving Train (documentary film), 43, 176, 178, 305n51
You Can't Be Neutral on a Moving Train (Zinn
 memoir), 43, 131, 150, 156–157, 272n31
Young, Alfred F., 26, 204–205
Young, Marilyn, 221, 222–223, 224–225,
 228–229, 301n199
Young People's History of the United States, A
 (book), 5, 6–7, 262

Zimmerman, Jonathan, 54
Zimmerman, Robert, 183, 201
Zinn, Howard: activism, 17, 18, 44, 130, 131,
 134, 149, 251; history education and, 229,
 289n15; inhumanity of war and, 1, 14;
 moralism, 95, 96, 215; papers of, 3, 4, 5;
 prisoners' rights activism, 3, 14, 21–22,
 154–155, 208, 234, 287n72; as revisionist

historian, 1, 31, 38, 81, 82, 89, 92, 135, 139,
 226; at Spelman College, 15, 17, 20, 39; student letters, 62, 67, 73, 80, 81–92; as teacher,
 158, 159–163, 167; teacher collaborations,
 158–159, 163–167, 172–178; teacher letters,
 62, 65–67; Vietnam War activism, 17, 20, 24,
 39, 131, 207, 221; working-class roots, 16, 17,
 156, 270–271n22; World War II service, 2,
 17, 18, 220–221. *See also* American Revolution: Zinn's treatment of; Jackson, Andrew;
 Patterson, Bill; slavery: Zinn's treatment of;
 working class: Zinn's treatment of; World
 War II: Zinn's treatment of
—works of: *Declarations of Independence*, 43,
 131; *Disobedience and Democracy*, 39; *Justice
 in Everyday Life*, 154; *Marx in Soho*, 242,
 243, 264; *SNCC: The New Abolitionists*, 15,
 39, 229, 275n62; *Vietnam*, 39, 304n28; *Voices
 of a People's History* (ed. with Arnove),
 5–6, 43, 243–250, 256–257, 263–266, 272n32,
 303n13, 303–304n19, 305n31; *You Can't Be
 Neutral on a Moving Train*, 43, 131, 150,
 156–157, 272n31. See also *People Speak, The*;
 People's History, A
Zinn Education Project (zep): impact, 5,
 12, 42, 92, 178; origins, 5, 65, 164, 175–176,
 280n60; *A People's History for the Classroom* and, 167–168. *See also* Bigelow, Bill;
 Menkart, Deborah